CW01218212

Repo and Stock Lending

A Practitioner's Guide

Consulting Editor **Guy Usher**

Consulting editor
Guy Usher

Managing director
Sian O'Neill

Editorial services director
Carolyn Boyle

Production manager
Neal Honney

Group publishing director
Tony Harriss

Repo and Stock Lending: A Practitioner's Guide
is published by
Globe Law and Business
Globe Business Publishing Ltd
New Hibernia House
Winchester Walk
London SE1 9AG
United Kingdom
Tel +44 20 7234 0606
Fax +44 20 7234 0808
www.GlobeLawandBusiness.com

Print and bound by Gomer Press

Repo and Stock Lending: A Practitioner's Guide
ISBN 9781909416581

© 2015 Globe Business Publishing Ltd

All rights reserved. No part of this publication may be reproduced in any material form (including photocopying, storing in any medium by electronic means or transmitting) without the written permission of the copyright owner, except in accordance with the provisions of the Copyright, Designs and Patents Act 1988 or under terms of a licence issued by the Copyright Licensing Agency Ltd, 6-10 Kirby Street, London EC1N 8TS, United Kingdom (www.cla.co.uk, email: licence@cla.co.uk). Applications for the copyright owner's written permission to reproduce any part of this publication should be addressed to the publisher.

DISCLAIMER
This publication is intended as a general guide only. The information and opinions which it contains are not intended to be a comprehensive study, nor to provide legal advice, and should not be treated as a substitute for legal advice concerning particular situations. Legal advice should always be sought before taking any action based on the information provided. The publishers bear no responsibility for any errors or omissions contained herein.

Table of contents

Foreword —— 5
    Guy Usher
    Fieldfisher

Repo and securities —— 7
lending: an overview
    Iain Colquhoun
    ICBC Standard Bank
    Marissa Dearden
    Fieldfisher

Lifecycle of transactions —— 23
    Guy Usher
    Fieldfisher

Agent lending/agency repo —— 41
    Sarah Reid
    Fieldfisher

Tri-party repo and —— 49
stock lending
    Guy Usher
    Fieldfisher

Central counterparty model —— 53
    Eric Bystrom
    Director
    Samit Desai
    Ivelina Dimtscheva
    Capco UK
    Swen Werner
    Securities services & collateral
    management expert

Structured repo transactions —— 69
    Daniel Franks
    Norton Rose Fulbright

Structured securities —— 81
lending transactions
    Daniel Franks
    Norton Rose Fulbright

Legal and regulatory issues —— 97
    Emma Spiers
    Fieldfisher

Industry documentation —— 113
    Edward Miller
    Jamie Pullen
    Fieldfisher

Accounting —— 183
    Andrew Spooner
    Deloitte LLP

UK taxation of repo —— 199
and stock lending transactions
    Nicholas Noble
    Fieldfisher

Appendices —— 253

Glossary —— 379

About the authors —— 387

Index —— 391

Foreword

Guy Usher
Fieldfisher

This book was initially conceived due to the absence of any generally available comprehensive text on the securities lending market practices and documentation. The primary aim of the book is to try to plug that gap.

While several existing texts give a good account of the repo markets and documentation, there have been so many developments since many of them were published that it was felt timely to provide a more up-to-date reference source for that product as well.

Part of the reason for covering both products in one volume is the growing convergence in these markets and in their documentation. To an increasing extent, both formats are now (often agnostically) used to trade products that, from an economic perspective, are essentially the same.

However, that convergence also highlights some of the differences – sometimes subtle and often in the detail – that in certain scenarios can become much more significant. We have sought to identify those key differences.

As a result, some chapters deal with both products together, whereas others deal with them separately. There was no right way to do this, so contributors adopted whichever route made the text easier to follow from the reader's perspective. I am conscious that not all readers will feel that this was done correctly, so I can only apologise and hope that those readers are in the minority.

As with other Globe Law and Business publications, this book is intended as a practitioner's guide. It therefore does not seek to explain every issue or intricacy of either the way the products are traded or the terms of the trade, but we have tried to highlight some of the many nuances which feature. The idea behind the book is that it should provide a leg-up, rather than a total solution, to those who deal in the products. We acknowledge that specialists will know their subjects better than the chapters of this book can describe them, but it is hoped that the trader might find it useful to have a resource in order to understand the legal terms, the accounting or tax treatment a little better. If this book achieves this purpose, then it will have been a success.

This book looks at both the repo and securities lending markets from a European market perspective and, in some chapters, from a largely English law perspective. The documentation of the transactions, as well as market conventions, regulatory requirements and tax treatment, will inevitably vary across different jurisdictions; but hopefully, we have provided enough detail for readers to be able to identify the issues so that they can then apply them in the context of their local trading, legal and regulatory environment. One specific word of warning: repo and stock lending transactions in the US markets, for example, have a different legal structure from that which prevails outside the United States and are documented under different industry agreements. It would therefore be unwise to assume that the same principles apply in the US markets.

I am extremely grateful to those who have authored and contributed to this book, without whose efforts it would not have come to exist. In addition to the named authors, I would also like to offer thanks for the work and insights provided by Stuart Cullen, head of repo finance at ICBC Standard Bank, who enumerated real trade details for the lifecycle chapter. Last, but by no means least, my thanks to Gary Walker, without whose efforts in driving the project forward this book may not have come into print at all.

Guy Usher
Head of derivatives and structured finance group, Fieldfisher
March 2015

Repo and securities lending: an overview

Iain Colquhoun
ICBC Standard Bank
Marissa Dearden
Fieldfisher

This chapter provides an introduction to the repo and securities lending products and markets and sets out the background and concepts which are used elsewhere in this book. It also explains some of the frequently used terminology, although readers may also refer to the Glossary in Appendix 1.

While this chapter, like a number of others in this book, looks at repo and securities lending separately, increasingly both products are being used interchangeably for the same fundamental transactions in economic terms.

The market and regulators increasingly refer to both products together as being 'securities financing' transactions, and so that term is used in the same way in this book.

1. Repo

1.1 What is a repo?

A repurchase transaction (or repo) is a simple product. It comprises a sale of securities for cash, with a commitment by the seller to repurchase equivalent securities from the buyer at a later date for a pre-agreed price. A simple (or vanilla) repo has the same key economic characteristics as a loan of cash secured against the asset which, in a repo context, has been sold (or repoed) to the buyer (or economic cash lender).

With a repo, the difference between the price of the securities when sold at the outset, and the price at which they are repurchased at a later date, represents a predetermined amount of interest payable by the repo seller (or cash borrower). A 'reverse repo' is simply the term used to describe the same transaction, but from the perspective of the repo buyer (or cash lender).

The terms of repo transactions have more potential variants than ever, and yet the fundamental payment and delivery flows are broadly the same. While other chapters consider how economic drivers and characteristics of repo have developed in the context of structured, agency, tri-party and cleared transactions, this chapter gives an overview of the origins of the repo market, and the uses and basic structure of a vanilla repo entered into on a bilateral basis.

1.2 The repo market

Despite its inherent simplicity, repo is now an essential instrument within the capital markets. Its origins can be traced to the US Federal Reserve, which began using repo in 1918 to manage liquidity within the banking system. The rapid growth of the US treasury market in the 1970s fuelled the parallel development of the interbank market for these instruments, due largely to two interrelated motivations.

First, the necessity to fund positions economically led banks to provide assets as collateral against cash borrowing. This provided a cheaper source of funding than unsecured inter-bank markets, allowing the construction of larger outright treasury positions than would have been possible within a model reliant solely on unsecured borrowing.

Secondly, the existence of a repo market facilitated settlement flows in securities transactions by providing liquidity – in particular, by enabling market participants (through transacting as repo buyer) to cover delivery obligations under short positions. The ability to sell a treasury note without owning it, either for a day or two, or as a long-term 'naked short' position, became important in the mechanical operations of prime dealers and in the development of interest rate trading strategies. Put simply, the repo market gave banks ready access to securities for settlement purposes, without the need to hold long positions in those assets.

Over time, the market developed to cover a huge variety of underlying securities and now encompasses a much wider range of participants in jurisdictions across the globe. In addition to broker-dealers, repo is now traded by corporates, pension funds, insurers, hedge funds, mutual funds, UCITS, sovereigns and central banks – each with its own drivers and issues.

The results of a bi-annual survey by the International Capital Markets Association (ICMA)[1] in the first half of 2014 recorded an approximate €5.8 trillion of repo trades outstanding as at the survey reference date (June 11 2014), which figure reflects volumes traded by only a sample of participating financial institutions in the European market alone. At least half of that amount was attributable to cross-border trades both within and outside the Eurozone. ICMA's 'frequently asked questions' published in 2013 cites sources estimating a global market of up to €15 trillion.[2]

1.3 Basic economics

When illustrating the economic flow of a repo, it is necessary to differentiate between two distinct types of transaction: classic repos and buy/sell-back transactions. These two transaction types have the same fundamental motivations and, while certain cash flows are constructed differently, they have an equivalent net economic result. The lifecycle of these transactions is illustrated elsewhere in this book, but the basic economic concepts are described below.

(a) Commencement of trade

The initial sale and purchase under a repo is made by the delivery of securities to the repo buyer, against payment to the repo seller of the purchase price for those securities. This constitutes an outright sale under which legal and beneficial ownership of the relevant securities is transferred outright to the buyer.

The purchase price may be the spot price (ie, the then-current market value) of

---

1   *European repo market survey* (number 27 – conducted June 2014), published in September 2014 by the ICMA.
2   *Frequently asked questions on repo*, published in February 2013 by the ICMA.

the securities sold (which would usually be agreed according to the prevailing market quote from a generally recognised source, such as Bloomberg) or, more typically where a repo is entered into for cash funding purposes, a price which is lower than the market value of the securities on the initial purchase date. This is because the buyer (or economic cash lender) will generally require the application of a haircut to the value of the purchased securities in order to protect itself against potential price volatility of those securities over the life of the trade. In other words, the lender of cash wants to be over-collateralised in case the cash borrower defaults.

This haircut is essentially a discount on the market value of the securities. For example, the repo buyer might agree to pay (ie, lend) only 98% (or any other pre-agreed percentage) of the market value of the securities purchased. In fact, the haircut is more usually expressed the other way around – that is, the value of securities required in order to borrow 100 of cash – for example, 102%. Note, however, that in economic terms an initial margin requirement of 102% of the purchase price is not the same as a 2% haircut applied to collateral value; the equivalent haircut would be very slightly less than 2%.

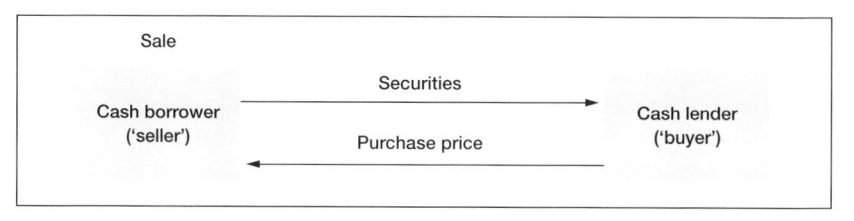

```
         Sale
                          Securities
   Cash borrower    ───────────────────▶    Cash lender
      ('seller')                               ('buyer')
                        Purchase price
                   ◀───────────────────
```

(b) *Termination or repurchase*

On maturity of the trade (referred to as the 'repurchase date'), the initial buyer of securities will deliver to the seller securities which are equivalent (ie, the same but not necessarily identical) to the original securities, in return for payment by the repo seller (cash borrower) of the repurchase price. As with the outward sale and purchase leg of the trade, this redelivery of securities (or the 'return leg') takes effect as an outright transfer of legal and beneficial ownership.

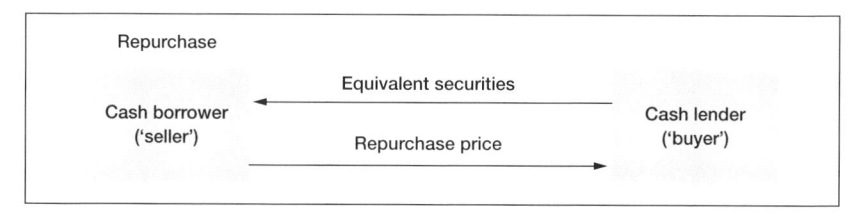

```
        Repurchase
                       Equivalent securities
   Cash borrower   ◀───────────────────      Cash lender
      ('seller')                               ('buyer')
                        Repurchase price
                   ───────────────────▶
```

(c) *Interest*

The amount of cash paid by the initial repo seller to repurchase the securities will equal the price for which they were originally purchased, plus interest on that purchase price, accrued over the term of the trade. The rate of interest is agreed at the outset and is typically referred to as the 'repo rate'. This will be a fixed rate for a vanilla repo transaction.

Hence the repurchase price is not determined by reference to the market value of the securities at maturity – it is simply a factor of the amount which was paid at the outset plus repo interest on that amount for the term of the transaction.

(d) *Margining*

Of critical importance to repo transactions is the requirement to maintain the level of over-collateralisation at the outset of the transaction.

During the life of a repo transaction, fluctuations in the underlying value of the repoed securities will occur. In order to avoid a change in the relative credit exposure between the parties, the transaction will be subject to margining procedures. Within the repo market there are two standard ways in which to handle this process. The first is the most common, particularly when dealing with trades which have a pre-agreed end date. The party who is exposed by the market movement will provide margin to the other party to the trade. This margin will be subject to pre-agreed parameters often set out in the repo agreement. For example, prior to transacting a repo transaction (or many individual repo transactions) both parties will agree to revalue the portfolio on a daily basis. If the value of the underlying collateral is at variance with the initial cash agreed on the portfolio in an amount greater than the margin threshold amount (specified within the repo agreement as a minimum transfer amount), margin will move between the counterparties. The industry standard master agreement for repos – the Global Master Repurchase Agreement (GMRA) – will typically stipulate each of the following:

- margin threshold amount (usually between $250,000 and $500,000);
- value date basis for collateralisation (typically T+2, but increasingly likely to be T+0 in newer agreements);
- minimum requirement for the margin security (often A-rated, non-subordinated paper, but can be limited to only AAA-rated government bonds). This requirement is controlled by the appetite for credit risk of the parties. It is also possible that margin collateral will be cash.

As an alternative to this process, it is possible to reprice trades. This method is often used when the trade is transacted on an open basis (see 'Term' below). If an existing trade has a pre-agreed end date, it is important to remember that a reprice of the trade will alter its economics. In addition to the change in the cash amount subjected to interest, a reprice will also settle the interest accrued up to that point. This will impact the compounding of interest on the transaction to the benefit of the initial cash lender (or repo buyer).

These margin mechanics are described more fully elsewhere in this book.

(e) *Term*

Repo trades are relatively short term (having developed in the United States mostly as overnight positions), although longer-dated trades, including term-trades of one year or more, are becoming more common in certain markets. Parties to a repo usually agree a fixed term at the outset, but it is also possible to trade without a pre-agreed end date (so that the repo continues until terminated by either party, upon notice). These open or on-demand transactions are common, particularly within the corporate market, or when the nominal size of the asset involved is relatively small. Longer-term, structured repos are considered elsewhere in this book.

(f) *Asset types*
Where repo is used for cash funding purposes, the cash provider will typically require the securities provided as collateral by the repo seller to be as liquid and non-volatile as possible. For this reason, the repo markets have historically been – and still are – predominantly in government debt securities. ICMA's bi-annual market survey in June 2014 reported government bonds forming an approximate 80% share of collateral provided under repo trades in the European market.

Cash providers may, however, accept other types of security (usually then requiring a higher haircut) and the use of repo to source specific assets, and in structured transactions, now means that other asset-types have increased their market share. Examples include corporate bonds, equities, asset-backed securities, certificates of deposit and commercial paper. Markets for repos of loans and commodities are now also developing, although they have some specific issues which do not apply to securities.

1.4 Ownership transfer and the (partial) undoing of its effects

The fact that repoed securities are transferred outright to the buyer raises a number of issues which distinguish a repo from a secured loan transaction. The concept is a recurring theme throughout this book. Indeed, it is such a fundamental feature that it is also appropriate to list the key implications here.

The outright transfer of ownership of the securities means:
- Buyer free to deal – the buyer is free to sell or otherwise deal with the securities purchased in any way it wishes. In fact, it is common for a repo buyer to onward repo the securities it has purchased in order to finance its own lending business or balance sheet. All the buyer needs to do is to ensure that it will be in a position to redeliver equivalent securities at maturity of the repo.
- Voting rights – the buyer will be the person entitled to vote on any decisions in respect of the securities, if it still holds them.
- Payment on the securities – any coupons or repayments of principal on the securities purchased will belong to the buyer, if it still owns them at the time.
- Corporate actions – the buyer will receive the benefit of these if it still holds the securities at the time they arise.
- Credit risk – the seller is exposed to the risk that the buyer may not return the securities at maturity of the repo, and the buyer is exposed to the risk that the seller might not return the cash lent. However, in a default situation, no actual return or repayment is made; instead, the parties' respective obligations are valued and offset against each other, so that a party's exposure is only in respect of the net difference between the values of those obligations. In practice, this normally means that it is the seller who will be exposed to the buyer on a net basis as it sold securities which were worth more than the cash it borrowed. This is over-collateralisation risk (ie, the risk of loss on default).

The terms of the repo transaction will address some – but not all – of these issues, so as to seek to put the parties into the position which would have prevailed had the securities not been sold at all but had simply been provided as security for the cash lent. This reflects the accounting treatment which generally applies to repo; for accounting purposes the seller of the securities will still recognise them as if it still owned them and, correspondingly, the buyer will show a receivable representing the cash it has lent and not show the securities as its asset. The accounting treatment of repos is considered more fully elsewhere in this book.

The features of ownership of the securities having passed to the buyer that will be addressed in the terms of the repo (at least if documented under standard industry terms or similar) include:

- Income – the buyer will be required to pay to the seller an amount equal to any coupons, cash dividends or other distributions paid on the securities during the term of the trade. These amounts are referred to as 'manufactured dividends'. The obligation arises as and when the payment is made by the relevant issuer. No manufactured payments are required in the case of a buy/sell-back transaction; instead, the expected coupon payment is rolled up into the repurchase price (and so paid to the seller at maturity).
- Corporate actions – the buyer will be required to redeliver equivalent securities to the seller on maturity of the transaction. This means that, even if something happens to the securities during the term of the repo, the buyer must redeliver assets which the seller would have had if it had owned the securities throughout. So, if the securities are converted into other assets, it is those other assets which would have to be redelivered. If the securities had been redeemed in whole or in part, then an amount equal to the redemption proceeds would have to be returned at maturity of the repo.
- Credit risk – the terms of the repo will provide ongoing obligations on the buyer and seller to maintain the agreed initial level of over-collateralisation represented by the haircut applied to the market value of the purchased securities at the outset. This is most commonly achieved by daily revaluations and posting and/or returns of variation margin – which may be in the form of cash or securities. The precise margining mechanics are described and illustrated elsewhere in this book.

The terms of the repo transaction do not typically provide for:

- Restrictions on dealing – the buyer is always free to deal in the securities purchased and this is a necessary feature of the product and market. It provides essential liquidity to the markets in securities.
- Direction of voting rights – there is no requirement for the seller to be able to direct that voting rights be exercised in a particular way. This reflects the fact that the buyer is free to deal with the securities as it wishes. To provide otherwise could also have implications in terms of the accounting treatment afforded to repo transactions.
- Over-collateralisation risk – standard repo terms do not seek to mitigate against this other than to maintain the initial level through the posting of

variation margin. However, there are structures which are increasingly used to reduce or eliminate such risk if the parties are concerned about this from a credit or regulatory capital perspective.

Where a party to the repo transfers margin in the form of securities, this will similarly be made by way of outright transfer of ownership of the margin securities. Any such securities are therefore treated in the same way as the purchased securities in terms of the foregoing issues.

1.5 Buy/sell-back transactions

Buy/sell-back (or sell/buy-back) transactions are economically equivalent to repo and these days are also invariably documented under the same form of master agreement used for repo, the Global Master Repurchase Ageeement (GMRA). Buy/sell-backs are particularly popular, for example, in the Italian government bond markets.

Originally, buy/sell-back transactions were effected by way of an initial sale of an asset and a separate, but economically linked, second transaction for the seller to buy the assets back at an agreed price at a future date (with the future price being the original sale price, plus an effective interest charge representing the use of funds). There was, at the time, no master agreement to provide for ongoing margining, close-out on default or manufactured income payments for these types of trade.

In recognition of the shortcomings of these stand-alone transactions – especially with the increased significance for banks and other financial institutions of ensuring that the two legs of the transaction could be offset against each other – a specific form of Annex was created for the GMRA to allow for some of the features of the GMRA to be applied to buy/sell-backs in the same way as they apply to repo. So, for example, parties entering into buy/sell-backs have the same default and close-out regime as well as the ability to apply ongoing margin maintenance.

However, the trade terms for buy/sell-backs are still largely preserved as they would have been had two stand-alone sale and purchase contracts been entered into between the parties. So, with a buy/sell-back transaction, the repurchase price (which incorporates the effective repo interest charge) will be agreed at the outset based on a fixed repurchase date. Because the interest amount is settled at the outset, buy/sell-backs have to be fixed-term transactions and cannot be on-demand transactions. Another feature which is preserved is the retention by the buyer of the coupons on the underlying securities. That is, when a coupon is received on a fixed-income security, it is not manufactured back to the original owner of the asset (as is the case with a classic repo) but instead becomes part of the closing cash flow of the trade. The repurchase price agreed at the outset has built into it an adjustment for the fact that the buyer will receive and retain the coupon. The adjustment will take into account not just the coupon itself, but also the fact that the buyer had the use of the cash from the coupon payment date until the repurchase date.

1.6 Uses of repo and market conventions

(a) Cash financing

The essence of traditional repo trading is the provision or receipt of cash funding on a secured basis. For a repo buyer, the characteristics of repo make it a relatively low-risk means of investing (lending out) cash in a ready market. The rate of return for the buyer may be greater than the interest earned from leaving funds on deposit and less risky for the buyer or cash lender, as bank deposits are unsecured obligations whereas repo is a secured financing. For a repo seller, who may be long on certain asset-types which are suitable to provide as collateral, repo provides a relatively cheap and flexible source of funding.

'General collateral' (GC) is the term given to a range of securities – each conforming to a certain set of characteristics – which repo buyers across the market will accept as collateral under trades entered into for cash funding purposes. The 'general collateral rate' (GC rate) is the standardised rate at which repo buyers in the market are prepared to lend cash against the provision of such general collateral. Fundamentally, the GC rate is driven by the creditworthiness of the relevant issuer. The seller of a basket of AAA-rated German government bonds would, for example, expect to achieve a significant discount on the cost of borrowing in the repo market in comparison with the seller of a basket of A-rated corporate assets.

The GC rate will also be quoted in a variety of standard maturity terms (typically from one day to one year in length) and, in practice, may vary further to reflect any restrictions imposed on the general collateral pool. For example, there will be a commonly quoted rate for 'French Government GC' or 'Sub 10 year French Government GC' where the asset pool is restricted to securities with less than ten years to final maturity – or even 'Sub 10 year French Government GC, ex linkers', where index-linked securities are excluded.

The concept of GC collateral is taken to its logical conclusion with the tri-party segment of the market. The tri-party repo model is considered in more detail elsewhere in this book but essentially involves a third party moving collateral in any of the eligible forms (based on pre-agreed haircuts) between accounts of the buyer and seller.

(b) Securities financing

From the repo buyer's perspective, repo can also be an effective (and widely used) method of obtaining securities to cover delivery obligations under other transactions – including short sales, physically deliverable derivative transactions and collateral or margin obligations under other transaction-types.

When a repo transaction is motivated by demand for an individual security, the asset in question is referred to as a 'special' and, accordingly, the trade is a special repo. The primary motivation for the buyer in the special repo market will be to cover a requirement to hold or obtain a position in the specific asset. The level of demand for each individual security will impact upon the repo rate for such a security. Typically the special rate is less than the GC rate reflecting the value of buying the securities (so cash borrowing is cheaper). Where demand for a security is particularly high, the rate may even be negative (ie, the repo buyer may have to pay the repo rate to the seller, not the other way around). The difference between the repo rate for a 'special' and the relevant GC rate is termed the 'speciality' of the security in question. It is common for the market to quote in these terms. A trader will, for example, refer to a particular asset as trading '10bps through GC', meaning that the repo buyer will earn 0.10% less on the cash lent than if transacting at the GC rate for that security.

The existence of the specials market allows for a trader to speculate as to the future value of an individual security. It is possible for an A-rated corporate bond to acquire such special value as to allow the seller to generate cash at a cheaper rate than the owner of higher-grade government collateral. The degree of speciality for each security will be caused to fluctuate by a variety of factors (eg, its scarcity within the market, its presence in the futures delivery market or the anticipation of a market event relating to the underlying issuer).

(c) *Leverage*

A further use of repo is to provide leverage. In this context, a repo seller might borrow cash under a repo transaction to obtain most of the cash it needs to purchase a holding of securities which it then uses for that repo. Alternatively, a repo seller may own a portfolio of securities and use those securities to raise cash through a repo and then reinvest that cash by purchasing other securities under a second repo (under which is it a buyer), then raise further cash by selling those securities purchased and so on – with the net effect of maximising the return on the initial securities portfolio. If a haircut of 2% is applied to each repo, it is theoretically possible to achieve close to 50x leverage in this way, although the actual number is less than 50 and additional liquidity would also be needed to meet margin calls.

(d) *Central banks*

Repo and reverse repo transactions are routinely employed by central banks – both as a means of managing monetary policy during normal market conditions and as an emergency measure to boost liquidity in times of market stress.

(e) *Market conventions*

As discussed above, a primary use of the repo market is to facilitate settlement flows. The majority of market conventions and norms are therefore driven by this. Settlement conventions in repo, where possible, will allow for usual market settlement on the day preceding the usual cash settlement in the bond or equity market in question. For example, if the cash market in an asset settles T+2, the usual repo trade will settle T+1. This follows for all interest calculations (eg, where bond interest is calculated on a 360-day basis, the repo convention will follow the underlying asset).

Certain nuances remain within these general conventions, by reason of characteristics which are peculiar to repo. The interest rate applied to a trade and the haircut taken (usually, but not always, by the provider of cash) can vary widely according to the market and the relative credit profile of the counterparties involved.

Although the interdealer market rate in a benchmark security can be regarded as largely commoditised (trading as a function of the relevant overnight indexed swap (OIS) curve in current market conditions), any variation in participant or underlying security can make this interest rate fluctuate widely. This is also true of the haircut applied to the trade. As discussed elsewhere in this book, the haircut is the difference, in percentage terms, between the actual asset value and the cash transferred against it. In investment grade bonds for a standard repo period (one week to one year) and in a single currency transaction this can vary from 0–20% depending on the relative credit strength of the participants to the trade. The repo market will, in this respect, be governed by credit risk appetite, but there is certainly an element of competitiveness in pricing when a haircut is set by a dealer for client business.

The following table sets out the repo conventions in the major markets:

Market	Settlement convention	Usual trade type	Day count
UST	T+0	classic repo	360
UK gilt	T+0	classic repo	365
Euroclear govt	T+1	classic repo	360
Italian govt	T+1	buy/sell-back	360
Japan govt	T+3	classic repo	365 on shore, 360 off shore
Euroclear corp	T+1 or T+2 (depending on ISIN and country of issue)	classic repo	360
GBP corp	T+2	classic repo	360

2. Securities lending

2.1 What is a stock loan?

A securities (or stock) loan is similar to a repo transaction. The lender of the securities transfers legal and beneficial ownership in them to the borrower, with an agreement that the borrower will deliver back to the lender equivalent securities at maturity of the loan.

In exchange for the loaned securities, the borrower provides collateral to the lender of the securities to secure its obligation to return the securities it has borrowed. This collateral may be in the form of cash or other securities. Ownership of the collateral is also transferred outright and, at the end of the loan, the lender must repay or redeliver the collateral (whether cash or equivalent securities) back to the borrower.

The key economic motivation for the lender is the rate of return generated on the loan of its securities, being the lending fee which the borrower is prepared to pay for the use of the securities borrowed.

Like repo, securities lending is a form of secured financing. The key difference is that with securities lending it is not cash which is lent (ie, financed) but securities. This difference reflects the contrast in the relative position and the underlying incentives of the parties as seen in the trade itself.

As the legal structure and basic payment and delivery flows of the two transaction-types are fundamentally the same, the two forms of trade can be used interchangeably for the same purpose, whether that purpose is raising cash or sourcing a specific security. Hence the specials repo market essentially fulfils the same function as a stock loan.

2.2 The securities lending markets

Securities lending materialised in the United Kingdom as far back as the 19th century, when the growth of securities trading created a niche market in sourcing gilts for market-makers and middlemen. The modern, global market in these instruments has its beginnings in US inter-dealer securities-financing activity which arose and developed during the 1960s and 70s. US custodian banks shortly thereafter spotted the opportunity to lend out assets on behalf of clients, initially in local markets then, increasingly throughout the 1980s, on an international basis. The development and globalisation of the securities lending market has been further propelled by the parallel development of the repo market, the expansion of derivatives trading and the relaxing of regulatory restrictions in a number of key jurisdictions.[3]

In the third quarter of 2011, the Bank of England estimated there to be approximately $2 trillion of securities on loan.[4] This market comprises a range of institution-types sitting on either side of the trade.

Borrowers of stock are commonly large institutions such as investment banks and broker-dealers, who may also source securities for their clients, such as hedge funds and investment funds. Such entities may need specific stock for settlement or 'collateral upgrade' purposes, to hedge derivative transactions, or for specific trading strategies (employing 'shorting' or capitalising on arbitrage opportunities).

Securities lenders are generally institutional investors seeking to generate higher returns on what might otherwise be a largely static pool of assets. It is common for this type of lender – which may include pension funds, insurers, investment funds and sovereign wealth funds – to use an agent, such as a global custodian, to arrange loans of assets they are holding for clients in return for a fee. Agency lending is discussed in greater detail elsewhere in this book.

---

[3] See Securities Lending Transactions: Market Development and Implications, published by the Technical Committee of the International Organization of Securities Commissions (IOSCO), July 1999.

[4] See Developments in the Global Securities Lending Market, 2011 *Quarterly Bulletin* Q3, by Matthew Dive, Ronan Hodge and Catrin Jones. The extent to which the figure quoted also captures the specials repo market is not specified.

2.3 Basic economics

(a) Commencement of loan

On commencement of the loan, the lender delivers the specific loaned securities to the borrower, and the borrower pays or delivers collateral to the lender. Title to both the loaned securities and any collateral in the form of securities is transferred outright to the receiving party.[5]

The lender is generally agnostic as to the precise collateral which is provided to secure the loan but there will typically be a pre-agreed schedule of acceptable collateral types and haircuts which are to be applied to their market value in order to establish their collateral value. So, if developed market government bonds are to be posted as collateral a haircut of 102% might be agreed. If the borrower chooses to post those bonds as collateral for the loan it will therefore post bonds having a market value equal to 102% of the market value of the loaned securities. If it chose to post collateral in the form of cash, a 100% haircut might apply and, if it chose to post equities (which are more volatile), then the haircut might be 5% (although the actual percentage applied can vary widely).

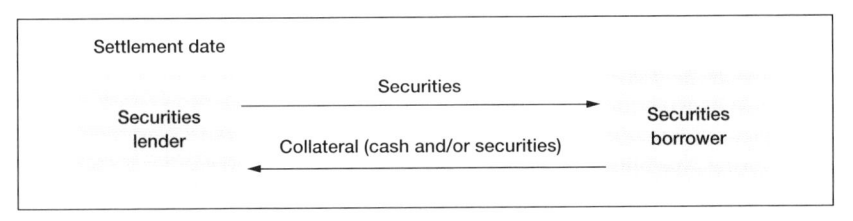

```
Settlement date

                       Securities
 Securities      ──────────────────────>      Securities
 lender          <──────────────────────      borrower
                 Collateral (cash and/or securities)
```

(b) Termination

At the end of a loan, the borrower redelivers securities which are equivalent to the loaned securities, and the lender repays any cash collateral and redelivers securities which are equivalent to any collateral securities. To the extent that the parties have agreed not to pay stock lending fees or interest on cash collateral on a periodic basis throughout the term of the loan, these amounts would also be paid (and offset, if applicable) at maturity of the trade.

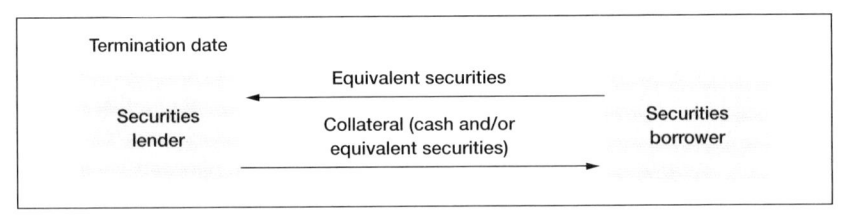

```
Termination date

                    Equivalent securities
 Securities      <──────────────────────      Securities
 lender          ──────────────────────>      borrower
                 Collateral (cash and/or
                 equivalent securities)
```

---

5   This assumes that the loan is documented under one of the English law-governed forms of the Global Master Securities Lending Agreement as published by ISLA. Under the New York law-governed SIFMA Master Securities Loan Agreements (1993 and 2000 versions), the analysis is less clear insofar as the collateral provider grants a security interest over the collateral in favour of the collateral taker.

(c) ***Lending fees***

The lending fee payable by the borrower is usually calculated by applying an agreed rate to the market value of the securities borrowed. If collateral is provided in the form of cash, it may be agreed that the lender will reinvest the cash and rebate back to the borrower a portion of the interest received (which may be paid by offsetting this rebated amount against the amount of stock lending fees payable by the borrower). Lending fees are typically paid on a monthly basis.

(d) ***Collateral***

It is a fundamental feature of a stock loan that the parties are required to maintain the amount of collateral for the loan.

Much like a repo, in order to avoid a change in the relative credit exposure between the parties over the life of a loan, there will be an obligation to provide additional collateral or to return collateral as the value of the loaned securities increases or decreases during the life of the loan. The stock lending agreement will set out an agreed list of eligible collateral types and the haircuts (or discounts to market value, for collateralisation purposes) that will apply. In the stock lending market, some borrowers provide letters of credit to lenders instead of posting collateral.

These collateralisation mechanics are described more fully elsewhere in this book.

(e) ***Term***

Unless the parties have agreed on a loan for a fixed term, the loan will be terminable on demand by either party. The borrower can simply redeliver equivalent loaned securities to the lender at any time, upon which the lender must return the collateral. Alternatively, the lender can recall the loaned securities at any time, upon which the borrower is required to redeliver the securities within the standard settlement period in the relevant market (eg, two days for UK equities).

(f) ***Asset types***

While the bulk of repo trading is still largely executed for cash financing (where secured against GC), the stock lending market is generally driven by demand for a specific security. As a result, while the repo market is still predominantly centred on debt securities, the securities lending market is focused much more on equities.

2.4 **Ownership transfer and the (partial) undoing of its effects**

As with repo, the fact that loaned securities are transferred outright to the borrower carries a host of issues. Again, the key features are described here.

The outright transfer of ownership of the securities means:
- Borrower free to deal – the borrower is free to sell or otherwise deal with the loaned securities in any way it wishes. In fact, it is common for a borrower to sell the securities it has borrowed in order to create a short position or to lend them on to the borrower's client for them to be able to do so. All the borrower needs to do is to ensure that it will be in a position to redeliver equivalent securities at maturity of the loan.

- Voting rights – the borrower will be the person entitled to vote on any decisions in respect of the loaned securities, if it still holds them.
- Payment on the securities – any dividends, coupons or repayments of principal on the loaned securities will belong to the borrower, if it still owns them at the time.
- Corporate actions – the borrower will receive the benefit of these if it still holds the securities at the time.
- Credit risk – the lender is exposed to the risk that the borrower may not return the loaned securities at the end of the loan and the borrower is exposed to the risk that the lender might not return the collateral it has received. However, in a default situation, no actual returns are made. Instead, the parties' respective obligations are valued and offset against each other, so that a party's exposure is only in respect of the net difference between the values of those obligations. In practice, this normally means that the borrower will always be exposed to the lender on a net basis as it sold securities which were worth more than the value of the securities it borrowed. This is over-collateralisation risk (ie, the risk of loss on default).

The terms of the loan will address some (but not all) of these issues, so as to seek to put the parties into the position which would have prevailed had the securities not been lent at all. This reflects the accounting treatment which generally applies to securities loans; for accounting purposes the lender of the securities will still recognise them as if it still owned them and, correspondingly, the borrower will show the assets it has provided as collateral as if they were still owned and will not show the loaned securities as its asset. This treatment is considered more fully elsewhere in this book.

The features of ownership of the securities having passed to the borrower that will be addressed in the terms of the loan (at least if documented under standard industry terms or similar) include:

- Income – the borrower will be required to pay to the lender an amount equal to any cash dividends or distributions paid on the loaned securities during the term of the loan. These amounts are referred to as 'manufactured dividends'. The obligation arises as and when the payment is made by the issuer.
- Corporate actions – the borrower will be required to redeliver equivalent securities to the lender at the end of the loan. This means that even if something happens to the securities during the term of the loan, the borrower will have to redeliver assets which the lender would have had if it had owned the securities throughout. So, if the securities are converted into other assets, it is those other assets which would have to be redelivered. If elective rights arise, then the lender can elect if it wants to receive back assets as if those rights had been exercised.
- Credit risk – the terms of the loan will provide ongoing obligations on the borrower and lender to maintain collateral for the loan. So, if the value of the loaned securities increases, the borrower will have to post more collateral. If

the value of the posted collateral were to increase then the lender would have to return the excess. Under a standard stock loan, the amount of securities loaned will remain static, and only the collateral leg is rebalanced. The precise mechanics for this are described and illustrated elsewhere in this book.

The terms of the loan will not typically provide for:
- Restrictions on dealing – the borrower is always free to deal in the loaned securities and this is a necessary feature of the product and market. It provides essential liquidity to the markets in securities and the borrower to on-lend them or create a short position by selling them.
- Direction of voting rights – there is no requirement for the lender to be able to direct that voting rights be exercised in a particular way. This reflects the fact that the borrower is free to deal with the loaned securities as it wishes.
- Over-collateralisation risk – standard securities lending terms do not seek to mitigate against this but it can be limited by the borrower providing only cash collateral. However, if lower grade collateral is provided there are structures which can be adopted to reduce or eliminate it if the parties are concerned about this from a credit or regulatory capital perspective.

Where a party to the loan transfers collateral in the form of securities this will similarly be by way of outright transfer of ownership of the securities, and so those collateral securities are treated in the same way as the loaned securities in terms of these issues.[6]

2.5 Uses of stock lending

(a) *Securities financing*

Much like the specials repo market, stock lending offers a means by which market participants (from a borrower's perspective) can source securities for a particular purpose. As discussed previously in this chapter, this might be:
- to cover short positions;
- to meet delivery obligations under physically deliverable derivative trades, repo transactions or other stock loans;
- to source a particular collateral-type (eg, by providing illiquid, lower quality collateral, such as mortgage-backed securities, in return for a loan of more liquid securities, such as gilts or US treasury instruments, which can then be provided as collateral under a separate trade);
- to effect hedging strategies (eg, if physically hedging an equity derivative transaction);
- to be in a position to vote on those securities; or
- to execute trading strategies (eg, tax, regulatory or futures price arbitrage).

---

6   See footnote 5 above.

Borrowers may also enter into securities loans specifically to obtain liquid assets for compliance with regulatory capital requirements.

(b) *Cash financing*

Securities loans are increasingly used as instruments for cash financing. A securities loan under which collateral is provided solely in the form of cash is economically equivalent to a GC repo (provided that the securities lender – in these circumstances, also the cash borrower – is under-collateralised for the securities loan). This type of transaction typically requires bespoke changes to the governing documentation to ensure that the margining mechanics and fee payments (and other key economic components) reflect the intended characteristics of the trade.

Lifecycle of transactions

Guy Usher
Fieldfisher

This chapter looks at the lifecycle of a repo and securities lending transaction, from inception (trading and settlement), during its term (income payments and corporate events) through to maturity or early unwind.

For a more precise understanding of the contractual obligations which underpin much of what is said in this chapter, reference should be made to the provisions of the underlying documentation between the parties. This chapter assumes the underlying documentation to be the 2000 Global Master Repurchase Agreement (GMRA) (for repo and buy/sell-backs) or the 2010 Global Master Securities Lending Agreement (GMSLA) (for securities lending), in each case discussed in detail elsewhere in this book. There would be slight differences if other versions of those documents had been used. Some, but not all, of these differences are noted.

Additional guidance on market practices, conventions and best or recommended practices can be obtained from the "Guide to Best Practice in the European Repo Market" published by ICMA (latest edition October 2014) and the "Securities Borrowing and Lending Code of Guidance" published by the SLRC (latest edition July 2009, but in the process of being updated at the time of writing).

1. Doing the trade

The trade itself may arise in any number of ways depending on the circumstances.

A holder of stock may proactively offer its securities as being available for borrowing by a panel of approved borrowers. In practice, this will often be arranged through an agent lender on its behalf who will enter into stock loans for their lender client.

A corporate treasurer looking to invest cash may call up a relationship bank and request that an amount of cash it holds be invested in repo. Alternatively, an owner of securities may use repo to seek to raise finance on the inventory that it is holding or is about to purchase.

The trade may also come to exist through one of the many automatic borrowing and lending facilities operated by the clearing systems or through a trading platform.

The trade may be agreed via the telephone, by email or via an electronic messaging system or it may be generated automatically or through an order matching system. The date on which the deal is struck is then the trade date. Where the trade is only agreed orally or otherwise than through a matching system there will be a separate trade confirmation generated by either or both parties which will be exchanged and agreed – which may itself occur by physical signature of paper confirmations, email exchange or through an electronic messaging system. The confirmation, once agreed, will then become the definitive source of the terms of the trade and will supersede the initial oral agreement. Until that time, however, there is still a binding contract as long as all the key trade terms are sufficiently clear at the outset. Confirmations are typically issued and agreed on the same day as the trade date.

It is also increasingly best practice periodically to reconcile trade details subsequent to the trade in order to affirm its terms and so identify any breaks (mismatches) and hopefully avoid future disputes.

2. Pricing rates, initial margin and collateral

How the trade is priced will depend on the type of transaction and is best shown by reference to simple illustrations.

Repo rates are usually bilaterally agreed specifically for each transaction but there are quoted repo rates for general collateral repo published by the major pricing sources. Central banks also have published rates at which they will buy back government bonds from the banks that they regulate. Since the financial crisis, central banks have also been purchasing by way of repo asset-backed securities subject to certain qualification criteria being met.

Stock lending fees are similarly bilaterally agreed. There are standard lending fee rates for very liquid stocks on the main markets but fees can be significantly higher for stocks that are less liquid or are 'special' (ie, in demand). Where cash collateral is posted to the lender of stock the fee may be quoted as a 'rebate', reflecting the fact that the lender will earn interest on the cash collateral and 'rebate' it to the borrower of the stock.

The following paragraphs give some example transactions.

2.1 Classic repo

The holder of €100 million principal (or face) amount of 1.5% 10-year German Bunds wishes to raise finance on them for one week. It approaches the repo desk of one of its relationship banks and agrees a repo rate of 0.1% for the financing. A 2% haircut for repos of G7 government bonds is agreed. The deal is done. The trade will settle (ie, the purchase date will occur) on T+1[1] (the day after the trade date).

The settlement date for a repo is usually a day earlier than in the conventional settlement cycle for transactions in the cash market for the securities themselves, as repo market settlement conventions follow money-market conventions and earlier settlement is required in order to enable repo securities to be used by the buyer for settlement of onward sales. Non-bank sellers might need to extend this settlement to correspond to the cycle in the cash market for the securities.

Assume that the clean market value of the Bunds is €106,330,000. The accrued interest on the holding of the Bunds at the purchase date is €719,180 giving a 'dirty' price (including the accrued coupon) of €107,049,180. Applying a 2% haircut to the market value of the Bunds means that the seller of the Bunds (ie, the person borrowing the cash) can raise €104,908,200 (or €107,049,180 × 98%) from its holding. This is the initial purchase price.

---

1   With the European cash bond markets moving to T+2 in October 2014, the repo settlement convention changed to T+1.

It should be noted that the initial margin under the GMRA is actually expressed as the value of collateral (purchased securities), as a percentage of the purchase price, not as a discount to the value of collateral (purchased securities).[2] Mathematically, an initial margin of 102% is the same as applying a haircut of 1.961% to the value of the Bunds, not 2%.

Slightly different repo rates will apply to different financing periods and different haircuts will apply to different types of asset, although there are conventional categorisations and haircuts for the main asset classes. The more volatile the price of the security and the less liquid, the higher the haircut. As it is this which protects the buyer in case the seller defaults, the haircut should be adequate to allow for possible changes in value of the collateral for the period of time it takes to close-out and then liquidate the collateral since the last movement of margin was made. Haircuts may also be higher to reflect the term of the transaction and the creditworthiness of the counterparty.

2.2 Buy/sell-back

With a buy/sell-back transaction it is the repurchase price that needs to be agreed. So in the above example, had the parties instead entered into a buy/sell-back, they would have instead agreed an initial purchase price of €104,908,200, a repurchase date seven days after the initial settlement date and a repurchase price of:

$$€104{,}908{,}200 + [€104{,}908{,}200 \times 7/360 \times 0.1\%] = €104{,}910{,}240.$$

The implicit repo rate (0.1%) can be derived from the repurchase price as the daily rate of accrual of the excess of the repurchase price over the purchase price.

In practice, however, the parties will still actually agree the repo rate and then use it to calculate the repurchase price. This calculation is not always as straightforward as in the above example for reasons which are explained later in this chapter.

2.3 Stock loan

With a conventional stock loan the parties will agree what securities are to be lent, what period they are to be lent for (if not open-ended, on demand) and what lending fee will apply. The types of collateral which can be posted and the haircuts which will apply to each type are typically pre-agreed in the GMSLA.

Take an example of 1 million shares in SAP AG being lent for a week against non-cash collateral at a fee of 0.5%. The initial price of SAP AG shares is €53.70. Collateral having a margin (or 'haircutted') value of €53,700,000 will therefore be required to be posted to the lender of the stock. The borrower chooses to post 3.75% five-year OATs (French government bonds) as collateral which have a pre-agreed 'margin percentage' of 105%. The clean price of the OATs is 117.22 and there is accrued interest on the OATs giving a dirty price of 117.34. The borrower of the SAP AG shares will have to provide OATs to the lender of the stock by way of collateral having a market value of:

---

[2] The 2011 GMRA now allows for both methods of expressing initial margin to be used.

€53,700,000 × 105% = €56,385,000.

The principal amount of OATs to be provided will therefore be:

€56,385,000 ÷ 117.34% = €48,052,667.

3. **Settlement at the outset**
In all cases, initial settlement will occur on the agreed or customary standard settlement date (by reference to the applicable market convention and trade date). On that date there will be a transfer of securities against cash or collateral.

In the repo example, on the initial settlement date, the seller will transfer €100 million principal amount of the Bunds to the buyer, who will pay €104,908,200 to the seller. In the stock loan example, the lender will transfer 1 million shares in SAP AG to the borrower and the borrower will transfer to the lender €48,052,667 principal amount of the OATs.

Transfers are almost always made on a delivery-versus-payment (DvP) basis through one of the international or local clearing systems that settle transactions in the relevant securities or by debiting and crediting cash and securities accounts held by the parties with a tri-party agent. DvP settlement removes inter-day settlement risk (ie, the risk of one party meeting its transfer obligation and the other party failing to meet its corresponding payment or transfer obligation).

4. **Interest/fee accrual**

4.1 Classic repo
Repo interest accrues at the agreed repo rate for each day during the term of the repo on the amount of cash lent. In the classic repo example, with a repo rate of 0.1%, accrued repo interest on day three is therefore:

€104,908,200 × 3/360 × 0.1% = €870.

4.2 Buy/sell-back
The same rate applies to the buy/sell-back example but the way to view it is that the accrued repurchase price as at day three is €104,909,070, being the original purchase price plus accrued repo interest at the repo rate *implicit* in the trade terms.

4.3 Stock loan
With the stock loan example, there is no interest as such (as the collateral posted was not cash) but there is an accrued lending fee. In order to determine that fee we need to know the SAP AG share price for each of the three days on which the stock loan has been outstanding. Assuming an average share price for the three days of €52.57, the accrued lending fee (at an agreed rate of 0.5%) will therefore be:

€52.57 × 1,000,000 × 3/360 × 0.5% = €2,190.

Note that repo interest and lending fees are not paid each day; they are either paid at maturity (in the case of a repo) or periodically (typically monthly in the case of on-demand (or 'open') stock loans). With longer-dated term transactions, periodic payments may also be required and the repo rate itself may be reset during the term of the transaction.

5. Margin/collateral maintenance

Both repos and stock loans are collateralised transactions from the outset. The initial securities sold to the buyer in a repo secure the seller's obligation to repay the cash it has borrowed and, in the stock loan, the initial collateral posted to the lender secures the borrower's obligation to return the stock borrowed. However, that is not the end of the story. There are also obligations to maintain the agreed collateralisation on an ongoing (daily) basis. This margining is also referred to as 'variation margin', as opposed to the initial margin which determined the amount of collateralisation required at inception.

The purpose of posting variation margin is to maintain the initial collateralisation level so that, if there were a default by one of the parties, the other party would be covered to the same extent throughout the term of the trade.

The following assumes that there have been no collateral movements before day three, although in practice the calculation will be made each day.

5.1 Classic repo and buy/sell-back

In terms of the classic repo, the position on day three would look like this:

Seller-side obligation: cash borrowed plus accrued repo interest = €104,909,070.

Buyer-side obligation: Bunds purchased (current market value of the holding including then accrued coupon) = €107,061,680.

By applying the agreed 2% haircut to the market value of the Bunds on day three, it can be seen that the margin (or haircutted) value of the Bunds is now €104,920,450 which is more than the accrued seller's obligation at that time. This is entirely expected given that the Bunds are accruing coupon at a rate of 1.5% a day and the repo interest is accruing at a rate of only 0.1%.

In this case the seller has over-collateralised the buyer by €12,070 and so makes a margin call on the buyer. The buyer has to transfer margin to the seller equal to that amount. If the call is made before the pre-agreed cut-off time, the margin call will be satisfied by the payment of cash in the pre-agreed base currency to the seller on the day the call is made (or within the period the parties have specified in their GMRA). If the margin call is made after the pre-agreed cut-off time, the payment will only have to be made on the following business day. The buyer and seller will agree at the time what interest is to be paid by the seller to the buyer on that cash – typically based upon an overnight benchmark rate from which a spread may be deducted.

Alternatively, the buyer may deliver non-cash collateral to cover the differential in obligation values. Under the GMRA, any non-cash collateral has to be reasonably acceptable to the party receiving it. It is a market practice recommendation to accept as collateral securities which are recognised as being general collateral in the repo market or which are at least as good as the purchased securities from a quality perspective.

Haircuts do not apply to variation margin posted under the GMRA unless they are agreed at the time the collateral is posted.[3] It would be unusual to apply a haircut to cash collateral (at least in a major currency) but it might be appropriate to agree to apply a haircut to non-cash collateral. The effect of a buyer posting cash collateral to the seller is economically the same as the buyer lending more money, albeit probably at a different rate of interest to the repo rate. The effect of a seller posting cash collateral economically reduces the cash lent and so economically increases the initial margin/haircut (smaller cash exposure compared with the purchased securities). When accepting non-cash margin, the person making the margin call should also consider that it might not be possible for the other party to deliver non-cash collateral as quickly as cash, which means accepting credit risk of its counterparty over that extended period.

The margin calculation methodology is the same for the buy/sell-back – if documented under a GMRA – as for a repo, although in the case of a buy/sell-back it is usual to use repricing as a means of rebalancing the credit exposure between the parties.

With either repo or buy/sell-back transactions, the GMRA gives the parties the option to agree to have a transaction 'repriced' or 'adjusted' instead of being margined in the conventional manner as just described. There are provisions in the GMRA specifying how this will occur but, essentially, either the cash leg or the securities leg of the transaction is re-sized in order to eliminate the exposure represented by the differential in obligation values which has arisen due to price movements and repo interest/coupon accrual. Legally this takes effect as a termination of the original transaction and its replacement with a new transaction. Repricing is not uncommon; adjustment is rarely used.

If the parties had agreed to reprice the illustrative buy/sell-back transaction instead of posting margin, they would agree to a new transaction for the same amount of the purchased securities. However, the purchase price would be increased to reflect the fact that the securities are worth more than they were at inception and the repurchase price would similarly be increased to reflect the fact that the cash lent – which has to be returned – had been increased and that interest will have to be paid on the additional amount during the remainder of the term. The GMRA provides for net settlement to occur across the two transactions (the original and the replacement) so that only a small cash or securities movement occurs (as would be the case with a conventional margin call). Accrued interest to the repricing date will usually be paid and not rolled forward into the new transaction.

There are standard provisions for the margining of forward transactions, starting from the date which is one settlement cycle before the initial purchase date is due to occur. This reflects the fact that there is almost certainly going to be an exposure at initial settlement reflecting market value movements on the purchased securities

---

3   The 2011 GMRA contemplates that haircuts may apply to collateral posted as variation margin.

since the trade date. In practice, this re-balancing may be effected using either repricing or adjustment.

The GMRA assumes that the market value of any purchased securities – or margin securities – is objectively observable for margin maintenance purposes and so does not specify which party will determine market value for margining purposes; nor does it contain a mechanism for resolving any disputes which may arise. With very liquid assets whose prices are quoted on recognised pricing sources – such as Bloomberg – it is generally the case that either party can observe the same price provided they use the same pricing source. That is why it is provided in the GMRA for the parties to agree a pricing source for obtaining market values of securities. When less liquid assets are repoed this no longer holds true and the parties should legislate who makes the determination, the valuation basis and a mechanism for the other party to challenge the determination.

For both classic repo and buy/sell-backs, the GMRA provides for margining of transactions on a global net basis for all transactions outstanding between the two parties. The parties can, however, agree to provide for transaction-by-transaction margining to occur instead. Repricing and adjustment work only on a transaction-by-transaction basis. Where global net margining applies, the parties may also agree a minimum transfer amount which has to be exceeded before collateral has to be transferred.

5.2 Stock loan

For the stock loan, the margin requirement is similarly determined by comparing the values of the loaned securities with the haircutted value of the collateral. The requirement is to maintain collateral with a haircutted value equal to the market value of the securities lent. So, on day three the position would look like this:

Collateral: OATs held (assume a current market value of the holding including then accrued coupon) = €56,400,054, having a haircutted value of €56,400,054 ÷ 105% = €53,714,337.

Securities: SAP AG shares (current price = €52.8 per share) = €52,800,000.

The borrower has over-collateralised the lender in the amount of €914,337 and so the lender will have to return collateral (OATs) to the borrower in an amount which has that value (ie, €914,337 ÷ dirty price of 117.37 = €779,021 in principal amount of OATs). Under the 2010 GMLSA, it is now provided that it is the lender of the stock who determines where prices should be sourced (ie, from a pricing information source or, if unavailable, from a dealer in the relevant market) for both the market value of the securities lent and any collateral in the form of securities.

Unlike repo interest, the accrued lending fee does not feature in the collateral maintenance calculation for a stock loan. In a situation where the borrower has to post collateral to the lender it can transfer any of the pre-agreed eligible collateral types applying the pre-agreed haircuts.

Collateral is called on a daily basis and often same-day delivery periods will be agreed, provided that the demand (or 'call') is made by the pre-agreed cut-off time for same-day margin deliveries. Otherwise it will be posted on the following day. Where securities collateral is posted, then (other than for UK Gilts and US Treasuries) same-day margining may not be possible due to the minimum settlement cycles which apply to transfers of such securities.

6. **Income/manufactured dividends**

For the purpose of the remainder of this chapter, it needs to be borne in mind that the securities sold or lent and the collateral transferred are legally an outright transfer of the securities in question. That is, the receiver of the securities becomes the outright owner of them and is free to sell or otherwise use them in any way it wishes. The receiver may not necessarily, therefore, retain ownership of those securities during the term of the trade. It is for this reason that the obligation to redeliver or return the securities is only an obligation to redeliver or return 'equivalent' securities (ie, the same type of securities but not the exact same specific securities which were originally transferred).

Notwithstanding this legal construct, market participants in the stock lending market in particular commonly – and technically incorrectly – refer to the lender as being the 'beneficial owner' of the loaned securities. This reflects the position that the lender is substantially in the same economic position as if it had not lent the loaned securities.

6.1 **Classic repo**

Under a classic repo, the buyer of the purchased securities – as well as the person holding non-cash collateral, which could be the buyer or seller – is required to pay to the other party an amount equal to any income (coupon in the case of a bond) paid on those securities which have been transferred to it. This is irrespective of whether that person is actually holding those securities at the time the income is paid. This payment is called a manufactured dividend or manufactured payment.

So, if on day four in the example given, the Bunds were to pay their semi-annual coupon (0.75%), the buyer would be obliged under the GMRA to pay to the seller €750,000, being an amount equal to six months' interest on the holding of the Bunds which have been repoed. At the same time, the market value of the Bunds for margining purposes (which is a dirty price and so includes the accrued coupon) will have reduced and there will be a margin call made by the buyer on the seller as a consequence of the differential this creates between the buyer-side and the seller-side obligations at that time.

6.2 **Buy/sell-back**

With a buy/sell-back transaction, the payment of the coupon on the purchased securities would have been anticipated in the agreed repurchase price. The coupon – or a manufactured dividend equal to it – is not paid by the buyer to the seller; instead, it is retained by the buyer. So, if there were a scheduled coupon payment on the repoed securities before the repurchase date, the implicit repo rate in the buy-sell example would not be the same as the classic repo and, indeed, in this example the repurchase price would actually be less than the purchase price as the buyer received the entire semi-annual coupon on the bonds it bought (and has had the use of the cash from the coupon payment date until maturity of the transaction). The derivation of the implicit repo rate in buy/sell-back is therefore complex where coupon payment dates occur. If the issuer were to fail to pay the coupon on a security which was the subject of a buy/sell-back, the buyer would suffer the loss as a consequence, as the buy-back leg is priced to assume that it will be paid. This contrasts with a repo, as the obligation to make a manufactured dividend payment arises only when the income is actually paid.

6.3 Stock loan

With the stock loan, assume that, instead of a coupon being paid on the OATs collateral (which would be treated in the same way as the coupon paid on the Bunds in the classic repo example above), a dividend of €0.60 is declared in respect of the SAP AG shares – they are now trading ex-dividend at a price of €52.20. No dividend has been paid yet, but the holder of the SAP AG stock at the record date for the dividend which has been declared is now legally entitled to receive the dividend when it is paid. Under the GMSLA, when the dividend is paid by SAP AG, the borrower of the stock will have to pay an amount equal to that dividend to the lender (ie, put the lender in the same position as it would have been in had it not lent the stock). The obligation to pay this amount (again referred to as a manufactured dividend) arises whether or not the borrower of the stock is actually holding the SAP AG shares on the date the dividend is declared or paid. There is an option in the 2010 GMSLA for the parties to agree also to include the unpaid dividends in the collateral calculation, which marks it out as different from earlier versions.

6.4 Non-cash distributions

The GMRA and GMSLA also provide for what is to happen in the case of non-cash distributions on, and redemptions of, securities. The treatment varies slightly depending on the vintage of master agreement and the nature of the securities in question – fixed income or equity securities – but, in broad terms, the principle is that these do not give rise to obligations to make manufactured dividend payments but are treated as forming part of, or replacing in whole or in part, the purchased or loaned securities (or the collateral securities if applicable) and therefore form part of the 'equivalent' securities to be returned to the seller/lender.[4]

7. Voting rights

In a repo, buy/sell-back or a stock loan, the holder of securities (whether securities purchased, stock borrowed or securities collateral transferred) does not have to exercise voting rights on those securities in accordance with the wishes of the person who sold, lent or transferred them. This feature is more relevant where the underlying securities are equities rather than fixed-income instruments.

---

4   The 2011 GMRA now takes the opposite position as regards the treatment of redemption amounts.

It may be critical to a lender of stock to be in a position to vote on the securities it has lent. If so, it would need specifically to agree this with the borrower – which may be difficult if the borrower wants to use or sell the stock it has borrowed – or it needs to be able to recall the stock, perhaps substituting another asset for it.

Alternatively, a person may borrow stock precisely in order to obtain the right to vote on key issues affecting the issuer of the shares. The SLRC Code of Guidance states that there is a consensus that borrowing stock solely for this purpose is not appropriate due to concerns about decisions being influenced by people who do not have a permanent or long-term economic interest in the outcome. In addition, prospective borrowers should be aware that the GMSLA contains a warranty from the borrower of stock that it is not borrowing the securities primarily for the purposes of exercising voting rights on them.

8. Corporate events

Variations to securities (whether securities sold, stock lent or securities collateral transferred) can occur during the term of a trade and the impact of these variations needs to be accommodated in the trade terms. Such events may include conversion, sub-division, consolidation, take-over or the right to receive other securities or property.

While under a repo and a stock loan the legal ownership of securities is transferred to the person receiving them, the economic interest in the securities – market value, issuer default risk, etc – remains with the person who transferred them. It is for this reason that the securities remain on the balance sheet of the seller/lender from an accounting perspective, something that is discussed in more detail elsewhere in this book.

8.1 Classic repo and buy/sell-back

With a repo under the GMRA, the position is that the obligation to redeliver or return equivalent securities includes an obligation to return any cash or securities which arise from a holding of the securities in question – other than cash income payments – which have to be paid over when received by way of manufactured dividend payments. So, if there were a conversion of a bond which was a purchased security under a repo into a different type of security, then the obligation would be to return a quantity of the replacement security equal to the amount which would have been received by a holder of the original security had it held the amount of bonds which had been purchased under the repo.

8.2 Stock loan (and equity repo)

In the case of a stock loan, the position is similar to a repo but there are additional provisions reflecting the fact that, with equities, corporate events are more common and diverse in terms of the range of events which can occur. So, for example, under a stock loan, the lender of stock – or a party which has posted equities as collateral – can elect to have assets returned to it when the time for redelivery occurs on the basis that rights attaching to the stock have been exercised in a particular way. If there is a payment required to be made by the holder in order to exercise those rights, then that has to be paid by the person specifying that it wishes to receive back assets as if those rights had been exercised.

With an equity repo, additional provisions are included in the GMRA through the application of the Equities Annex to deal with corporate events so that the position is then broadly the same as would apply to a stock loan under the GMSLA.

Practical issues frequently arise in the context of corporate actions as it is often impractical and sometimes impossible for the person who received the securities to commit to return the assets which the original owner would like to receive. This can be a particular issue for agent lenders who lend out their clients' stock.

9. Substitutions and recalls

9.1 Classic repo and buy/sell-back

During the term of a repo, the seller (ie, the borrower of the cash) may wish to take back the original securities it sold to the buyer and, instead, provide alternative securities as collateral for the cash it has borrowed. This is contemplated under the GMRA but the substitution requires the consent of the buyer. The buyer will commonly agree to this as long as the replacement securities are of a similar quality and market value as the securities being substituted and the repo buyer did not enter into the transaction to obtain the particular purchased securities. If a substitution of purchased securities is agreed, the exchange is to be simultaneous where that is possible.

A corresponding provision applies to the substitution of margin in the form of securities.

In a general collateral repo the buyer is generally agnostic as to the precise purchased securities and, in a tri-party repo arrangement, the seller will be entitled to provide and replace any collateral with other collateral of an eligible type at any time. The right to substitute can also be included in a non-general collateral (GC) repo, although there are likely to be restrictions on this in terms of the number of substitutions permitted and notice periods. The existence of the right may affect the repo's pricing as the buyer may be restricted in terms of what it can do with purchased securities knowing that it might be required to return them to the seller at any time.

9.2 Stock loan

With a stock loan, there is no contemplated right to substitute the securities lent under the GMSLA, reflecting the fact that the purpose of the transaction is typically for a borrower to have a particular stock for a particular purpose. The parties can, of course, agree to substitutions if they wish and, in more structured transactions, a right to substitute the loaned securities may be specified.

Substitutions of collateral securities are common and the borrower of stock is allowed under the GMSLA to make substitutions without the consent of the lender provided that the replacement collateral is of a type which the parties have agreed may be provided as collateral and the required amount is delivered to the lender (based on the market value and pre-agreed haircut for collateral of the relevant type).

With a stock loan there are additional rights for the lender and borrower to terminate the loan at any time unless the terms of the stock loan otherwise provide. Absent a more specific provision which excludes the right to terminate, any stock loan may be terminated. For a lender to effectively recall the loaned securities in this way, it has to give notice to the borrower at least one settlement cycle for the relevant securities prior to the date it wants the loaned securities to be returned. For a borrower to effectively terminate the loan in this way, it simply has to deliver back securities equivalent to the loaned securities. In either case the lender is obliged to return equivalent collateral to the borrower, simultaneously if possible.

10. Settlement at maturity

At maturity the trade will unwind by the parties returning the securities they originally bought or borrowed, repaying the cash originally paid or returning the collateral originally received and also paying interest and fees.

10.1 Classic repo and buy/sell-back

So, in the case of the classic repo example, at the end of the seven-day term of that trade, the seller will repay the cash borrowed (€104,908,200) and pay the repo interest for the seven-day period (€2,040). The payment by the seller is a single payment of the repurchase price (ie, the cost of repurchasing the securities it sold at the outset will be higher than the purchase price paid by the buyer for the securities by an amount equal to seven days of repo interest on the purchase price). The repurchase price is therefore €104,910,240.

The buyer will simultaneously deliver securities equivalent to those it purchased (€100 million principal amount of Bunds) against payment of the repurchase price.

There is no correlation between the market value of the securities at the time of repurchase and the repurchase price paid. That differential would have been reflected instead by variation margin transferred throughout the life of the trade. Once the trade is unwound, then the seller or buyer will be required to return any variation margin it may have received to the extent not previously returned. Only one of the buyer or seller will be holding (and so will have to return) variation margin at any particular time.

Once the trade is settled there will cease to be any exposure and so the €12,070 cash collateral posted by the buyer to the seller pursuant to the margin call made on day three would then be demanded back by the buyer.

10.2 Stock loan

With a stock loan, the position is the same; the borrower will return stock which is 'equivalent' to the stock it borrowed and the lender will return cash or securities equivalent to the collateral it received. The borrower will also pay a fee to the lender or the fee will be rebated from the interest that the borrower will pay to the lender by way of an interest cost on any cash collateral it receives. Any variation collateral will then also be returned to the party which provided it.

So, in the illustrative stock loan, the lender will deliver the 1 million SAP AG shares to the borrower and the borrower will deliver €47,273,646 principal amount of OATs to the lender (assuming no further OATs were delivered back to the borrower after day three). The lending fee paid for the seven days will be the average price of the SAP AG shares on each day that the stock loan was outstanding × 0.5% × 7/365.

11. Delivery failures: 'mini close-outs' and buy-ins

It is not uncommon in securities markets for delivery failures to occur for a variety of reasons and that applies as much to the securities financing markets as it does to the cash markets in the securities.

For this reason, there are special provisions and remedies provided in the GMRA and GMSLA dealing with delivery fails. Such failures are treated differently from other forms of default because they are frequent and, more likely than not, do not arise as a result of any deterioration in the creditworthiness of the party responsible for the failed delivery.

11.1 Classic repo and buy/sell-back

Under the GMRA, in the event of a failure to deliver purchased securities at the outset of the transaction or to deliver back equivalent securities at maturity, the parties are given various rights including the ability to initiate what is called a 'mini close-out'. These rights entitle the person who is due to pay the cash leg to withhold payment or, if already paid, require repayment of the cash. The transaction, however, remains in place unless the party due to receive the securities decides to terminate the transaction (if it never settled at inception) or close-out the transaction (if it settled at the outset but failed to settle at maturity).

The fact that the transaction remains open means that the delivering party remains obliged to make the delivery and, if it does so, the other party is required to make the corresponding cash payment. There is no express entitlement to make partial deliveries[5] but the ERC Guide to Best Practice recommends that partial deliveries are accepted as they mitigate the extent of the issues arising from a failure to deliver.

If it is a seller who fails to deliver the purchased securities, whether the transaction is terminated or not, the seller has to pay repo interest from the scheduled purchase date even though it may not have received – or may have had to return – the purchase price.

It is not uncommon for non-GC repo rates to be negative where the securities to be repoed are special – and where the buyer is motivated not by the desire to earn interest on its cash but by a desire to own and use the purchased securities for the term of the repo transaction. In that respect the transaction is more like a stock loan than a repo. In that situation it is common to include wording in a GMRA so as to ensure that the seller does not benefit from a failure to deliver the purchased securities to the buyer if the transaction is not immediately terminated due to a failure to deliver.

If it is the buyer who fails to redeliver securities equivalent to the purchased securities on the repurchase date, then this is where the mini close-out occurs. A mini

---

5   Although this is now contemplated in the 2011 GMRA.

close-out is equivalent to a 'buy-in' in the cash securities markets, which means that the transaction is closed-out at the seller's side of the market (ie, the price at which the seller is able to buy the securities in the market). This can be costly for the buyer.

Where a transaction is terminated or closed-out due to a failure to deliver or redeliver purchased securities, the person to whom delivery has been made may also claim the cost of entering into a replacement transaction or hedging its exposure.

These rights do not apply to a failure to deliver non-cash collateral and the sole remedy would be for the person to whom it was to be delivered to close-out on the basis of an event of default.[6]

11.2 Stock loan

Under the GMSLA, there are similar rights for a party when the other party fails to make a delivery (on the return leg only) of equivalent loaned securities or equivalent securities to any collateral delivered. There is no corresponding termination right if the delivery of loaned securities on the outward leg fails. In the case of a return leg delivery failure, the party which was to receive the securities may elect to continue the loan until the delivery is made (and may call for margin accordingly) or to terminate the loan and, if applicable, undertake a mini close-out of the affected loan only. It is also entitled to compensation for interest costs and other expenses as a result of the failure and to claim from the other party any costs that are suffered from any buy-in exercised against it by third parties.

Although in both repo, buy/sell-back and stock loans, economic buy-in rights exist under the mini close-out regimes, they are not frequently used due to their economic impact. It is for this reason that the ICMA and the ERC are opposed to the mandatory buy-in rights proposed by the EU Regulation on central securities depositories and securities settlement (CSDR).[7]

12. Default and close-out

Aside from the position of failed deliveries just discussed, the description of the lifecycle of a typical repo or stock loan so far assumes that the transactions proceed to maturity. The position is quite different, and more complex, in the case where one of the parties defaults prior to the scheduled settlement of the trade at maturity. A default could occur at any time, either due to a failure by one of the parties to meet its obligations to the other party or for reasons, such as bankruptcy, which are not directly connected to the trade itself. The following assumes that the parties have not defaulted in their specific obligations in respect of the transaction but that, nevertheless, an early termination has occurred due to an event of default occurring with respect to one of the parties (eg, supervening bankruptcy).

12.1 Classic repo

With the classic repo, assume that an event of default occurs with respect to the seller

---

6   The 2011 GMRA has modified events of default which apply in this situation.
7   See "CSDR Mandatory Buy-ins and the treatment of SFTs: An ICMA-ERC Briefing Note" (September 2014).

and that the buyer has elected to terminate the trade immediately by serving a default notice on the seller. This occurs on day four, just after the buyer has made its first transfer of variation margin to the seller. The position is as follows:

The seller has borrowed cash in the amount of €104,908,200; now four days' repo interest (of €1,165.64) has accrued and the seller has received cash margin of €12,070 on day three. The parties agreed that interest at EONIA minus 0.125% is payable on the cash margin posted.

The buyer has bought the €10 million principal amount of Bunds.

By virtue of giving the termination notice, the repurchase date is accelerated so that the repo becomes a four-day repo instead of its originally scheduled seven days. That brings forward the date on which the settlement obligations arise. However, instead of delivering back the securities purchased, the securities are instead valued so as to create a cash value of the delivery obligation. The same would apply to an obligation to return variation margin in the form of securities, but in the illustration, the variation margin is in the form of cash.

The buyer is the non-defaulting party and so is required to determine who owes what as a consequence of the early termination of the repo. It is also the party which has to value the purchased securities for this purpose.

So, in the illustration, the buyer must determine the value of the Bunds it has purchased for the purpose of the calculation – referred to as the default market value in the GMRA.[8] The buyer has several choices and a period of five dealing days from the date of termination of the trade within which to make its determination. It can determine the default market value based upon the cost – including fees and expenses – at which it sells Bunds in the market on or after the date of termination of the trade. Alternatively, the buyer can determine the default market value based upon the prices quoted by a recognised dealer for the purchase by the dealer of Bunds on or after that date (in which case the buyer may deduct the notional transaction costs it would have incurred had it actually sold the Bunds based upon that quoted price). Otherwise, if the buyer is unable either to sell Bunds or obtain such quoted price (or it considers that it is not commercially viable to obtain quotes or to use the quotes), it must establish the 'fair market value' of the securities (using such pricing sources, methods and proxies as are available and, again, deducting notional transaction costs which would apply on a sale by it of Bunds). The buyer may use any of these alternatives – in the five-day window allowed if under the GMRA – and, once it has chosen which one to use, it is required to notify the seller. If it has not done so within the five dealing days then the default market value can only be the fair market value at the end of that five-day period.

The sale cost is to be established in the example as the buyer is not in default and is the person who would have been required to deliver the Bunds back to the seller. This will mean that the Bunds are valued at their lowest price. Had the buyer, not the seller, defaulted in the illustration, it is the seller who would have established the purchase cost of Bunds and added notional transaction costs if not included already.

---

8   The position under the 2011 GMRA is different to that described here in a number of respects. These are described in more detail in the industry documentation chapter.

The principle is that the valuation should be at the side of the market which is most favourable to the non-defaulting party.

Assume that the buyer uses a price quoted by a dealer three days after the termination date and gives notice of that to the seller. The buyer has obtained quotes showing that the all-in (dirty) price based on the €100 million holding of Bunds is €107,080,403 and the notional costs of selling would have been 0.25%, giving a net default market value of €106,812,702.

Once the default market value is established, the buyer then offsets the cash values of the obligations of the parties as at the accelerated repurchase date (ie, at day four in the originally repo). In the examples these obligations are shown below.

Seller-side obligations:
 (A) Repurchase price (purchase price plus four days' accrued repo interest): €104,909,366.
 (B) Margin return (cash margin posted plus one day's interest at the agreed rate (at €zero)): €12,070.
 (C) Total ((A) plus (B)): €104,921,436.

Buyer-side obligations:
 (D) Default market value (quoted price, plus accrued coupon on the Bunds less notional costs): €106,812,702.

Net amount payable (D) minus (C): €1,891,266.

As the buyer-side obligations are more than the seller-side obligations, the buyer must pay this amount to the seller. This is what you would expect as the trade was entered into on the basis that the buyer is over-collateralised for the cash it has lent to the seller.

What can be seen from this calculation is that the amount which the buyer has to pay to the seller is actually increased due to the accrual of coupon on the Bunds for the three days after the accelerated repurchase date it took the buyer to establish the default market value, whereas the repo interest on the cash it lent to the seller ceased to accrue from the date of termination of the trade. There is therefore a cost to the buyer of using the flexibility allowed to it in the five-day window.

The termination payment, when calculated, is due on the early termination date and, under the GMRA, interest is payable from that date until the date is it paid, at one month LIBOR. In our example, therefore, the buyer must also pay at least three days' interest on the amount it has to pay on termination, even if it is paid immediately upon the calculation being made.

There is no element of compensation payable; the termination mechanism simply provides for an accrual to the accelerated repurchase date and there is no value attached to the unperformed future element of the trade. The only way that that is claimable is if the buyer incurs a cost in entering into a replacement transaction (although the buyer would also have to pay over any profits or gains it made in so doing). Alternatively, it may enter into, unwind or replace a hedging transaction in respect of the terminated trade and claim the costs of so doing, or account to the seller from the profit or gain arising from that.

12.2 Buy/sell-back

The termination of a buy/sell-back is effectively the same as for a repo. The difference is that the determination of the equivalent of the repurchase price as at the accelerated repurchase date also requires any assumed coupon payments on the purchased securities made during the term of the transaction (applying a discount for the time value of those) to be factored into the accrual calculation.

12.3 Stock loan

With a stock loan, the consequences of termination are economically the same as those in the case of a repo, with only very minor differences.

So, in the stock loan example, if the lender defaults on day four just after the lender has made its first transfer of variation collateral to the borrower, the position would be as follows:

The borrower has borrowed 1 million SAP AG shares, and the accrued lending fees are, say, €2,920.

The lender is now holding €47,273,646 principal amount of OATs, having just returned €779,021 in principal amount of them pursuant to the previous day's margin call.

Assume that the borrower uses the sale price of SAP AG shares on the date of termination and the purchase price quoted three days after the termination date for the OATs and gives notice of those determinations to the lender within the five-day window permitted under the 2010 GMSLA. The sale price of the SAP AG shares is €52.90 and the cost of sale was 0.5%. The (clean) purchase price of the OATs is still 117.22 and the notional costs of purchase would have been 0.25%.

Once the default market values of the SAP AG shares and the OATs are established, the borrower then offsets the cash value of the parties' obligations as at the termination date. That is:

Lender-side obligations:
   (A) Default market value of OATs to be returned to the borrower (clean price of €55,414,206 plus notional costs of €138,535 plus accrued coupon of €34,470): €55,587,211.

Borrower-side obligations:
   (B) Default market value of SAP AG shares to be returned to the lender ([€52.90 less notional costs of 0.5%] × 1,000,000): €52,635,500 plus
   (C) Accrued stock lending fee payable to lender: €2,920.
   (D) Total ((B) plus (C)): €52,638,420.

Net amount payable ((A) minus (D)): €2,948,791.

As the lender-side obligations are more than the borrower-side obligations, the lender must pay this amount to the borrower. Again, this is what you would expect as the trade was entered into on the basis that the lender is over-collateralised for the stock it has lent to the borrower.

Here it is the borrower who is benefiting from the accrued interest on the OATs for the period from the termination date until the date on which it decided to lock in the value of the OATs for default valuation purposes.

The borrower is also entitled to interest (at overnight LIBOR) on the termination payment from the termination date.

The borrower is unable to claim for the costs of entering into any replacement transaction or entering into or replacing or unwinding any hedge position. This reflects the fact that stock loans are more typically terminable on a daily basis at any time, rather than entered into as term trades. With term trades, especially for stock which is considered to be 'special', compensation provisions (effectively break costs) are therefore commonly added.

Agent lending/agency repo

Sarah Reid
Fieldfisher

An agency relationship is a relationship between two parties whereby one party (the principal) authorises the other (the agent) to take certain actions on its behalf, such as entering into contractual relations with third parties which are then binding on the principal. The authority given by a principal to an agent may be as wide or as limited as the parties agree.

Agency relationships are used throughout the financial markets, particularly in the securities financing markets. This chapter gives an overview of agency stock loan and agency repo practices.

1. Background to the market

In the 1970s, US custodian banks began to offer a service whereby they would lend out long securities positions from their clients' custody accounts. This gave borrowers access to a wide range of securities and enabled the custodians' clients to make additional returns on their existing securities positions. Clients which started to lend out their securities under these agency-lending programmes were mainly institutional investors with traditional, long-only investment policies.

Custodian banks also offered a service whereby they would lend out their clients' positive cash balances by entering into reverse repurchase transactions with market counterparties that were looking to raise cash finance, under which clients would receive high-quality securities, such as government bonds, as collateral. Agent lenders were also able to act as repo agents for their client base by reusing cash collateral received under securities loans to generate an increased return by entering into reverse repos on behalf of their lender clients.

A number of institutional asset managers (which typically do not have custody of their clients' assets but manage them) have stock lending and repo desks in order to lend or repo their clients' securities. However, these have been reduced in recent years, with the managers outsourcing this function to clients' custodians, enabling their clients to benefit from greater market access and the cost efficiencies afforded by the scale of their operations.

According to one recent industry estimate, the global total value of securities on loan is $2.0 trillion.[1]

---

1   Estimate based on Markit® data.

2. Participants

Most of the global inventory of securities is held by institutional investors which hold positions with their custodians by way of long-term investment. As a result, intermediaries such as agent lenders and repo agents are important to the securities finance markets to tap into this source of securities and, in turn, provide an ancillary source of income for the institutional investors. In the past, these agent lenders and repo agents were custodian banks and asset managers, but today there are also a number of other non-custodial agents which act as intermediaries in the securities financing markets.

2.1 Beneficial owners

Any beneficial owner of securities can access the securities finance markets, but the main categories of lender consist of institutional investors such as pension funds, insurance companies, mutual funds and endowments. These beneficial owners use agency lending and/or repo programmes for a number of reasons, but often the volume of their securities finance transactions would not be enough to warrant the set-up and ongoing operational costs of direct trading activity. By participating in an agency programme, a beneficial owner will benefit from economies of scale with access to the agent lender's operational infrastructure, market intelligence, counterparty relationships and technology. An agent lender with a significant client base will have a larger, wider and more consistent inventory of securities to offer than a single beneficial owner lending out its securities direct to the market and will therefore be more attractive to prospective borrowers.

2.2 Global custodians

Custodians of securities are ideally placed to offer an agency lending and/or repo programme for a number of reasons. First, as they are holding the securities on behalf of the beneficial owners, they have absolute visibility of the inventory of securities which are available for lending at any time. Second, they can offer the service to existing clients as an add-on, which will give beneficial owners the opportunity to raise additional revenue without any action on their part (other than completing the documentation to give the agent the authority to trade).

2.3 Non-custodian agents

As outsourcing became a popular business practice in the early 2000s, parties that were not custodians started to offer agency lending and repo agency services. These are sometimes referred to as 'third-party' agent lenders or repo agents. These third-party agents offer the same services as their custodian competitors, but have needed to find solutions around visibility and access to the clients' securities.

2.4 Borrowers

Demand for securities and for leverage is largely generated by the trading activities of broker-dealers and their hedge fund and other clients. Prime brokers make cash and securities loans available to clients by sourcing cash and securities from the market and, in particular, by themselves transacting as principal with agent lenders and repo agents.

Agent lenders and repo agents are attractive to borrowers for a number of reasons. They provide constant availability of cash and securities and a wide variety of securities, and require only a single point of contact for transactions and operations. The time and cost for a borrower of using an agent lender's umbrella documentation are also significantly less than negotiating individual agreements with all of the underlying beneficial owners.

3. The agency relationship

The diagram below illustrates the structure of a transaction (in this case a securities loan; but it would look the same, apart from the terminology, if it were a repo). The following paragraphs consider in more detail some of the specific features of the agency arrangements using the agency securities lending market and terminology, as that is more prevalent than agency repo. However, the principles apply equally to both products.

Agency lending documentation framework

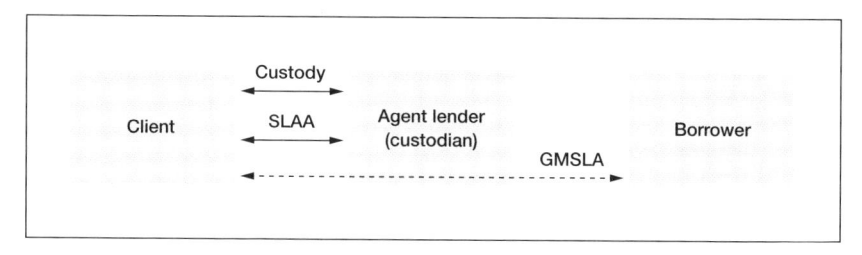

```
                    Custody
                  ◄─────────►
    Client          SLAA         Agent lender                    Borrower
                  ◄─────────►   (custodian)
                                          GMSLA
                  ◄─────────────────────────────►
```

'SLAA' in the diagram is the stock lending agency agreement between the client of the agent lender and the agent lender (which, as illustrated, is also the custodian of the client, although these roles can be bifurcated so that different entities fulfil the roles of agent lender and custodian). 'GMSLA' is the industry standard master stock lending agreement which the agent lender has entered into with its relationship borrowers as agent for its portfolio of lender clients.

3.1 The agent and the borrower

The terms of an agency loan or an agency repo transaction are the same as for a bilateral loan or bilateral repo, except that they are negotiated between the agent and the counterparty. Once the loan or repo is executed by the agent, it will create a binding transaction between the beneficial owner and the counterparty as the parties to the contract.

Using industry standard documentation, it is a condition of an agency transaction that the agent has authority to enter into the transaction on behalf of its underlying client and the agent accepts an obligation to inform the counterparty in the event that it becomes aware of a default with respect to the principal lender. Even in the absence of an express provision to that effect, legally the agent will generally be deemed to warrant that it has authority to bind the principal which it is purportedly representing in any event, at least in common law jurisdictions.

Once the trade is done, the agent will manage the transaction on behalf of its client.

At the commencement of the transaction, the agent will deliver the securities (or pay the cash) to the borrower on behalf of the beneficial owner, and the borrower will deliver collateral (or purchased securities in the case of a reverse repo) to the agent for the account of the beneficial owner.

For the duration of the loan or repo, the loaned or purchased securities and any non-cash collateral will be valued daily so that the agreed economics of the loan or repo can be maintained. The agent will manage these valuations on behalf of the beneficial owner and demand, pay or deliver any additional margin to the counterparty when required.

The agent will also manage recalls requested by the beneficial owner as well as corporate actions and manufactured dividend payments.

When the loan is terminated, equivalent securities are returned to the agent for the account of the beneficial owner and equivalent collateral is returned by the agent to the borrower.

In return for lending out the securities, the borrower pays a fee in the usual way. As noted elsewhere, lending fees can vary greatly depending on a number of factors, including the nature, size and duration of the transaction and the demand to borrow the particular securities.

3.2 The agency agreement

An agent and its client will enter into an agreement to give the agent authority to undertake securities lending/repo transactions on behalf of the client, and to set out the services which the agent will provide to the client in relation to such securities lending/repo transactions.

There is no industry standard form of agency agreement; instead, bespoke service-level agreements are drafted by the agent depending on its particular set-up and product offering. However, aspects of the agreement need to be considered and addressed:

(a) *Commitment*

The agent will not be committed to make any loans of securities/repos and will not usually guarantee to the client any amount of return on its portfolio. Among other things, the agent must also allocate opportunities to lend or repo among its lender clients where demand is less than supply.

(b) *Scope of authority*

The agent's authority under the agency agreement is likely to include:

- approval for the disclosure and marketing of the client's portfolio to prospective borrowers;
- authority to execute industry standard master agreements with approved borrowers on behalf of the client; and
- authority to negotiate the terms of each individual transaction or any exclusivity arrangement with an approved borrower.

(c) *Available assets*

Generally, the agent will be free to lend out all securities of the beneficial owner in a particular custody account unless the beneficial owner notifies the agent that they are blocked. The agent may also be authorised to sell (sometimes by way of auction) the right for a period of time for a borrower to call for the loan of a quantity of particular securities – in exchange for a commitment fee.

Accordingly, if the beneficial owner sells securities, these may have to be recalled or the lending commitment cancelled in order to settle the transaction. Securities loans are generally callable on demand. Repos may be for a term and so costs could be incurred in breaking a repo which the client would have to meet if it were to require them back early.

(d) *Approved counterparties and collateral*

The agent may be restricted in terms of the borrowers to which the client is willing to lend its securities and there may be specific requirements as to the types of collateral and haircuts which will apply. An agent will often have very limited ability to change these provisions on an individual client basis, as they will typically be agreed with its borrowers and/or any tri-party agents which are being used.

(e) *Holding of collateral*

The agency authorisation agreement may also set out custody terms for any collateral that is held on the client's behalf, including how any cash collateral received by the agent on behalf of the client may be reinvested (which may include reverse repo).

(f) *Reporting*

The agency agreement will set out the agent's reporting obligations to the client in respect of the portfolio.

(g) *Fees*

The parties will agree fees and any allocation of costs. While legally the fee is due to the beneficial owner as the contractual lender, agent lenders are typically compensated for their services through an agreed split of the revenue generated by the lending for the particular client. The percentage of such splits may vary depending on a number of factors, such as the services and protection (ie, loss indemnification) provided by the agent lender and the type and size of the client's portfolio of assets.

(h) *Liability*

The parties should negotiate limitations on liability and loss, give relevant representations and articulate the extent of reliance on statements made by the agent to the lender and vice versa, as well as documenting any indemnities (see further below).

(i) *Borrower default*

As the transaction is a direct contractual arrangement between the beneficial owner and borrower, each faces the risk and consequences of each other's default. The agency agreement will state what actions, if any, are to be taken on a default; but typically, the agent will not be required to take any action other than to notify the client if a default occurs.

(j)   *Indemnities*
In 1994 the sharp increase in US short-term interest rates led to losses for many securities lenders that had taken US dollar cash as collateral and were reinvesting it in a variety of money market instruments. In many cases their agents, typically custodian banks, compensated their underlying clients for these losses even though they were not legally obliged to do so. Lessons learnt included improved risk management procedures, better documentation and clear reinvestment guidelines. Indemnities from agents to their clients for borrower defaults also became more common.

Many agent lenders now give indemnities to their clients against the risk of borrower default. The scope and terms of these indemnities vary considerably in their detail. However, in general, such an indemnity will mean that, following a default by a borrower, if the amount of collateral held is insufficient for the agent to be able to buy in the securities that were loaned to that borrower, the agent will make up the shortfall (ie, the agent will assure that the securities that have been loaned are returned).

The indemnity needs to consider the events that would constitute a borrower default and the extent of the obligations of the agent to the beneficial owner (eg, does it just cover the return of securities to the lender or does it also cover fees and dividends/corporate actions? Additionally, does it deal with the situation whereby the agent is unable to buy in the securities so that they cannot be returned to the lender?).

From the agent's perspective, it will typically expect to be in the driving seat once it has indemnified the client and to be subrogated to the lender's rights to pursue the borrower.

3.3   Agent lender disclosure

On May 2 2008 the International Securities Lending Association (ISLA) published a consultation setting out proposals requiring agents to disclose on a daily basis details of exposure to underlying principals. The aim was to provide firms which were borrowing securities with information to manage counterparty credit exposure and calculate regulatory capital requirements under Basel II, and in general, to put in place in Europe a regulatory framework similar to that operating in the United States. Various updates have been made by ISLA to the original proposals, most recently on October 24 2014.

The Securities and Exchange Commission (SEC) has been similarly concerned with how broker-dealers and agent lenders monitor the credit and capital impact of agency lending arrangements and with the transparency of underlying exposures to principal lenders. Under the SEC's agency lending disclosure initiative, agents are now required to send detailed standard information to broker-dealers. This information allows broker-dealers to approve or reject specific underlying principals. The agent is also required to send to broker-dealers periodic master lists showing approved or rejected principals.

Traditionally, for the purposes of calculating regulatory capital exposure, a broker-dealer would calculate this as against the agent. However, this approach is no longer recognised as valid, so broker-dealers must now calculate exposure as per each underlying principal.

3.4 Pooled principals

An agent may enter into a single loan with a borrower on behalf of more than one principal or may pool its clients for collateral call aggregation or both.

Where acting for multiple principals in this way, agents need to establish systems that clearly show which principal's assets are being loaned and how collateral is being allocated between the principals. This is essential in case there is a borrower default, as the agents will need to know which securities they can claim for and which collateral belongs to them.

The industry standard documentation for securities lending (GMSLA) and repo (GMRA) contain specific provisions dealing with the situation where the agents are acting on behalf of multiple clients on a pooled principal basis.

These provisions consider the aggregation and subsequent allocation of collateral as well as the transactions themselves and are described in more detail elsewhere in this book.

Tri-party repo and stock lending

Guy Usher
Fieldfisher

This chapter seeks to explain the features of the tri-party market and transactions. There are a number of similarities to agency transactions as well as cleared transactions and these are considered in chapters 3 and 5 respectively, but it is just as important to understand how they differ.

Tri-party occur primarily in the repo market. Although the concepts are the same for securities lending, agency lending largely provides the functionality of tri-party as regards lenders who use agents. Tri-party stock lending, therefore, really only occurs in the directly traded (bilateral) universe. For this reason, the chapter focuses on the more commonly used repo product and the terminology used reflects this approach.

1. **What is tri-party repo?**
Tri-party repo is a service which deals with the post-trade processing of transactions, comprising collateral selection, settlement, custody and lifecycle activity management (ie, margin maintenance, manufactured payments, substitutions and corporate actions). Effectively, it is an outsourcing of these services to a third-party, the tri-party agent.

2. **An agency relationship**
Tri-party is an agency relationship. This means that, unlike in the centrally cleared market but in the same way as with agency transactions, the primary contractual relationship in respect of the transaction is and remains between the buyer and the seller. The key differences between agency lending and tri-party repo are that the tri-party agent does not execute the transactions (it only provides its services post-trade) and is appointed as agent by both the buyer and the seller.

3. **The role**
The repo trade itself may be agreed bilaterally between the parties (either by telephone or electronic messaging) or may come to exist through an automated repo trading system or platform. There are providers of electronic cash auctions which do this.

The tri-party agent receives details of the trade from the parties and makes sure that they match. Alternatively, it may receive the details via a direct feed from the trading system or venue which has been used. Armed with that information, the tri-party agent then arranges for settlement of the transaction by debiting the buyer's cash account with the purchase price and paying it to the seller. It then selects the collateral (the purchased securities) from the seller's account with the agent which satisfies the criteria for eligibility as agreed between the buyer, seller and tri-party agent. In addition to specifying the classes of collateral that are acceptable, such eligibility criteria usually include credit and liquidity criteria, concentration limits etc and the haircuts which are to be applied to each collateral type.

The buyer is otherwise agnostic as to the actual collateral provided, which is why tri-party is not appropriate for repo of securities which are special. Equally, tri-party repo facilitates the use of a broad range of assets as potential collateral. Whereas in the bilateral world the most prevalent form of collateral is government bonds, in the tri-party world, corporate bonds, equities and asset-backed securities are also used, as are convertibles.

Once the trade has settled, the tri-party agent will revalue the collateral and the accrued cash leg on a daily basis and debit and credit accounts of the seller and buyer with collateral so that the post-haircut value of the collateral matches the cash exposure. It also monitors ongoing eligibility criteria and effects substitutions of collateral where these criteria cease to be satisfied. It will also effect substitutions over income payment dates on collateral if there would be adverse tax consequences for the buyer or seller. Finally, substitutions may be made at the request of the seller, for example if it requires the securities which have been provided as collateral for another purpose or if it wishes to sell them.

Unless substituted, the tri-party agent will pay over any coupons and dividends on the collateral to the seller and will recall collateral in order to enable the seller to exercise voting and other corporate actions on the collateral securities.

Importantly, tri-party agents do not assure performance by the parties to the transactions. Instead, if a party notifies the tri-party agent that the other party has defaulted and the transactions have been terminated as a result, it will lock down the collateral accounts pending instructions from the non-defaulting party.

4. **Documentation**

Tri-party agents have developed standard forms of agreement for their tri-party offerings. As they are generally drafted to accommodate the fact that the tri-party agent is agent for both parties and they have systems in place to run the service, there is limited scope to adapt these to the specific needs of the parties save as to collateral eligibility and haircuts.

The transactions themselves will invariably be documented under a bilateral master repo agreement (eg, the Global Master Repurchase Agreement (GMRA)) between the parties but the tri-party document(s) will override this in certain respects as regards the mechanical aspects. Specifically, the tri-party agent will determine the market value of the collateral using its own pricing sources and methodologies which will take precedence over the bilateral agreement where they differ. For example, the GMRA assumes that the initial collateral (the purchased securities) will have been agreed by the parties and the over-collateralisation is determined by reference to the differential between the initial market value of that collateral and the purchase price. In the tri-party world, a haircut is instead applied to the collateral and this will depend on what has been provided at any given time.

Traditionally, tri-party agents developed a form of documentation which was a single three-way agreement that each of the parties and the tri-party agent would sign – a tri-party agreement. More usually these days, the parties will each separately sign an agreement with the tri-party agent. They may just sign a single agreement where they are only ever a collateral receiver or giver (covering a number of potential counterparties) or may sign up to both on the basis that, at any time, they could use the service as a repo buyer or seller. It is important that parties using this "plug and play" documentation framework clearly understand its features as they have no direct relationship with the other parties other than the underlying GMRA or equivalent.

There has been a further development in documentation terms which is intended to facilitate the use of tri-party repo by the likes of corporate treasurers. In recognition of the fact that it can be time-consuming to negotiate individual GMRAs with each potential counterparty, Clearstream has developed its own form of master repo agreement (the Clearstream Repurchase Conditions or CRC) which can be automatically applied to users of its service. While this is convenient for corporates, matters are not so simple for regulated firms. As discussed in chapter 7, regulated firms have to be satisfied that the netting arrangements (cash versus collateral) would be enforceable in an insolvency of each counterparty. The availability of industry opinions on the GMRA greatly facilitates that need, whereas the same does not apply to the CRC.

5. **Market participants**

Because of the nature of the services provided, tri-party agents are custodians and, in Europe, the market is dominated by Bank of New York Mellon, JP Morgan, Euroclear and Clearstream. According to the International Capital Market Association (ICMA), about 10–12 per cent of the European repo market is settled through tri-party agents.

The tri-party segment of the repo market is attractive to those, like corporate treasurers, who do not have the operational capability to manage the transaction lifecycle. While hold-in-custody (HIC) repo (where the collateral is held in a client custody account by the seller for the buyer) also obviates the need for much of the functionality that is otherwise associated with repo trading, it carries with it a much greater degree of risk of loss on default than tri-party repo.

The market is also very significant for prime brokers who want to have the ability to raise cash on a range of assets they may be holding. It enables them to optimise those assets by using the lowest quality collateral that is acceptable to their buyers to raise finance, keeping the higher quality assets for use as collateral for purposes where there is less flexibility.

6. **Recent developments**

Tri-party repo results in the custodian providers of that service holding very large amounts of collateral, and an active broker will probably have an arrangement with all or most such providers to give it access to the widest range of potential cash lenders. However, this introduces a certain amount of inefficiency and fragmentation as pools of assets which can potentially be available as collateral have to be maintained with each of the providers. In response to this, there has been a move by the European international clearing systems, Euroclear and Clearstream, to enable inter-operability to enhance the movement of collateral across Europe.

There have also been moves to integrate tri-party services more closely with trading platforms so as to provide a more complete offering to users, not just the "back-office" function that has historically been provided.

In light of the increased need for collateral in financial transactions generally, it is now possible for collateral receivers in tri-party to re-use the collateral outside the tri-party system. This might, for example, enable a repo cash lender to use collateral for margining of derivative positions that it might have. However, this does mean that the collateral receiver assumes responsibility (and associated risks) in being able to ensure that the collateral can be returned to the tri-party agent when the trade is unwound or on a substitution which, for some participants, removes one of the key attractions of using tri-party in the first place.

Central counterparty clearing

Eric Bystrom
Director
Samit Desai
Ivelina Dimtscheva
Capco UK
Swen Werner
Securities services & collateral management expert

This chapter looks at the process of central clearing and the impacts it has on the repo and securities lending markets. For the repo market, the key drivers to central clearing are considered. While the securities lending market looks very similar to the repo market, the structural challenges and different business drivers underpinning stock loans compared to repo highlight some of the reasons why central clearing has historically struggled to enter the securities lending market.

Finally, some thoughts are given on the impact of impending regulation on the future of central clearing for repo and securities lending transactions. This is particularly relevant in the debate around the "shadow banking" system and the potential supply-demand situation of high grade collateral.

1. The drivers for repo and securities lending central clearing counterparties (CCPs)

This section considers some of the drivers for central clearing in the repo and securities lending markets and identifies the differences for each market segment. Unlike OTC derivatives, central clearing is not mandatory for the repo and securities lending markets, even though the relevant transactions are typically traded "over the counter". Instead, CCPs for securities financing have emerged to the extent they can deliver benefits to specific market participants.

1.1 Repo

CCPs have been active in the repo markets for over 10 years. For example, LCH's RepoClear service was launched in 1999.[1] The initial driver was to facilitate transaction netting but, more recently, the focus has shifted towards other risk mitigation functions. While CCPs for repo also exist in North America and Asia, the proportion of centrally cleared repo in Europe has been higher than in other regions. Due to the lack of data and statistics, little empirical research has been done to explain this, especially the gap between US and European markets.

The proportion of tri-party repo in the US is about double that of Europe.[2] As discussed in section 3, many of the drivers that led to the introduction of CCPs for securities financing are similar to those that led to the emergence of the tri-party

---

1 London Clearing House, 1999 Report and Financial Statements (1999).
2 Viral V. Acharya and T. Sabri Oncu, The Repurchase Agreement (Repo) Market (2010).

model (eg, mitigation of counterparty risk, operational efficiencies, etc). Additionally, the historic fragmentation of the European securities markets along national borders may have encouraged CCPs to provide an alternative solution where tri-party repo has not been available in that specific market or segment or is less effective at mitigating the associated risks.

As illustrated in Table 1, approximately one third of the European repo market is centrally cleared today. Over the course of the financial crisis (during the second half of 2008), the volume of centrally cleared repo was much more stable than bilateral repo, arguably providing testament to the benefits of having CCPs. Tri-party volumes experienced only volume reductions in that period.

Table 1

	Dec-08	Dec-09	Dec-10	Dec-11	Dec-12	Dec-13
%CCP	33	29	32	32	32	30
%tri-party	11	12	12	11	10	10
%bilateral	56	59	56	57	58	60
EUR billion	4,633	5,758	5,908	6,127	5,611	5,499

Source: ICMA, European Repo Market Survey (2013).

2. Drivers for CCP clearing in the repo market

Here is a summary of the drivers for central clearing in the repo markets:

2.1 Mitigating counterparty credit risk

While repo is a collateralised transaction, it is not free of credit risk. The residual credit risk arises from three primary areas:
- The inability to meet the mark-to-market obligations under the repo transaction (ie, failure to post margin);
- On a default by the collateral provider (repo seller), the inability of the cash lender (repo buyer) to liquidate the repo collateral and recoup the amount of cash lent;
- On a default by the cash lender (the repo buyer), the inability of the collateral provider (repo seller) to recoup the amount of over-collateralisation given to the collateral receiver (repo buyer) by virtue of the haircut applied to the collateral.

With the introduction of a CCP, these credit risks are mitigated as the central counterparty assumes the following functions:
- As the CCP interposes itself between the counterparties and assumes responsibility for margining both counterparties, the mark-to-market risk is decoupled from the repo transaction. Instead, each counterparty is then only

exposed to the credit risk of the CCP. In order to assume this principal risk, CCPs typically operate through various lines of defences (discussed below) in addition to applying haircuts and concentration limits to collateral. The effect is that risk is transferred from bilateral exposures to trading counterparties to the credit risk of the CCP in question.
- A CCP assumes the liquidation function, and returns cash to the cash lender (repo buyer) in the event of default of the collateral provider (repo seller).

2.2 **Overcollateralisation and haircuts are posted to the CCP, not the repo counterparty, and so are removed from a default of the cash lender (repo buyer).** Tri-party repo, on the other hand, is an agency service and so lacks the principal risk component of CCP clearing. Reduction of credit risk is also a key component of tri-party repo. However, the mechanics by which tri-party repo agents achieve this are different as tri-party agents do not guarantee the performance of the repo transaction itself; put another way, there is no principal risk of the tri-party repo agent. Instead credit risk is mitigated (to a degree) from a practical perspective through the segregation of collateral at the tri-party repo agent.

Connection to electronic platforms and anonymous trading: Connection to electronic trading platforms facilitates the ability both to trade and to clear repo anonymously. Cash lenders are not able to distinguish or discriminate against cash borrowers and hence are unable to cherry pick who they lend cash to. In such arrangements, CCPs provide post-trade anonymity. However, this depends on the actual trading pattern. For example, trades can be negotiated through voice brokers and then entered into an electronic system afterwards. In this case, the counterparties would know the identity of their initial trading counterparty even for CCP cleared transactions. Several trading platforms (such as BrokerTec or MTS) offer such functionality. Post-trade anonymity can be particularly important in times of stress when market rumours or perception may pose an obstacle to certain institutions raising short term liquidity in the repo markets. Similarly, collateral providers may wish to avoid creating or enhancing negative perception about their short term liquidity positions if they are seen to borrow cash in the repo markets. The market infrastructure of having anonymous execution and clearing is therefore a key driver for market liquidity in repo among brokers.

Balance sheet and capital usage: The involvement of a CCP as the single counterparty provides certain capital benefits depending on the type of activity. For example, repo participants are able to net cash receivables and liabilities through a CCP, regardless of the identity of trading counterparties, and thus can achieve balance sheet netting across the entire universe of trading counterparties. Additionally, exposures to CCPs (regardless of the cleared product) may attract beneficial risk weighting for capital adequacy purposes compared to exposures to bilateral trading counterparties. The new Basel III rules concerning the capitalisation of bank exposures to CCPs, as far as the exposure relates to repos and securities lending transactions, will however increase the risk weight for exposures to CCPs (although exposures to 'qualifying' CCPs will still be lower than for exposures to bilateral trading counterparties).

Operational efficiency: As a central 'hub' in the market, CCPs can reduce the operational overhead of post-trade processing. In particular, efficiencies are gained across the following functions:
- Trade settlement – both as a result of having the ability to net settle obligations, but also through automated settlement linkages to counterparties and central securities depositaries (CSDs) like Euroclear and Clearstream;
- Confirmation and trade matching – reducing mismatches and reconciliation of trades by individual counterparties;
- Risk management and margining – central valuation and collateral management across the market on a consistent basis.

In the bilateral repo markets, these functions are performed by each counterparty on each and every transaction creating an operational burden and an enhanced risk of breaks (or mismatches) and disputes.

Tri-party agents perform several of these operational functions, especially in respect of risk management and margining. In order to manage non-cash collateral, CCPs have in some cases become clients of tri-party agents. This can provide additional benefits for counterparties as it allows market participants to allocate collateral for multiple exposures (cleared or non-cleared repos or other financial market transactions) through a tri-party arrangement.

Market transparency: The existence of electronic trading platforms and CCPs allows regulators to have better market and pricing transparency in the absence of any central reporting requirements for repo transactions. With growing concern over the shadow banking system, the ability to gain critical visibility in securities financing markets is a key benefit for the regulators.[3]

3. Transaction lifecycle

The lifecycle of a CCP cleared repo transaction shows how many of the drivers feature. Diagram 1 opposite illustrates the transaction lifecycle for a cleared repo transaction.

2.1 Pre-trade

The legal agreements and documentation are the first step towards executing a repo. Repo transactions in the European market are typically contracted under a bilateral Global Master Repo Agreement (GMRA) between the cash lender and the cash borrower. Where a CCP is used, this contract is either complemented or overtaken by clearing and settlement agreements with the CCP.

---

3   See paragraph 4.2 below and paragraph 3.2 of Chapter 7 (Legal and Regulatory Issues) for a discussion of regulatory initiatives in this connection.

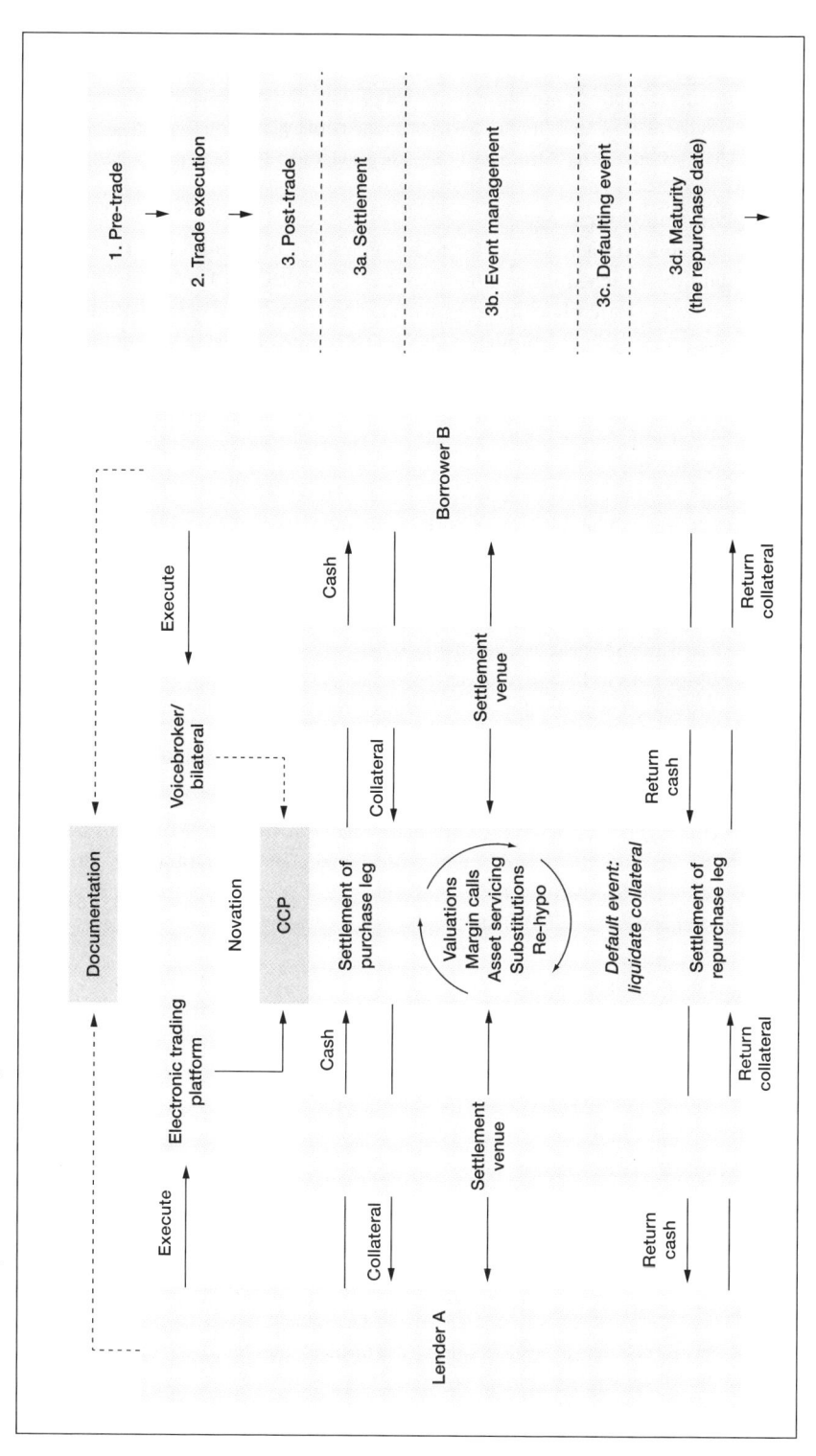

Eric Bystrom, Samit Desai, Ivelina Dimtscheva, Swen Werner

Diagram 1: Lifecycle of a cleared repo transaction

3.2 Trade execution
Repo transactions are typically agreed bilaterally via an electronic trading platform, voicebroker or by telephone/e-mail. Electronic platforms tend to be connected to a CCP, so providing automated clearing services to the executing counterparties.

3.3 Post-trade matching
For transactions made on an electronic trading platform, that platform will usually send pre-matched instructions to the CCP for clearing. For transactions agreed to be centrally cleared but not executed on an electronic trading platform, the bilateral trade terms will go through a give-up (novation) process, subsequently interposing the CCP as counterparty between the cash lender and the cash borrower. However, matching is still required in order for clearing to complete.

3.4 Settlement
Settlement occurs automatically at the agreed settlement venue between Lender A and CCP, and CCP and Borrower B. The settlement risk is assumed by the CCP.

3.5 Collateral management
Post-settlement, until the repurchase date, transactions are managed by the CCP. The CCP will undertake regular mark-to-market valuations of the transactions and will call for margin to mitigate the credit risks it faces to its clearing members. Collateral substitution will usually also be allowed by the clearing service in order to optimise the use of collateral.

3.6 Corporate events, etc
Typically, the buyer of the repo has to pay the coupon amount to the seller of the repo because the seller remains the beneficial owner of the securities from an economic perspective. A CCP will provide this compensation for income events. Other corporate events may require a substitution of collateral.

3.7 Default management
CCPs typically have an organised default management process in place which comprises set procedures, designed to facilitate the orderly liquidation process of complex portfolios. They apply a framework of safeguards, the so-called lines of defence (see Table 2 below), to rebalance themselves and protect the market.

Table 2: CCPs lines of defence

Level 1	Initial and variation margin provided by the Defaulting Member
Level 2	Contributions of the Defaulting Member to the Default Fund
Level 3	CCP's contribution – "skin-in-the-game"[4]

continued on next page

Level 4	Contribution of non-Defaulting Members to the Default Fund
Level 5	Further contributions of non-Defaulting Members in line with CCP rules/member guarantees
Level 6	CCP's own capital and reserves
Level 7	Other possible sources: • Insurance • Financial guarantees, eg, from bank, parent of CCP etc. • Bailout from government, monetary or fiscal authorities

3.8 Maturity

On maturity, the repurchase leg occurs between Borrower B and the CCP and Lender A and the CCP. The settlement risk is assumed by the CCP, not by the original counterparties.

4. Securities lending

Unlike repo, CCPs have to date not been as prevalent in the securities lending market. By way of comparison, the amount of centrally cleared securities lending transactions is estimated to be less than 1.5% of the aggregate value of transactions outstanding[5] (with OCC in the US being the only currently active CCP for securities lending globally). After the collapse of Lehman Brothers, CCP services were being offered by two electronic platforms, Quadriserv in the US, and SecFinex in Europe. SecFinex has since exited the market due to limited trade volumes on the platform. Limited trade volumes similarly led to SIS X-Clear and LCH suspending services for securities lending. Table 3 below outlines the active CCPs in both repo and securities lending. While each CCP listed in the table operates slightly differently, the general functions they perform are consistent.

Table 2: Active repo and securities lending CCPs

Asset	Active repo CCPs	Active securities lending CCPs
Euro Area	Eurex Clearing AG, CC&G, LCH.Clearnet SA, LCH.Clearnet Ltd	Eurex Clearing AG (LCH. Clearnet SA. and SIX x-clear have a CCP service which is inactive)

continued on next page

---

[4] This is a European Union requirement for CCPs to place 25% of their total minimum capital ahead of non-defaulting clearing members within the lines of defence. Some CCPs decided not to follow this example, eg, the Options Clearing Corporation (OCC) and the Korean Exchange (KRX).
[5] Size of global securities lending market data source: Bank of England, Developments in the global securities lending market, *Quarterly Bulletin* (2011 Q3).

Central counterparty clearing

Asset	Active repo CCPs	Active securities lending CCPs
US	FICC-GSD (for clearing GCF repos)	OCC
Canada	CDCC, FINet	N/A
Spain	MEFFRepo	
Sweden	NASDAQ OMX DM	Eurex Clearing AG
Switzerland	Eurex Clearing AG	Eurex Clearing AG
Hong Kong	N/A[6]	N/A
Japan	JGBCC	N/A
United Kingdom	LCH.Clearnet Ltd	Eurex Clearing AG
Russia	National Clearing Centre (NCC)	N/A

4.1 CCPs in securities lending markets

So what are the challenges with introducing a CCP structure into the securities lending markets? The market structure of repo and securities lending markets have some important differences and, as a result, a CCP model for securities lending would have certain unique features compared to a repo CCP model. These include:

- Market participants – unlike a repo transaction, a securities lending transaction has a beneficial owner who lends securities (generally via an agent lender). The borrower on the other side of the securities lending transaction would typically be a prime broker servicing an end borrower such as a hedge fund.
- Only CCP clearing members can be counterparties to the CCP – in the securities lending model the ultimate lending clients of an agent lender and ultimate borrowers of the prime broker may well not be clearing members of a CCP. In such a scenario, the lender and ultimate borrower would need to appoint a general clearing member who would then become an additional counterparty in the transaction chain. The additional cost and risk management processes this requires mean that a securities lending CCP is less obviously attractive.
- The term nature of the trades – repos tend to be fixed term transactions whereas securities lending trades are generally open, ie, the securities lent can

---

6 The Central Moneymarkets Unit (CMU) offers intraday and overnight repo facilities but without a guarantee mechanism.

- be demanded back by the lender at any time. This makes securities lending transactions less attractive to CCPs as well as lenders and borrowers of stocks.
- Operational requirements – most agent lenders run global, multi-asset class programs, and a securities lending model would have limited operational benefits unless the CCP was able to clear all the transactions of that agent lender.
- Importance of specials – the securities lending market is more relationship-driven, characterised by a strong relationship culture between borrowers and their (often agent) lenders and specific product nuances, for example "specials" where there is increased demand for particular assets that are in short supply for lending at a given time. As a result, electronic trading platforms are less prevalent in the securities lending market, leading to lower CCP adoption as well.

These structural differences between the securities lending markets and the repo markets then shape the CCP model as depicted in Diagram 2 on the next page.

5. Challenges facing a securities lending CCP

There follow some of the challenges for a CCP structure in the securities lending market.

5.1 Participation in CCPs

It is more challenging for CCPs to target the relevant market participants directly in the securities lending market as long as the beneficial owners of securities should not become clearing members of CCPs, and therefore still need to maintain a principal relationship with their agent lender. In fact, the number of intermediaries in the process could actually increase in the event that the agent lenders are also not clearing members of the CCP.

5.2 Margining

In the traditional CCP structure, the CCP effectively assumes the obligation to return of both the security lent, and the collateral posted. Both the securities and the collateral are physically transferred between the clearing members and the CCP on both sides of the transaction. The issue arises as the CCP is therefore exposed to a default of either party and as a result requires additional margin to protect itself against the mark-to-market fluctuations of the trade. The lending side would thus be required to post additional margin and this would be a significant deviation from bilateral securities lending markets where the lender of stock is typically only ever a recipient of collateral.

CCPs are attempting to address some of these challenges through offering beneficial owners direct participation and certain exemptions for lenders from additional margin requirements.

5.3 Cost challenges

The operational and technological costs associated with a large scale structural shift

Central counterparty clearing

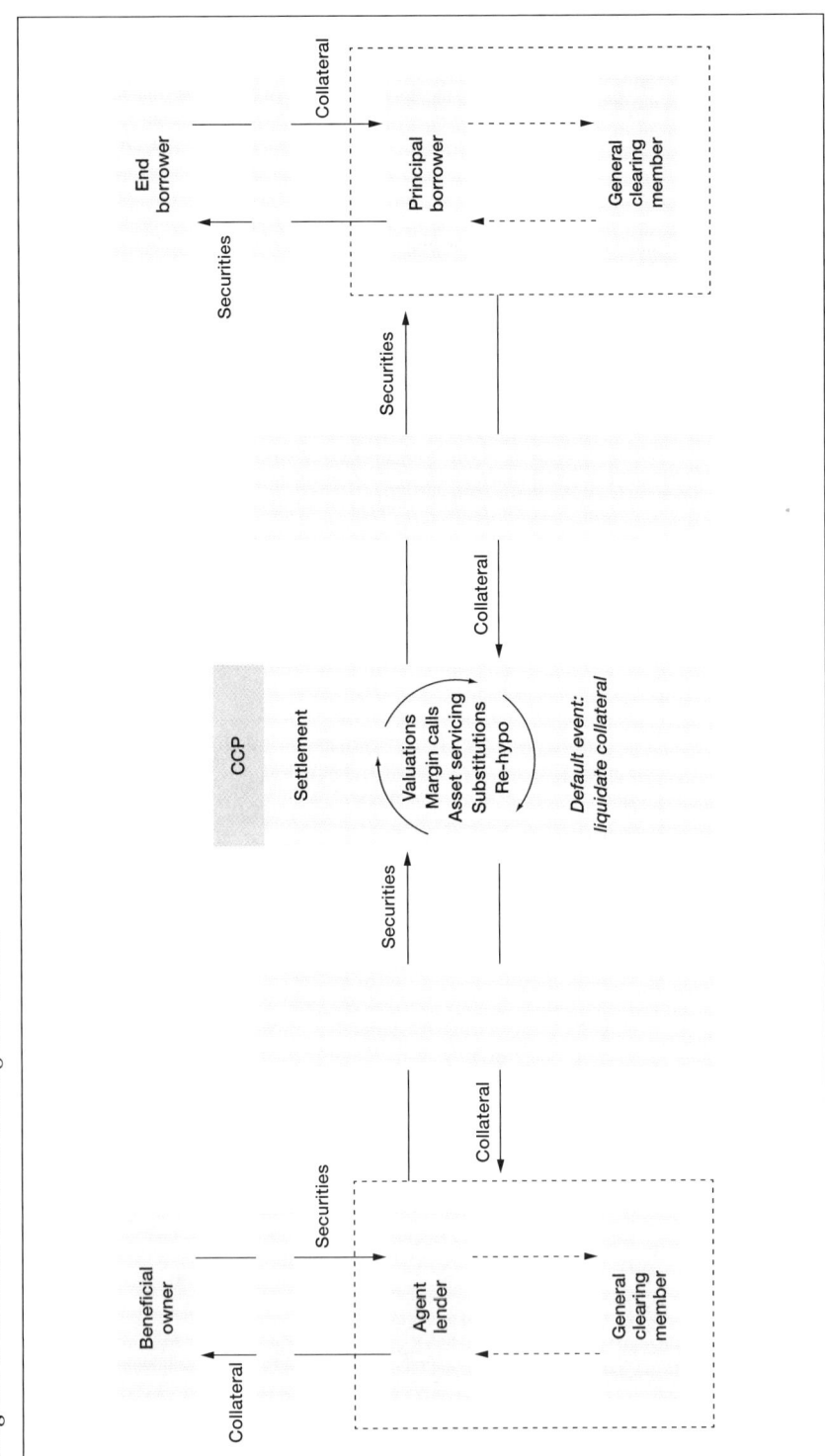

Diagram 2: Potential securities lending CCP model

62

that would occur in moving to a centrally cleared operating model should not be underestimated and could outweigh the benefits. The securities lending market is a relatively low-margin business and may not be capable of bearing any of these additional costs. By introducing additional intermediaries into the market structure, questions have been asked about the overall economics the CCP model would bring.

6. **CCPs compared to tri-party and bilateral trading of repo and securities lending**

The various approaches to risk mitigation provided in the bilateral, tri-party and centrally cleared models feature both similarities and differences. Market participants are offered a choice between these models, and may participate in more than one approach depending on the market or the preference of their counterparties.

Table 4 outlines some of the key functions performed by CCPs, tri-party agents and bilateral trading counterparties.

Table 4: CCPs functions compared to tri-party and bilateral

Description	CCPs	Tri-party	Bilateral
Parties	Repo: Cash lender, cash borrower, CCP SL: Beneficial owner, agent lender, CCP, broker/dealer, borrower	Repo: Cash lender, cash borrower, tri-party agent SL: Beneficial owner, agent lender, tri-party agent, broker/dealer, borrower	Repo: Cash lender and cash borrower SL: Beneficial owner, agent lender, broker/dealer, borrower
Pre-trade	Clearing agreements between CCP and its members Repo: GMRA between trading counterparties SL: GMSLA between trading counterparties	Tri-party service agreement(s) between tri-party agents and their members Repo: GMRA between trading counterparties SL: GMSLA between trading counterparties	Repo: GMRA between trading counterparties SL: GMSLA between trading counterparties
Trade execution	Through electronic trading platforms (can be anonymous) for automated clearing Bilateral trades can also be given-up to CCP	Bilaterally (phone/email)	Through voice brokers or bilaterally (telephone/email)

continued on next page

Description	CCPs	Tri-party	Bilateral
Post-trade			
Operational trade and securities processing (including corporate actions, valuations, margining, settlement, etc)	Supported by the CCP	Supported by the tri-party agent	Managed by each counterparty
Risk management	Credit risk is centralised at the CCP and zero/reduced risk-weights apply Collateral eligibility is determined by the CCP	Credit risk is partially mitigated through the collateral management functions of the tri-party agent Collateral eligibility is determined by the trading counterparties but monitored and collected by the tri-party agent	Managed by each trading counterparty Collateral eligibility determined and monitored/called by trading counterparties
Default management	CCPs assure return of securities and cash CCPs perform liquidation function	Collateral is held segregated but no guarantee of trade performance is provided Tri-party agents do not perform liquidation function	Managed by each trading counterparty

7. Perspectives on central clearing

It is difficult to describe the impact of CCP clearing generally across both repo and securities lending markets given the different market structures supporting these segments. However, there are some common themes around capital and operational changes involving CCPs as an additional intermediary in both these markets.

7.1 Central Counterparties

CCPs have expanded into the clearing of repo and are slowly expanding into securities lending for various reasons, including achieving larger scale to spread the cost of their operations. A CCP that is able to service clients that already use the CCP in other markets (eg, bond futures) could provide margin offset advantages if it could offer repo and securities lending services within the same CCP service. Additionally, further efficiency could materialise from clearing member participants only having to make a single default fund contribution for a CCP clearing multiple asset classes. This should reduce the cost from the additional margin requirements of a CCP model leveraging the portfolio effect of opposite exposures for those firms which are active in a number of different markets and asset classes. However, these benefits would need to be balanced with the concerns around risk concentration if more collateral requirements were pooled in fewer CCPs and how "contamination risk" between different asset classes and their markets could be mitigated.

7.2 Tri-party agents

Existing tri-party agents are likely to continue to play a role by managing the non-cash collateral flowing between the CCP and its member participants at least for the time being. As such, the involvement of CCPs in securities lending would probably make CCPs a significant client of tri-party collateral services. Given that brokers are likely to interact with a number of CCPs, tri-party agents can help to allocate collateral across different CCPs.

7.3 Banks and brokers

The conditions set by accounting rules to allow for balance sheet netting of the different legs of repo transactions are very specific. For instance, cash receivables and liabilities of the opening and closed leg to transactions can be offset only against the same counterparty using the same clearing system and same end date of a transaction. The involvement of a CCP can help provide the basis to meet these requirements.

The precondition for balance sheeting netting through CCPs to be effective is a market structure where firms intensively trade with each other. Furthermore, the netting and settlement procedures of the CCP will need to meet specific standards as described under the relevant accounting standards such as FASB Interpretation No. 41.

Balance sheet netting cannot be achieved if the counterparties are using different CCPs. However, a few CCPs (eg, LCH, Eurex and CC&G, the Italian domestic CCP) have built interoperability arrangements for repo transactions which would allow balance sheet netting even if the counterparty is using another CCP.

From a bank or broker's perspective, having a single counterparty enables the bank or broker to take a more simplified approach to counterparty credit risk. As noted in chapter 7, there is a universal requirement for regulated entities to be satisfied that on a counterparty default they will be able to achieve a net outcome and dealing with multiple counterparties of different types in various jurisdictions makes this more difficult. This is much more of an issue in the securities lending markets where the agent lenders are often acting as agents for a multitude of ultimate lenders, all of which have to be looked at individually from the point of view of the bank/broker borrower.

7.4 Agent lenders and beneficial owners

The involvement of CCPs in securities lending markets is more complex than for repo transactions given the important role agent lenders play in this segment. This has puzzled regulators. For example, the Bank of England commented that the lack of success for CCPs in the securities lending market could be the result of "a collective action problem".[7]

---

7   Bank of England, *Quarterly Bulletin* 2011 Q3 (2011).

However, the market structure of the securities lending market is different to the repo market. Many agent lenders would require the support of a clearing member to provide them with indirect access to the CCP in question for them and their clients. The agent lender's trading book is typically one-way (ie their clients are only lenders) and thus allows for limited netting opportunities through a CCP from the lender's perspective. Additionally, the CCP model may necessitate the absorption of the costs of the involvement of at least two additional intermediaries (the CCP and the clearing member) compared to securities lending transactions through tri-party arrangements.

In the traditional agent lending arrangement, the beneficial owner of a security is only ever a receiver of collateral. The involvement of a CCP would require that beneficial owners would have to post collateral, depending on the CCP model in question. The involvement of a CCP thus can have a fundamental impact on the economics of the trading activity. Equally, the benefits from a risk perspective are not straightforward. Agent lenders commonly offer beneficial owners indemnification protection against the risk of default by the borrowers (ie banks and brokers) by collecting appropriate collateral. As a result, the benefits associated with CCP clearing for the lenders (ie, counterparty default protection) are not as obvious compared to the non-cleared model operated by agent lenders. These features may explain why securities lending CCPs have so far faced an uphill struggle to position their services.

8. Industry Outlook

8.1 Unintended consequences for securities financing as a result of OTC derivatives regulation

The OTC derivatives market aims to increase the level of collateralisation supporting derivatives activity by, amongst other measures, requiring such trades to be cleared through CCPs more widely. In contrast to bilateral collateralisation, participants in a CCP are partly exposed to the risk that their collateral (eg, their contribution to the default fund) could be used to absorb mutualised losses of other participants. This risk applies independently of the underlying transactions. Regulators have responded to this by defining stricter rules around collateral segregation, even extending to the clients of the clearing members. As such, regulation is trying to square the circle to increase the use of a centralised risk model without the mutualisation risk that typically comes with it. Whilst such risks are important considerations also when considering the benefits of CCP clearing for repo or securities lending transactions, the policy implications go much further.

This new regulation could increase the interconnectedness between repo and securities financing markets and OTC derivatives as they are mandated for clearing. This is due to the fact that repo and securities lending activity is expected to be increasingly used to provide CCP-eligible collateral for OTC derivatives margining (eg, as a result of collateral transformation activities). The potential size of this activity could be significant. Projections for the increased CCP collateral requirements for cleared OTC derivatives reach from $500–$800 billion[8] to $2 trillion[9] or even up to $7 trillion.[10]

This market development has the potential to both increase the amount of repo/securities lending volume, and therefore the potential for CCPs to clear the products, but also may lead to consolidation as synergies can be realised across clearing OTC derivatives as well as repo and securities lending transactions. If CCPs increasingly clear all these transaction types in the same entity, this would create interesting market dynamics for regulators and market participants as CCPs would be the driver of a significant demand for collateral transformation whilst also operating the supply side if they increasingly were to clear in the repo and securities lending markets.

8.2 Shadow banking

Under the term 'shadow banking', global regulators have been considering the impact of leveraged credit intermediation on financial stability if involving institutions outside the banking system such as corporates and funds. Regulators have noted that there can be pro-cyclical effects as a consequence of institutional investors shifting their investment pattern to favour safe but liquid assets, such as short-term claims secured through repo contracts, over holding unsecured claims such as bank deposits. As a result, changing asset (collateral) prices could limit or expand the capacity for cash borrowers to secure finance from lenders.

9. Conclusions

Central clearing provides a number of tangible benefits to the various participants in the repo markets. CCPs have historically (before Basel 3) had comparably little success in establishing themselves for securities lending. But there are also geographical differences. In Europe, the penetration of CCPs is relatively high compared to the US. A plausible reason for this is the partly similar functions that tri-party repo agents perform in the US. The fragmented European market has enabled CCPs to provide services where tri-party repo agents are not present or where tri-party services have been structured in silos (ie, central bank financing vs. other usages). While CCPs and tri-party models cater for different market needs, the market structure has evolved around the presence of either of them.

CCPs seem to work best for markets where trading is concentrated between direct CCP participants that as result can run a matched book. Where this is not the case and parties to a transaction require agents to intermediate the CCP access, the benefits may not outweigh the cost.

It is, however, not accurate to view CCPs and tri-party repo agents as competing services; rather they are complementary. CCPs provide additional risk mitigation services over and above those of a tri-party agent especially in terms of assuming the performance by the counterparty. In doing so, their risk techniques differ for instance in terms of default management. Tri-party repo agents on the other hand provide custody and collateral management services which are complementary to

---

8   Morgan Stanley and Oliver Wyman, Wholesale & Investment Banking Outlook, March 2012.
9   IMF Working Paper, Making OTC Derivatives Safe – A Fresh Look, March 2011.
10 *Risk Magazine*, New regulations could cause $7 trillion "collateral shock" date?.

those activities performed by CCPs. As a result, one emerging trend is that CCPs are increasingly becoming clients of tri-party repo agents to manage the post-trade collateral management and custody functions. Furthermore, tri-party agents can help to optimise collateral across multiple CCPs.

There is also a potential drawback to central clearing of OTC derivatives which could impact securities lending or repo markets. As new prudential rules continue to encourage mandatory clearing for OTC derivatives, this may create a large scale liquidity squeeze on 'safe assets'. If regulators were also to mandate clearing in the securities financing markets, the risk of creating a large scale liquidity squeeze would only heighten and could lead to financial instability. The IMF summarised this risk:

The shrinking set of assets perceived as safe, now limited to mostly high-quality sovereign debt, coupled with growing demand, can have negative implications for global financial stability. It will increase the price of safety and compel investors to move down the safety scale as they scramble to obtain scarce assets. Safe asset scarcity could lead to more short-term volatility jumps, herding behaviour, and runs on sovereign debt.[11]

It will be interesting to see how market participants seek to deal with the challenges faced by central clearing of securities financing and how the regulators may directly or even inadvertently cause changes to market activity to occur in this important aspect of the trading of these products.

---

11   International Monetary Fund; Safe Assets: Financial System Cornerstone? (April 2012).

Structured repo transactions

Daniel Franks
Norton Rose Fulbright

Repos originated as a form of overnight financing. To this day, a significant majority of repos are overnight trades, with another substantial proportion still being short-term (ie, three months or less) or rolling overnight trades. Similarly, repos have traditionally been used in respect of liquid assets, primarily as a result of their short-term nature. However, the use of repos as a source of longer-term funding has continued to grow and they have filled the funding gap left by the inactivity in certain other credit markets, most notably securitisation, or otherwise supplemented those markets. The versatility of repos – particularly as a result of their bilateral nature, and the ability to call for margin on a daily or even intra-day basis – has attracted many participants and allowed for those participants' specific funding, credit and legal requirements to be satisfied. This chapter looks at some of the structured trades that are more commonly used and identifies their distinguishing features and associated risks when compared with more short-term vanilla trades.

1. Floating rate repo

1.1 **Background**
Because of the nature of a standard overnight trade, overnight interest rates at the time of trading (together with any applicable spread reflecting the margining terms and the credit profiles of the parties and of the securities) are used to fix the repo rate and so no consideration is required as to payment dates, reset dates or interest breakage.

Medium- and long-term repos are likely to require additional considerations, even where the trade has a fixed maturity equal to a single interest period.

1.2 **Additional considerations**
While the following considerations apply equally to repos of any maturity (other than overnight trades), they are in practice typically addressed only if the trade has a scheduled maturity longer than three months.

(a) *Periodic payments*
If the repo interest is to be paid in instalments on a periodic basis during the term of the repo (eg, quarterly payments during a one-year trade), bespoke payment obligations will need to be included in the documentation. Consequential definitions and provisions will also be required, such as interest rate reset dates,

calculation periods and rate disruption fallbacks. These periodic payments are often structured as partial payments of the repurchase price, rather than payments of interest, particularly where characterisation is a concern.

(b) **Additional events of default**
The standard industry documentation does not include a generic 'failure to pay' event of default. The standard events of default relate to specific payment obligations (eg, the obligations to pay the purchase price, repurchase price and manufactured dividends/income payments). The generic failure to perform obligations event of default has a 30-day grace period, which is generally considered to be too long for a failure to make a payment. If periodic payments of the repo rate have been introduced, parties should consider including a bespoke event of default for failure to pay those periodic payments, even if they are structured as interim payments of the repurchase price.

(c) **Calculation agent**
A standard repo does not require a calculation agent, since each party may conduct its own valuation of the assets (in accordance with the definition of market value) and make a margin call as appropriate (with a dispute arising if both parties make a call on the same day). However, parties may consider it prudent, following the introduction of periodic repo rate reset and payment provisions, to introduce the role of a calculation agent, identifying one or both of the parties, or a third party, to make calculations and act in accordance with a specified standard of care. If the purchased securities are illiquid, such as certain types of asset-backed security, it may also be appropriate for a calculation agent to determine their market value.

(d) **Interest breakage**
Parties may wish to consider whether interest breakage costs should be payable upon termination of the repo prior to its scheduled maturity. Early termination may be due to an event of default, mini close-out, tax event or any termination option included in the terms of the repo itself. As with all interest breakage provisions, parties should consider whether the non-defaulting party (or non-breaking party) should be required to account for break gains as well as being able to recover break costs. This is likely to depend on the negotiating position of each party, as well as other considerations, such as whether the transaction is considered to be closer to a secured loan (where it is unusual for break gains to be addressed) rather than a derivative (where both gains and losses are typically accounted for). Parties should also consider whether the ability to claim for the cost of unwinding or replacing a transaction in the circumstances described in the standard documents is appropriate or sufficient to address the associated interest rate risk.

(e) **Ancillary amendments**
Parties should also ensure that any bespoke provisions of the types described above are adequately incorporated into the document so that they are captured within the close-out calculation and avoid double counting.

2. Committed repo facilities

2.1 Background

A standard repo relationship involves the parties from time to time agreeing to enter into transactions, without the obligation to do so. As parties have sought to supplement or replace other committed funding facilities, the use of various committed repo structures has increased. The committed nature of these arrangements introduces additional risks that the parties will need to consider and, if appropriate, mitigate.

Unlike secured lending facilities (eg, revolving credit facilities), which give the cash borrower the right to draw down and the cash lender the obligation to lend funds, the committed party in a repo can be either the repo seller (cash borrower) or the repo buyer (cash lender). For example, a committed repo facility may provide that the buyer may from time to time be required by the seller to enter into repurchase transactions under which the buyer is required to purchase from the seller eligible securities. Such a facility would economically be similar to a secured lending facility where the cash lender is subject to the obligation to lend. Conversely, a committed repo facility may provide that the seller may from time to time be required by the buyer to enter into repurchase transactions under which the seller is required to sell to the buyer eligible securities.

2.2 Types of structure

Committed repo facilities can take one of a number of forms, each of which may give rise to its own legal, tax, accounting and documentation considerations:

- Facility transaction (with separate transactions for each 'drawdown') – in this structure, a transaction, which itself is not a repurchase transaction, is entered into under or by reference to the repurchase agreement, permitting one party to require the other party to enter into repos from time to time. Each drawdown then comprises a separate transaction under the repurchase agreement.
- Revolving transaction – in this structure, a repurchase transaction is entered into between the parties but, unlike in a vanilla repo, one party can elect to increase and/or decrease the size of the trade from time to time. The transaction may itself be a portfolio transaction, with the purchase price allocated among multiple securities.
- Evergreen repo – in this structure, a repurchase transaction is entered into between the parties but, unlike in a vanilla repo, the maturity date automatically 'rolls' for a specified period unless one of the parties elects to prevent further rolls. Again, the transaction may be a portfolio transaction.
- Facility annex – in this structure, the repurchase agreement is supplemented by an additional annex (or by additional provisions in an existing annex) which commits one party to enter into repurchase transactions upon the demand of the other party. The provisions in this annex form part of the repurchase agreement itself.
- Standalone facility document – this operates in the same way as the facility annex, except that the commitment is contained in a bespoke standalone document that does not form part of the repurchase agreement itself.

2.3 Additional considerations

Depending on the type of structure being used, parties should consider the following.

(a) **Extent of commitment**

The circumstances in which the party that is subject to the commitment (the 'committed party') may refrain from entering into a repo (or refrain from adjusting the terms of an existing repo, as appropriate) will be of particular concern, with each party having opposing interests. The committed party may wish to ensure that it is not required to enter into a repo if it would cause an adverse regulatory (including regulatory capital), tax or legal consequence (including if it would be unlawful to enter into the transaction, hold the securities or acquire an associated hedge position). The potential impact of the EU financial transaction tax on future transactions may, for example, result in the trade being commercially unviable for the committed party.

Similarly, the committed party may wish to ensure that it is not compelled to deliver or receive securities in contravention of its own legal, regulatory or quasi-regulatory requirements or guidance, or in a manner that would otherwise subject it to onerous requirements. For example, a committed party may wish to avoid being required to receive equity securities during a takeover period or being party to a transaction which breaches a securities lending code of conduct. It may also wish to avoid being required to deliver securities which it is unable to source or deliver due to legal or market constraints.

The other party (the 'non-committed party') will, on the other hand, wish to ensure that the commitment is as robust as possible, in particular if it is to take any liquidity benefit from the facility from an accounting and regulatory capital perspective.

(b) **Commercial terms (non-committed party)**

The non-committed party will wish to ensure that the commercial terms of the repo are as robust as possible. Key commercial terms that the non-committed party is likely to want to agree at the outset of the facility (or for which a methodology is likely to be agreed) include the size of the haircut and the repo rate.

(c) **Commercial terms (committed party)**

The committed party will wish to ensure that the securities comply with certain eligibility criteria, concentration limits and portfolio guidelines. The terms applicable to any commitment fee will also need to be clear.

(d) **Consequences of a failure under the facility**

While a default under a transaction, once entered into, is likely to fall within the standard events of default in the repurchase agreement, the parties should consider the appropriate consequences for a failure by either party to comply with the commitment terms of the facility. These include the following:

- Failure to pay the commitment fee – should this constitute an event of

default under the repurchase agreement and, if so, what is the appropriate grace period?
- Failure by the committed party to comply with the commitment in accordance with the facility – should this constitute an event of default and, if so, what are the remedies of the non-committed party? In particular, a standard repo close-out calculation (which compares the repurchase price with the market value of the securities) may be insufficient to protect the non-committed party against a default by the committed party in complying with the commitment.
- Breach of the eligibility criteria, concentration limits or portfolio guidelines – should these constitute an event of default, or should there be an alternative remedy (eg, an ability to remove the ineligible assets)?

2.4 Comparison with secured lending facilities

Given the economic similarities between a repo and a secured loan, and the similarity between the commitment offered in connection with a committed repo facility and that offered pursuant to a revolving credit facility (at least where the buyer is the committed party), it is common for parties to consider the two as interchangeable. However, there are important differences between the repo markets and the secured lending (bank debt) markets, and parties should consider whether any of these differences affect the way in which the committed repo facility should be structured.

(a) Margining

Typically, a repo will be margined daily (or even intra-day), while secured lending facilities do not always permit the lender to request more collateral and often do not require the lender to return excess collateral until the debt has been discharged.

(b) Covenants

Typically, a revolving credit facility might contain several covenants, including financial covenants, with which the borrower must comply. In the repo markets, such covenants are less common (due, in most part, to the additional credit protection afforded by daily margining).

(c) Title transfer

Typically, a secured lending facility will involve the granting of security over the collateral, while repos involve the transfer of full ownership to the buyer (cash lender). In addition to the direct impact of a title transfer arrangement on cost of funds (since the buyer can use the assets, its cost of funding is reduced, which may also reduce the repo rate when compared with a secured funding interest rate), the title transfer may have other indirect benefits. For example, upon a default by the seller (cash borrower), the buyer may have the right to offset its obligation to account for excess collateral, which is a simple debt obligation, against other exposures between the parties, which in essence permits the buyer to treat the value of the securities as quasi-collateral for other exposures. A lender under a secured loan facility is less likely to have such broad powers over non-cash collateral.

Structured repo transactions

(d) Syndication
While there are established markets and standard form documents for syndicating secured debt, there are no such markets or documents in the repo markets. As such, syndication will require bespoke documentation to be put in place, which will need to take into account the constraints of provisions in repurchase agreements which were not designed for syndicated facilities (eg, prohibitions on assignment).

(e) Lender default
In a typical secured lending facility, the parties do not include representations, covenants or events of default in respect of the lender. Neither does a typical secured lending facility include contractual consequences upon bankruptcy of the lender. Each of these is present in a standard repurchase agreement.

3. Credit-linked repo

3.1 Background

A vanilla repo simply provides for the buyer (cash lender) to return equivalent securities at maturity of the transaction. Accordingly, the seller (cash borrower) remains economically exposed to the value of the securities (and therefore the credit risk of the issuer) throughout the life of the transaction. Absent a default by either party, the repo should not result in the reallocation of credit risk in relation to the securities or the issuer. In recent years, parties have introduced additional credit-risk exposures into repos, primarily as a way of reducing the repo rate.

While there are various types of credit-linked repo, the most common involve:
- the repurchase price being accelerated upon the occurrence of specified credit events;
- upon the occurrence of a credit event, instead of delivering equivalent securities (ie, equivalent to the securities that were transferred on the purchase date), the buyer being permitted to deliver securities satisfying certain categories and characteristics (a 'cheapest to deliver option'), similar to a typical physically settled credit derivative; and
- the repo rate payable by the seller being reduced because of the buyer's cheapest to deliver option (essentially, due to the cost of the embedded credit derivative within the repo).

Diagrams setting out the primary cashflows of a typical credit-linked repo are shown below.

Purchase date

```
                  Purchased securities
         Seller  ─────────────────────→  Buyer
                  Purchase price
                 ←─────────────────────
```

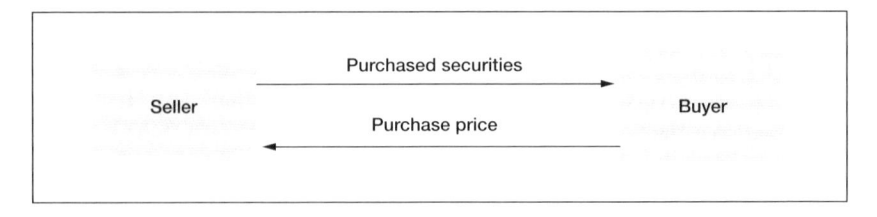

Repurchase date (if no intervening credit event)

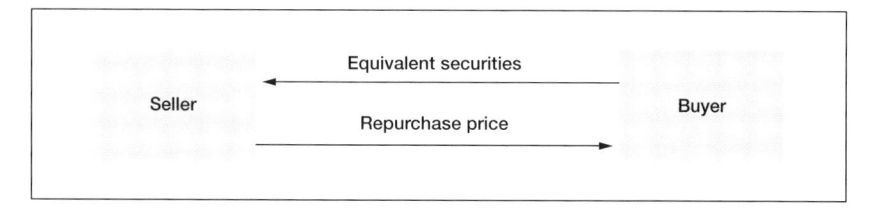

```
         ←——— Equivalent securities ———
Seller                                      Buyer
         ——— Repurchase price ———→
```

Accelerated repurchase date following occurrence of credit event

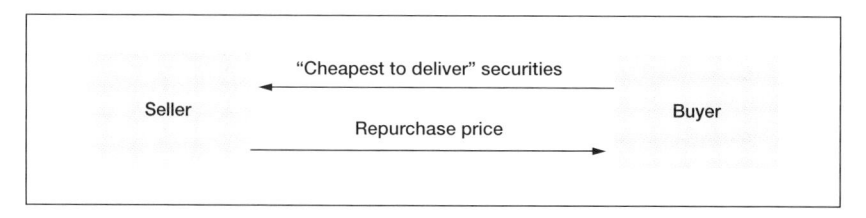

```
         ←——— "Cheapest to deliver" securities ———
Seller                                              Buyer
         ——— Repurchase price ———→
```

3.2   **Additional considerations**

Parties should consider the following when entering into a credit-linked repo such as the one described above:

(a)   *Credit-linked provisions*

The documentation will need to incorporate provisions identifying the credit events that may trigger an accelerated repurchase date and the criteria and characteristics for determining which obligations may be delivered as part of the cheapest to deliver option. Typically, these may be defined by reference to the International Swaps and Derivatives Association (ISDA) Credit Derivatives Definitions, although parties should consider whether the Credit Derivatives Definitions booklet should be incorporated by reference (together, where appropriate, with the elections in ISDA's most recent Physical Settlement Matrix) or whether the relevant provisions should be included in long-form in the repo confirmation itself. Parties should also consider whether it is appropriate, given the circumstances of their transaction, for the embedded credit-linked element to be phrased in derivatives terminology or whether the credit-linked provisions might better be described in language that is less closely associated with derivatives.

(b)   *Hedging*

Parties will need to consider the potential impact on their hedging arrangements of any departures from standard credit derivatives practice, such as amendments to the standard Credit Events and Deliverable Obligation Characteristics in the ISDA Credit Derivatives Definitions. In addition, since a single-name credit default swap typically ties the parties to resolutions made by an ISDA determinations committee, parties should consider whether such resolutions should have any impact on their repo or, if not, whether this gives rise to hedging basis risk.

Structured repo transactions

(c) *Margining*
The standard margining provisions applicable to a vanilla repo compare the current market value of the securities with the repurchase price. Parties should consider whether, and if so how, to amend these margining provisions so that the mark-to-market calculations take into account the embedded credit-linked provisions (both the potential acceleration of the repurchase date and the cheapest to deliver option).

(d) *Consequences of default*
If an event of default occurs, standard repo terms will provide for the value of equivalent securities to be determined and set off against the repurchase price. In addition, the defaulting party may be responsible for any loss or expense incurred by the non-defaulting party in entering into a replacement transaction or unwinding a hedging transaction. The parties may wish to consider whether these remedies are sufficient to capture costs (or value) associated with terminating the embedded credit-linked element, or whether bespoke provisions are required to address this more specifically.

(e) *Consequences of early termination*
Similarly, if the transaction terminates early for any other reason (eg, because a party has exercised a termination option upon the occurrence of a tax event relating to the securities), the parties should consider whether breakage costs, hedging unwind or replacement costs are recoverable.

(f) *Additional termination provisions*
Parties should consider whether the inclusion of the credit-linked provisions introduces additional legal risks that require mitigation by termination rights. For example, standard repo documentation does not include termination provisions in the event that it becomes illegal for the parties to perform their obligations, or if the parties are prevented by a force majeure event from performing their obligations, while such provisions would normally apply to credit derivatives entered into under an ISDA Master Agreement. While parties may consider that the likelihood of such events occurring in respect of a vanilla repo is low, they should consider whether the risk is increased as a result of the inclusion of the credit-linked provisions.

(g) *Accounting*
While parties should consider the appropriate accounting treatment of all transactions which they may enter into, the combination of two types of transaction/exposure (repos and credit derivatives) is likely to require particular accounting attention. In addition to considering their own accounting treatment, parties may wish to consider whether it is appropriate to enquire into the accounting treatment being given to the trade by their counterparty.

4. **Loan repo**

4.1 Background
The types of asset that are subject to repos have historically been limited to debt

securities and equities. In more recent years, market participants have looked to repo other types of asset, including loans (ie, credit exposures arising under bilateral or multilateral credit agreements not taking the form of securities). While the general principles applicable to repos, such as title transfer, apply equally to all product types, loan repo gives rise to specific considerations.

4.2 Additional considerations

The following additional considerations arise as a result of the unique nature of loans as underlying assets.

(a) Transfer restrictions

For a loan to be capable of being sold under a repo, it must be possible for the seller to transfer full ownership in the loan to the buyer and for the buyer to transfer full ownership back to the seller at maturity of the repo transaction. The parties should consider the impact of any provisions in the facility agreement or related documentation (eg, an intercreditor agreement) that contain prohibitions on transfer by lenders, or require certain formalities to be performed before any such transfer can become effective.

(b) Confidentiality

Loan agreements typically contain confidentiality undertakings prohibiting lenders from disclosing to third parties information relating to the borrowers save in specific circumstances. For the parties to consider entering into a repo, the seller will usually need to disclose information to the buyer (and, if not to the buyer, to a third-party collateral agent). Similarly, for a repo to operate effectively, the parties will generally need to disclose information between themselves relating to the borrower and the underlying loan, for example for the purposes of determining the value of the loan, the occurrence of an income payment date or a default by the borrower. Parties should therefore consider whether the loan documentation permits the seller to disclose information to the buyer in advance of the repo being entered into and for the buyer to disclose information to the seller during the term of the repo. The buyer should also consider whether it would continue to have access to sufficient information during the term of the repo if it were to decide to sell or otherwise deal with the loan. The parties should also consider, in addition to these contractual confidentiality undertakings, similar issues arising out of local bank secrecy laws.

(c) Additional payment obligations

The parties should consider whether the lender may be required to make additional payments to the borrower or to a third party (eg, an agent) and, if so, make appropriate arrangements for corresponding payments to be made between the seller and the buyer under the repo. For example, in the case of a revolving credit facility, the buyer (in its capacity as lender) may be required to make additional advances to the borrower (either because the loan is repaid and then redrawn or because it is not fully drawn when the repo is entered into). Similarly, a term loan facility which is not fully drawn but for which the utilisation period has not expired may require the buyer (in its capacity as lender) to advance further funds.

(d) **Syndicated loans**
If the loan is syndicated, there are likely to be pro-rata sharing provisions requiring the lender to account to the facility agent if the lender receives more than its appropriate share of principal repayments or interest payments. Parties should consider whether the repo documentation adequately defines what constitutes a repayment or income distribution, and whether additional provisions may be required if the buyer pays amounts to the seller in respect of principal repayments/income payments which are then clawed back by the facility agent or other lenders.

(e) **Valuation**
Parties should consider whether there is a generally recognised source for the purposes of determining the value of the loan for margining calculations. Similarly, parties should consider whether there is a sufficiently liquid secondary market for the loan such that the standard default valuation mechanics and timings continue to be appropriate.

(f) **Tax**
The parties should consider whether, by virtue of the loan having been transferred to the buyer (even if the borrower is not aware of this), the withholding tax and/or gross-up obligations of the borrower under the loan are affected.

(g) **Equivalent assets**
The parties should address the question of whether the true sale characterisation under any applicable laws is adversely affected by virtue of the fact that the repo buyer is required to redeliver the same loan at maturity of the repo, as opposed to an equivalent loan (since there is unlikely to be a fungible equivalent loan).

5. Commodity repo

5.1 **Background**
Because of broader economic trends, including the increased relative value of certain commodities, such assets are increasingly being identified as suitable for repos. Like loans, commodities as an asset class give rise to specific issues that are less prevalent in other asset classes – primarily due to their tangible nature, but also as they may be perishable and need to be stored and insured. The issues also differ depending on whether the repo is in respect of a specific or a generic commodity asset.

5.2 **Additional considerations**

(a) **Transfer mechanics**
The asset being sold under the repo may be the commodity itself or, more likely, a

warrant or other traded instrument. The way in which the asset is transferred and the impact that this may have on the documentation will depend on the category into which it falls.

(b) *Allocation of risks and insurance*
As the value of commodities depends on their physical state, the parties should consider whether the commodities are appropriately insured against various risks of loss or damage. Since both parties have an interest in making sure that those risks are adequately covered, they should decide who will be responsible for obtaining and maintaining the insurance, who will pay for the insurance and the minimum terms of the insurance. Similarly, parties should consider whether the repo buyer should be under any obligation in respect of the care and custody of the commodity, although they should be careful to ensure that any such obligations do not increase the risk that the seller is considered to have retained an ownership interest in the commodity.

(c) *Environmental liability*
The owner of a commodity may be responsible, under either specific national or international laws or conventions (eg, maritime conventions for commodities transported by sea) or more general tortious principles, to account for any environmental damage caused by those commodities while in its ownership. Parties to a commodity repo should consider who should bear the risk associated with any such damage during the term of the repo, and in particular whether the repo seller should indemnify the buyer for losses incurred as a result.

(d) *Regulatory impact*
Certain types of commodity trading are given particular treatment in various jurisdictions, including under the US Bankruptcy Code or the EU Markets in Financial Instruments Directive. Accordingly, parties should consider how their commodity repo is likely to be treated for the purposes of any relevant regulatory or legislative requirements.

6. Repo of asset-backed securities

6.1 Background
Repos of asset-backed securities have been used for various purposes, but their primary use is as a substitute or supplement to direct investment in the asset-backed securities themselves. Central bank liquidity schemes are often structured as repos and in recent years they have allowed originators to access funding in respect of asset-backed securities where the direct investment market has been illiquid. Bilateral repos have also been used for similar purposes. When compared with a direct investment in the asset-backed security, repos offer various benefits to investors, including a maturity that is shorter than the asset-backed security itself and enhanced credit protection in the form of a commitment by the originator to repurchase the asset, which commitment is backed by ongoing margin maintenance.

6.2 Additional considerations

(a) *Illiquidity*

Compared with ordinary debt securities, many types of asset-backed security are illiquid. As well as potentially affecting the reliability of valuations, illiquidity is likely to give rise to other issues. The repo buyer is likely to require a greater haircut to reflect the increased volatility – the greater haircut will in turn increase the credit risk for the seller. Because of this additional credit risk, the seller may then wish to put in place haircut segregation procedures (eg, security rather than title transfer). Illiquidity may also result in the typical default valuation window applicable to repos (between one and five days) being extended or disapplied if it is considered that a short timeframe is inappropriate for purposes of determining an accurate value of the asset-backed securities.

(b) *Valuation*

Many types of asset-backed security are difficult to value with adequate certainty, with potentially large differences of opinion as to the appropriate value. While this is likely to result in the repo buyer requiring significant discretion in determining the value for margining and close-out purposes, the seller is likely to want some protection against arbitrary and unreasonable pricing, in particular if there are different views as to whether to value the asset-backed security or the underlying pool of assets.

(c) *Amortisation*

Since asset-backed securities often amortise (and may also suffer principal write-downs and reimbursements), parties should consider how to address principal repayments during the life of the repo. There are different ways in which amortisation may potentially be addressed, including:
- treating the repo as a vanilla trade, which means that principal repayments will be rolled up until maturity, with no interim cashflows to reflect amortisation;
- reducing the size of the repo by the repo buyer accounting to the seller for the principal repayments when paid by the issuer (in the same way as income payments) and the seller being required to repay a proportionate amount of the repo purchase price; and
- treating the principal repayment as a form of income, which means that the repo buyer will account to the seller for the principal repayments when paid by the issuer. This will likely result in a margin call being made by the buyer reflecting the corresponding decrease in value of the securities.

Structured securities lending transactions

Daniel Franks
Norton Rose Fulbright

Securities lending transactions originated as a method of obtaining access to securities for a particular purpose or for a particular period. To this day, a significant majority of securities lending transactions are vanilla on-demand trades, where the securities are lent on an open basis against liquid collateral of an eligible type. Similarly, securities lending transactions have traditionally been in respect of equity or debt securities. However, the use of securities lending transactions as a source of funding has continued to grow, and they have filled or supplemented the funding gap left by the inactivity in certain other credit markets, most notably securitisation. The versatility of securities lending transactions, particularly as a result of their bilateral nature and the ability to call for collateral on a daily or even intra-day basis, has attracted many participants and allowed for their specific funding, credit and legal requirements to be satisfied. This chapter looks at some of the structured trades that are more commonly used and identifies their distinguishing features and associated risks when compared with more short-term vanilla trades.

1. Floating rate transactions

1.1 Background
Because of the on-demand nature of vanilla securities lending transactions, fixed rates or standard overnight interest rates are used to determine the fee payable by the borrower to the lender (together with any applicable spread reflecting the margining terms and the credit profiles of the parties and of the securities), and so no consideration is required as to payment dates, reset dates or interest breakage.

Medium- and long-term securities lending transactions – particularly where they have a fixed maturity – are likely to require additional considerations, even where the trade has a fixed maturity equal to a standard interest period.

1.2 Additional considerations
While the following considerations apply equally to securities lending transactions of any maturity (other than overnight trades), they are in practice typically addressed only if the trade has a scheduled maturity longer than three months.

(a) Periodic payments
If the securities lending fee is to be paid in instalments on a periodic basis during the term of the securities lending transaction (eg, quarterly payments during a one-year

trade), bespoke payment obligations will need to be included in the documentation. Consequential definitions and provisions may also be required to allow for interest rate reset dates, calculation periods and rate disruption fallbacks.

(b) *Additional events of default*

The standard industry documentation does not include a generic 'failure to pay' event of default. The standard events of default relate to specific payment obligations (eg, the obligations to pay cash collateral and manufactured dividends/income payments) and the generic 'failure to perform obligations' event of default has a 30-day grace period, which is generally considered to be too long for non-payment. If periodic payments of the fee or interest on cash collateral have been introduced, parties should consider including a bespoke event of default for failure to pay those periodic payments.

(c) *Calculation agent*

A standard securities lending transaction does not require a calculation agent, since each party can conduct its own valuation of the assets (in accordance with the definition of market value) and make a margin call as appropriate. However, parties may consider it prudent, following the introduction of periodic reset and payment provisions, to introduce the role of a calculation agent, identifying one or both of the parties or a third party to make calculations and act in accordance with a specified standard of care. If the borrowed or collateral securities are illiquid, such as certain types of asset-backed security, it may also be appropriate for a calculation agent to determine their market value.

(d) *Breakage costs*

Parties may wish to consider whether breakage costs should be payable upon termination of the securities lending transaction prior to its scheduled maturity. Early termination may be due to an event of default or mini close-out or the on-demand nature of the transaction itself. As with all breakage provisions, parties should consider whether the non-defaulting party (or non-breaking party) should be required to account for break gains as well as being able to recover break costs. This is likely to depend on the negotiating position of each party, as well as other considerations such as whether the transaction is considered to be closer to a secured loan (where it is unusual for break gains to be addressed) rather than a derivative (where both gains and losses are typically accounted for). Parties should also consider whether the ability to claim for the cost of unwinding or replacing a transaction in the circumstances described in the standard documents is appropriate or sufficient to address the associated risks in the transaction.

(e) *Ancillary amendments*

Parties should also ensure that any bespoke provisions of the types described above are adequately incorporated into the document so that they are captured within the close-out calculation and avoid double counting.

2. Committed facilities

2.1 Background

A standard securities lending relationship involves the parties from time to time agreeing to enter into transactions, without the obligation to do so. As parties have sought to supplement or replace other committed funding facilities, the use of various committed securities lending structures has increased. The committed nature of these arrangements introduces additional risks that the parties will need to consider and, if appropriate, mitigate.

Unlike secured lending facilities (eg, revolving credit facilities), which give the cash borrower the right to draw down and the cash lender the obligation to lend funds, the committed party in a securities lending transaction can be either the lender or the borrower. For example, a committed securities lending facility may provide that the borrower may from time to time be required by the lender to enter into securities lending transactions under which the borrower is required to borrow from the lender eligible securities against the provision by the borrower of collateral. Where the collateral must be cash, such a facility will be similar to a secured lending facility where the cash lender is subject to the obligation to lend. Conversely, a committed securities lending facility may provide that the lender may from time to time be required by the borrower to enter into securities lending transactions under which the lender is required to lend to the borrower eligible securities.

2.2 Types of structure

Committed securities lending facilities can take one of a number of forms, each of which may give rise to its own legal, tax, accounting and documentation considerations:

- Facility transaction (with separate transactions for each 'drawdown') – in this structure, a transaction which itself is not a securities lending transaction is entered into under or by reference to the securities lending agreement, permitting one party to require the other to enter into transactions from time to time. Each drawdown then comprises a separate transaction under the securities lending agreement.
- Revolving transaction – in this structure, a securities lending transaction is entered into between the parties but, unlike in a vanilla trade, one party can elect to increase and/or decrease the size of the trade from time to time. The transaction may itself be a portfolio transaction, with the collateral allocated among multiple securities.
- Evergreen – in this structure, a securities lending transaction is entered into between the parties and the maturity date automatically 'rolls' for a specified period unless one of the parties elects to prevent further rolls. Again, the transaction may be a portfolio transaction.
- Facility annex – in this structure, the securities lending agreement is supplemented by an additional annex (or by additional provisions in the schedule) which commits one party to enter into transactions upon the demand of the other party. The annex forms part of the securities lending agreement itself.

- Standalone facility document – this operates in the same way as the facility annex, except that the commitment is contained in a bespoke standalone document that does not form part of the securities lending agreement itself.

2.3 Additional considerations

Depending on the type of structure being used, parties should consider the following.

(a) Extent of commitment

The circumstances in which the party that is subject to the commitment (the 'committed party') may refrain from entering into a securities lending transaction (or refrain from adjusting the terms of an existing transaction, as appropriate) will be of particular concern, with each party having opposing interests. The committed party may wish to ensure that it is not required to enter into a transaction if it would cause an adverse regulatory (including regulatory capital), tax or legal consequence (including if it would be unlawful to enter into the transaction, hold the securities or acquire an associated hedge position). In particular, the potential impact of the EU financial transaction tax on future transactions may, for example, result in the trade being commercially unviable for the committed party.

Similarly, the committed party may wish to ensure that it is not compelled to deliver or receive securities in contravention of its own legal, regulatory or quasi-regulatory requirements or guidance, or in a manner that would otherwise subject it to onerous requirements. For example, a committed party may wish to avoid being required to receive equity securities during a takeover period or being party to a transaction which breaches a securities lending code of practice. It may also wish to avoid being required to deliver securities which it is unable to source or deliver due to legal or market constraints.

The other party (the 'non-committed party') will, on the other hand, wish to ensure that the commitment is as robust as possible, in particular if it is to take any liquidity benefit from the facility from an accounting and regulatory capital perspective.

(b) Commercial terms (committed party)

The non-committed party will wish to ensure that the commercial terms of the transaction are as robust as possible. Key commercial terms that the non-committed party is likely to want to agree at the outset of the facility (or for which a methodology is likely to be agreed) include the eligible collateral, the size of the margin, the lending fee and interest rate on cash collateral.

(c) Commercial terms (non-committed party)

The committed party will wish to ensure that the securities comply with eligibility criteria for the securities, concentration limits and portfolio guidelines. The terms applicable to any commitment fee will also need to be specified.

(d)   Consequences of a failure under the facility
While a default under a transaction, once entered into, is likely to fall within the standard events of default in the securities lending agreement, the parties should consider the appropriate consequences for a failure by either party to comply with the commitment terms of the facility. These include the following:
- Failure to pay the commitment fee – should this constitute an event of default under the securities lending agreement and, if so, what is the appropriate grace period?
- Failure by the committed party to comply with the commitment in accordance with the facility – should this constitute an event of default and, if so, what are the remedies of the non-committed party? In particular, a standard securities lending close-out calculation (which compares the current market value of the loaned securities with the current market value of the collateral) may be insufficient to protect the non-committed party against a default by the committed party before the facility has been drawn down.
- Breach of the eligibility criteria, concentration limits or portfolio guidelines – should these constitute an event of default, or should there be an alternative remedy (eg, an ability to remove the ineligible assets)?

2.4   Comparison with secured cash lending facilities

Given the economic similarities between a securities lending transaction (particularly if the collateral is cash collateral) and a secured loan, and the similarity between the 'commitment' offered in connection with a committed securities lending facility and that offered pursuant to a revolving credit facility, it is common for parties to consider the two as interchangeable. However, there are important differences between the securities lending market and the secured lending (bank debt) markets, and parties should consider whether any of these differences affect the way in which the securities lending facility should be structured.

(a)   Collateral
Typically, a securities lending transaction will be subject to daily (or even intra-day) marking to market, while secured lending facilities do not always permit the lender to request more collateral and often do not require the lender to return excess collateral until the debt has been discharged.

(b)   Covenants
Typically, a revolving credit facility might contain several covenants, including financial covenants, with which the borrower must comply. In the securities lending markets, such covenants are less common (due, in most part, to the additional credit protection afforded by daily marking to market).

(c)   Title transfer
Typically, a secured lending facility will involve the granting of security over the collateral, while securities lending transactions involve the transfer of full ownership of both the loaned securities and the collateral.

(d) Syndication
While there are established markets and standard form documents for syndicating secured debt, there are no such markets or documents in the securities lending markets. As such, syndication would require bespoke documentation to be put in place which would need to take into account the constraints of provisions in securities lending agreements which were not designed for syndicated facilities (eg, prohibitions on assignment).

(e) Lender default
In a typical secured lending facility, the parties do not include representations, covenants or events of default in respect of the cash lender. Neither does a typical secured lending facility include contractual consequences upon bankruptcy of the cash lender. Each of these is present in a standard securities lending agreement.

3. Documenting repos under a securities lending agreement (switching the roles of borrower and lender)

3.1 Background

Under a typical securities lending transaction, the loaned securities are specific, less liquid securities, while the collateral is more liquid. Because the loaned securities are the primary driver behind a typical securities lending transaction and the collateral is seen as supporting the borrower's obligations in relation to that primary obligation, the borrower is required to provide the lender with excess collateral. For the same reason, the borrower is the party that pays the fee in connection with the transaction.

However, if the primary purpose of the transaction does not relate to the loaned securities themselves (eg, if the transaction is principally a liquidity swap whose purpose is to permit the lender to exchange its illiquid assets for cash or other liquid assets), then the parties may wish to apply a haircut to the loaned securities (such that the lender is required to provide excess loaned securities when compared to the value of the collateral) and require the lender, rather than the borrower, to pay a fee. Adjusting the transaction in this way may result in the cashflows being similar to those of a repo, where the cash borrower (seller) provides excess collateral (the securities) to the cash lender (buyer) and pays a fee (the repo rate) for the funding.

3.2 Additional considerations

(a) Amendments to payment and delivery obligations
Parties will wish to make certain adjustments to the payment and delivery obligations to achieve the desired result, including some or all of the following:
- providing that the only type of eligible collateral is cash or near-cash assets;
- amending the haircut so that the value of the loaned securities is greater than the value of the collateral, rather than the other way around;
- amending the way in which the haircut is calculated so that it is expressed as a loan-to-value percentage similar to a repo, rather than a discount to the value of particular types of securities; and

- providing that the fees payable in connection with the transaction are rates in respect of cash collateral, equivalent to the repo rate in a repo or, if non-cash collateral is provided, introducing a new fee payable by the lender to the borrower.

(b) *Characterisation*

Parties may wish to check that the characterisation given by the parties would be respected by the courts, regulatory authorities and taxing authorities in all relevant jurisdictions. In particular, parties may wish to check, to the extent that characterisation is important to them for any reason, that the transaction would continue to be characterised as a securities lending transaction and would not be recharacterised as a repo by virtue of the substantive economic characteristics of the transaction. For example, if the purpose of entering into such a transaction under a Global Master Securities Lending Agreement is because one of the parties lacks the capacity to enter into repos, parties should ensure that the courts would recognise the transaction as a securities lending transaction and that the transaction would not continue to be beyond the relevant party's capacity by virtue of the substantive economic characteristics of the transaction. The issue of characterisation is dealt with more generally elsewhere in this book.

(c) *Reliance on opinions*

As with other types of structured transaction, parties should ensure that their transaction is of a type covered by any opinion on which they are seeking to rely, and that any amendments to the agreement do not contravene any assumptions or qualifications in that opinion.

4. Constant collateral amount securities lending transaction

4.1 Background

A typical securities lending transaction involves the transfer of a specified amount of loaned securities and the provision of collateral whose value is at least equal to the value of the loaned securities. Accordingly, the loaned securities represent the 'fixed' leg of a securities lending transaction, with the collateral being the leg that adjusts from time to time. This reflects the nature of a vanilla securities lending transaction as being one in which the borrower wishes to gain access to a particular quantity of the specified securities – any requirement of the borrower to return those securities simply because their value has increased might defeat this primary purpose. The amount of collateral from time to time may therefore be greater than the amount initially provided at the beginning of the securities lending transaction.

Parties may wish to amend the terms of the trade to ensure that the amount of collateral provided to the lender either is fixed or does not exceed a specified fixed amount (which is likely to be equal to, or within a specified tolerance of, the initial amount of collateral). This will result in the loaned securities being subject to periodic adjustment.

While there are various types of structure which limit the amount of collateral, a

Structured securities lending transactions

typical structure will involve:
- the loaned securities being subject to periodic marking to market, such that if the value of the loaned securities were to increase (or increase above a specified level), the borrower would be required to return an amount equal to the excess, and if the value of the loaned securities were to fall (or fall below a specified level), the lender would be required to provide additional loaned securities to eliminate the shortfall; and
- the collateral being subject to periodic marking to market by reference to a specified fixed amount, rather than by reference to the value of the loaned securities from time to time, such that if the value of the collateral were to increase above that specified fixed amount, the lender would be required to return an amount equal to the excess; and if the value of the collateral were to fall below a specified fixed amount, the borrower would be required to provide additional collateral to eliminate the shortfall.

The specified level of loaned securities and the specified fixed amount of collateral may be equal, or they may be different amounts. Each may also be subject to a tolerance, such that the excess collateral or loaned securities are required to be returned only once the excess is greater than a specified number and the shortfall is required to be eliminated only once the shortfall is greater than a specified number.

Diagrams setting out the primary cashflows of such a securities lending transaction are shown below.

Initial transfer

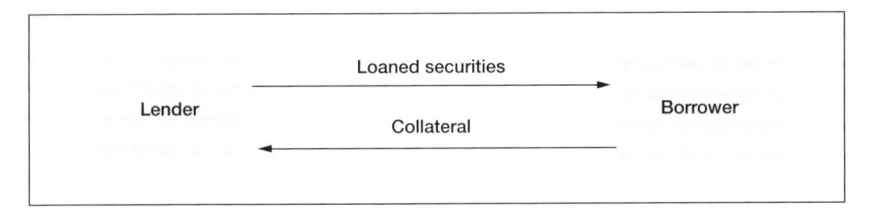

```
                    Loaned securities
Lender         ───────────────────────▶      Borrower
                    Collateral
               ◀───────────────────────
```

Marking to market of loaned securities

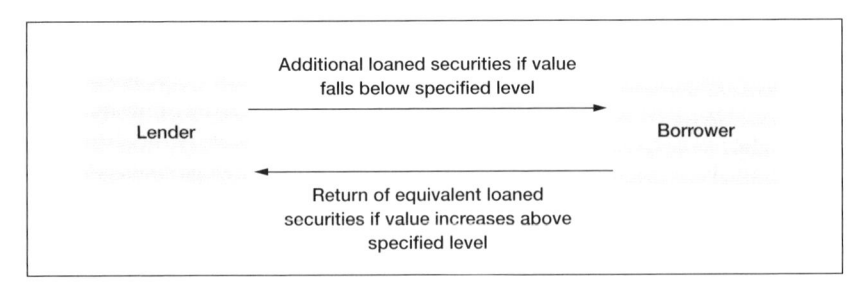

```
              Additional loaned securities if value
                   falls below specified level
Lender         ───────────────────────▶      Borrower
                  Return of equivalent loaned
               ◀───────────────────────
                securities if value increases above
                       specified level
```

Marking to market of collateral

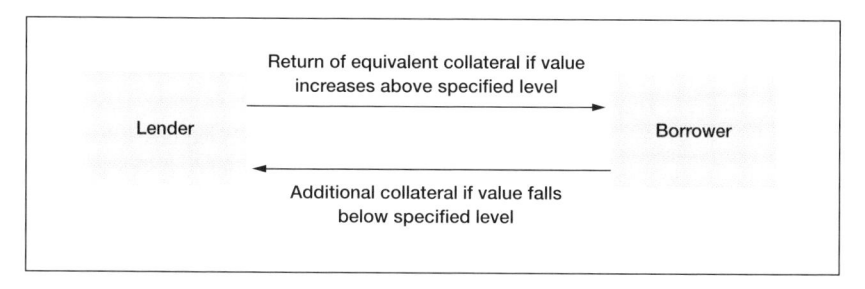

```
                    Return of equivalent collateral if value
                      increases above specified level
                   ─────────────────────────────────▶
        Lender                                              Borrower
                   ◀─────────────────────────────────
                    Additional collateral if value falls
                           below specified level
```

4.2 Additional considerations

(a) *Consequences of failure to transfer loaned securities on the settlement date*
Standard securities lending documentation does not contain a specific remedy relating to a failure to transfer loaned securities on the settlement date. This is because the amount of collateral required to be maintained is typically at least equal to the value of the loaned securities, and if no loaned securities have been transferred, no collateral is required to be transferred. If collateral has been transferred under a standard securities lending transaction before the loaned securities have been transferred, the borrower will be entitled to call for a return of the collateral. If the required amount of collateral is divorced from the amount of loaned securities, parties may wish to consider including an event of default or other consequence relating to a failure to transfer the loaned securities.

(b) *Additional events of default*
Since the marking to market provisions relating to the loaned securities are bespoke, they will not be subject to a standard event of default other than the generic 'failure to perform obligations' event of default, which has a long grace period. Parties may wish to consider including a specific event of default if either party does not comply with its obligations to provide additional loaned securities or return excess loaned securities.

(c) *Double counting*
Typically, the collateral marking to market provisions take into account various payments between the parties, such as unpaid amounts or accrued but unpaid interest or fees. Parties should ensure that such amounts are not double counted in the separate loaned securities and collateral marking to market provisions.

(d) *Timing of delivery of additional loaned securities or return of excess loaned securities*
Standard securities lending agreements provide for a period within which additional collateral must be provided or excess collateral returned following a demand. That period is typically short, reflecting the fact that collateral is likely to be liquid and have short settlement periods for spot transfers. Bespoke transfer timings will need to be included for the delivery of additional loaned securities or the return of excess

loaned securities. Such timings may not necessarily match those applicable to collateral, since the settlement period for spot transfers of loaned securities may be greater than that applicable to collateral.

(e) *Settlement risk*
The revised provisions may result in both parties being required to make a transfer on the same day. For example, if there are excess loaned securities and excess collateral, the lender will be required to return the excess collateral and the borrower will be required to return the excess loaned securities. Parties may wish to consider whether the securities lending agreement adequately addresses any concerns relating to the so-called Herstatt risk (ie, the overnight settlement risk that one party makes a transfer to the other party, but does not receive the corresponding transfer expected to be received from the other party on the same day).

(f) *Rates in respect of loaned securities*
Standard securities lending documentation provides that the rates payable by the borrower to the lender are applied to the market value of the loaned securities from time to time. Parties may wish to consider amending this to refer to the specified amount of loaned securities that are required to be maintained from time to time, rather than the actual amount of loaned securities outstanding.

5. Uncollateralised securities lending

5.1 Background
A typical securities lending transaction involves the borrower providing collateral in exchange for the loaned securities. The primary purpose of the collateral is to protect the lender against the risk of the borrower's failure to return the loaned securities, since if the borrower were to default, the lender would simply have a debt claim against the borrower for an amount equal to the value of the loaned securities. In fact, the lender does have such a claim in any event, but can offset against it the value of the collateral it is holding and which it ceases to be required to return.

Parties may be willing to enter into a securities lending transaction where the borrower is not required to provide collateral. This may be because the borrower's creditworthiness is sufficiently strong that the lender does not have credit concerns, or the borrower's creditworthiness is significantly greater than the lender's creditworthiness. Another reason that the lender may be willing to enter into an uncollateralised securities lending transaction is because there may be other relationships between the parties under which the borrower has a credit exposure to the lender, such that the effect of the securities lending transaction is to collaterise that other credit exposure of the borrower to the lender.

5.2 Additional considerations

(a) *Set-off*
Because an uncollateralised securities lending transaction results in the lender taking

a gross credit exposure to the borrower in respect of that transaction, it is likely to be important that both the lender and the borrower can rely on rights of set-off against other exposures between them to mitigate their respective gross exposures in the event of default. As such, parties should consider whether they have sufficient contractual set-off rights (including in other agreements between them). They should also consider whether they have sufficient legal comfort as to the enforceability of those set-off rights, and whether there are any circumstances in which those rights might be disturbed (eg, the ability of either party to transfer a gross claim without the consent of the other party).

(b) *Disapplication of provisions*
Because standard securities lending agreements anticipate that collateral will be provided, the parties should consider whether, and if so how, to disapply those provisions that become redundant where no collateral is required. Parties should check that the disapplication of core provisions of the securities lending agreement does not cause that agreement to fall outside the scope of any industry or bespoke netting opinion on which they are relying.

6. Net stocklending

6.1 Background

Under a typical securities lending transaction, the borrower must pay a manufactured dividend to the lender representing income paid on the loaned securities, and the lender must pay a manufactured dividend to the borrower representing income paid on any non-cash collateral. In addition to the possibility that the income paid by the issuer of the relevant securities may be subject to a withholding tax, the manufactured dividend payment may itself also be subject to a withholding tax, depending on the jurisdictions involved. As such, lending the securities under a securities lending transaction may result in additional tax burdens on the parties.

Parties may wish to adjust the cashflows of the securities lending transaction to reduce the likelihood of a manufactured dividend being payable. If the manufactured dividend payable by the borrower on the loaned securities is likely to attract a withholding tax, parties may wish to disapply the manufactured dividend requirements and instead permit the borrower to retain the income, with the other economics of the transaction having been adjusted (at the time of trading) to reflect the expected dividend. For example, the collateral provided by the borrower to the lender might also be an income-producing asset, and may generate an income that is at least equal to the expected dividend on the loaned securities – if the manufactured dividend provisions were to be disapplied in respect of both the collateral and the loaned securities, parties may (depending on the tax treatment of the transaction as a whole) be put in the same economic position as if they had not loaned the securities, notwithstanding that there are no manufactured dividends to which a withholding tax might apply.

Structured securities lending transactions

6.2 Additional considerations

(a) Tax treatment and characterisation

Parties may wish to ensure that the arrangements that replace the manufactured dividend would not be subject to the same withholding tax that would have applied to the relevant manufactured dividend. In particular, they may wish to ensure that all relevant taxing authorities would respect the characterisation given to the arrangements by the parties, and would not recharacterise them as manufactured dividend payment obligations.

(b) Shortfall and excess

In a typical securities lending transaction, the lender would expect to receive full credit for any income paid on the loaned securities, and the borrower would expect to receive full credit for any income paid on the collateral. Parties may wish to ensure that the arrangements that they have put in place do not affect this ultimate commercial position. For example, if the actual income on the collateral is greater than was initially expected, parties may wish to ensure that the lender is required to account to the borrower for the excess.

7. Credit-linked securities lending transactions

7.1 Background

A vanilla securities lending transaction simply provides for the borrower to return equivalent securities and the lender to return equivalent collateral at maturity of the transaction. Accordingly, the lender remains economically exposed to the value of the loaned securities (and therefore the credit risk of their issuer), and the borrower remains economically exposed to the value of the collateral (and therefore the credit risk of its issuer, if applicable) throughout the life of the transaction. Absent a default by either party, the securities lending transaction should not result in the reallocation of credit risk in relation to the securities, the collateral or their issuers. In recent years, parties have introduced additional credit-risk exposures into securities lending transactions.

Whether the credit-linked provisions apply to the loaned securities or the collateral (or both) will depend on the way in which the broader transaction has been structured – for example, whether the less liquid assets comprise the loaned securities or the collateral.

While there are various types of credit-linked trade, the most common involve:
- the termination date being accelerated upon the occurrence of specified credit events in respect of the loaned securities;
- upon the occurrence of a credit event in respect of the loaned securities, instead of delivering equivalent loaned securities (ie, equivalent to the securities that were loaned), the borrower being permitted to deliver securities satisfying certain categories and characteristics (a 'cheapest to deliver option'), similar to a typical physically settled credit derivative; and
- the fee payable in connection with the transaction being increased to reflect

the cheapest to deliver option (essentially, due to the cost of the embedded credit derivative within the transaction).

Diagrams setting out the primary cashflows of a typical credit-linked securities lending transaction are shown below.

Settlement date

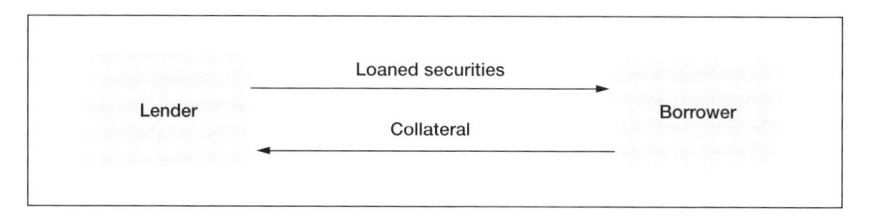

```
Lender  --- Loaned securities --->  Borrower
        <--- Collateral ---
```

Termination date (if no intervening credit event)

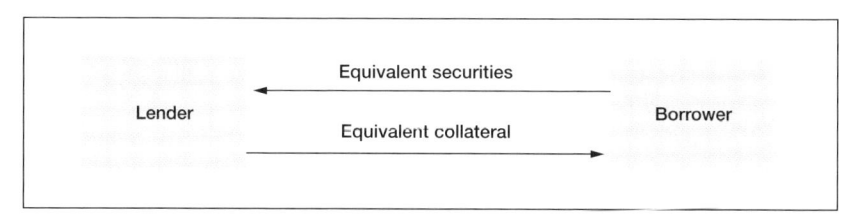

```
Lender  <--- Equivalent securities ---  Borrower
        --- Equivalent collateral --->
```

Accelerated termination date following occurrence of credit event

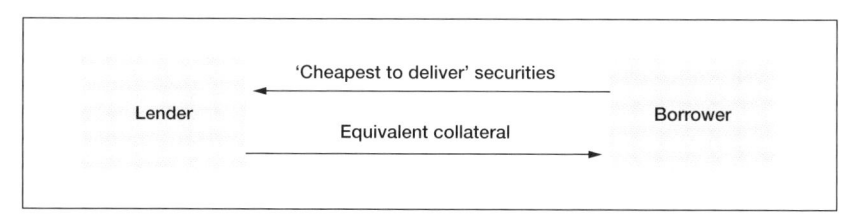

```
Lender  <--- 'Cheapest to deliver' securities ---  Borrower
        --- Equivalent collateral --->
```

7.2 Additional considerations

Parties should consider the following when entering into a credit-linked securities lending transaction such as that described above.

(a) *Credit-linked provisions*

The documentation will need to incorporate provisions identifying the credit events that may trigger an accelerated termination date and the criteria and characteristics for determining which obligations may be delivered as part of the cheapest to deliver option. Typically, these may be defined by reference to the International Swaps and Derivatives Association (ISDA) Credit Derivatives Definitions, although parties should consider whether the Credit Derivatives Definitions booklet should be incorporated by reference (together, where appropriate, with the elections in ISDA's most recent Physical Settlement Matrix) or whether the relevant provisions should be included in long-form in the securities loan confirmation itself. Parties should also consider whether it is appropriate, given the circumstances of their transaction, for the embedded credit-linked element to be phrased in derivatives terminology or whether the credit-linked provisions might better be described in language that is less closely associated with derivatives.

(b) *Hedging*
Parties will need to consider the potential impact on their hedging arrangements of any departures from standard credit derivatives practice, such as amendments to the standard Credit Events and Deliverable Obligation Characteristics in the ISDA Credit Derivatives Definitions. In addition, since a single-name credit default swap typically ties the parties to resolutions made by an ISDA determinations committee, parties should consider whether such resolutions should have any impact on their securities lending transaction or, if not, whether this gives rise to hedging basis risk.

(c) *Collateral*
The standard collateral provisions applicable to a vanilla securities lending transaction compare the current market value of the collateral with the current market value of the loaned securities, after adjustment,

To reflect the agreed haircut, parties should consider whether, and if so how, to amend these collateral provisions so that the mark-to-market calculations take into account the embedded credit-linked provisions (both the potential acceleration to the termination date and the cheapest to deliver option).

(d) *Consequences of default*
If an event of default occurs, standard securities lending terms will provide for the value of equivalent securities to be determined and offset against the value of the collateral. In addition, the defaulting party may be responsible for any loss or expense incurred by the non-defaulting party in entering into a replacement transaction or unwinding a hedging transaction. Parties may wish to consider whether these remedies are sufficient to capture costs associated with (or value derived from) terminating the embedded credit-linked element, or whether bespoke provisions are required to address this more specifically.

(e) *Consequences of early termination*
Similarly, if the transaction terminates early for any other reason (eg, because a party has accelerated an on-demand trade), parties should consider whether breakage costs, hedging unwind or replacement costs should be recoverable and, in the interim, be margined.

(f) *Additional termination provisions*
Parties should consider whether the inclusion of the credit-linked provisions introduces additional legal risks that require mitigation by termination rights. For example, standard securities lending documentation does not include termination

provisions in the event that it becomes illegal for the parties to perform, or the parties are prevented by a force majeure from performing, their obligations, while such provisions would normally apply to credit derivatives entered into under an ISDA Master Agreement. While parties may consider that the likelihood of such events occurring in respect of a vanilla trade is low or would otherwise be mitigated by the on-demand nature of a vanilla securities lending transaction, they should consider whether the risk is increased as a result of the inclusion of the credit-linked provisions in a term trade.

(g) *Accounting*
While parties should consider the appropriate accounting treatment of all transactions which they may enter into, the combination of two types of transaction/exposure (securities lending transactions and credit derivatives) is likely to require particular accounting attention. In addition to considering their own accounting treatment, parties may wish to consider whether it is appropriate to enquire into the accounting treatment being given to the trade by their counterparty. The accounting treatment of securities lending transactions is dealt with generally elsewhere in this book.

8. Loans of asset-backed securities

8.1 Background

Loans of asset-backed securities (ABSs) (either as loaned securities or as collateral) have been used for various purposes, but their primary use is as a substitute or supplement to direct investment in the ABSs themselves. Central bank liquidity schemes are often structured as repos, while some (eg, the Bank of England's special liquidity scheme) have been structured as securities lending transactions, and in recent years they have allowed originators to access funding in respect of ABSs where the direct investment market has been illiquid. Bilateral repos and securities lending transactions have also been used for similar purposes. When compared with a direct investment in the ABS, securities lending transactions offer various benefits to investors, including a maturity that is shorter than the ABS itself and enhanced credit protection in the form of a commitment by the originator to re-acquire the asset, supported by ongoing mark-to-market collateralisation.

8.2 Additional considerations

(a) *Illiquidity*
Compared with ordinary debt securities, many types of ABS are illiquid. As well as potentially affecting the reliability of valuations, illiquidity is likely to give rise to other issues. The recipient of the ABS (the borrower if the ABSs are the loaned securities; the lender if the ABSs are collateral) is likely to apply a greater haircut to them to reflect the increased volatility – the greater haircut will in turn affect the credit risk taken between the parties. Because of the potentially greater credit risks, parties may then wish to put in place segregation procedures (eg, security rather than

title transfer). Illiquidity may also result in the typical default valuation window applicable to securities lending transactions (five days) being extended or disapplied if it is considered that a short timeframe is inappropriate for purposes of determining an accurate value.

(b) *Valuation*
Many types of ABS are difficult to value with adequate certainty, with potentially large differences of opinion as to the appropriate value. While this is likely to result in one party requiring significant discretion in determining the value for margining and close-out purposes, the other party is likely to want some protection against arbitrary and unreasonable pricing, in particular if there are different views as to whether to value the ABS or the underlying pool of assets.

(c) *Amortisation*
Since ABSs often amortise (and may also suffer principal write-downs and write-backs), parties should consider how the securities lending transaction should address principal repayments during the life of the trade.

Legal and regulatory issues

Emma Spiers
Fieldfisher

1. Legal issues

1.1 Nature of transactions

From an economic perspective, a repo or a stock loan could be considered either as a sale and repurchase transaction or as a secured loan. In each case, the lender of the cash or securities is equally 'secured' for the return of the cash or those securities. However, from a legal perspective, the difference between a sale and repurchase (on the one hand) and a secured loan (on the other) is extremely important.

The legal form of both a repo and a stock loan is fundamentally intended to be one of outright sale and subsequent repurchase/return, in that all transfers of securities or cash are made by way of full title transfer from one party to the other. Any obligation to 'return' securities is no more than an obligation to transfer securities that are 'equivalent' to the securities originally transferred. The term 'equivalent' in this context means that the securities must be issued by the same issuer, part of the same issue, and identical as to type, nominal value, description and amount. This means that the equivalent securities must be identical in all respects including, for example, the International Securities Identification Number (ISIN), save – in the case of a certificated security – for the precise certificate numbers.

1.2 Title transfer and recharacterisation risk

The characterisation of a repo or stock loan as an outright title transfer arrangement (as opposed to a secured loan) has a number of important implications, albeit that some of these have assumed lesser significance for counterparties in the European Union with the advent of the Financial Collateral Arrangements Directive.[1] The standard industry documentation for both repos and stock loans goes to some length to ensure that the transactions would be characterised title transfer arrangements. Although the standard securities lending master agreements use loan-based terminology, they nevertheless clarify that notwithstanding the use of terms such as 'borrow' and 'lend', full title to any transferred securities passes from the transferring party to the recipient.

In many jurisdictions, the characterisation of a legal arrangement is not dependent solely on the label attached to it by the parties, but on the parties'

---

1 Directive 2002/47/EC of the European Parliament and of the Council of June 6 2002 on financial collateral arrangements (OJ 2002 L168/43).

Legal and regulatory issues

intentions and the commercial reality of the arrangements. The possibility of a court determining that a repo or stock loan is in fact a secured loan, despite the express language used in the documentation, is known as 'recharacterisation risk'.

The following are some of the issues which could arise if a repo or stock loan were to be recharacterised in this way.

(a) **Registration**

If a repo or stock loan is recharacterised as a secured loan, the security interest created may require registration under local laws. In the United Kingdom, for example, the Companies Act 2006 requires registration of most types of security interest created by a UK company. In the vast majority of cases, this security would not have been registered if the parties intended for it to take effect as an outright transfer arrangement, and so any security interest that was created might – if not registered – consequently be void on the insolvency of the security provider. Since the Financial Collateral Arrangements Regulations[2] came into force on December 26 2003, this registration requirement has fallen away for UK counterparties to the extent that the recharacterised repo or stock loan constitutes a 'security financial collateral arrangement'. The Financial Collateral Arrangements Regulations are discussed further below, but (at least since April 2011, when the FCA Amendment Regulations 2010[3] came into force) it is likely that a recharacterised repo or stock loan would now constitute a security financial collateral arrangement as a result of which the security interest would not require registration.

(b) **Enforcement procedures**

In a title transfer arrangement, full ownership of transferred securities is obtained by the recipient. This means that in the event of a party defaulting (or indeed at any other time), the recipient of the securities can simply sell them, retain the proceeds and recover amounts due to it from the defaulting party by first deducting amounts due to it before accounting to the defaulting party for the proceeds. If, on the other hand, the securities had been transferred by way of security, the holder of the security interest may be obliged to follow various procedural steps before it can enforce its security. It might also be subject to additional duties and obligations, such as the duty to act with reasonable care and skill and to obtain the best price reasonably obtainable for the securities which are subject to the security interest.

(c) **Preferential creditors**

If a repo or stock loan is recharacterised as a secured loan, it is possible that, on the insolvency of the security provider, local insolvency laws will give certain preferential creditors priority over the secured party.

---

2   Financial Collateral Arrangements (No 2) Regulations 2003 (SI 2003/3226).
3   Financial Markets and Insolvency (Settlement Finality and Financial Collateral Arrangements) (Amendment) Regulations 2010 (SI 2010/2993).

(d)   Negative pledge

The party providing the assets, if those assets are characterised as having been granted as security, may breach negative pledge provisions which apply to it (eg, in loan and bond instruments).

Given the potential impact of these issues on the contracting parties' relationship, the relevant industry associations have obtained legal opinions in respect of repos and securities loans addressing – amongst other things – the question of the recharacterisation risk in the relevant jurisdiction. However, these opinions relate only to transactions entered into on standard terms under the industry standard documentation. If entering into bespoke arrangements, the parties should still consider these issues if the terms of the transactions are such that they fall outside the scope of the industry opinions.

The following are some of the legal and practical factors which may increase the likelihood of recharacterisation.

(e)   Equity of redemption

Even though repos and stock loans may specify an outright transfer of title to the securities, if the recipient is obliged to redeliver the identical securities (as opposed to equivalent securities) at maturity of the transaction, this would increase the recharacterisation risk as it would indicate that the transferring party had retained an interest in those specific securities. This is consistent with the concept of a person granting a security interest in assets but retaining an 'equity of redemption' in them (ie, a right to have them returned once the debt secured by them is satisfied).

(f)   Voting rights

The voting rights attached to securities transferred under a repo or stock loan should belong exclusively to the recipient, as the outright legal owner of the securities. Any suggestion that the person who transferred the securities is entitled to direct how the recipient should exercise voting rights on them would indicate both that the transferor has retained some of the incidents of ownership in the securities and also that the recipient of the securities is effectively obliged to retain the securities in order to fulfil its obligation to vote in accordance with the directions of the transferor. This would increase the recharacterisation risk.

(g)   Income

The industry documentation for repo and securities loans provides for payments of what is known as 'manufactured' income. This means that the party which has transferred securities receives an amount equivalent to any coupons, dividends or other income earned on those securities. If the recipient of the securities were instead required to transfer the actual income earned on those securities, this might again imply that the recipient's right to dispose of the securities is impaired and could therefore undermine the principle that a true sale had occurred.

None of these factors alone would necessarily result in recharacterisation being made but care should be taken when introducing any of these features into a transaction.

1.3 Netting and set-off

A key aspect of repos and stock loans is that, on default, the obligations of the parties are accelerated, redelivery obligations are valued and the cash equivalent of each party's obligations to the other are set off to give a single, net termination payment owed by one party to the other.

Where transactions are entered into under an industry standard master agreement, this set-off is taken a step further (save, in certain cases, where the default is limited to a delivery failure under a single transaction) such that the net termination payment under each transaction is netted down to a single net termination payment in respect of all outstanding transactions between the parties under the master agreement and not just the two 'legs' of one transaction. This process is known as 'close-out netting'.

This has obvious benefits in terms of reducing counterparty credit risk as an effective netting arrangement reduces a party's exposure to the net market value differential between the different legs of each individual transaction and also across all outstanding transactions. As a result of the adoption of the regulatory capital standards set by the Basel Committee on Banking Supervision, regulators in most jurisdictions (including the United Kingdom) recognise the benefits of this risk reduction, allowing regulated entities to report their exposures under repo and securities lending transactions on a net basis for regulatory capital purposes. This treatment applies only to the extent that the regulated entity has a written netting agreement in place and the benefit of legal opinions which confirm the enforceability of that netting agreement:

- under its governing law;
- in the jurisdiction of incorporation of its counterparty; and
- in the jurisdiction of any branch through which the counterparty is trading under the agreement.

A key feature for close-out netting being effective in a number of jurisdictions is that all individual repo or securities lending transactions entered into under a master agreement are treated – together with the master agreement itself – as a single agreement. The purpose of this feature is to reduce the risk that an insolvency official appointed in respect of a party is able to disclaim its obligations under the individual legs of transactions (or under unprofitable transactions) whilst enforcing its rights to claim for any amounts which are owed to it. To obtain the risk-reducing benefits of close-out netting, it is important to ensure that the master agreement, including the 'single agreement' concept, is enforceable in the event of the bankruptcy of the counterparty. The legal opinions obtained by industry bodies – the International Capital Market Association (ICMA) and the International Securities Lending Association (ISLA) – in respect of repo and securities lending documentation address these questions.

1.4 Capacity and authority

In any contractual relationship, a party would expect to carry out basic legal due diligence on the counterparty in order to establish that the counterparty has the capacity to enter into the contract and also that the execution of it has been duly authorised. This due diligence may take the form of an examination of constitutional documents and decisions of the governing body or a formal legal opinion may be obtained.

These due diligence requirements apply equally to repo and stock lending transactions. It would be risky to assume that any corporate or other body has the ability, without restriction, to enter into a repo or stock loan transaction. Some pension schemes and funds, for example, are subject to restrictions on both repo and stock lending activities and care should be taken to understand the effect of any trading not being in compliance with any applicable restrictions.

1.5 Financial Collateral Arrangements Directive

The Financial Collateral Arrangements Directive[4] came into force on June 27 2002 and required implementation into the local law of each EU Member State by December 27 2003.

The purpose of the directive was to develop an EU-wide framework for financial collateral, and to require Member States to repeal certain provisions of local law to ensure the enforceability of financial collateral arrangements.

The directive imposed the following fundamental requirements:

- the creation, perfection, validity, enforceability or admissibility of a financial collateral arrangement must not be dependent on any formal procedure or act;
- the collateral-taker must be entitled to realise financial collateral by way of sale, set-off or – if agreed between the collateral-provider and collateral-taker – appropriation (although not all remedies apply to all types of financial collateral);
- financial collateral arrangements, including rights of use and close-out netting provisions, must be given effect in accordance with their terms (even if a party is subject to winding-up or reorganisation procedures); and
- insolvency laws must be amended or repealed to remove certain restrictions on enforcement of financial collateral arrangements.

The directive also sets out certain conflict of laws rules in relation to financial collateral.

Financial collateral arrangements under the directive can fall into one of two categories: 'security financial collateral arrangements' and 'title transfer collateral arrangements'. They must be in writing and made between two non-natural persons, one of which must be a public authority, central bank, regulated financial institution or central counterparty. A 'security financial collateral arrangement' is where a security interest arises over the financial collateral to secure amounts owed to the collateral taker but ownership of the financial collateral remains with the collateral-provider. A 'title transfer collateral arrangement' is where full ownership to the collateral is transferred to the collateral-taker for the purpose of securing or otherwise covering the

---

4   See footnote 1 above.

Legal and regulatory issues

obligations of the collateral-provider. The definition of title transfer collateral arrangement in the directive expressly includes reference to repurchase agreements.

'Financial collateral' for the purposes of the directive is limited to cash, financial instruments (which covers shares and bonds, amongst others) and credit claims.

The directive was implemented in the United Kingdom by the Financial Collateral Arrangements Regulations (FCARs).[5] As with the implementation of any EU directive, the directive has no direct effect in Member States so it is important to look carefully at the implementing regulations of the applicable Member State as the drafting of the directive may not have been precisely transposed into local law.

While the definition of title transfer collateral arrangement in the FCARs does not include the express reference to repos which is in the directive, it is nonetheless the clear view in the United Kingdom that a repo or stock loan between two non-natural persons (note that the requirement for one party to fall into the more limited categories set out in the directive has not been transposed into the FCARs) pursuant to an industry standard master agreement would constitute a title transfer financial collateral arrangement, provided that the assets being lent or repoed are within the definition of 'financial collateral' and that the arrangement was entered into after the FCARs came into force on December 26 2003.

If a repo or stock loan were to be recharacterised as a secured loan rather than a title transfer arrangement, it would then be necessary to consider whether or not the recharacterised arrangements constitute a security financial collateral arrangement. Pursuant to the FCARs, the key issue in assessing this is that the financial collateral must be 'delivered, transferred, held, registered or otherwise designated so as to be in the possession or under the control of the collateral-taker or a person acting on its behalf'. The FCARs go on to clarify that a right of the collateral-provider to – amongst other things – substitute financial collateral of the same or greater value or withdraw excess financial collateral does not prevent the financial collateral from being in the possession or under the control of the collateral-taker. The requirement for possession or control has been considered in a number of cases in England, but as far as repos and securities loans are concerned, it is almost certainly the case that a recharacterised repo or securities loan would nevertheless constitute a security financial collateral arrangement for the purposes of the FCARs.

The key consequences of a repo or stock loan constituting a financial collateral arrangement for the purposes of the FCARs (or equivalent implementing regulations in other EU Member States) include the following:

- the close-out netting provisions applicable to the repos or stock loans will be enforceable, even on the winding-up or reorganisation of a party, unless the other party was (or should have been) aware of those proceedings when entering into the financial collateral arrangement;
- a liquidator's power to disclaim onerous property (such as unprofitable contracts) will not apply;
- certain claims or creditors which might otherwise have received preferential treatment over the collateral-taker on enforcement will not apply;

---

5   See footnote 2 above.

- provisions of insolvency law which would void certain disposals made after the commencement of insolvency proceedings will not apply; and
- if a repo or stock loan were recharacterised and the resulting security interest would otherwise be registrable, registration would not be required.

2. Regulatory issues

2.1 Framework

The regulation of repo and securities lending activities stems from a wide variety of sources, ranging from global organisations to local regulators. Examples are set out below.

- International bodies, such as:
- Bank for International Settlements (BIS): an international financial organisation which serves as a bank for central banks and seeks to foster international cooperation in matters of monetary and financial stability. One of the standing committees of the BIS is the Basel Committee on Banking Supervision, which provides an international forum for banking supervisory matters (most notably capital requirements for financial institutions).
- Financial Stability Board (FSB): an international body which monitors and makes recommendations about the global financial system. Its recommendations are not legally binding; it relies on its members for implementation. The FSB coordinates the financial regulatory reform agenda agreed by the Group of Twenty (G20) forum.
- Supranational bodies, such as the European Union, which provides economic and political union between its Member States. Laws emanating from the European Union largely fall into two categories: regulations (such as the European Market Infrastructure Regulation[6]), which are directly applicable to all Member States; and directives (such as the Financial Collateral Directive), which require implementation in each Member State.
- National regulators, such as (in the United Kingdom) the Financial Conduct Authority and Prudential Regulation Authority. These entities oversee, regulate and enforce compliance with financial law and regulation. In the context of the European Union, the national regulators in each Member State are generally responsible for the regulation of their own markets and domestic implementation of EU directives. It is, therefore, not uncommon for EU directives to be implemented slightly differently in each Member State and also individual Member States often impose further requirements over and above the EU requirements. Where a Member State chooses to impose more onerous requirements than those required by the directive, this is sometimes referred to as 'gold-plating'.
- Local rules applicable to transactions in particular securities and markets, such as the rules of any applicable stock exchange.

---

[6] Regulation on OTC derivative transactions, central counterparties (CCPs) and trade repositories (Regulation 648/2012).

2.2 Regulated activities and authorisation

Market participants may require authorisation to carry out certain types of repo or securities lending transactions as they involve dealings in securities (which are financial instruments) and also include as part of the contract a forward settlement component.

In the United Kingdom, both repo and stock lending business (whether carried out as principal or agent) may involve regulated activities under the Regulated Activities Order.[7] As a result, unless an exemption applies, any person conducting repo or stock lending business must be authorised by the Financial Conduct Authority (FCA) or the Prudential Regulation Authority (PRA) and will then be regulated by the FCA for these activities. Regulated entities are subject to the rules set out in the FCA's handbook of rules and guidance, which include rules relating to conduct of business, transparency and transaction reporting as well as the requirements (including maintenance of adequate capital reserves) for entities to be and remain authorised to carry on business.

In the United Kingdom, buying, selling or arranging transactions in securities is a regulated activity. This is the case whether or not the person acts as principal for their own account. However, a person dealing in securities as principal is not required to be authorised unless it is:

- acting as a market-maker in the securities;
- engaging in the business of buying the securities with a view to selling them;
- an underwriter of the securities or regularly soliciting members of the public to induce them to deal with the securities.

The forward leg of a repo and, arguably, a stock loan, may be considered to be a forward transaction which itself is a financial instrument separate from the securities which are the subject matter of the forward. As with dealings in securities, there is also an exception relevant to the activity of dealing in these kinds of investment as principal. The exception applies where a person is dealing as principal with authorised firms or overseas parties that would have to be authorised if carrying on business in the United Kingdom. For a corporate end user of repo or a stock loan, these exceptions would generally apply to both the initial spot sale or purchase of securities and to the forward repurchase or resale of equivalent securities as they typically are not securities dealers and they typically trade with regulated entities. Even where this is not the case, however, there may be other exceptions which mean that authorisation is not required.

2.3 Short selling regulations

Short selling is the practice of agreeing to sell a security which the seller does not own. The short seller satisfies its delivery obligations under the sale by borrowing the securities, usually by way of a stock loan or repo. When the short seller needs to redeliver the securities to the lender under the stock loan or repo, it purchases them

---

[7] Financial Services and Markets Act 2000 (Regulated Activities) Order 2001 (SI 2001/544), Articles 14, 76, 77 and 84.

in the market which then gives it an economic benefit if the securities have fallen in value in the meantime. This can be shown in the following diagram:

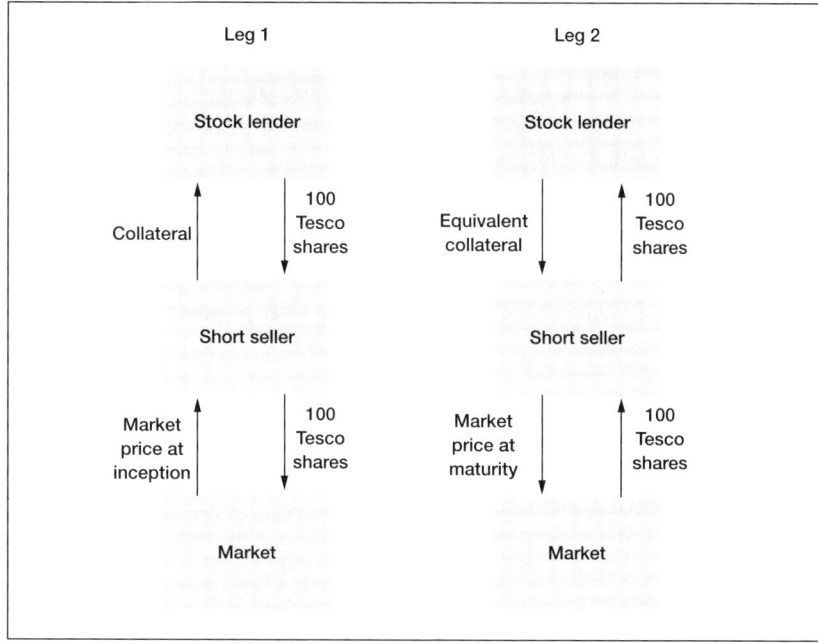

```
                    Leg 1                              Leg 2

                Stock lender                       Stock lender

                          ↑ 100                              ↑ 100
    Collateral |          Tesco      Equivalent   |          Tesco
               ↓          shares     collateral   ↓          shares

                Short seller                       Short seller

    Market     ↑          ↑ 100      Market       ↑          ↑ 100
    price at   |          Tesco      price at     |          Tesco
    inception  ↓          shares     maturity     ↓          shares

                   Market                              Market
```

The short seller's hope is that it will have to pay less for the securities when settling leg 2 than it sold them for in leg 1. In this way the short seller profits when the value of the securities decreases.

There are two types of short sale: a 'naked' short sale, meaning that the seller does not possess the securities at the time it agrees to sell them; and a 'covered' short sale, meaning that the seller has the securities prior to agreeing the short sale and is simply using the short sale to reduce its exposure in case the securities fall in value.[8]

There are two distinct risks inherent in short selling. First, the risk that the short seller is unable to purchase securities in the market to satisfy its delivery obligations under the stock loan or repo in leg 2, and secondly, the fact that the potential losses which could be incurred by the short seller are unlimited (because the price to which the security could potentially rise between the two legs of the short sale is theoretically unlimited). In addition, regulators have expressed the concern that naked short selling (in particular) permits a security to be effectively sold an unlimited number of times, thus potentially distorting the market and – in extreme cases – causing a 'run' on the securities which could have a significant effect on the issuer.

---

[8] Note that if the short seller actually acquires the securities by way of a stock loan prior to, and for the purpose of, the short sale (known as a 'pre-borrow'), and the lender of the securities imposes conditions on the borrower as to its use of those securities (ie, for the settlement of the short sale), there is an argument that a trust may arise and that outright title to the loaned securities might not, in fact, transfer to the borrower. See Daniel A Harris, *A bird in the hand: pre-borrows examined* (Trusts & Trustees, 2014).

Legal and regulatory issues

Since the financial crisis in 2008 there has been an increased focus by regulators on short selling, which has in turn brought repos and stock loans under scrutiny. In June 2009, the Technical Committee of IOSCO[9] released a report on short selling, which set out four high-level principles for the effective regulation of short selling. These principles state that:

- short selling should be subject to appropriate controls to reduce or minimise the potential risks that could affect the orderly and efficient functioning and stability of financial markets;
- short selling should be subject to a reporting regime that provides timely information to the market or to market authorities;
- short selling should be subject to an effective compliance and enforcement system; and
- short selling regulations should allow appropriate exceptions for certain types of transactions for efficient market functioning and development.

In the European Union, the Short Selling Regulation[10] (which came into force on November 1 2012) prohibits naked short sales of government bonds or listed equities in Europe, save where the naked short seller is (in either case) a market-maker or (in the case of naked short sales of government bonds) a bank involved in the issuance of government bonds. Covered short sales of government bonds or listed equities are not prohibited but are subject to disclosure obligations, unless a market making or primary market operations exemption applies. Similar restrictions exist in a number of other jurisdictions.

2.4 Disclosure and transparency

Most jurisdictions impose certain disclosure obligations in relation to equities in publicly traded companies. These requirements generally fall into the following categories.

(a) Disclosure on acquisition or disposal of equities

It is common for regulators to require disclosure of an acquisition or disposal of shares which results in a person's control over the voting power of a listed company passing a specified threshold. The purpose of these rules is to ensure that the board of the listed company knows the identity of its significant shareholders and can track or anticipate any potential takeover threat.

Where an acquisition or disposal arises out of a stock loan or repo, however, the same issues do not necessarily arise. There are a number of reasons for this. One is that stock loans are commonly 'on demand' (which effectively means that the lender retains control over voting rights as it could recall the securities to exercise them) and repos are generally overnight only (so the buyer would not have time to exercise any voting rights). Another is that the borrower/buyer often disposes of the shares very quickly after acquiring them, particularly in the case of a stock loan. Therefore, if all

---

9   International Organization of Securities Commissions.
10   Regulation on short selling and certain aspects of credit default swaps (236/2012).

of these transfers fell within the disclosure rules, they could result in a high volume of potentially misleading notifications.

Therefore, it is often the case that acquisitions and disposals which occur under a stock loan or repo benefit from exemptions from the disclosure rules.

In the European Union, the notification requirements on acquisition or disposal of shares are primarily set out in the Transparency Directive.[11] The directive sets out only the minimum notification requirements required across the European Union, and expressly provides that Member States may impose more stringent requirements. In the United Kingdom, the disclosure requirements of the Transparency Directive have been transposed into local law in the FCA Disclosure Rules and Transparency Rules Sourcebook (the DTRs). The DTRs contain two exemptions[12] applicable to stock lending agreements:

- a delivery of securities by a lender under a stock lending agreement which gives the lender the right to call for redelivery of the lent shares does not – as far as the lender is concerned – constitute a disposal of those shares for the purposes of the notification rules; and
- the acquisition of securities by a borrower under a stock lending agreement does not give rise to a notification obligation if the borrower:
  - on-lends or otherwise disposes of the shares by the close of business on the next trading day; and
  - does not exercise or declare any intention of exercising the voting rights attached to the shares.

While the DTRs do not refer specifically to repo transactions, the general view is that they should be treated in the same way as stock lending transactions for the purposes of the DTRs. However, given the differences in the way the two products are traded, it may be that the exemptions do not, as a matter of fact, apply to repo transactions to the same extent.

(b) *Disclosure requirements on a takeover*

In many jurisdictions, additional disclosure obligations arise when a company is subject to a potential takeover, and the extent to which these obligations apply to securities, which have been subject to a stock lending or repo transaction, may vary between jurisdictions.

In the United Kingdom, the requirements are set out in the City Code on

---

11 Directive 2004/109/EC of the European Parliament and of the Council of December 15 2004 on the harmonisation of transparency requirements in relation to information about issuers whose securities are admitted to trading on a regulated market and amending Directive 2001/34/EC as amended by Directive 2013/50/EU of the European Parliament and of the Council of October 22 2013 amending Directive 2004/109/EC of the European Parliament and of the Council on the harmonisation of transparency requirements in relation to information about issuers whose securities are admitted to trading on a regulated market; Directive 2003/71/EC of the European Parliament and of the Council on the prospectus to be published when securities are offered to the public or admitted to trading; and Commission Directive 2007/14/EC laying down detailed rules for the implementation of certain provisions of Directive 2004/109/EC.

12 An amendment to the Transparency Directive, which will come into force by November 26 2015, is likely to result in a removal of these exemptions.

Legal and regulatory issues

Takeovers and Mergers (the Takeover Code). If a takeover has been announced in respect of a company resident in the United Kingdom and traded on a regulated exchange, dealings in shares by a person with an 'interest' of 1% or more must be disclosed. The Takeover Code provides that, for these purposes, only the lender of shares under a stock loan will be treated as 'interested' in the shares.

The Takeover Code also contains a requirement for a person to announce a takeover offer where their interest in shares of a company resident in the United Kingdom and traded on a regulated exchange reaches 30% or more. In these circumstances, the Takeover Code provides that both the borrower and the lender under a stock loan must be treated as 'interested' in the shares (unless, in the case of the borrower, it has on-lent or sold the securities).

The Takeover Code does not expressly refer to repo transactions but, in practice, shares which have been subject to a repo transaction are treated in the same way as those which have been lent out under a stock lending transaction.

(c) **Disclosure of interests in shares**

Finally, it is likely that a publicly traded company will be entitled to require disclosure by any person of that person's interests in the company's shares. Again, what constitutes an 'interest' in shares which have been subject to a stock loan or repo transaction may differ from jurisdiction to jurisdiction.

In the United Kingdom, the relevant requirements are set out in the Companies Act 2006.[13] Both the borrower/buyer and the lender/seller under a stock loan or repo would be treated as having an interest for this purpose (unless, in the case of the borrower/buyer, it has sold the securities on).[14]

2.5 **Industry codes of practice**

A number of industry bodies have published codes of practice relating to trading repo and stock loans. These codes serve a variety of functions, including codifying market conventions and setting out recommended practices to ensure smooth running markets.

Codes of practice are not endorsed by regulators and are subject to all applicable laws and regulations. There are no specific consequences of breach of a code of practice; parties are free to depart from the recommendations if they are happy to accept the increased risks which may result.

Codes of practice which currently exist in relation to the UK market include the following:

- A Guide to Best Practice in the European Repo Market, published by the European Repo Council of ICMA, which also includes margin guidelines;
- Securities Borrowing and Lending Code of Guidance, published by the Securities Lending and Repo Committee of the Bank of England (SLRC);
- Securities Lending: Agent Disclosure Code of Guidance, published by SLRC; and
- Gilt Repo Code of Best Practice, published by the Bank of England.

---

14 Section 793.
14 Section 820 of the Companies Act 2006.

3. Recent and imminent developments in the repo and securities lending markets

3.1 Basel III

Following the financial crisis of 2007/08, the Basel Committee on Banking Supervision developed wide-ranging reforms to the international regulatory framework for banks. The reforms are designed to deal with some of the issues which arose during the financial crisis and which were not adequately addressed by the previous framework (known as Basel II).

The reforms are extensive and it is not possible here to provide a full-scale review or analysis. Below are a few of the reforms which are likely to have a direct impact on the repo and stock lending markets.

- CCR exposures – Basel III imposes some significantly strengthened capital requirements for counterparty credit risk (CCR) exposures. It became apparent during the financial crisis that the fear of a counterparty default can (of itself) cause systemic problems, such as a significant reduction in interbank liquidity, and that the CCR measures need to protect against those systemic issues as well as entity-specific default risk. Basel III seeks to address those issues, as well as simply increasing the capital buffers required to be held against CCR exposures. In addition, the Basel Committee on Banking Supervision (BCBS) has used the CCR exposure measures in Basel III as a means of encouraging central counterparty clearing.
- Leverage ratio – Basel III introduces a new leverage ratio, aimed at restricting the leverage levels of banks. The test requires a bank to divide its tier 1 capital by its 'total exposure'. The exposure measure includes exposures under repo and stock lending transactions, although if certain conditions are met, those exposures can be determined on a net basis.

  The BCBS's initial proposals for the leverage ratio required securities financing transactions to be measured on a gross basis for the purposes of the 'total exposure' calculation, which market participants agreed would have effectively forced bigger banks to remove themselves from those markets. Even on a net basis, however, the leverage ratio may reduce the size of the repo and stock lending markets. To stay within the ratio, banks need to choose between raising capital and selling assets.
- Liquidity ratios – The Basel III reforms introduce two new liquidity ratios: the liquidity coverage ratio and the net stable funding ratio. These ratios are intended to encourage banks to hold higher levels of unencumbered, high-quality liquid assets which can be converted into cash to meet a bank's liquidity requirements over a 30-day period of market stress.

  There are a number of reasons for the new liquidity ratios, one of which is that it became clear during the financial crisis that it is not in fact correct to assume that a highly capitalised bank would always be able to obtain liquidity. In addition, the questionable (and, as ICMA has been keen to point out, unusual) accounting treatment of Lehman's 'Repo 105' and 'Repo 108' transactions and MF Global's 'repo to maturity' product has led regulators to

Legal and regulatory issues

focus on increasing the balance sheet transparency of repo and stock lending transactions, one facet of which is ensuring that those transactions are not used to mask the quality of a bank's assets. The new Basel III liquidity ratios are one way in which regulators are addressing those issues.

The Basel III reforms are subject to a phased implementation. Certain reforms – such as those relating to CCR exposures – have already been implemented in the European Union. Others are not due for implementation until between 2015 and 2019.

The cumulative impact of these reforms on the repo and stock lending market could be significant. It is generally accepted in the market that the cost to banks of repo and stock lending volumes will increase, and that activity in those markets will therefore decline. This could have a number of knock-on effects, including reduced market liquidity, higher spreads (particularly for 'safe' assets) and a reduction of balance sheet availability for transactions with buy side clients.

One of the initial consequences of the financial crisis was that commercial banks found themselves needing to rely increasingly on repo or stock lending transactions to cover (amongst other things) the funding gap left by the collapse in interbank lending. This also provided buy side firms with opportunities to make returns in an otherwise difficult market. These regulatory reforms could have the effect of reducing a valuable source of investment return for the buy side and increase the cost of investing across the market.

3.2 Shadow banking

An area which has seen a great deal of regulatory attention recently is the shadow banking sector. This is where credit activities – such as extending credit or accepting deposits – are carried out outside the usual (regulated) banking sphere. Repos and stock loans (often collectively referred to as 'securities financing transactions' or 'SFTs' in this context) are two key activities which fall into the shadow banking sphere.

One reason for the increased focus on shadow banking is that, following the Liikanen Report[15] in the European Union, and similar work in other jurisdictions, there are proposals to implement regulations preventing banks which are considered 'too big to fail' from engaging in proprietary trading and to give supervisors the power to require those banks to separate risky trading activities from their deposit-taking business. Regulators are concerned that the banks could circumvent these rules by moving their activities to the shadow banking sector.

In August 2013, following a consultation period, the Financial Stability Board (FSB) published a document entitled 'Policy framework for addressing shadow banking risks in securities lending and repos' which sets out a number of policy recommendations to address the risks of shadow banking in the repo and stock lending markets. The recommendations related to increased transparency, regulation and structural aspects of the repo and stock lending markets.

---

15 Final report of the High-level Expert Group on reforming the structure of the EU banking sector (chaired by Erkki Liikanen), published on October 2 2012.

This was followed in October 2014 by a further FSB document entitled 'Regulatory framework for haircuts on non-centrally cleared securities financing transactions' which sets out a regulatory framework based on consultation and a quantitative impact study. The framework proposed by the October 2014 document would require implementation by national/regional authorities. The FSB also intends to publish further recommendations relating to the transparency proposals.

In January 2014, the European Commission published a legislative proposal for a regulation aimed at increasing the transparency of securities financing transactions outside of the regulated banking sector. The proposal aims to increase transparency in three ways:

- requiring all transactions to be reported to a trade repository;
- requiring detailed reporting by UCITS management companies, UCITS investment companies and alternative investment fund managers to investors on the securities financing activities of the relevant investment funds; and
- imposing minimum conditions to be met before rehypothecation is permitted by the collateral-taker. These conditions include obtaining the consent of the counterparty,[16] disclosing the potential risks of rehypothecation and that the rehypothecation takes place pursuant to a written agreement.

The proposed regulations apply to all counterparties in the stock lending and repo markets, all UCITS management companies and UCITS investment companies, alternative investment fund managers and counterparties engaging in rehypothecation.

3.3 MiFID II and MiFIR

As from January 2017, the Markets in Financial Instruments Directive[17] (MiFID) is to be significantly updated and amended by a new Markets in Financial Instruments Directive[18] (MiFID II) and the new Markets in Financial Instruments Regulation[19] (MiFIR) will take effect. MiFID II and MiFIR (like the original MiFID) are the main legislative instruments in a suite of EU rules aimed at an EU-wide regulation of financial markets, focusing particularly on regulating intermediaries which provide investment services in financial instruments to clients and ensuring the organised trading of financial instruments.

MiFIR will be directly applicable in all Member States but the directive requires implementation in each Member State. However, for both to occur the European Securities and Markets Authority (ESMA) will also prepare a raft of technical standards and advice in relation to the more complex aspects of the rules. These technical standards are currently going through consultation and discussion phases and are due for publication in 2015.

---

16 Following a recent (May 2015) development, it appears that consent will no longer be required in relation to collateral provided under a title transfer collateral arrangement (such as a repo or stock loan).
17 Markets in Financial Instruments Directive (2004/39/EC).
18 Markets in Financial Instruments II Directive (2014/65/EU).
19 Markets in Financial Instruments Regulation (600/2014).

The scope of MiFID II and MiFIR is very wide, but it is likely that the main impact of these reforms will be felt more in the OTC derivatives market rather than the securities financing markets. From the perspective of repo and stock lending, there are two key themes which arise out of the reforms. The first is an increased focus on market transparency – a common theme across many of the current regulatory reforms. This is achieved (amongst other things) through additional trade transparency and trade reporting requirements.

The second theme (relevant to stock loans, rather than repos) is the move to restrict the use of title transfer collateral arrangements. MiFID II prohibits the use of title transfer collateral arrangements with retail clients, and the consultation paper issued by ESMA in connection with the proposed technical standards suggests that further guidance is necessary to ensure that title transfer collateral arrangements are not used 'indiscriminately' with non-retail clients, thus jeopardising the effectiveness of the regime to protect client assets. ISLA has expressed concern that such guidance might restrict the ability of clients to engage in securities lending arrangements which use title transfer collateral arrangements. It remains to be seen how the published technical standards will address this issue.

3.4 Central Securities Depositories Regulation

A subject of ongoing concern to the repo and stock lending markets is the Central Securities Depositories Regulation[20] – in particular Article 7 on settlement discipline. Under Article 7, any participant to a securities settlement system operated by a central securities depository that fails to deliver the relevant financial instruments on the agreed settlement date will be subject to cash penalties and a mandatory buy-in procedure, whereby those financial instruments are bought in and delivered in a timely manner to the receiving party. ESMA and ICMA continue to debate precisely how this general principle will be transposed into technical standards – ICMA is generally against mandatory buy-ins and in favour of exemptions for the first leg of relevant transactions and tri-party arrangements, among other things. The argument will have to be settled by June 2015, when ESMA is required to submit its proposals to the European Commission. The question of settlement fails and mandatory buy-ins are considered elsewhere in this book.

---

20   Central Securities Depositories Regulation (909/2014).

Industry documentation

Edward Miller
Jamie Pullen
Fieldfisher

1. **Overview**

This chapter looks at the industry standard documentation for trading repo and stock loans in the London and European markets,[1] and focuses on the forms of master agreement most commonly used today for new agreements. It includes an in-depth, clause-by-clause examination of the terms and their legal implications.

1.1 **Why standard documents?**

As with over-the-counter (OTC) derivatives, but unlike the more traditional capital markets (eg, loans and bonds), there is a long history – since the early 1990s – of using industry standard documentation in the repo and stock lending markets in the form of master agreements. There are a number of reasons for this, including:

- There is a practical advantage in being able to document efficiently the (often complicated) terms of a large number of transactions. Standard form master agreements achieve this.
- As a party could be a seller or lender for one transaction and a buyer or borrower for another, and any transaction could at one time be an asset for a party and at another a liability for that party, the parties' interests are typically more even. Terms which may benefit a party at one time could be used against that party at another.
- A standard form master agreement facilitates close-out netting. This is examined in more detail later on in this chapter, but one consequence of the delivery of securities under any repo or stock lending transaction being on a title-transfer basis is that, if there is default by one party leading to early termination of transactions, it is highly desirable for there to be a mechanism that allows for the amounts owed in respect of those terminated transactions to be netted against each other, resulting in a single net amount owed by one party to the other. Further, many repo and stock lending dealers are regulated entities and are subject to detailed requirements as to the capital cover which they must maintain in respect of losses that they might suffer – including on a counterparty default under repo or stock lending transactions. Although the relevant regulatory rules[2] will typically permit the capital cover requirement to be calculated by reference to the net potential loss, this is

---

1   As opposed to the US markets, in which different documentation (such as SIFMA's 1996 Master Repurchase Agreement and 2000 Master Securities Loan Agreement) is used.

subject to the requirement of a netting agreement that is legally effective and enforceable, including in the event of a counterparty's bankruptcy or insolvency. For standardised netting agreements, instead of each bank needing to obtain legal opinions – or similar – as to effectiveness and enforceability, credit institutions can rely on legal opinions obtained by the sponsors of the standardised netting agreements.

1.2 Structure of chapter

This chapter contains a paragraph-by-paragraph analysis of the most commonly used master agreements for repos – the 2000 Global Master Repurchase Agreement (GMRA), and for stock loans – the 2010 Global Master Securities Lending Agreement (GMSLA). These are in sections 2 and 3 of this chapter respectively.

As the termination and close-out netting provisions in both these master agreements are closely aligned, and given their importance, these are analysed in a separate section – see below in section 4 of this chapter.

Section 5 examines the termination and close-out netting provisions as set out in the 2011 Global Master Repurchase Agreement.

2. Global Master Repurchase Agreement

The GMRA is published by the Securities Industry and Financial Markets Association (SIFMA)[3] and the International Capital Market Association (ICMA).[4] There have been a number of versions of the GMRA, each incorporating perceived improvements in the documents, namely:

- the 1992 Global Master Repurchase Agreement;
- the 1995 Global Master Repurchase Agreement;
- the 2000 Global Master Repurchase Agreement; and
- the 2011 Global Master Repurchase Agreement.

At the time of writing, the 2000 version of the GMRA remains the predominantly used version for newly originated agreements. This chapter will focus on the 2000 version, and for the remaining sections of this chapter 'GMRA' will be used to refer to the 2000 version. In section 5 of this chapter, the close-out netting provisions of the 2011 GMRA (which are substantially altered from the 2000 GMRA) are examined.

The GMRA has a typical 'master agreement' structure. There is a pre-printed form (often referred to as the 'front-end') which is not amended, and then an Annex I in

---

2   For EU credit institutions, this is Regulation (EU) No 575/2013 of the European Parliament and of the Council of June 26 2013 on prudential requirements for credit institutions and investment firms (the 'Capital Requirements Regulation' or 'CRR') and Directive 2013/36/EU of the European Parliament and of the Council of June 26 2013 on access to the activity of credit institutions and the prudential supervision of credit institutions and investment firms ('Capital Requirements Directive IV' or 'CRD IV'). The CRR and CRD IV became effective on January 1 2014 (with some exceptions), and the Prudential Regulation Authority (PRA) and Financial Conduct Authority (FCA) are in the process of implementing CRD IV in the United Kingdom as amendments to the FCA and PRA handbooks.
3   SIFMA was originally called the Public Securities Association (PSA). It changed its name to the Bond Market Association (TBMA) and, in 2006, merged with the Securities Industry Association to form SIFMA.
4   ICMA was created in 2005 on the merger of the International Securities Market Association (ISMA) with the International Primary Market Association (IPMA).

which the parties make various elections contemplated by the front-end and also any amendments or additions to the terms in the front-end.

There are also a number of standard form annexes for the GMRA which include:
- the agency annex (to allow a party to enter into repo transactions as the agent for another person, referred to as the 'principal');
- the buy/sell back annex (for buy/sell back transactions);
- the equities annex (setting out provisions where the securities under a repo are equities); and
- a number of jurisdiction-specific annexes (including for Canada, Italy, Japan and the Netherlands) containing provisions for where a party is based in that jurisdiction and/or the securities under a repo transaction are issued in that jurisdiction.

The following analysis covers each of the agency annexes, the buy/sell back annex and the equities annex, together with suggested provisions published by ICMA to address issues arising out of the US Foreign Account Tax Compliance Act.

The trade-specific terms of individual repo transactions are set out in separate confirmations. The pre-printed GMRA front-end includes (as Annex II) a pro-forma confirmation.

The basic layout of the GMRA front-end is:
- definitions;
- commencement and termination of transactions;
- margining;
- income payments and distributions;
- events of default and the consequences of early termination; and
- boilerplate clauses, such as notices, etc

2000 Global Master Repurchase Agreement

No.	Paragraph Heading/Description	Summary
1	Applicability	Paragraph 1 sets out the scope of the GMRA, under which the two parties to the GMRA will enter into transactions under which one party (defined as the 'Seller') sells securities (defined as 'Securities') to the other party (defined as the 'Buyer') against the payment of a purchase price, together with a simultaneous agreement by the Buyer to sell to the Seller securities 'equivalent' to such securities in the future against the payment by the Seller of the repurchase price. Such transactions are defined as 'Transactions' and can be either repurchase transactions or (if the parties so elect in paragraph 1(a) of Annex I)

buy/sell-back transactions.

The term 'Securities' is defined as any securities or financial instruments, although:

(a) if the parties wish to include 'Net Paying Securities' within the scope of the GMRA, an election for their inclusion needs to be made in paragraph 1(b) of Annex I; and

(b) if the parties wish to include equities within the scope of the GMRA, then the Equities Annex needs to be attached and form part of the GMRA.

2	Definitions	Paragraph 2 sets outs the various defined terms that are used in the GMRA. This summary only considers those definitions which are particularly useful in understanding the mechanics of the GMRA.
2(d)	'Base Currency'	This is to be specified in Annex I and is the currency into which prices, sums or values are converted. It is used for both margining and close-out purposes.
2(e)	'Business Day'	This term has different meanings depending on the context:

(i) for Transaction settled through Clearstream or Euroclear, a day on which they are open to settle business in the currency in which the Purchase Price and the Repurchase Price are denominated;

(ii) for Transactions not settled through Clearstream or Euroclear, a day on which the applicable settlement system is open to settle such Transaction;

(iii) for delivery of Securities not settled through a settlement system, a day on which banks are open for business in the place where the Securities are being delivered;

(iv) for payments not made through a settlement system:
- for payments in EUR, a day on which TARGET operates; or
- for payments in currencies other than EUR, a day other than a Saturday or Sunday on which banks are open for business (a) in the principal financial centre of the country of which the currency in which the payment is

		denominated is the official currency and (b) in the place where any account designated by the parties for the making or receipt of payment is situated.
2(t)	'equivalent'	Securities are 'equivalent' to other Securities if they are part of the same issue and of an identical type, nominal value and description as those other Securities. However, if Securities have been converted, subdivided, consolidated or been the subject of a takeover, or if holders of Securities have become entitled to receive or acquire other property, then 'equivalent to' also means such additional or replacement Securities or other property receivable by the holders of the original Securities. Where the Securities are equities (and assuming the Equities Annex is part of the GMRA), then a more detailed definition of 'equivalent' applies – see below.[5]
2(z)	'Margin Ratio'	For each Transaction, this is the Market Value of the Purchased Securities (at the time the Transaction was entered into) divided by the Purchase Price, although the parties can agree a different ratio. The Margin Ratio is one of the elements used in determining the margin requirements under Paragraph 4 (Margin Maintenance) and, in essence, is the ratio that needs to be maintained following changes to the Market Value.
2(aa)	'Margin Securities'	These are the Securities that can be transferred following a call for a Margin Transfer under Paragraph 4. As defined in the GMRA, these are simply those Securities 'reasonably acceptable' to the party calling for the Margin Transfer, although it is open for parties to agree in advance what would be acceptable.
2(bb)	'Margin Transfer'	This term covers both (a) the payment of Cash Margin and the transfer of Margin Securities and (b) the repayment of Cash Margin and the transfer of Equivalent Margin Securities.
2(cc)	'Market Value'	The Market Value of Securities is determined by reference to a generally recognised pricing source agreed to by the parties plus the aggregate amount

---

[5] The summary table for the Equities Annex follows this summary table for the GMRA.

of Income which, as at the date of determination, has accrued but not been paid to the extent not already included in the price (ie, the 'dirty' price). With respect to suspended Securities, (i) for the purposes of Paragraph 4 (Margin Maintenance), the Market Value is nil, and (ii) for all other purposes (effectively substitution under Paragraph 8), the Market Value is the price as of the close of business on the last dealing day in the relevant market prior to suspension.

It is not uncommon for the definition of Market Value to be tailored in Annex I to reflect operational realities and/or commercial agreement reached between the parties. In particular, the parties can agree in Annex I what the 'generally recognised pricing source' will be (together, where appropriate, with fallbacks if the selected pricing source is not available on the relevant day). Also, as Paragraph 4 (Margin Maintenance) contains no provisions to deal with a dispute between the parties as to Market Value, parties may add dispute resolution provisions in Annex I.

2(ee)   'Net Margin'   This term refers to the amount of margin already transferred between the parties, and is used in the formula set out in Paragraph 4(c) (Margin Maintenance) in order to determine the Net Exposure (and thus which party is required to make a Margin Transfer to the other).

The Net Margin is the excess at any time of:

(i)   the Cash Margin paid by a party (Party X) to the other party (Party Y) plus the Market Value of Margin Securities transferred by Party X to Party Y

over

(ii)   the Cash Margin paid by Party Y to Party X plus the Market Value of Margin Securities transferred by Party Y to Party X.

For this purpose, Cash Margin includes accrued but unpaid interest.

2(ii)   'Price Differential'   This is, in effect, the amount of interest to be paid in respect of the cash financing under a Transaction. The Price Differential is the amount determined by daily application of the Pricing Rate to the Purchase Price, for the number of days during the period from (and including) the

		Purchase Date until (but excluding) the date of calculation or the Repurchase Date. The Price Differential is used to determine what the Repurchase Price would be on any given date during the term of a Transaction and is thus a component of determining the Transaction Exposure, the Net Exposure and the direction of the Margin Transfer.
2(jj)	'Pricing Rate'	This is the per annum percentage rate that the parties agree, in connection with a Transaction, is to be applied to the Purchase Price for that Transaction. It in effect represents the rate of interest to be paid on the cash financing under the Transaction. The Pricing Rate is used in the Price Differential calculation.
2(mm)	'Purchased Securities'	This term refers to the Securities that are the subject of a Transaction.
2(pp)	'Repurchase Price'	This is defined as the sum of the Purchase Price of a Transaction plus the Price Differential of a Transaction at the relevant date. It is used both to determine the amount payable on termination of a Transaction and in the Margin calculations during the term of a Transaction.
2(rr)	'Spot Rate'	This is the rate for converting into the Base Currency amounts denominated in other currencies. Unless otherwise agreed in Annex I, this will be the rate quoted by Barclays Bank PLC in the London inter-bank market.
2(ww)	'Transaction Exposure'	This refers to the exposure for each Transaction and is used in the formula set out in Paragraph 4(c) (Margin Maintenance) in order to determine the Net Exposure. The Transaction Exposure is, on any date, the difference between: (i) the Repurchase Price on the date of calculation multiplied by the applicable Margin Ratio and (ii) the Market Value on the date of calculation of the Purchased Securities, such that, if (i) is greater than (ii), the Buyer has a Transaction Exposure to the Seller equal to that excess and, if (ii) is greater than (i), the Seller has a Transaction Exposure to the Buyer equal to that excess. In other words, if (i) is greater than (ii), the Buyer has less 'cover' (in the form of Purchased Securities)

Industry documentation

		margin than it should have in relation to the Seller's future obligation to pay the Repurchase Price and, if (ii) is greater than (i), the Seller has provided more 'cover' (in the form of Purchased Securities) than it should have in relation to that future obligation.
3	Initiation; Confirmation; Termination	Paragraph 3 sets out how Transactions can be entered into, the requirements for Confirmations, how the Repurchase Date for Transactions is to be determined and outlines the payments and deliveries to be made on the Purchase Date and the Repurchase Date.
3(b)	Confirmations	The parties are to agree whether one or both parties are to deliver Confirmations following the entry into a Transaction (and, if one party only, which one).
		The key terms of a Transaction are to be set out in the Confirmation (which may be in the form set out in Annex II). However, each Transaction is effective from the initial oral or written agreement, rather than from when the Confirmation is generated.
		The GMRA is silent as to the consequences of each party delivering to the other Confirmations which conflict. It is recommended therefore that a party promptly notifies the other party of any objections to the received Confirmation. It is not uncommon for this issue to be specifically addressed in Annex I with the inclusion of bespoke wording.
		In the event of any conflict between the Confirmation and the GMRA, the Confirmation will prevail for the purposes of that particular Transaction.
3(c)	Transfers on Purchase Date	On the Purchase Date, the Seller is required to transfer to the Buyer the Purchased Securities against payment of the Purchase Price by the Buyer. Paragraph 6 (Payments and Transfers) contains provisions specifying how payments and deliveries are to be effected.
3(d)	Termination of Transactions	This provides that Transactions can be 'on demand' and terminate when specified in a demand or be 'fixed term' and terminate on the date fixed for termination.

3(e)	On demand Transactions	Either party may serve a demand for termination of an 'on demand' Transaction. The minimum notice period for termination is the minimum settlement period for the relevant cash payment or the relevant delivery of Equivalent Securities.
3(f)	Transfers on Repurchase Date	On the Repurchase Date, the Buyer is required to transfer to the Seller Equivalent Securities (ie, Securities that are 'equivalent' to the Purchased Securities) against payment of the Repurchase Price by the Seller (less any amount then payable but unpaid by the Buyer under Paragraph 5 (Income Payments)). Paragraph 6 (Payments and Transfers) contains provisions specifying how payments and deliveries are to be effected.
4	Margin Maintenance	Paragraph 4 contains provisions dealing with the margin to be provided (in the form of cash or Securities) when one party has an exposure to the other under the Transactions. Paragraph 4 also contains alternative methods of dealing with such exposure – repricing (Paragraph 4(j)) and adjustments of Transactions (Paragraph 4(k)).
4(a)	Right to Margin Transfer if Net Exposure	A party which has a Net Exposure[6] to the other party can demand (orally or in writing) that a Margin Transfer be made to it which is at least equal to that Net Exposure. Paragraph 4(c) sets out how Net Exposure is to be calculated. It should be noted that such a demand can be made 'at any time' that the relevant party has a Net Exposure. The GMRA does not contain any provision for the minimum amount below which Margin Transfers may not be called, and so it is not uncommon for parties to agree to a minimum transfer amount in Annex I so as to avoid the operational burden of transferring de minimis amounts of margin.
4(c)	Definition of 'Net Exposure'	A party (Party X) will have a Net Exposure to the other party (Party Y) equal to the amount by which: (i) Party X's Transaction Exposures plus (ii) any amounts payable to Party X under paragraph 5 (Income Payments) but unpaid minus

---

6   Paragraph 4(c) sets out how the net exposure is to be calculated.

(iii) any Net Margin provided to Party X exceeds
   (i) Party Y's Transaction Exposures
   plus
   (ii) any amounts payable to Party Y under paragraph 5 (Income Payments) but unpaid
   minus
   (iii) any Net Margin provided to Party Y.

It is not uncommon for parties to agree to remove both elements (ii) from this calculation, typically for operational reasons, or simply to not include elements (ii) in practice. Also, as Income Payments under Paragraph 5 only become payable on the date the relevant payment is made by the issuer (the Income Payment Date), if there could be a delay between the date that the holders of Securities are identified as being entitled to Income and the date of actual payment of Income by the issuer (during which period the Market Value of the Securities will likely have fallen), the parties should consider whether or not this unpaid Income amount should be collateralised.

For the purposes of these calculations, any amounts not denominated in the Base Currency should be converted into the Base Currency at the Spot Rate.

4(d)	Composition of Margin Transfer		Where a party, which has delivered margin (whether Cash Margin or Margin Securities) to the other party, subsequently becomes entitled to demand a Margin Transfer – in effect, for a return of margin – that party can demand the return of margin in the form originally delivered (ie, Cash Margin in the same currency or Equivalent Securities). Subject to that right, however, the party making the Margin Transfer can determine the composition of the Margin Transfer.
4(e)	Currency of Cash Margin		Any Cash Margin must be in the Base Currency or any other currency agreed between the parties.
4(f)	Nature of payment of Cash Margin		The payment of Cash Margin gives rise to a debt owing by the receiver to the payer. This debt will accrue interest at a rate, and will be payable at such times, as specified in Annex I.
4(g)	Time for Margin Transfer		Unless otherwise agreed in Annex I, Margin Transfers must be satisfied within the minimum period customarily required for the settlement of

		the relevant Cash Margin or Margin Securities being transferred or delivered.
4(h)	Separate margining for Transactions	This sub-paragraph allows the parties to agree that, in relation to a Transaction, the margin provisions of Paragraphs 4(a) to (g) do not apply but, instead, that Transaction is margined separately.
4(j)	Repricing	Instead of eliminating Net Exposure by means of Margin Transfers, the parties can agree to eliminate Net Exposure by 'repricing' Transactions.
		If a Transaction is repriced, the Repurchase Date is brought forward to the date on which the repricing takes effect (the 'Repricing Date') and, simultaneously, the parties are deemed to have entered into a new Transaction (the 'Repriced Transaction') on the Repricing Date on the following terms:
		Purchase Date: Repricing Date
		Purchase Price: Market Value of the Purchased Securities on the Repricing Date multiplied by the original Margin Ratio
		All of the other trade terms are identical to those under the original Transaction (including the Repurchase Date, the Pricing Rate and the Margin Ratio).
		In respect of the original Transaction, the Seller would be required to pay the Repurchase Price and the Buyer would be required to deliver Equivalent Securities. In respect of the Repriced Transaction, the Buyer would be required to pay the Purchase Price and the Seller would be required to deliver the Purchased Securities. Each of these obligations is due on the Repricing Date but is set off against each other such that only a net cash sum will be paid by one party to the other, depending on which party would have been required to make the Margin Transfer.
4(k)	Adjustment of Transactions	Instead of eliminating Net Exposure by means of Margin Transfers (or repricing under Paragraph 4(j)), the parties can agree to eliminate Net Exposure by 'adjusting' Transactions.
		If a Transaction is adjusted, the Transaction is terminated on the date that the adjustment is to take effect (the 'Adjustment Date') and simultaneously the parties enter into a new

			Transaction (the 'Replacement Transaction') on the Adjustment Date on the following terms:
			Purchase Date: Adjustment Date
			Purchased Securities: Such securities as the parties may agree and that have a Market Value which is substantially equal to the Repurchase Price under the original Transaction multiplied by the original Margin Ratio
			All of the other terms shall be as agreed between the parties on or before the Adjustment Date.
			The payments and deliveries for both the termination of the original Transaction and the entry into of the Replacement Transaction are made in accordance with Paragraph 6 (on the basis that it is not practicable to set off the delivery of Equivalent Securities against the delivery of different Purchased Securities).
			In practice, repricing is much more common than adjustment.
	5	Income Payments	If a Transaction extends over an Income Payment Date for the relevant Purchased Securities, the Buyer is to pay to the Seller an amount equal to the amount paid by the issuer.
			If Margin Securities have been transferred, and an Income Payment Date arises before Equivalent Margin Securities are returned, the transferee of such Margin Securities is to pay to the other party an amount equal to the amount of Income paid by the issuer.
			In both cases, the amount to pay is the gross amount (ie, without withholding or deduction on account of taxes), even if such payment by the issuer is subject to a withholding or deduction. Each such payment is to be made on the same day that such Income is paid by the issuer.
	6	Payment and Transfer	Paragraph 6 sets out the mechanics of how payments of cash and transfers of Securities are to be effected.
	6(a)	Formalities of payment and transfer	All money paid must be in immediately available freely convertible funds of the relevant currency.
			All Securities transferred must be:
			(i) in suitable form for transfer and accompanied by duly executed instruments of transfer or assignment in blank (where required) and such

			other documentation as the transferee may reasonably request; or
			(ii) transferred through Euroclear or Clearstream; or
			(iii) transferred through any other securities clearance system; or
			(iv) transferred by any other method mutually agreed.
	6(b)	No withholdings or deductions	This requires that all payments in respect of a Transaction are made on a gross basis. If a withholding or deduction is required by law, the paying party is to pay an additional amount such that the amount actually received by the other party is equal to the amount it would have received had no withholding or deduction been applied.
	6(c)	Simultaneous transfer and payment	The transfer of Purchased Securities and the Purchase Price at the start of a trade and Equivalent Securities and the Repurchase Price at the end of a trade must be simultaneous unless otherwise agreed. 'Simultaneous' in this context effectively means delivery versus payment so the parties should ensure that they (or their settlement agents) have the operational functionality to accommodate this requirement or else agree alternative arrangements or a waiver – under Paragraph 6(d), a party may waive its right to receive simultaneous transfer in respect of a particular Transaction (although the relevant transfer should nevertheless be made on the same day).
	6(f)	Full transfer of title in cash and Securities	This sub-paragraph makes it clear that, notwithstanding the use of market-based terminology such as 'Repurchase Date' and 'Repurchase Price', all title and interest in any Purchased Securities, Margin Securities, Equivalent Securities and any Equivalent Margin Securities passes to the transferee and that the obligation of the transferee of Purchased Securities or Margin Securities is to transfer Equivalent Securities and any Equivalent Margin Securities. This provision is important to address recharacterisation risk.[7]
	6(h)	Payment netting	This provides for payment netting. Amounts in the same currency and payable on the same day shall be combined, so that only a net sum is payable by

---

[7] See elsewhere in this book for a discussion of this risk.

		one party in satisfaction of all relevant payment obligations of both parties.
6(i)	Settlement netting	This provides for settlement netting. Securities of the same issue, denomination and series that are deliverable on the same day shall be combined, so that only a net quantity of those Securities is transferable by one party in satisfaction of all relevant delivery obligations of both parties.
6(j)	Optional condition precedent to payment/transfer obligations	The parties can agree that each of their obligations under the GMRA is subject to the condition precedent that certain of the events listed in Paragraph 10(a) (Events of Default) have not occurred and are not continuing with respect to the other party (in other words, a party can withhold performance if any of those events has occurred and is continuing). This is an election that should be made in Annex I and, if applied, the relevant events set out in Paragraph 10(a) should also be specified. Although there is no specific case law on this provision, parties should consider case law in respect of the equivalent provision in the ISDA Master Agreement (Section 2(a)(iii)).[8]
7	Contractual Currency	Paragraph 7 deals with the currency in which payments are to be made. All payments made in respect of the Purchase Price or the Repurchase Price are to be made in the currency of the Purchase Price (the 'Contract Currency'). If, however, the payee at its option accepts an alternative currency, then any shortfall on the currency conversion is at the payer's risk and (under Paragraph 7(b)) the payee is obliged to pay the shortfall.
8	Substitution	Paragraph 8 deals with substitutions – both of Purchased Securities and of Margin Securities.
8(a)	Varying Purchased Securities	The parties can agree to vary the Securities which comprise the Purchased Securities under a Transaction. In that event, the Buyer is to transfer Equivalent Securities and the Seller is to transfer new Purchased Securities – the Market Value of the latter at the date of transfer should be at least equal to the Market Value of the former.

---

8   In particular, *Lomas v Firth Rixson Inc* [2012] EWCA Civ 419 (CA).

8(b)	Simultaneous transfer on variation	The transfer of the Equivalent Securities and new Purchased Securities under Paragraph 8(a) should be simultaneous.
8(c)	Effect of variation	Notwithstanding a substitution under Paragraph 8(a), the Transaction continues in effect, with the new Purchased Securities being the Purchased Securities under that Transaction.
8(d)	Substitution of Margin Securities	This provides for the substitution of Margin Securities. Such substitution is at the election of the party that transferred the Margin Securities, but requires the consent of the other party. The new Margin Securities should have a Market Value at least equal to the Market Value of the Equivalent Margin Securities.
		The transfer of the new Margin Securities and of the Equivalent Margin Securities should be simultaneous. Paragraph 8(d) provides that, if the settlement system for such transfers gives rise to a payment by or for the account of either party, the parties are to arrange for additional payments outside the settlement system to ensure that, overall, there is no net payment of cash by either party.
9	Representations	Paragraph 9 sets out representations that each party is to make to the other. In contrast with the GMSLA, the representations do not differ depending on whether a party is acting as Buyer or Seller for a particular Transaction. These representations are deemed to be given by both parties on the date on which a Transaction is entered into and on each date that Securities are transferred by either party to the other under a Transaction.
		The representations cover matters including due authority, the possession of all necessary authorisations and full title of any Securities transferred. In addition, each party makes non-reliance representations and a representation that each party acts as principal.
10	Events of Default	Paragraph 10 sets out the events that can give rise to an Event of Default and the consequences of the occurrence of an Event of Default. Section 5 of this Chapter analyses in more detail the consequences of Events of Default.

10(a)		Default Notice	With the exception of certain Acts of Insolvency (see Paragraph 10(a)(vi)), an event listed in Paragraph 10.1 will not constitute an Event of Default unless the Non-Defaulting Party serves written notice (defined as a 'Default Notice') on the Defaulting Party stating that an Event of Default has occurred.
			The Default Notice may be given in any manner set out in Paragraph 14(b) and the date/time of effective delivery will vary with the manner chosen. The parties should ensure that the relevant addresses or numbers are readily available such that notices may be delivered without delay if necessary. It is therefore common for key contact details to be specified in paragraph 1(o) of Annex I.
	10(a)(i)	Failure to pay cash	There are two events covered: • the Buyer fails to pay the Purchase Price on the Purchase Date; and • the Seller fails to pay the Repurchase Price on the Repurchase Date.
	10(a)(ii)	Failure to deliver Securities	It is optional for this event to be capable of giving rise to an Event of Default. For it to apply, the parties must specify its application in Annex I. There are two events covered: • the Seller fails to deliver Purchased Securities on the Purchase Date; and • the Buyer fails to deliver Equivalent Securities on the Repurchase Date. However, if either event occurs, then the intended recipient may (instead, where applicable, of serving a Default Notice) exercise the remedies set out: • in Paragraph 10(g) in relation to a failure to deliver Purchased Securities on the Purchase Date; and • in Paragraph 10(h) in relation to a failure to deliver Equivalent Securities on the Repurchase Date.
	10(a)(iii)	Failure to pay the cash settlement amount under Paragraph 10(g) or 10(h)	This refers to a failure by a party to pay the cash settlement amount following the exercise of a party's remedies under Paragraph 10(g) or 10(h) (these paragraphs apply following the occurrence of a failure to deliver Purchased Securities on the Purchase Date or Equivalent Securities on the Repurchase Date). With regard to the timing of such payments, by

		virtue of Paragraph 10(c)(ii), the cash settlement amount is payable on the Business Day following the determination of such amount. Therefore, the earliest that this Event of Default could be triggered is at the end of that Business Day.
10(a)(iv)	Failure to comply with margin provisions	This event covers any failure to comply with the provisions of Paragraph 4 (Margin Maintenance), in particular the obligations to pay or repay Cash Margin, to deliver Margin Securities or to redeliver Equivalent Margin Securities when required following a demand for a Margin Transfer. In that regard, parties should ensure that the delivery period(s) referred to in Paragraph 4(g) (or specified in Annex I) is/are viable from a collateral management operations perspective. Due to time differences, consideration of these period(s) is particularly important where the collateral management functions are being administered out of different jurisdictions.
10(a)(v)	Failure to make manufactured payments	This event covers any failure to comply with the provisions of Paragraph 5 (Income Payments). As mentioned above, Paragraph 5 obliges each party to make the required payment on the same day as the payment is made by the issuer of the relevant Securities. Again, parties should ensure that they are able to monitor this and make the required payments within these time frames.
10(a)(vi)	Occurrence of Act of Insolvency	Each of the events listed in the definition of 'Act of Insolvency'[9] will constitute an Event of Default with the service by the Non-Defaulting Party of a Default Notice.
		However, if the Act of Insolvency is 'the presentation of a petition for winding up or analogous proceeding or the appointment of a liquidator or analogous officer', no Default Notice is required for such event to constitute an Event of Default (ie, the Event of Default shall be deemed to have automatically occurred).
		It should be noted that, unlike the 2010 GMSLA, the GMRA does not provide for the parties to elect whether or not these Acts of Insolvency should automatically trigger an Event of Default. In the

---

[9] These are extensive but may not cover all the bases. Regard should be had to the relevant local legal opinion in this connection.

		2011 GMRA, however, provisions were inserted to specify whether the relevant Acts of Insolvency with respect to either or both parties would automatically trigger early termination.[10]
10(a)(vii)	Breach of representation	This event refers to any representations by either party being 'incorrect or untrue in any material respect'. It is not limited to the representations set out in Paragraph 9 and so would, for example, include additional representations set out in Annex I.
10(a)(viii)	Admission of inability or intention not to perform obligations	This event covers any admission to this effect (and is not limited to obligations, the breach of which could give rise to an Event of Default).
10(a)(ix)	Suspension/ expulsion from exchange, etc	This event seeks to address situations which would not be captured by the definition of Act of Insolvency but which are nonetheless important factors for counterparty risk assessment. The equivalent event in the 2011 GMRA has been brought into line with the equivalent event in the 2010 GMSLA, by specifying that the occurrence of such an event must be on the grounds that the party in question has failed to meet any requirement relating to financial resources or credit rating.
10(a)(x)	Failure to perform any other obligation	This event covers a failure to perform any obligation under the GMRA, which is not captured by the other events set out in Paragraph 10(a), if such failure is not remedied within 30 days of written notice from the other party requiring remedy. This event would also cover any additional obligation that the parties have agreed in Annex I, unless the parties also amend Paragraph 10(a) to include a failure to perform such additional obligation as an additional event that is capable of giving rise to an Event of Default.
10(b) to (f)	Close-out	Following the occurrence of an Event of Default (which includes, where applicable, the Non-Defaulting Party having served a Default Notice on the Defaulting Party), the close-out mechanics set out in Paragraphs 10(b) to 10(f) would be triggered. These mechanics are materially the same as the equivalent provisions in the GMSLA and are discussed in detail in section 5 of this chapter.

---

10 Paragraph 10(b) of the 2011 GMRA.

10(g)	Seller's failure to deliver Purchased Securities	If the Seller fails to deliver the Purchased Securities on the Purchase Date (ie, at the beginning of the Transaction), the Buyer may: (i) demand that the Seller repays the Purchase Price (if already paid); (ii) demand Cash Margin from the Seller (to the extent that a Transaction Exposure exists); or (iii) if the failure is continuing, terminate the Transaction by written notice, subject to which the Seller will be required to pay the Buyer the difference between the Purchase Price and the Repurchase Price at the date of termination (effectively the interest accrued on the cash financing extended during that period). Subject to the requirement in (iii) that the failure is continuing, the exercise of one of the above remedies does not preclude the exercise of another.
10(h)	Buyer's failure to deliver Equivalent Securities	If the Buyer fails to deliver Equivalent Securities on the Repurchase Date (ie, at the end of the Transaction), the Seller may: (i) demand that the Buyer repays the Repurchase Price (if already paid); (ii) demand Cash Margin from the Buyer (to the extent that a Transaction Exposure exists); (iii) if the failure is continuing, terminate the Transaction by written notice in accordance with Paragraph 10(c) as if an Event of Default, but only with respect to that Transaction, had occurred in respect of the Buyer (and so, in effect, the Transaction is valued by the Seller on the Seller's side of the market and cash settled). It should be noted that the remedies in (i) and (ii) would mean that, pending a termination under (iii) above, there is in effect a rolling of the Transaction by the Seller. The remedy in (iii) is known as a 'mini close-out'. The contrast between this remedy and the equivalent position where Seller fails to deliver Purchased Securities (see Paragraph 10(g)) should be noted. In Paragraph 10(h) the mini close-out amount is calculated on the basis that the relevant Securities were initially delivered but never returned (ie, more akin to an actual default scenario).

10(l)	Notification of Event of Default or potential Event of Default	There is a positive obligation on a party immediately to notify the other party if an Event of Default (or event which would constitute an Event of Default with the giving of a Default Notice) occurs in relation to it.
11	Tax Event	This Paragraph deals with the situation where there has been a change in the tax position that applied when the parties decided to enter into a Transaction.[11] If: (i) action is taken by a tax authority, or (ii) there is a change to the fiscal or regulatory regime (but excluding a change in tax rate), which has or will have a material adverse effect on a Transaction (eg, rendering it no longer economically viable), the affected party (referred to as the 'notifying party') may terminate the affected Transaction upon at least 30 days' notice. In this case, the notifying party will be required to indemnify the other party against reasonable legal and other professional expenses (but not consequential loss or damage) incurred as a result of the termination. If so requested, the notifying party will also provide an opinion from a suitably qualified adviser as to the existence or occurrence of one of the above tax events. During this 30-day notice period, the other party is permitted to override the termination notice with a counter-notice, the effect of which is that the affected Transaction is not terminated and will continue until the original maturity date. In this case, the party serving the counter-notice is deemed to agree to indemnify the notifying party against any 'adverse effect' which triggered the notifying party's termination. While a new requirement in respect of a tax withholding or deduction may constitute a tax event as described above (and be the basis on which the notifying party is seeking to terminate the affected Transaction), the obligation to gross-up under Paragraph 6(b) will remain.
12	Interest	Any sum of money payable under the GMRA,

---

11 For tax generally, see elsewhere in this book.

		which is not paid when due, will accrue interest at the greater of (i) the Pricing Rate under the Transaction to which the payment relates (if applicable), and (ii) LIBOR on a 360 or 365 day basis in accordance with the applicable ISMA convention, for the number of days such amount remains outstanding, including the due date but excluding the actual payment date. This applies to any net amount due under Paragraph 10(c) following an Event of Default.
13	Single Agreement	Paragraph 13 makes it clear that the parties' intention is that the GMRA and each Transaction form part of a single agreement. This provision is important to ensure the effectiveness of close-out netting in certain jurisdictions.
14	Notices and Other Communications	Notice details for each party are set out in paragraph 1(o) of Annex I and the date on which a notice is deemed effective will depend on the means by which it was sent: (i) if in writing and delivered in person or by courier, on the date the notice is delivered; (ii) if by telex, at the time when the recipient's answerback is received; (iii) if by fax, at the time a legible transmission is received by a responsible employee of the recipient – a transmission report generated by the sender's fax machine will not be sufficient proof of effective delivery; (iv) if by certified or registered mail, the date that mail is delivered or its delivery attempted; and (v) if by electronic messaging system, the date on which the message is received. If the notice is delivered after close of business or on a day on which commercial banks are not open for business in the place where the notice is being given, it shall be effective at the opening of business on the next following day on which commercial banks are open for business in such place. Given the decision in *Greenclose Limited v National Westminster Bank Plc*,[12] the parties may wish to add email as an express additional means of delivering notice.

---

[12] [2014] EWHC 1156 (Ch).

14(c)	Special Default Notice	Paragraph 14(c) deals with the situation where a Non-Defaulting Party, having attempted delivery using at least two of telex, fax and electronic messaging system, has been unable to effectively serve a Default Notice on the Defaulting Party. In that event, the Non-Defaulting Party may 'sign' a Special Default Notice which shall be effective from the date and time so specified in that notice. A Special Default Notice must: • specify the relevant event under Paragraph 10(a); • state that the Non-Defaulting Party has been unable to serve a normal Default Notice on the Defaulting Party; • specify the date and time on which the Special Default Notice was signed by the Non-Defaulting Party; and • state that the relevant event will be treated as an Event of Default with effect from the date and time so specified. The effect of a Special Default Notice is that the specified event will constitute an Event of Default with effect from the date and time specified in the Special Default Notice – notwithstanding that the Special Default Notice has not been effectively served on the Defaulting Party. The Non-Defaulting Party does have to give the Special Default Notice to the Defaulting Party as soon as practicable after signing.
15	Entire Agreement; Severability	Paragraph 15 provides that the GMRA supersedes existing agreements between the parties containing general terms for Transactions. Unlike other 'entire agreement' provisions, there is no express supersession of prior oral or written communications. Paragraph 15 also provides that each provision in the GMRA is to be treated as separate from other provisions and as enforceable notwithstanding the unenforceability of any other provision.
16	Non-assignability; Termination	This Paragraph sets out the limits on each party's right to assign its rights under the GMRA and sets out the right for termination of the GMRA on notice.
16(a)	No assignment without consent	Neither party may assign its rights or obligations under the GMRA without the written consent of

		the other party. Each party may, however, assign or otherwise deal with its rights in respect of amounts owing to it under Paragraphs 10(c) and 10(f) (being amounts due after an Event of Default). It should be noted that this right extends to a Defaulting Party that is owed the Paragraph 10(c) amount (by way of contrast to, for example, the ISDA Master Agreement where it is only the Non-Defaulting Party that may assign its rights under the equivalent provision).
16(b)	Termination on notice	Either party can terminate the GMRA by written notice to the other party provided that the GMRA will not be effective with respect to any outstanding Transactions.
17	Governing Law	The GMRA and any non-contractual obligations arising out of or in connection with it are governed by English law. The parties also submit to the non-exclusive jurisdiction of the English courts, although this does not limit the right of a party to commence proceedings in the courts of any other country of competent jurisdiction. There is provision for each party to appoint a process agent in England, whose contact details should be specified in Annex I. If a process agent is appointed by a party, that party is obliged to appoint, and notify the other party of, a replacement agent.
18	No Waivers, etc	Paragraph 18 provides that no waiver of an Event of Default constitutes a waiver of any other Event of Default. Any modification or waiver must be in writing and signed by both parties.
19	Waiver of Immunity	Each party waives all immunity (sovereign or otherwise) from jurisdiction, attachment or execution to which it might be entitled.
20	Recording	The parties are entitled to electronically record telephone conversations between them.
21	Third Party Rights	There is an exclusion of the rights of third parties under the Contracts (Rights of Third Parties) Act 1999.

Industry documentation

Forward Transactions – Para 2(b) and (c) of Annex I

No.	Paragraph Heading/ Description	Summary
2(b)	Forward Transactions[13]	The published form of the GMRA includes in its template Annex I pro-forma paragraphs 2(b) and (c) that cover 'Forward Transactions'.
2(b)(i)(A)	Definition of 'Forward Transaction'	A 'Forward Transaction' is defined as a Transaction where the Purchase Date is at least [three][14] Business Days after the date on which the Transaction was entered into. A Transaction is only a Forward Transaction for the period before its Purchase Date.
2(b)(ii)	Agreement of Purchased Securities	If the Confirmation merely describes the Purchased Securities under a Forward Transaction by reference to a type or class of Securities, then, not less than two Business Days before the Purchase Date, the parties must agree the actual Purchased Securities.
2(c)(i)	Amendment to 'Transaction Exposure' definition	This sub-paragraph amends the definition of 'Transaction Exposure' for Forward Transactions: (i) for the period from the 'Forward Repricing Date' (being the number of days before the Purchase Date that equals the minimum period for the delivery of Margin) to the Purchase Date, the difference between the Market Value of the Purchased Securities and the Purchase Price; and (ii) for the period (if any) from the Purchase Date to the date on which the Purchased Securities are delivered to the Buyer, the difference between the Market Value of the Purchased Securities and the Repurchase Price.
2(c)(ii)	Amendments to 'Net Exposure' definition	This sub-paragraph makes a couple of consequential amendments to Paragraph 4(c) – which defines when a Net Exposure arises – to exclude unpaid amounts under Paragraph 5 that would otherwise have become payable in the period from the Forward Repricing Date to the Purchase Date.

---

13   These account for less than 10% of total volumes according to a 2013 survey by ICMA.
14   The published form suggests 'three' in square brackets, which is consistent with the pre-October 2014 generally considered settlement horizon for repo of T+2. Since October 2014, this is now T+1. The parties are free to designate a different period.

Agency Annex

No.	Paragraph Heading/ Description	Summary
1	Scope	Either a Buyer or a Seller (referred to as an 'Agent') may enter into a Transaction (referred to as an 'Agency Transaction') as agent for a third party (referred to as a 'Principal'). The Agency Annex amends the GMRA when an Agency Transaction is entered into. Agents are most commonly custodian banks and financial institutions managing the repo business of institutional investors (such as pension funds, insurance companies and investment funds). See chapter 3 generally on agency transactions.
1(d)	Multiple Principals	The parties can agree that an Agency Transaction may be entered into on behalf of more than one Principal. In this event, the addendum for multiple principal transactions (see below) applies.
2	Initiation; Confirmation	This Paragraph sets out how Agency Transactions are entered into.
2(a)	Conditions for Agency Transactions	In order to enter into an Agency Transaction, the Agent must specify that the Transaction is an Agency Transaction when it is entered into and must disclose the identity of the Principal (either by name or by a code or identifier that the parties have previously agreed). In addition, an Agency Transaction can only be entered into if the Agent has actual authority to enter into and perform the Transaction on behalf of the Principal. If the Agent does not have actual authority, then the party that is purporting to be an Agent will be liable as principal for obligations under the Transaction.
2(b)	Only one Agent	Only one party may be an Agent in relation to a Transaction, but an Agent can act on behalf of the Buyer or the Seller.
3	Notification	An Agent is required to notify the other party if it becomes aware of any Event of Default affecting the Principal or if it becomes aware that the Agent is not authorised to enter into and perform an Agency Transaction on behalf of the Principal.

4	Separate Agreement	This paragraph provides that: (i) the Agent has no liability as principal under an Agency Transaction, which is a Transaction between the Principal and the other party; and (ii) if an Agent enters into Agency Transactions on behalf of more than one Principal, there is a separate agreement between each Principal and the other party. If an Event of Default (or an event that could give rise to an Event of Default) occurs in relation to the Agent, then the other party can give notice that such Event of Default or event shall be treated as having occurred in relation to the Principal: the effect of this would be to trigger a close-out under each separate GMRA between a Principal and the other party.
5	Representations and Warranties	This paragraph sets out some consequential amendments to the warranties set out in the GMRA and additional warranties in relation to Agency Transactions.

Addendum to Agency Annex for Multiple Principal Transactions

No.	Paragraph Heading/ Description	Summary
1	Scope	The Addendum applies if a party wishes to enter into an Agency Transaction on behalf of more than one Principal.
2	Interpretations	This paragraph sets out some additional definitions for Transactions where there are multiple Principals.
3	Modifications to the Agency Annex	This paragraph makes some consequential amendments for the purposes of Transactions where there are multiple Principals.
4	Allocation of Agency Transactions	This paragraph sets out how Agency Transactions are to be allocated between multiple Principals.
4(a)	Allocation before Purchase Date	If, at the time an Agency Transaction is entered into, the Agent allocates that Transaction to one or more Principals before the relevant Purchase Date, it must promptly notify the other party of the identity of the Principal(s).
4(b)	Effect of allocation	Upon allocation (and not only upon notification):

			(i) if to a single Principal, the Agency Transaction takes effect as a Transaction between the Principal and the other party; and
			(ii) if to more than one Principal, the Agency Transaction takes effect as a number of separate Transactions, each between a Principal and the other party, and each in relation to the appropriate proportion of the Purchased Securities.
5		Allocation of Margin	This paragraph sets out how Margin and Margin Transfers are to be allocated where there are multiple Principals.
	5(a)	Express allocation	Unless the Agent expressly allocates a Margin Transfer, the deemed allocation provisions of paragraph 6(c) (see below) apply. If an allocation of a Margin Transfer is made, then paragraph 5(b) applies.
	5(b)	General rule for transfer or receipt of Margin	If a Margin Transfer is made by the Agent or received by the Agent, in either case on behalf of more than one Principal, such transfer is allocated in proportion to each relevant Principal's Net Transaction Exposure. This does not apply to Margin Transfers to which paragraph 6(c) (see below) applies.
6		Pooled Principals: rebalancing of margin	The parties can agree that, where the Agent is acting on behalf of more than one Principal (together, the 'Pooled Principals'), Margin Transfers will be made on an aggregate net basis in respect of all Agency Transactions with the Pooled Principals ('Pooled Transactions'). The purpose of these is to ensure that Cash Margin and Margin Securities are held uniformly as between the Pooled Principals in respect of their Pooled Transactions. This is effected by there being (after the close of business on each Business Day) Margin Transfers, which are made by the relevant entries in the Agent's accounting systems, from those Pooled Principals to which the other party has a Net Transaction Exposure and to those Pooled Principals which have a Net Transaction Exposure to the other party.

Buy/Sell Back Annex

No.	Paragraph Heading/ Description	Summary
1	Scope	If the parties have elected in Annex I that Buy/Sell Back Transactions[15] may be entered into under the GMRA, then the provisions of Buy/Sell Back Annex – which amend certain provisions of the GMRA in relation to any Buy/Sell Back Transactions – apply. The Buy/Sell Back Annex does not need to be separately entered into: it applies automatically if the parties agree to enter into a Buy/Sell Back Transaction.
2	Interpretation	This sets out some additional definitions for Buy/Sell Back Transactions.
2(a)(i)	Definition of 'Accrued Interest'	This is defined as, for any date, any unpaid Income on the Purchased Securities that has accrued from the previous Income Payment Date (or date of issue, if there has been no Income Payment Date) until such date.
2(a)(iii)	Definition of 'Sell Back Price'	As mentioned in Chapters 1 and 2, a key feature of Buy/Sell Back Transactions which differs from repo transactions is that Income in respect of the Purchased Securities does not give rise to a separate, manufactured, payment. Instead, the price payable by the Seller on the Repurchase Date is adjusted to reflect the Income payable on the Purchased Securities. The definition of 'Sell Back Price' is, accordingly: (a) in relation to the originally agreed Repurchase Date, the price agreed between the parties; and (b) in relation to any other date, the same definition as 'Repurchase Price' but adjusted to include (i) Accrued Interest and (ii) any Income payable between the Purchase Date and such other date of calculation (plus interest on that Income, if any). Paragraph 2(b) provides that, in the GMRA, references to the Repurchase Price shall be references to the Sell Back Price for Buy/Sell Back Transactions.

No.	Paragraph Heading/Description	Summary
3	Initiation; Confirmation; Termination	This paragraph amends the mechanics of a Transaction where it is a Buy/Sell Back Transaction.
3(c)	Sell Back Price	The parties are required to agree the Sell Back Price at the time of entering into a Buy/Sell Back Transaction.
3(e) and (f)	Accrued Interest	The Purchase Price under a Buy/Sell Back Transaction is exclusive of Accrued Interest on the Purchased Securities. Accordingly, on the Purchase Date, the Buyer is to pay an amount equal to the Accrued Interest as well as the Purchase Price.
4	Margin Maintenance: 'repricing'	If a Buy/Sell Back Transaction is to be subject to repricing under Paragraph 4 (Margin Maintenance) of the GMRA, the parties are to agree the Sell Back Price at the time of repricing.
5	Income Payments	Paragraph 5 (Income Payments) of the GMRA does not apply to Buy/Sell Back Transactions.

Equities Annex

No.	Paragraph Heading/Description	Summary
1	Scope	As mentioned in Chapter 1, the origins of the repo market are in the secondary bond market, and the terms of the GMRA still reflect that and do not contain provisions that would be expected when entering into repos of equity securities. If the parties wish to enter into repos of equities (and/or to use equities as Margins Securities), then the Equities Annex should be attached to the GMRA between the parties. Paragraph 1 of the Equities Annex states that the provisions of the Equities Annex apply if there are Transactions where the Purchased Securities include equities or if Margin Securities may include equities.
2	Interpretation	This sets out the additional definitions needed for the Equities Annex.
2(a)(i)	Definition of 'Equivalent Margin Securities' and 'Equivalent Securities'	This definition expands the GMRA definition of 'equivalent' to include the cash or securities that would result from the following events occurring in relation to the relevant Purchased Securities or Margin Securities: a conversion or consolidation; a

---

15 See elsewhere in this book for more detail on buy/sell back transactions.

			redemption; a take-over; a call on partly-paid securities; a capitalisation issue; a rights issue; or income in the form of securities.
	3	Income Payments	Paragraph 5 (Income Payments) of the GMRA is amended, so that: (i) for equities that are Purchased Securities, the Seller should seek a substitution of those Purchased Securities under Paragraph 8 of the GMRA, failing which the Seller can notify the Buyer that the Repurchase Date is to occur on the Business Day prior to the Income Payment Date; (ii) for equities that are Margin Securities, the transferor of those securities can notify the transferee that it wishes to transfer new Margin Securities in exchange for the transfer of Equivalent Margin Securities, although such exchange is subject to the transferee indicating that the new Margin Securities are acceptable to it; (iii) (subject to (iv) below) if the substitution/transfer does not take place, the Buyer/transferee is to pay to the Seller/transferor on the date that Income is paid by the issuer an amount equal to (a) the amount of Income that would have been paid in cash to the Buyer/transferee if it held the securities plus (b) any tax or tax benefit that the Buyer is entitled to recover from the issuer's jurisdiction in respect of that Income payment; and (iv) if the Buyer/transferee has not made reasonable efforts to substitute Purchased Securities or exchange Margin Securities when required to, the Buyer/transferee is to indemnify the Seller/transferor for any loss (including loss of Income Payment) that it suffers.
	4	Corporate actions and voting	Unlike the front-end GMRA,[16] the Equities Annex sets out provisions that deal with the exercise of voting rights, etc in relation to Purchased Securities and Margin Securities.
	4(a)	Notice of proposed corporate action	The Buyer of Purchased Securities and the transferee of Margin Securities is obliged to notify

---

16 Although the definition of 'equivalent to' does deal with the consequences of certain types of corporate action.

		the Seller/transferor of any notice by the issuer of the securities of any proposed corporate action (including conversion, sub-division, consolidation, take-over, option, etc).
		Where a corporate action is to take place:
		(i) the Seller can terminate the Transaction early;
		(ii) the transferor can request an exchange of Margin Securities; and/or
		(iii) (if applicable) the Buyer/transferee can, in relation to an option under the relevant securities, notify the Seller/transferor that it wishes to receive Equivalent Securities or Equivalent Margin Securities in a particular form if that option is exercised, subject to the Buyer/transferee giving sufficient notice.
4(b)	Voting rights	Neither the Buyer of Purchased Securities nor the transferee of Margin Securities is obliged to arrange for any voting rights under such Purchased Securities or Margin Securities to be exercised in accordance with the other party's instructions.
5	Transfer	The Seller is to pay any transfer or similar duties chargeable in connection with the transfer of Purchased Securities or Equivalent Securities.
		The transferor of Margin Securities is to pay any transfer or similar duties chargeable in connection with the transfer of Margin Securities or Equivalent Margin Securities.

FATCA Approaches

No.	Paragraph Heading/ Description	Summary
		Although not strictly an 'Annex' to be attached to a GMRA, ICMA has published a set of standard amendments to address issues arising out of the US Foreign Account Tax Compliance Act (FATCA). These amendments affect the following provisions: • definition of 'Equivalent Securities' • Paragraph 5 (Income Payments) • Paragraph 6(b) (Payments and Transfer) and add new provisions to: • Paragraph 6 (Payments and Transfer) • Paragraph 10 • paragraph 5 of the Equities Annex, in all cases, to make it clear that no withholdings

or deductions that are required to be made under FATCA will be the subject of any gross-up or other compensation under the terms of the GMRA.

3. **Global Master Securities Lending Agreement**

The GMSLA is published by ISLA (the International Securities Lending Association). There have been a number of versions of stock lending master agreements, initially covering different types of underlying securities and more recently incorporating perceived improvements in the documents, namely:
- the 1994 Overseas Securities Lender's Agreement;
- the 1995 Overseas Securities Lender's Agreement;
- the 1995 Master Gilt Edged Stock Lending Agreement;
- the 1996 Master Equity and Fixed Interest Stock Lending Agreement;
- the 2000 Global Master Securities Lending Agreement;
- the 2009 Global Master Securities Lending Agreement; and
- the 2010 Global Master Securities Lending Agreement.

The 2010 GMSLA is the version that, at the time of writing, is most commonly used for newly originated agreements, although there are many 2000 GMSLAs in place that are still being used. This chapter will focus on the 2010 version, and for the remaining sections of this chapter 'GMSLA' will be used to refer to the 2010 version.

The GMSLA has a typical 'master agreement' structure. There is a pre-printed form – often referred to as the 'front-end' – which is not amended, and then a Schedule in which the parties make various elections contemplated by the front-end and also any amendments or additions to the terms in the front-end.

There are also a number of standard form annexes for the GMSLA, including:
- a standard form Agency Annex (to allow a party to enter into stock lending transactions as the agent for another person, referred to as the 'principal');
- an Addendum for Pooled Principal Agency Loans;
- a UK Tax Addendum (updated in 2014); and
- a US Tax Addendum (updated in 2014).

The following analysis covers the Agency Annex, the Addendum for Pooled Principal Agency Loans, the UK Tax Addendum and the US Tax Addendum.

The trade-specific terms of individual stock lending transactions are set out in separate confirmations.

The basic layout of the GMSLA front-end is:
- definitions;
- commencement of transactions;
- collateral;
- income payments, distributions and corporate actions;
- termination of transactions;
- events of default and the consequences of early termination; and
- boilerplate clauses, such as notices, etc

2010 Global Master Securities Lending Agreement

No.	Paragraph Heading/ Description	Summary
1	Applicability	Paragraph 1 sets out the scope of the GMSLA, under which the two parties to the GMSLA will enter into transactions (defined as 'Loans') under which one party (defined as the 'Lender') transfers securities (defined as 'Securities') to the other party (defined as the 'Borrower') against the transfer by that other party of collateral, together with a simultaneous agreement by the Borrower to transfer in the future to the Lender securities 'equivalent' to the Securities against the transfer by the Lender of assets 'equivalent' to the collateral.
2	Interpretation	Paragraph 2 sets outs the various defined terms that are used in the GMSLA, along with some basic principles of interpretation. This summary considers those terms which are particularly useful in understanding the mechanics of the GMSLA.
2.1	'Base Currency'	This is specified in paragraph 2 of the Schedule and is the currency into which prices, sums or values are converted. It is used for both margining and close-out purposes.
2.1	'Business Day'	This term is used throughout the GMSLA and has different meanings depending on the context: (a) for Deliveries in respect of a Loan, it is a day (other than a Saturday or Sunday) on which banks and securities markets are open for business generally in the place where the Securities are being delivered; (b) for payments, it is (i) a day (other than a Saturday or Sunday) on which banks are open for business generally in the place where the account designated for the making or receipt of payment is situated, or (ii) if it is an EUR payment, a day on which TARGET operates; (c) for notices or communications, it is a day (other than a Saturday or Sunday) on which banks are open for business generally in the place designated for delivery; (d) for any other case, a day (other than a Saturday or Sunday) on which banks are open for business generally in the place(s) specified

		in the Designated Offices section in paragraph 6 of the Schedule.
2.1	'Collateral'	The parties can agree in the Schedule what types of assets (ie, securities, financial instruments or transfers of currency) shall constitute eligible forms of collateral to be provided by the Borrower to the Lender under a Loan, including Alternative Collateral following a substitution pursuant to paragraph 5.3.
		The eligible forms of Collateral, along with the applicable Margin Percentage, are specified in paragraph 1.1 of the Schedule. The parties can also specify whether certain types of assets will constitute eligible forms of Collateral for both parties or only one of the parties (eg, when a party acts as Borrower or as Lender).
2.1	'Equivalent' or 'equivalent to'	This term is used in the context of Loaned Securities and Collateral in the form of Securities and clarifies what type of assets are to be returned to a party (eg, the return of Equivalent Securities to the Lender at the end of the Loan or the return of Equivalent Collateral to the Borrower under the marking to market or substitution provisions). The importance of 'equivalency' to the legal analysis is considered in Chapter 7.
		The meaning of this term will vary depending on whether a corporate event or similar has occurred in relation to the relevant Securities during the term of the Loan.
		If there has been no such change to the Securities, 'equivalent' refers to a Security which is of the identical type, nominal value, description and amount (but not the identically numbered securities) originally transferred.
		If, however, the Securities are partly paid or have changed in some way following an event (eg, a corporate action), the term will also include securities or other assets to which the relevant party would be entitled following the occurrence of such event (subject to the necessary notice having been delivered pursuant to Paragraph 6.7 and provided sums due in respect thereof having been paid). In such circumstance, the term 'equivalent' shall refer to:
		(a) if the Securities have been redeemed, a sum of

money equivalent to the proceeds of redemption;

(b) if partly paid Securities are subject to a call, Securities in relation to which the Lender (in the case of Loaned Securities) or the Borrower (in the case of Collateral) has paid an amount equal to the sum due in respect of the call;

(c) if a capitalisation, equivalent Securities plus the bonus Securities issued; and

(d) in all other cases, equivalent Securities and/or a cash equivalent, in each case resulting from the event.

2.1 'Market Value' This term describes the manner in which Loan Securities and Collateral (and thus margin requirements) are valued and is calculated by the Lender on a mid-price basis by reference to a reputable pricing source chosen reasonably by the Lender in good faith (in the 2000 GMSLA, the reference was to 'bid price'). Any accrued income is added to the valuation if it is not already included in the price (ie, the Market Value should be the 'dirty' price).

With respect to suspended securities and those which cannot be legally transferred (or can only be transferred to a government or trustee or third party), the parties must agree in a commercially reasonable manner as the value of such Securities. If the parties cannot agree, they must appoint a third party dealer or, in the absence of agreement, the party determining Market Value must obtain price quotations from four leading dealers in the relevant Securities selected by such party. If more than three quotations are obtained, the Market Value is the arithmetic mean; if three quotations are obtained, the Market Value is the middle quotation; if fewer than three quotations, the Market Value is as determined by the relevant party.[17]

It is not uncommon for the definition of Market Value to be tailored in paragraph 4 of the Schedule to reflect operational realities and/or commercial agreement reached between the parties.

2.1 'Margin' This term is also widely referred to as the 'haircut' and represents the discount (usually expressed as a

---

17 The dispute mechanism is new to the 2010 GMSLA; it was not in the 2000 version.

			percentage in paragraph 1.1 of the Schedule) which is to be applied to the Market Value of the Collateral. This allows the parties to assign an appropriate level of overcollateralisation for each Loan based upon the type of asset being posted as Collateral (ie, it is common for less liquid and/or more volatile assets to be assigned a higher haircut than liquid and/or less liquid assets).
	2.3	Market terminology	Notwithstanding the fact that the commercial impetus behind Loans entered into under the GMSLA is to 'borrow' certain Securities with an intention to return them at a later date, Securities and Collateral are transferred on a full title transfer basis and the transferee party is free to use and dispose of the relevant Securities or Collateral in its discretion. On termination of a Loan, the party receiving the Securities or Collateral is not required to return the same Securities or Collateral to the other party but is obliged to return Securities or Collateral which are 'Equivalent' to those received.
	2.4	Currency Conversion	Currency conversions are to be effected by the Lender obtaining a spot FX rate from a reputable bank in the London interbank market on the day of calculation.
	3	Loans of Securities	Paragraph 3 provides that the terms of a Loan can be agreed orally or in writing (including by any agreed form of electronic communication) – the date of such agreement will be the 'Trade Date'. Such agreement will then usually be confirmed in such form as agreed between the parties (eg, one party prepares a Confirmation and the other approves it). Unless otherwise agreed, a Confirmation prepared by one party will not on its own prevail over the initial oral or written agreement.
	4	Deliveries	Paragraph 4 deals with how deliveries of Securities are to be effected.
	4.2	Requirements to effect Delivery	Each party must ensure that the Securities or Collateral (as the case may be) will be transferred to the other with full title guarantee, free from all liens, charges and encumbrances. The party receiving the Securities or Collateral is not required to return the same Securities or Collateral to the other party but is obliged to return Securities or Collateral which are Equivalent to those received.

4.3	Deliveries to be simultaneous unless otherwise agreed	Subject to each party's right under Paragraph 8.6 to withhold payment or delivery, in recognition of the operational limitations of effecting simultaneous delivery, a party can waive its right to require simultaneous delivery. Such waiver can be by course of conduct or otherwise.
5	Collateral	Paragraph 5 deals with the determination of the amounts of Collateral to be provided for Loans and with the delivery and return of Collateral.
5.1	Delivery of Collateral on commencement of Loan	The Borrower is required to deliver Collateral simultaneously with the delivery of the Loaned Securities to which the Collateral relates and in any event no later than close of business on the date upon which the Loaned Securities are due to be transferred to the Borrower. It is not uncommon for a Lender to require the Borrower to provide Collateral before the transfer of the Loaned Securities (known as pre-collateralisation).
5.2	Deliveries through securities settlement systems generating automatic payments	Where a clearing or settlement system is not operationally configured to accept securities on a 'free-of-payment' basis (ie, delivery of securities with no corresponding payment of funds), an automatically generated knock-on payment or delivery could be inadvertently effected by the relevant clearing or settlement system. This knock-on payment or delivery can either be (a) credited against any outstanding obligation to deliver Securities or Collateral which the transferee may owe to the transferor (until such time as alternative Securities or Collateral are posted by the transferee to the transferor), or (b) if no such obligation exists, the transferor must make a delivery or payment equivalent to the knock-on payment to the transferee outside of the clearing or settlement system on the same day.
5.3	Substitution of Collateral	At any time during the term of a Loan, the Borrower can recall Collateral from the Lender (without the consent of the Lender), provided that the Borrower has (i) delivered alternative Collateral to the Lender and acceptable to the Lender, and (ii) there is no outstanding liability under the mark-to-market provisions. This is a unilateral right of the Borrower. This is in contrast with the position under the GMRA where

5.4 Marking to Market of Collateral during the currency of a Loan on aggregated basis

substitutions can be effected only with the agreement of both parties.

Loans under the GMSLA will be margined on an aggregated basis unless the parties have elected in paragraph 1.3 of the Schedule that Loans will be margined on a Loan by Loan basis (see Paragraph 5.5). It is more common amongst professional market participants for Loans to be margined on an aggregated basis for operational ease and in order to minimise counterparty exposure and settlement risk.

(a) At any time on any Business Day, the Market Value of the Collateral posted in respect of all Loans (this is referred to as 'Posted Collateral') must equal the Market Value of all Loaned Securities and the applicable Margin (this is referred to as 'Required Collateral Value'). Margin calls may be made intra-day and are not subject to any threshold or minimum transfer amount.

(b) The Borrower can demand the return of Equivalent Collateral from the Lender to the extent that the Market Value of the Posted Collateral exceeds the Required Collateral Value.

(c) The Lender can demand the delivery of further Collateral from the Borrower to the extent that the Market Value of the Posted Collateral falls below the Required Collateral Value.

Any unpaid amount due and payable by the Lender is added to the Market Value of the Posted Collateral.

If agreed between the parties, income payable on Non-Cash Collateral can also be added – this will often be subject to a party's operational capabilities or preferences. Note, however, that there may be a delay between the Income Record Date and the date on which the income is actually paid. As the manufactured payment does not become payable until the income is paid by the issuer, the parties should consider whether or not such amount should be collateralised.

Where the parties act as both Borrower and Lender under different Loans, there will be separate payment flows for margin in respect of Loans where a party is acting as Borrower and Loans

		where such party is acting as Lender (although see Paragraph 5.6 below).
5.5	Marking to Market of Collateral during the currency of a Loan on a Loan by Loan basis	Loans under the GMSLA will be margined on an aggregated basis (see Paragraph 5.4) unless the parties have elected in paragraph 1.3 of the Schedule that Loans will be margined on a Loan by Loan basis. It is less common for Loans to be margined on a Loan by Loan basis and is more often requested by counterparties with less operational functionality.
		The margining mechanics work in the same way as they do when effected on an aggregated basis except that there will be a separate payment flow of Collateral for each Loan.
5.6	Requirements to deliver excess Collateral	The separate payment flows of collateral under Paragraph 5.4 may be set off against each other so that only the net amount will be payable. It is effectively a Collateral netting provision.
		This Paragraph will apply unless dis-applied in paragraph 1.4 of the Schedule.
5.8	Timing of repayments of excess Collateral or deliveries of further Collateral	The Notification Time is the time by which a demand for Equivalent Collateral or further Collateral (as the case may be) must be made for Collateral to be due by close of business on the same Business Day. If the demand is made after the Notification Time, the Collateral is due by close of business on the next Business Day.
		The parties agree the Notification Time in paragraph 1.5 of the Schedule.
5.9	Substitutions and extensions of Letters of Credit	The Borrower may provide Collateral to the Lender in the form of a Letter of Credit. However, the Lender can on three Business Days' notice require the Borrower to substitute the Letter of Credit for cash or other forms of Collateral acceptable to the Lender.
		The Borrower must by 10:30am on the second Business Day prior to the expiration of a Letter of Credit provided as Collateral either (i) obtain an extension of the Letter of Credit or (ii) replace it with a different Letter of Credit in an amount at least equal to the expiring Letter of Credit.
6	Distributions and Corporate Actions	Paragraph 6 deals with events that can affect Loaned Securities or Collateral Securities – income payments, corporate actions, voting – during the term of Loan or while they are provided as Collateral.

6.2	Manufactured payments in respect of Loaned Securities		If a Loan extends over an Income Record Date, the parties can agree the sum of money or property that the Borrower will pay or deliver to the Lender in respect of the Income paid with respect to the Loaned Securities during the term of a Loan.

In the absence of agreement, the Borrower is to pay to the Lender an amount of money or property equivalent to the Income that the Lender would have received had the Lender not lent the Securities to the Borrower (ie, putting the Lender in the position it would have been in but for the Loan). This is payable on the date the Income is paid. It will be noted that this position does not take into account any circumstances specific to the Borrower which might reduce the amount actually received from the issuer (in contrast to the position in respect of Income paid on Non-cash Collateral – see Paragraph 6.3).

Failure to make the manufactured payment can give rise to an Event of Default under Paragraph 10.1(b).

6.3	Manufactured payments in respect of Non-cash Collateral	If an Income Record Date occurs in relation to Collateral Securities before they have been returned, the parties can agree the sum of money or property that the Lender will pay or deliver to the Borrower in respect of the Income with respect to the Collateral Securities.

In the absence of agreement, the Lender is to pay to the Borrower an amount of money or property equivalent to the Income that the Lender would have received assuming the Lender (a) had retained the Collateral Securities, and (b) is not entitled to any tax relief or benefit.

Therefore, this fallback position (a) requires the Lender to pay to the Borrower only what it actually receives or would receive (ie, it does take into account any circumstances specific to the Lender which might reduce the amount received from the issuer), and (b) allows the Lender to benefit from any tax reliefs to which it is entitled without passing such benefit on to the Borrower.

Failure to make the manufactured payment can give rise to an Event of Default under Paragraph 10.1(b).

| 6.4 | Indemnity for failure to redeliver Equivalent Non-cash Collateral | This provision deals with the circumstances where a Borrower seeks to substitute Collateral (rather than receive the manufactured dividend payment).
If (a) the Lender fails to make reasonable efforts to deliver Equivalent Securities back to the Borrower having accepted Alternative Collateral following substitution by the Borrower under Paragraph 5.3, and (b) the Borrower has given adequate notice and sufficient detail to the Lender in connection with the proposed substitution, the Lender must indemnify the Borrower for direct losses suffered which it would not have suffered had the Equivalent Securities been returned.
This indemnity will apply unless dis-applied in paragraph 1.6 of the Schedule. |
| 6.5 | Income in the form of Securities | Any Income paid to the Lender or Borrower which is in the form of Securities shall be automatically rolled up into the Collateral or Loaned Securities (as the case may be) until the end of the Loan. This could give rise to a margin call pursuant to Paragraph 5.4 or 5.5.
This provision is sometimes amended such that Income in the form of Securities will be paid to the other party during the term of the Loan. |
| 6.6 | Exercise of voting rights | The parties are not obliged to arrange for voting rights in respect of Securities to be exercised in accordance with the instructions of the other party. This should be contrasted with obligations with respect to corporate actions under Paragraph 6.7 (see below).
The Borrower warrants in Paragraph 14(e) that 'it is not entering into a Loan for the primary purpose of obtaining or exercising voting rights in respect of the Loaned Securities'. If the Borrower wishes to exercise voting rights in a particular manner, it may recall Posted Collateral under Paragraph 5.3 and a failure by the Lender to deliver may result in an obligation to indemnify under Paragraph 6.4 (to the extent of the Borrower's direct losses). The Lender does not have equivalent rights in respect of the Loaned Securities. |
| 6.7 | Corporate actions | If a corporate action is due to occur with respect to Loaned Securities or Collateral Securities, the Lender or Borrower can give written notice to the |

		other party prior to the corporate action taking place that when the relevant Equivalent Securities or Equivalent Collateral are subsequently returned, they should be in a form that would have arisen had a particular course of action been taken in respect of the corporate action.
		The written notice must be given within a reasonable time prior to the latest time the relevant right may be exercised.
7	Rate Applicable to Loaned Securities and Cash Collateral	Paragraph 7 deals with the fees payable by the Borrower in relation to Loans, as well as the amount payable in relation to Cash Collateral.
7.1	Rates in respect of Loaned Securities	The Borrower is required to pay a fee to the Lender for entering into the Loan, which accrues in a manner and is payable at intervals determined in accordance with Paragraph 7.3 (see below).
		The sum is calculated by reference to a rate which is applied to the daily Market Value of the Loaned Securities. This rate is typically described as a percentage. This rate is determined on a Loan by Loan basis and is sometimes a term specified in the relevant Confirmation.
		Amounts payable under Paragraph 7.1 may be set off against amounts payable by the Lender under Paragraph 7.2.
7.2	Rates in respect of Cash Collateral	The Lender is required to pay an amount to the Borrower in respect of Cash Collateral, which effectively represents interest on a cash deposit. This rate is determined on a Loan by Loan basis and is sometimes a term specified in the relevant Confirmation.
		Amounts payable under this paragraph may be set off against amounts payable by the Lender under Paragraph 7.1.
7.3	Payment of Rates	The rates mentioned in Paragraphs 7.1 and 7.2 each accrue daily and, unless otherwise agreed, are payable on a monthly basis in arrears by the 10th Business Day after the last Business Day of the relevant calendar month.
8	Delivery of Equivalent Securities	Paragraph 8 deals with the termination of Loans and the delivery by the Borrower of Equivalent Securities.
8.1	Lender's right to terminate a Loan	The Lender can terminate the Loan and recall the Loaned Securities at any time on a Business Day by giving notice of not less than the standard

			settlement time for the Securities on the relevant exchange or clearing system.
This is, however, subject to the terms of the relevant Confirmation, which may specify that the Loan is a 'term loan' with a fixed Termination Date, in which case the Lender would not be able to recall the Loan prior to such date.
8.2		Borrower's right to terminate a Loan	The Borrower can terminate the Loan at any time by returning Equivalent Securities to the Loaned Securities to the Lender.
8.3		Delivery of Equivalent Securities on termination of a Loan	The Borrower is required to ensure the return of Equivalent Securities to the Lender on the termination of the Loan.
If the Borrower fails to deliver Equivalent Securities, the Lender may effect a 'mini close-out' for the relevant Loan (see Paragraph 9.1).
8.4		Delivery of Equivalent Collateral on termination of a Loan	The Lender is required to ensure the simultaneous return of Equivalent Collateral to the Borrower on the date and time the Equivalent Securities are to be delivered by the Borrower under Paragraph 8.3.
If the Lender is not able to ensure the simultaneous return of the Equivalent Collateral as required, it is recommended that the Lender agrees with the Borrower that this obligation will be waived (see Paragraph 4.3).
If the Lender fails to deliver Equivalent Collateral, the Borrower may effect a 'mini close-out' for the relevant Loan (see Paragraph 9.2).
8.6		Delivery obligations to be reciprocal	A party's delivery obligations under the GMSLA are conditional upon the party being satisfied that the other party will fulfil its corresponding delivery obligation. If either party is not so satisfied, it shall notify the other party who must then make arrangements to assure full delivery.
9		Failure to Deliver	Paragraph 9 sets out the consequences of failure to deliver Equivalent Securities or Equivalent Non-Cash Collateral on the termination of a Loan.
9.1		Borrower's failure to deliver Equivalent Securities	If the Borrower fails to deliver Equivalent Securities on the termination of a Loan, the Lender may either:
(a) elect to continue the Loan; or
(b) terminate the Loan by written notice in accordance with Paragraph 11.2 as if an Event of Default had occurred in respect of the

Industry documentation

		Borrower (ie, the Loan will be valued by the Lender on the Lender's side of the market and cash settled). This is known as the 'mini close-out' mechanism and the Lender has this right only while the failure to deliver Equivalent Securities continues.
		The mini close-out will not itself constitute or give rise to an Event of Default, although a failure to pay the cash settlement amount can give rise to an Event of Default (see Paragraph 10.1(c)).
9.2	Lender's failure to deliver Equivalent Collateral	If the Lender fails to deliver Equivalent Non-Cash[18] Collateral on the termination of a Loan, the Borrower may either: (a) elect to continue the Loan; or (b) terminate the Loan by written notice in accordance with Paragraph 11.2 as if an Event of Default had occurred in respect of the Lender (ie, the Loan will be valued by the Borrower on the Borrower's side of the market and cash settled). This is known as the 'mini close-out' mechanism and the Borrower has this right only while the failure continues.
		The mini close-out will not itself constitute or give rise to an Event of Default, although a failure to pay the cash settlement amount can give rise to an Event of Default (see Paragraph 10.1(c)).
9.3	Failure by either party to deliver	A party that fails to deliver Equivalent Securities or Equivalent Collateral will reimburse the other party for (a) interest, overdraft or similar costs and expenses incurred, or (b) costs and expenses incurred as a direct result of a Buy-in[19] being exercised against it by a third party. Such reimbursement is payable one Business Day after demand.
10	Events of Default	Paragraph 10 sets out the events that can give rise to an Event of Default. Section 5 of this Chapter analyses in more detail the consequences of Events of Default.
10.1	Need for written notice	With the exception of certain Acts of Insolvency (see Paragraph 10.1(d)), an event listed in Paragraph 10.1 will not constitute an Event of

---

18 A lender's failure to repay cash collateral can give rise to an event of default.
19 A 'buy-in' is an arrangement where, following a failure by a seller or transferor to deliver securities, the buyer or transferee is entitled to acquire equivalent securities and recover the cost of doing so from the seller or transferor – here, the reference to 'seller or transferor' is to the party that is to take delivery of the equivalent securities under the GMSLA.

		Default unless the Non-Defaulting Party serves written notice on the Defaulting Party stating that an Event of Default has occurred.
		This notice may be given in any manner set out in Paragraph 20 and the date/time of effective delivery will vary with the manner chosen. The parties should ensure that the relevant addresses or numbers are readily available such that notices may be delivered without delay if necessary. It is therefore common for key contact details to be specified in paragraph 6 of the Schedule.
10.1(a)	Failure to pay or deliver	There are three events covered: • the Borrower failing to pay or deliver Collateral at the beginning of the Loan • the Borrower failing to pay or deliver further Collateral under the Marking to Market provisions • the Lender failing to repay Cash Collateral under the Marking to Market provisions or at the end of the Loan. In this drafting neither (i) the delivery of Loaned Securities by the Lender at the beginning of the Loan nor (ii) the redelivery of Equivalent Securities in relation to Collateral Securities by the Lender pursuant to the Marking to Market provisions in Paragraph 5 are covered (it should be noted that (ii) was covered in the equivalent provision in the 2000 GMSLA: it can also give rise to the Borrower's remedies under Paragraph 9.2).
10.1(b)	Failure to make manufactured payments	This can give rise to an Event of Default if the relevant payment is not made within 3 Business Days of written demand by the relevant party.
10.1(c)	Failure to pay the cash settlement amount following a mini close-out	This event applies to the cash settlement amounts payable under Paragraph 9.1 or 9.2 as well as to the additional costs payable under Paragraph 9.3. With regards to timing, by reason of Paragraph 11.2, such cash settlement amounts are payable on the Business Day following the determination of the relevant amount. Therefore, the earliest that this Event of Default could be triggered is at the end of that Business Day.
10.1(d)	Occurrence of Act of Insolvency	Each of the events listed in the definition of 'Act of Insolvency'[20] will constitute an Event of Default

---

20 These are extensive but may not cover all the bases. Regard should be had to the relevant local legal opinion in this connection.

with the service by the Non-Defaulting Party of a Default Notice.

However, if specified in paragraph 5 of the Schedule that Automatic Early Termination (AET) will apply with respect to the Defaulting Party, an Act of Insolvency event which is 'the presentation of a petition for winding up or analogous proceeding or the appointment of a liquidator or analogous officer' will not require the Non-Defaulting Party to serve notice on the Defaulting Party for such event to constitute an Event of Default (ie, the Event of Default shall be deemed to have automatically occurred).

In the 2000 GMSLA, AET always applied to both parties in this event. However, the 2010 GMSLA allows parties to elect whether or not it will apply to either or both parties. This allows greater flexibility for the Non-Defaulting Party to manage the close-out process. It also avoids situations where there is ambiguity as to whether or not AET has been triggered or where the parties are not aware that AET has been triggered.

The application of AET is ultimately a commercial decision, but generally it will be switched on only where a party is incorporated in a jurisdiction where the relevant industry opinion (commissioned by the relevant trade body and updated annually) expressly recommends it in order to ensure enforceability of the netting provisions in a local insolvency law context.

| 10.1(e) | Breach of warranties | It can give rise to an Event of Default if the warranties made by a party in Paragraph 13 or Paragraph 14 are 'incorrect or untrue in any material respect'. |

This event does not cover the warranty made by the Borrower in Paragraph 14(e) that it is 'not entering into a Loan for the primary purpose of obtaining or exercising voting rights' and, as such, a breach of this representation will not constitute a potential Event of Default.

It should also be noted that any other warranties – for example, if included in the Schedule – would not be covered by this event.

10.1(f)	Admission of inability or intention not to perform obligations under the GMSLA	The admission must relate to an obligation which would constitute an Event of Default with the service of notice or lapse of time. However, a failure to perform any obligation under the GMSLA can give rise to an Event of Default under Paragraph 10.1(i), and so an admission in relation to any of a party's obligations would be covered by this event.
10.1(g)	Material transfer of assets	This refers to the transfer of a material part of a party's assets to a trustee by the order of a regulator. This event seeks to address situations which would not be captured by the definition of Act of Insolvency but which are nonetheless important factors for counterparty risk assessment.
10.1(h)	Being declared in default, etc by an exchange or a regulatory authority	This event seeks to address situations which would not be captured by the definition of Act of Insolvency but which are nonetheless important factors for counterparty risk assessment. This provision is a refinement of the equivalent provision in the 2000 GMSLA, as the 2011 GMSLA specifies that the event must be on the grounds that the relevant party has failed to meet any requirement relating to financial resources or credit rating.
10.1(i)	Failure to perform any other obligation	A party has 30 days following written notice from the other party to remedy a failure to perform any obligation under the GMSLA which is not captured by the other events set out in Paragraph 10.1 before such failure can give rise to an Event of Default. This event captures obligations which are not expressly covered above in other sub-paragraphs of Paragraph 10.1. It would also cover additional obligations that the parties have agreed in the Schedule.
10.2	Notification	This paragraph places a positive obligation on each party to notify the other in writing of the occurrence of an Event of Default (which presumably refers to the occurrence of an Act of Insolvency that triggers Automatic Early Termination as all other events require notice to be served by the Non-Defaulting Party) or an event which would, with the service of notice or the passage of time, constitute an Event of Default.
11	Consequences of an Event of Default	Following the occurrence of an Event of Default (which includes the Non-Defaulting Party having served a default notice on the Defaulting Party), the

		close-out mechanics set out in Paragraph 11 would be triggered. These mechanics are materially the same as the equivalent provisions in the 2000 GMRA and are discussed in detail in Section 5 of this Chapter.
12	Taxes	Paragraph 12 deals with taxes that may occur in relation to Loans or payments under the GMSLA.
12.2	Withholding, gross-up and provision of information	If a party is required to make a deduction or withholding on account of Tax pursuant to any applicable law, such party is required to: (a) notify the other party, (b) pay the amount deducted or withheld to the relevant authority, (c) provide the other party with documentation evidencing such payment, and (d) gross-up the payment to the other party such that it is equal to the amount the other party would have received had the deduction or withholding not been made. Note, however, that the obligation to gross-up under (d) does not apply (i) to manufactured payments by the Lender to the Borrower under Paragraph 6.3, or (ii) if the other party fails to comply with its obligation under Paragraph 12.3 to provide such information or documentation that would have allowed the payment to be made without the deduction or withholding.
12.4	Stamp Tax	The Borrower is liable for any Stamp Tax chargeable in connection with the GMSLA, other than Stamp Tax which has arisen as a result of the Lender failing to comply with its obligations.
12.6	Sales Tax	Any Sales Tax which arises under the GMSLA is the responsibility of the party making the relevant payment and is not a liability that is transferred to the other party.
12.7	Retrospective changes in law	This provision makes it clear that it is the applicable law as at the date of the relevant payment that will be used to determine the amounts payable and that no adjustments will be made to amounts already paid as a result of a retrospective change in such applicable law.
13	Lender's Warranties	Each Party, when acting as Lender under a Loan, makes four representations which are deemed to be made on a continuing basis and will survive the termination of the Agreement. These representations are as follows: (a) it is duly authorised and empowered to

perform its duties and obligations under the GMSLA;

(b) it is not restricted by its constitution from lending Securities or performing its duties under the GMSLA;

(c) it is absolutely entitled to pass full legal and beneficial title in the Securities to the Borrower free from liens, charges and encumbrances; and

(d) it is acting as principal in respect of the GMSLA, other than under Agency Loans.

| 14 | Borrower's warranties |

Each Party, when acting as Borrower under a Loan, makes five representations which are deemed to be made on a continuing basis and will survive the termination of the Agreement. These representations are as follows:

(a) it has all necessary licences and approvals and will not do anything to jeopardise them and it is duly authorised and empowered to perform its duties and obligations under the GMSLA;

(b) it is not restricted by its constitution from lending Securities or performing its duties under the GMSLA;

(c) it is absolutely entitled to pass full legal and beneficial title in the Securities to the Borrower free from liens, charges and encumbrances;

(d) it is acting as principal in respect of the GMSLA; and

(e) it is not entering into a Loan for the primary purpose of obtaining or exercising voting rights.

Certain types of entities that typically act as Lenders (eg, pension funds) are often not permitted to face unregulated counterparties. The references to 'licences and approvals' in representation (a) is designed to give comfort to those Lenders as to the counterparties' authority to face the Lender (although it is recommended that any Lender or any Agent acting for a Lender should undertake due diligence as to what, if any, restrictions on counterparty types that Lender is subject to and should consider bespoke amendments to ensure that those restrictions are not breached).

Borrowing shares in order to exercise voting rights

Industry documentation

		is not in line with the Securities Borrowing and Lending Code of Guidance (prepared by the Securities Lending and Repo Committee) and the representation in Paragraph 14(e) recognises this view.
As the Agency Annex does not provide for a Borrower to act as Agent under a Loan and there is not generally much call in the markets for 'agency borrowing', there is no carve-out to the Borrower's acting-as-principal representation.
15	Interest on Outstanding Payments	The parties can specify in Paragraph 10 of the Schedule a rate of interest that will be applied to any net amounts payable and outstanding under the GMSLA. This is the same rate of interest which is applied under Paragraph 11.7 to costs and expenses incurred by a Non-Defaulting Party following an Event of Default.
If the parties have not agreed a rate of interest to be applied in these circumstances, the applicable rate shall be LIBOR as quoted on a reputable financial information service as at 11:00am (London time) on the date on which the amount payable is to be determined.
Such interest accrues daily on a compound basis and is payable upon demand.
16	Termination	Either party can terminate the GMSLA with 15 Business Days' written notice. If there are any outstanding Loans, then the parties' obligations under these Loans will need to be performed in accordance with the GMSLA, notwithstanding termination.
17	Single Agreement	Paragraph 17 makes it clear that the parties' intention is that the GMSLA and each Loan form part of a single agreement. This provision is important to ensure the effectiveness of close-out netting in certain jurisdictions.
18	Severance	Paragraph 18 provides that any provision of the GMSLA that is held to be void or unenforceable will be severed from the GMSLA and the remaining provisions are to remain in full force and effect.
19	Specific Performance	Each party agrees not to seek specific performance of the other party's obligations to deliver Securities.
20	Notices	Notices details for each party are set out in paragraph 6 of the Schedule and the date on which a notice is deemed effective will depend on the

means by which it was sent:

(a) if in writing and delivered in person or by courier, on the date the notice is delivered;

(b) if by fax, on the date that a legible transmission is received by a responsible employee of the recipient – a transmission report generated by the sender's fax machine will not be sufficient proof of effective delivery;

(c) if by certified or registered mail, the date that mail is delivered or its delivery attempted;

(d) if by electronic messaging system, the date on which the message is received.

If the notice is delivered or received after 'Close of Business', it shall be effective on the next following Business Day.[21]

Given the decision in *Greenclose Limited v National Westminster Bank Plc*,[22] the parties may wish to add email as an express additional means of delivering notice.

21	Assignment	Neither party may assign its rights or obligations under the GMSLA without the written consent of the other party. Each party may, however, assign or otherwise deal with its rights in respect of amounts owing to it under Paragraphs 11.2 and 11.7 (being amounts due after an Event of Default). It should be noted that this right extends to a Defaulting Party that is owed the Paragraph 11.2 amount (by way of contrast to, for example, the ISDA Master Agreement where it is only the Non-Defaulting Party that may assign its rights under the equivalent provision).
22	Non-Waiver	Paragraph 22 provides that failure or delay in enforcing a right does not act as a waiver.
23	Governing Law and Jurisdiction	The GMSLA and any non-contractual obligations arising out of or in connection with it are governed by English law. The parties also submit to the exclusive jurisdiction of the English courts. There is provision for each party to appoint a

---

21 As the definition of 'close of business' refers to the making of payments, rather than the delivery of notices, reliance should be placed on sub-paragraph (c) of the definition of 'business day' (ie, close of business is the time at which banks close business in the place designated for delivery of the relevant notice).

22 [2014] EWHC 1156 (Ch).

No.	Paragraph Heading/Description	Summary
		process agent in England, whose contact details should be specified in the Schedule. If a process agent is appointed by a party, that party is obliged to appoint, and notify the other party of, a replacement agent.
24	Time	Time is of the essence of the GMSLA.
25	Recording	Each party may record telephone conversations.
26	Waiver of Immunity	Each party waives all immunity (sovereign or otherwise) from jurisdiction, attachment or execution to which it might be entitled.
27	Miscellaneous	Paragraph 27 sets out some further boilerplate provisions.
27.2	Responsibility for conforming	One of the parties (referred to as the 'Relevant Party') must take responsibility for ensuring that the front end of the GMSLA conforms to the version published by the International Securities Lending Association and the Relevant Party warrants and undertakes to this effect. The Relevant Party is identified in paragraph 9 of the Schedule and is usually the party which has produced the first draft of the Schedule for the purposes of the relevant negotiation.
27.4	Existing securities lending agreements	The parties can specify in paragraph 11 of the Schedule any existing securities lending master agreements which should be superseded by the GMSLA. Any outstanding loans under such agreements will be treated as having been entered into under the GMSLA.

Agency Annex

No.	Paragraph Heading/Description	Summary
1	Transactions Entered into as Agent	This paragraph sets out the scope of the Agency Annex.
1.1	Power of Lender to enter into Loans as agent	A party acting as Lender under a Loan may enter into such Loan (referred to as an 'Agency Loan') as agent on behalf of a third party (referred to as the 'Principal'). This is an election which is made in paragraph 8 of the Schedule and can be applied to one or both of the parties. Each party can also specify whether it will enter into Loans as principal as well as agent or whether it will always be acting

in an agent capacity. It is common for the Principals to be listed in a separate Appendix to the Schedule which may be amended from time to time, although this is not itself a condition for an Agency Loan under paragraph 1.3 of the Agency Annex. Agent Lenders are most commonly custodian banks and financial institutions managing the securities lending business of institutional investors (such as pension funds, insurance companies and investment funds). See chapter 3 generally on agency stock lending.

1.2	Pooled Principal transactions	Where an Agent enters into a Loan on behalf of multiple Principals, the Addendum for Pooled Principal Agency Loans should be applied. The Addendum (see below) deals with the allocation of Loans and Collateral among the Principals.
1.3	Conditions for Agency Loan	An Agent may only enter into an Agency Loan if:

(a) prior to effecting the Agency Loan, the Borrower has been provided with any information it requests for the purpose of identifying the relevant Principal;

(b) the Agent enters into the Loan on behalf of a single Principal whose identity is disclosed to the Borrower either (i) on the Trade Date or (ii) by the time the relevant bank, securities settlement system or depositary in the business centre in which the Loaned Securities are to be delivered closes for business on the next Business Day after the Loaned Securities are transferred to the Borrower; and

(c) the Agent has actual authority to enter into the Agency Loan and to give effect to the provisions in paragraph 1.5 of the Agency Annex.

The Agent may only enter into Agency Loans on behalf of Principals that have been approved by the Borrower.

With respect to the information provided under (a) above, the Agent represents (in its personal capacity) that such information is true and accurate to the best of its knowledge and has been provided to the Agent by the Principal(s). However, the Agent is not required to provide confidential information regarding the financial status of the Principals.

1.4	Notification by Agent of certain events affecting any Principal		There is a positive obligation on the Agent (in its personal capacity) to notify the Borrower if it learns that (a) an Act of Insolvency has occurred in respect of a Principal, or (b) the warranty given in paragraph 1.6 of the Agency Annex have been breached or are no longer true.
			By virtue of paragraph 1.5(b) of the Agency Annex, the Principal is also itself subject to the obligation under Paragraph 10.2 of the GMSLA which provides that a party must notify the other party in writing of the occurrence of an Even of Default or Potential Event of Default.
1.5	Status of Agency Loans		It is made clear that Agency Loans are transactions between the Borrower and the relevant Principal and, subject to the obligations the Agent has under the Agency Annex, the Agent will not be liable in its personal capacity for the performance of an Agency Loan.
			There is deemed to be a separate agreement in place between the Borrower and each Principal that enters into an Agency Loan. However, if an Event of Default or an event set out in Paragraph 10.1 occurs in respect of the Agent, the Borrower can treat such event as having occurred in respect of the Principal.
			An Event of Default or a Paragraph 10.1 event in respect of one Principal will not trigger an Event of Default or a Paragraph 10.1 event in respect of another Principal.
1.6	Warranty of authority by Lender acting as Agent		The Agent warrants that it has been duly authorised to enter each Agency Loan and to perform all obligations of the relevant Principal under the deemed separate agreement under Paragraph 1.5(b) of the Agency Annex, which effectively means that the Agent may be treated as being the principal for the purposes of the day to day trading under the Agreement.

Addendum for Pooled Principal Agency Loans

No.	Paragraph Heading/ Description	Summary
1	Scope	The Addendum will apply where the Agent enters into a single Agency Loan on behalf of more than one Principal (ie, a block trade pursuant to which multiple Principals contribute towards a single Loan of Securities). These Principals are referred to as the 'Pooled Principals'.
2	Interpretation	This paragraph sets out some additional and amended definitions where the Agent is acting on behalf of more than one Principal.
2.1(b)	Definition of 'Net Loan Exposure'	This paragraph states that the 'Net Loan Exposure' is the aggregate exposure that may exist between the Borrower and each Principal in respect of all Agency Loans entered into between the Borrower and such Principal.
3	Modifications to the Agency Annex	Two drafting amendments are made to the Agency Annex such that the fact that the Agent may enter into an Agency Loan in respect of 'one or more Principals' is properly reflected.
4	Allocation of Agency Loans	This paragraph sets out provisions for the allocation of Loans where there is more than one Principal.
4.1	Obligation to allocate	The Agent is obliged (in its personal capacity) to allocate a relevant Loan to a Principal or several Principals either at the trade date of the Loan or by its settlement date. Each Principal is responsible only for the portion of the Loan that has been allocated to it, which is relevant for the purposes of calculating the Net Loan Exposure which exists between the Borrower and the relevant Principal and will be particularly important to the Borrower from a risk management perspective. The Agent is required to promptly notify the Borrower as to which Principal(s) the Loan has been allocated.
4.2	Effect of allocation	Once the Loan has been allocated to a Principal, there is deemed to be a separate Loan between the Borrower and the Principal in respect of the portion of the Loan for which the Principal is responsible.
5	Allocation of Collateral	This paragraph sets out provisions for the allocation of Collateral where there is more than one Principal.

5.1	Express allocation	Unless the Agent expressly allocates a transfer of Collateral to or by the Agent, the deemed allocation provisions of paragraph 6.3 will apply. If the Agent does make an allocation, then paragraph 5.2 (see below) applies.
5.2	Effect of allocation	If a transfer of Collateral is made by the Agent or received by the Agent, in either case on behalf of more than one Principal, such transfer is allocated in proportion to each relevant Principal's Net Loan Exposure. This does not apply to transfers of Collateral to which paragraph 6.3 (see below) applies.
6	Pooled Principals: Rebalancing of Margin	The parties can agree that, where the Agent is acting on behalf of more than one Principal (together, the 'Pooled Principals'), transfers of Collateral will be made on an aggregate net basis in respect of all Agency Loans with the Pooled Principals ('Pooled Loans'). The purpose of these is to ensure that Posted Collateral is held uniformly as between the Pooled Principals in respect of their Pooled Loans. This is effected by there being (after the close of business on each Business Day) transfers of Collateral, which are made by the relevant entries in the Agent's accounting systems, from those Pooled Principals to which the Borrower has a Net Loan Exposure and to those Pooled Principals which have a Net Loan Exposure to the Borrower.
7	Warranties	The Agent gives the following warranties in its personal capacity. These are in addition to those deemed to have been given by the Principal under paragraph 1.6 of the Agency Annex: (a) that all notifications of Loan allocations and Collateral Transfer statements are complete and accurate in all material respects; (b) at the time of each Loan allocation, the relevant Principal(s) is duly authorised to enter into the relevant Agency Loan; and (c) at the time of each Loan allocation, no Event of Default or event that could give rise to an Event of Default has occurred in relation to any Principal(s) to whom an Agency Loan has been allocated.

2014 UK Tax Addendum[23]

No.	Paragraph Heading/ Description	Summary
		This Addendum reflects changes to the UK tax regime on manufactured payments, by making it clear that, in determining whether the reference in Paragraph 12.1 (which requires that payments are not made subject to withholdings or deductions unless required by Applicable Law) to what is required by Applicable Law applies, where the Loaned Securities or Non-Cash Collateral are (a) shares in UK real estate investment trusts, (b) net paying UK securities or (c) shares in certain open-ended investment companies, the party making the payment should have regard to additional warranties to be given by the recipient as to its status for the purpose of UK tax law.

2014 US Tax Addendum

No.	Paragraph Heading/ Description	Summary
		This Addendum provides that, in determining whether the reference in Paragraph 12.1 (which requires that payments are not made subject to withholdings or deductions unless required by Applicable Law) to what is required by Applicable Law applies, the party making the payment should have regard to additional warranties to be given by the recipient as to its status for the purpose of US tax law.
		It also addresses issues arising out the US Foreign Account Tax Compliance Act (FATCA), by making it clear that no withholdings or deductions that are required to be made under FATCA will be the subject of any gross-up or other compensation under the terms of the GMSLA unless the tax forms required under FATCA are provided by the recipient.

---

23 See elsewhere in this book for a discussion of UK tax issues.

4. Close-out netting

As the ability to terminate all transactions and reduce all payment and delivery obligations to a single, net payment in the event of a counterparty's default – in particular, on a counterparty's bankruptcy or insolvency – is a key feature of the GMRA and the GMSLA, this section analyses the close-out netting provisions of the GMRA (paragraph 10) and the GMSLA (paragraphs 10 and 11) in more detail.

4.1 Events of default

The range of (non-insolvency) events that can lead to early termination is more limited in the GMRA and GMSLA than under many other agreements in the financial markets such as, for example, the ISDA Master Agreement or commercial loan agreements. This is due to the fact that repo and stock lending transactions have historically been seen as less risky because the transactions are inherently 'self-collateralising' and the underlying securities (and securities provided as collateral, if relevant) are typically high-grade with low price volatility. Therefore, there is less need for 'hair-trigger' early termination events. The key events – of failure to pay, failure to provide margin/collateral and acts of insolvency – are included. However, as can be seen, nothing outside the four corners of the parties' repo relationship, other than acts of insolvency, is included.

It might seem surprising that failure to deliver securities or redeliver equivalent securities is not an event that can automatically trigger early termination of all transactions under the GMRA/GMSLA. However, it should be noted that, in the GMRA, the parties can make an election in Annex I that such a failure can trigger early termination. The reason that a failure to deliver or redeliver is not necessarily an indicator of financial difficulties on the part of the delivering/redelivering party is that it can simply be a reflection of unavailability of the securities in the underlying markets.

In addition, both the GMRA and the GMSLA contain specific provisions dealing with the consequences of a failure to deliver/redeliver, which allow the recipient to elect to terminate just the relevant transaction, with a net cash payment being due from one party to the other – these provisions are in paragraphs 10(g) and 10(h) of the GMRA and paragraph 9 of the GMSLA.[24] The remedies in paragraph 10(h) of the GMRA and paragraph 9 of the GMSLA are sometimes referred to as a 'mini close-out'. Failure to make the payment under these provisions can trigger early termination under the GMRA and the GMSLA.

For all events, other than an act of insolvency (see below), an early termination occurs after the delivery of a notice (called a 'default notice' in the GMRA) by the non-defaulting party to the defaulting party. It is a slightly unusual feature of the GMRA and the GMSLA – and one which is often overlooked by those drafting

---

[24] In essence, these provisions, other than paragraph 10(g) of the GMRA, provide that only the affected transaction or loan is closed out with a net sum being determined solely in relation to the repayment/redelivery obligations under that transaction or loan (but otherwise in the same manner as described in this part of the chapter). Paragraph 10(g), which covers a failure to deliver purchased securities on the purchase date, simply provides for the seller to pay to the buyer an amount equal to the excess of the repurchase price as at the date of termination over the purchase price.

amendments and additional provisions for inclusion in Annex I or the Schedule – that the defined term 'event of default' refers not simply to the occurrence of one of the listed events, but to the occurrence of one of the listed events plus the delivery of the default notice.[25]

If certain types of an act of insolvency occur, this will automatically constitute an event of default (without the need for a default notice to be delivered). These include:
- under the GMRA;[26] and
- under the GMSLA if the parties have elected in the Schedule that 'automatic early termination' will apply if there is an act of insolvency affecting the defaulting party,[27] 'the presentation of a petition for winding up or analogous proceeding or the appointment of a liquidator or analogous officer'.

A number of the industry-standard legal opinions obtained in relation to the GMRA and the GMSLA will set out recommended amendments to be made to the definition of act of insolvency for some or all entity types incorporated in the relevant jurisdiction. Parties with access to the opinions that are negotiating a GMRA or GMSLA with such an entity will therefore typically look to include those amendments in order to be able to rely on the conclusions set out in those opinions.

A number of these legal opinions will, in relation to the GMSLA and the 2011 GMRA,[28] also make recommendations as to whether or not 'automatic early termination' should be specified as applying to parties incorporated in the relevant jurisdiction (in order to ensure, or reduce uncertainties surrounding, the enforceability of the close-out netting provisions against an insolvent entity incorporated in that jurisdiction).

4.2 Consequences of an event of default

On the occurrence of an event of default, the parties' obligations under each transaction or loan and with respect to margin and collateral are accelerated, so that under the GMRA:
- for each transaction, the repurchase price is payable (with the pricing rate having accrued until the date of the event of default)[29] and equivalent securities become deliverable (although, as will be seen below, a cash equivalent is payable);
- in relation to margin, a cash margin (including accrued interest) is payable and equivalent margin securities become deliverable (although again a cash equivalent is payable);[30] and

under the GMSLA:

---

25   For ease of reference, in the remainder of this section the term 'early termination' will be used to refer to what is strictly speaking an 'event of default'.
26   Paragraph 10(a)(vi) of the GMRA.
27   Paragraph 10.1(d) of the GMSLA.
28   See Section 5 below.
29   For buy/sell back transactions, it is the sell back price (with the accrued income and the pricing rate having accrued until the date of the event of default).
30   Paragraph 10(b) of the GMRA.

- for each loan, equivalent securities become deliverable (although again a cash equivalent is payable); and
- in relation to collateral, equivalent cash collateral is repayable and equivalent non-cash collateral becomes deliverable (although again a cash equivalent is payable).[31]

It should be noted that the GMSLA also provides that all delivery, payment and other obligations of the parties are accelerated to require performance on such accelerated early termination date.[32] This would include accrued loan fees (under paragraph 7.1), manufactured payments (under paragraphs 6.2 and 6.3) for which the record date precedes the early termination date but the payment date falls afterwards, and any amounts payable under paragraph 9.3 but yet to be demanded.

The GMRA does not include such a provision; it is only the repurchase date obligations (payment of repurchase price and delivery of equivalent securities) and the return of margin obligations (repayment of cash margin and delivery of equivalent margin securities) that are accelerated upon the occurrence of an event of default. Although other payment obligations (eg, manufactured dividend payments in respect of income) are not affected or cancelled by the early termination, they are not accelerated and should not be taken into account when determining the net amount payable.

4.3 Determination of default market values of securities

In order to be able to reduce the parties' obligations to a single, net amount payable by one party to the other, the accelerated delivery obligations of equivalent securities need to be converted into payment obligations. Both the GMRA and the GMSLA achieve this through similar provisions in which the 'default market values' of any equivalent securities are to be established.[33]

In both agreements, the default market value is intended to mirror the economic consequences for the non-defaulting party of the early termination of the transactions or loans. So, where the non-defaulting party is the party that would otherwise be delivering equivalent securities, the default market value is intended to reflect the proceeds that the non-defaulting party would receive by disposing of the equivalent securities elsewhere. These are defined as 'receivable securities' (as they were to be delivered to, or received by, the defaulting party).[34] Similarly, where the non-defaulting party is the party that would otherwise be receiving equivalent securities, the default market value is intended to reflect the cost for the non-defaulting party of acquiring the securities elsewhere. These are defined as 'deliverable securities' (as they are to be delivered by the defaulting party).[35] No distinction is made for these purposes between securities that were the subject of a transaction or loan and securities that were delivered as margin or collateral.

---

31 Paragraph 11.2(a) of the GMSLA.
32 Paragraph 11.2 (introductory sub-paragraph) of the GMSLA.
33 It should be noted that, although earlier versions of the GMRA use a similar concept for the calculations to be made after an event of default, the 2000 GMSLA and earlier standard form stock lending agreements have more convoluted provisions.
34 Paragraph 10(d)(v) of the GMRA and paragraph 11.3(e) of the GMSLA.
35 Paragraph 10(d)(iii) of the GMRA and paragraph 11.3(c) of the GMSLA.

Under both the GMRA and the GMSLA, there are three basic methods for the default market value to be established:
- by reference to the net proceeds[36] of an actual sale by the non-defaulting party of receivable securities or the aggregate cost[37] of an actual purchase by the non-defaulting party of deliverable securities;[38]
- by reference to quotations received by the non-defaulting party from (two or more) market-makers for the sale of deliverable securities or the purchase of receivable securities, adjusted for the transaction costs[39] that would be incurred for such a transaction;[40] and
- by reference to a determination by the non-defaulting party of the 'fair market value' of the deliverable securities or receivable securities, again adjusted for the transaction costs that would be incurred for such a sale or purchase, as applicable[41] – that adjusted fair market value being defined as the 'net value' (see below).

In the determination of the net amount payable (see below), the party that would ordinarily have been required to deliver the securities in question is instead obliged to pay the default market value of those securities to the other party.[42]

4.4 Default valuation time

In order to be used to determine the default market value, any purchases or sales have to be made after early termination and prior to the default valuation time and any quotations have to be received after early termination[43] and prior to the default valuation time.[44]

In both the GMRA and the GMSLA, the default valuation time is defined as the close of business (in the 'most appropriate' market for the securities in question) on the fifth dealing day after the day on which the early termination occurs.[45] Where

---

36 The 'net proceeds' are after the deduction of 'all reasonable costs, fees, and expenses' incurred in connection with the sale (paragraph 10(e)(i)(AA)(aa) of the GMRA) or 'the reasonable costs, commissions (including internal commissions), fees and expenses (including any mark-up or mark-down or premium paid for guaranteed delivery) incurred or reasonably anticipated' in connection with the sale (paragraph 11.3(f) of the GMSLA).
37 The 'aggregate cost' includes 'all reasonable costs, fees, and expenses' incurred in connection with the purchase (paragraph 10(e)(i)(AA)(bb) of the GMRA) or 'the reasonable costs, commissions (including internal commissions), fees and expenses (including any mark-up or mark-down or premium paid for guaranteed delivery) incurred or reasonably anticipated' in connection with the purchase (paragraph 11.3(f) of the GMSLA).
38 Paragraph 10(e)(i)(A) of the GMRA and paragraph 11.4(a) of the GMSLA.
39 Transaction costs are to be added in the case of deliverable securities (to replicate the purchase of securities by the non-defaulting party) and deducted in the case of receivable securities (to replicate the sale of securities by the non-defaulting party). In the GMRA, 'transaction costs' are 'the reasonable costs, commissions (including internal commissions), fees and expenses (including any mark-up or mark-down) that would be incurred in connection with the sale or purchase' (paragraph 10(d)(v)). In the GMSLA, 'transaction costs' are slightly wider in scope, being 'the reasonable costs, commissions (including internal commissions), fees and expenses (including any mark-up or mark-down or premium paid for guaranteed delivery) incurred or reasonably anticipated' in connection with the sale or purchase (paragraph 11.3(f)).
40 Paragraph 10(e)(i)(B) of the GMRA and paragraph 11.4(b) of the GMSLA.
41 Paragraphs 10(e)(i)(C) and 10(e)(ii) of the GMRA and paragraphs 11.5 and 11.6 of the GMSLA.
42 Paragraph 10(c)(ii) of the GMRA and paragraph 11.2(b) of the GMSLA.
43 The GMRA (unlike the GMSLA) does not specify that quotations have to be received after early termination.
44 Paragraphs 10(e)(i)(A) and 10(e)(i)(B) of the GMRA and paragraphs 11.4(a) and 11.4(b) of the GMSLA.
45 In other words, the day on which the event of default occurs does not count as the first day of this five-day dealing period.

early termination occurs automatically upon the occurrence of an act of insolvency, the default valuation time is the close of business on the fifth dealing day after the day on which the non-defaulting party first becomes aware of such act of insolvency.

4.5 **Default valuation notice – GMRA only**

The GMRA requires that, if the non-defaulting party wishes to rely on the proceeds/cost of an actual sale/purchase or quotations, it must deliver to the defaulting party, prior to the default valuation time, a written notice which states that the non-defaulting party has (as applicable) sold receivable securities, purchased deliverable securities or received quotations and is electing to treat the net proceeds, purchase costs or the quoted prices (adjusted for transaction costs) as the default market value. This notice is the 'default valuation notice'.[46]

Although it is not specifically stated in the GMRA, the implication is that this written notice must specify the amount of the net proceeds or aggregate cost if the actual sale/purchase method is elected. If the quotation method is elected, then the quoted prices and the transaction costs must be specified.[47]

More than one default valuation notice can be served to cover different deliverable securities or receivable securities (or, in the case of actual sales/purchases, different sales/purchases where the quantity sold/purchased is less than the total quantity of the deliverable securities or receivable securities in question).

In relation to the third method of determining the default market value (a determination of the 'fair market value'), the GMRA provisions are, on their face, confusing. A default valuation notice may be served – prior to the default valuation time – stating that the non-defaulting party has endeavoured, but not been able, to sell/purchase securities and/or obtain quotations or that the non-defaulting party has either determined that it would not be commercially reasonable to obtain quotations or to use quotations which have been obtained.[48] In that case, the net value is to be the default market value, although it is not specified as at what time the net value is to be determined.

However, if no default valuation notice is given on or prior to the default valuation time, then the default market value is to be the net value as at the default valuation time.[49] But, if the non-defaulting party reasonably determines that, as at the default valuation time, it is not possible to determine a commercially reasonable default market value, the non-defaulting party is to determine the default market value as soon as reasonably practicable after the default valuation time. No separate notice of such determination needs to be given.

There is no equivalent requirement in the GMSLA for a default valuation notice to be served.

4.6 **Timing of sales, purchases and quotations**

Under the GMRA, in order to be capable of being used to determine the default

---

46 Paragraph 10(e)(i) of the GMRA.
47 Paragraph 10(e)(i)(B) of the GMRA.
48 Paragraph 10(e)(i)(C) of the GMRA.
49 Paragraph 10(e)(ii) of the GMRA.

market value, it is a requirement that an actual sale or purchase is effected after early termination and, due to the default valuation notice requirement, before the default valuation time.[50] As far as quotations are concerned, although the default valuation notice requirement means that these must be obtained before the default valuation time, there is no actual requirement that these are obtained after the occurrence of early termination. It is submitted, though, that the use of quotations obtained prior to the occurrence of early termination would be open to challenge.

Under the GMSLA, in order to be capable of being used to determine the default market value, it is a requirement that an actual sale or purchase is effected or a quotation is obtained between the date on which early termination occurs[51] and the default valuation time.[52]

The five-dealing day window after the date on which early termination occurs does, of course, give rise to the potential for mismatches in relation to the accrual of coupons (for fixed income securities) or the payment of dividends (for equity securities). For repos, under the GMRA the pricing rate (ie, repo interest) ceases to accrue on the date of early termination, but default market value (certainly in the case of an actual sale/purchase or quotation; more arguably in the case of net value) would include the amount of accrued coupon on the purchased securities. In that case, the party that is accounting for the default market value is 'paying' for up to five dealing days' worth of coupon for which no equivalent repo interest is to be received. A similar issue could arise where there is a dividend payable under equity securities, if the income payment date (in the case of a repo) or an income record date (in the case of a stock loan) occurs between the date of early termination and the date as at which the default market value is determined.

4.7 Net value

Under the GMRA and the GMSLA:

- the default market value of the relevant securities may (at the election of the non-defaulting party) be the net value of those securities if the non-defaulting party has endeavoured, but not been able, to sell/purchase securities and/or obtain quotations or the non-defaulting party has either determined that it would not be commercially reasonable to obtain quotations or to use quotations which have been obtained;[53] and
- the default market value of the relevant securities will be the net value if the default market value has not been determined by an actual sale/purchase or quotation (or, in the case of the GMRA, by the non-defaulting party serving a default valuation notice electing to use the net value).[54]

The net value is defined as the:

---

50 Paragraph 10(e)(i)(A) of the GMRA.
51 This would include the period on the day of the early termination but prior to the actual occurrence of early termination – most typically, prior to the service of the relevant default notice.
52 Paragraph 11.4 (introductory paragraph) of the GMSLA.
53 Paragraph 10(e)(i)(C) of the GMRA and paragraph 11.5 of the GMSLA.
54 Paragraph 10(e)(ii) of the GMRA and paragraph 11.6 of the GMSLA.

amount which, in the reasonable opinion of the non-Defaulting Party, represents [the relevant securities'] fair market value, having regard to such pricing sources and methods (which may include, without limitation, available prices for Securities with similar maturities, terms and credit characteristics as [the relevant securities]) as the non-Defaulting Party considers appropriate, from which is deducted (in the case of Receivable Securities) or to which is added (in the case of Deliverable Securities) Transaction Costs in connection with the sale or purchase of the relevant securities.[55]

The GMRA refers to the transaction costs 'that would be incurred' in connection with the sale or purchase; the GMSLA refers to the transaction costs 'incurred or reasonably anticipated' in connection with the sale or purchase.

4.8 Standard of care

The GMRA and the GMSLA give the non-defaulting party the right and the obligation to determine the net amount payable – in particular, the default market values of the relevant securities. As the performance of such determination will require the non-defaulting party to make certain elections and exercise certain discretions, the question arises as to the extent to which the court will interfere with, or exercise control over, those elections and discretions.

In particular:

- the non-defaulting party can 'elect' to use the net proceeds or aggregate costs of an actual sale or purchase of securities as the basis for the default market value of the relevant securities (and can also elect to scale the proceeds up or down proportionately where the amount of securities sold or purchased does not equal the amount of securities for which the default market value is to be determined);
- the non-defaulting party can 'elect' to use quotations from two or more market makers or regular dealers as the basis for the default market value of the relevant securities (and the 'commercially reasonable' size of the quotations is to be determined by the non-defaulting party);
- the non-defaulting party may 'determine' that it would not be commercially reasonabe to obtain quotations (as mentioned above) or to use those quotations which have been obtained;
- the non-defaulting party can, in certain circumstances, 'elect' to use the net value as the basis for the default market value of the relevant securities;
- the non-defaulting party may 'reasonably determine' at the default valuation time that it is not possible to determine a net value of securities which is commercially reasonable (and so the net value is to be determined as soon as reasonably practicable after the default valuation time); and
- the net value is to be the amount which, in the 'reasonable opinion' of the non-defaulting party, represents their fair market value, having regard to such pricing sources and methods as the non-defaulting party 'considers appropriate'.

---

55   Paragraph 10(d)(iv) of the GMRA and paragraph 11.3(d) of the GMSLA.

The question of the extent to which the court will interfere with such discretions was considered by the Court of Appeal in *Socimer International Bank Ltd (in liquidation) v Standard Bank London Ltd*[56] which, although concerning a bank's own standard terms for the forward sale of securities,[57] does provide useful guidance in the absence of any decided case directly concerning the relevant provisions of the GMRA or GMSLA (or earlier versions).

Those terms provided that, following an event of default by the party (Socimer) that would otherwise have taken delivery of the securities on maturity, the other party (Standard Bank):

shall have the right, in its sole discretion ... to liquidate or retain sufficient [securities] and to apply the proceeds of their sale to satisfy to the extent possible any amount payable to [that other party].

The terms also provided that Standard Bank:

may in its sole and absolute discretion sell the [securities] at such time, in such manner and at such price as it deems reasonable and appropriate. The value of any [securities] liquidated or retained ... shall be determined on the date of termination by [Standard Bank].

In that case, a default did arise on the part of Socimer. For those securities that Standard Bank did not sell, it was held that the relevant provisions did not impose a duty of reasonable care on Standard Bank and did not require an objective inquiry into the true market value of the securities. Instead, Standard Bank could apply its own subjective criteria for the valuation, limited only by concepts such as good faith, honesty, rationality and capriciousness. The Court of Appeal also rejected the suggestion that there was any analogy to the position of a mortgagee in possession.

Although the specific wording in the Socimer case refers to the value being 'determined' by the relevant party, it is submitted that the same standard is likely to apply to the determination of net value, notwithstanding the presence of the words 'in the reasonable opinion' in the definition of net value.[58]

4.9 Determination of net amount

Once the default market values have been determined, an account is to be taken of the payments due from each party to the other as at the date of early termination. Sums denominated in a currency other than the base currency are to be converted into the base currency at the spot rate. Under the GMRA, the conversion is to be made as at the date of early termination; under the GMSLA, the non-defaulting party is to determine within reason the date and time of the conversion. The sums due from one party are to be setoff against the sums due from the other party with the balance or net amount payable by the party that was owed the lower amount prior to the set-off.[59]

---

56 [2008] EWCA Civ 116.
57 This forward sale was, in effect, the equivalent of the repurchase/redelivery leg of a repo.
58 See, for example, *Barclays Bank plc v Unicredit Bank AG (formerly known as Bayerische Hypo-und Vereinsbank AG)* [2014] EWCA Civ 302, where it was held that a provision for a bank's consent to be 'determined ... in a commercially reasonable manner' by the bank entitled the bank to have primary regard to its own commercial interests, in a manner akin to the *Socimer* case.
59 Paragraph 10(c)(ii) of the GMRA and paragraph 11.2(b) of the GMSLA.

It is unfortunate that neither the GMRA nor the GMSLA is perfectly clear as to the date on which the net sum is then payable. The GMRA[60] states that the amount is due and payable on the 'next following business day', without specifying what the payment date is to follow. It is likely (but not certain) that this would be the date of early termination. The GMSLA[61] states that the amount is payable on the 'next following Business Day after such account has been taken and such sums have been set off in accordance with [the relevant paragraph]'. Again, it is likely (but not certain) that this would be taken to refer to the date on which early termination occurred.

Under the GMRA and the GMSLA, interest is to accrue on sums that are not paid when due (including sums payable following early termination) for the period until actual payment at a rate equal to LIBOR or, in the case of GMSLA, the rate specified in the Schedule if the parties have specified a rate. Under the GMSLA, interest compounds daily, whereas under the GMRA it is simple interest only.[62]

4.10 Legal expenses

Both agreements provide for the defaulting party to be liable to the non-defaulting party for the amount of all legal and other expenses reasonably incurred by the non-defaulting party in connection with or as a consequence of an event of default (plus interest, at the same rate as it accrues for sums not paid when due).

4.11 Other heads of loss

The GMRA allows the non-defaulting party to recover from the defaulting party further amounts following the occurrence of an event of default, namely:

- if the non-defaulting party enters into a replacement transaction (as a result of a transaction terminating before its agreed repurchase date), any loss or expense incurred in entering into such replacement transaction; and
- if the non-defaulting party reasonably decides, instead of entering into replacement transactions, to replace or unwind any hedging transactions, the loss or expense incurred in entering into such replacement or unwind.

In both cases, the non-defaulting party must take into account any profit or gain made on any replacements or unwinding and, if the profits and gains are greater than the losses and expenses, the non-defaulting party is to pay the excess to the defaulting party.

Both the GMRA and the GMSLA provide that neither party may claim any sum by way of consequential loss or damage in the event of a failure by the other party to perform any of its obligations.[63]

Both the GMRA and the GMSLA provide that the close-out and netting provisions set out in the relevant agreements are a complete statement of the remedies available to each party in respect of any early termination.[64]

---

60   Paragraph 10(c)(ii) of the GMRA.
61   Paragraph 11.2(b) of the GMSLA.
62   Paragraph 12 of the GMRA and paragraph 15 of the GMSLA.
63   Paragraph 10(j) of the GMRA and paragraph 10.4 of the GMSLA.
64   Paragraph 10(i) of the GMRA and paragraph 10.3 of the GMSLA.

4.12 Set-off

The GMSLA contains[65] a set-off provision, which gives the non-defaulting party the option to setoff any amount payable under paragraph 11.2(b) (ie, the net amount described above) against any amount payable by the payee of such net amount under any other agreement or instrument between the parties.

The GMRA contains no set-off provision in its standard form, although it is always open to the parties to agree to the inclusion of a set-off provision in Annex I.

5. 2011 GMRA

In 2011, SIFMA and ICMA published the 2011 GMRA, incorporating perceived improvements, in particular in relation to the close-out netting provisions in paragraph 10 (on which this section focuses).[66]

At the same time, SIFMA and ICMA published the 2011 Global Master Repurchase Agreement Protocol. This would allow a party that formally 'adhered' to this protocol to amend any existing 1995 GMRAs and/or 2000 GMRAs that the party had in place with another party that also adhered to the protocol by essentially replacing[67] the existing paragraph 10 of such 1995 GMRAs and/or 2000 GMRAs with a paragraph 10 that reflected paragraph 10 of the 2011 GMRA.

Under paragraph 10(a) of the 2011 GMRA, the events listed in the relevant sub-paragraphs are each defined as an 'event of default' prior to (and without there being) any service of a default notice or other notice by the non-defaulting party.

Paragraph 10(b) provides that, following the occurrence of an event of default which is continuing, the non-defaulting party may serve notice on the defaulting party designating an early termination date. The early termination date may not be more than 20 days after that notice. If, however, 'automatic early termination' has been specified in Annex I in relation to the defaulting party then, if the event of default comprises an act of insolvency which is the presentation of a winding-up petition (or similar) or the appointment of a liquidator (or similar), an event of default occurs immediately prior to the occurrence of that event of default.

If an early termination date occurs, then by virtue of paragraph 10(c) the repurchase date for all transactions occurs on the early termination date with the result that:

- for each transaction, the repurchase price is payable – with the pricing rate having accrued until the early termination date – and equivalent securities become deliverable (although, as with the 2000 GMRA, a cash equivalent is payable); and
- in relation to margin, a cash margin – including accrued interest – is payable

---

65 In paragraph 11.8.
66 Other changes include: the inclusion of an alternative method of calculation of 'transaction exposure' (where the haircut is applied to the market value of securities instead of to the repurchase price) – the parties can elect which approach is to be used (paragraph 2(xx) of the GMRA 2011); and a set-off provision (paragraph 10(n) of the 2011 GMRA).
67 It should be noted that the amendments to paragraph 10 implemented by the 2011 Global Master Repurchase Agreement Protocol do not include amendments to the events listed in paragraph 10(a) that are capable of giving rise to an event of default. These amendments do, though, include the 2011 GMRA approach to defining the term 'event of default' and the procedure for designating an early termination date.

and equivalent margin securities become deliverable (although, again, a cash equivalent is payable).

As with the 2000 GMRA, for the equivalent securities and the equivalent margin securities which are deliverable on the early termination date, the default market value is to be established[68] and then the sums due under the GMRA from one party are to be setoff against the sums due from the other party, with the net amount being payable by the party owed the lower amount before the set-off.[69]

Unlike the 2000 GMRA, the 2011 GMRA[70] requires the non-defaulting party to deliver a statement to the defaulting party showing its calculations in reasonable detail[71] and setting out the amount payable. This statement is to be provided 'as soon as reasonably practicable' following the calculation of the amount payable. It is also made clear that this amount is payable on the business day following the date of the statement. Interest, however, accrues on the amount payable for the period from the early termination date. Although the 2011 GMRA does expressly specify the rate of interest, it is submitted that this should be the 'applicable rate', which is defined in the 2011 GMRA[72] as the 'rate selected in a commercially reasonable manner by the non-defaulting party'.

There are some important differences in the 2011 GMRA (as opposed to the 2000 GMRA) as to how the default market value is to be calculated. Most importantly, instead of there being a clear period – between the occurrence of the event of default and the default valuation time – in which purchases, sales and quotations can be used to determine default market value, the 2011 GMRA uses the formulation 'on or about the early termination date'.[73] This does seem to envisage that purchases, sales and quotations before the early termination date would be within scope for use, but it is also unclear as to how long before or after it would be permitted or required.

Further, in the 2011 GMRA, the use of the net value (see above) to establish the default market value is only available if the non-defaulting party has:

- endeavoured, but not been able, to sell or purchase securities and/or obtain quotations; or
- determined that it would not be commercially reasonable to either obtain quotations or to use quotations which have been obtained.[74]

There is no provision for the net value to be used to establish the default market value if the default market value has not been determined by an actual sale, purchase

---

68 Paragraph 10(d)(i) of the 2011 GMRA.
69 Paragraph 10(d)(ii) of the 2011 GMRA.
70 Paragraph 10(d)(iii) of the 2011 GMRA.
71 In relation to the question of what might constitute 'reasonable detail', it is instructive to consider the judgment in *Goldman Sachs International v Videocon Global Ltd* [2013] EWHC 2843 (Comm), which concerned the construction of a very similar provision in the 1992 ISDA Master Agreement. In that case, it was held that showing only the addition or subtraction of total sums was insufficient to meet the 'in reasonable detail' criterion and that part of the purpose of the requirement to show 'reasonable detail' was to allow the party receiving the statement to form a view as to whether the relevant determination of an early termination amount satisfied the contractual requirements relating to that determination.
72 Paragraph 2(c) of the 2011 GMRA.
73 See the introductory wording to paragraphs 10(f)(i) and 10(f)(ii) of the 2011 GMRA.
74 Paragraph 10(f)(iii) of the 2011 GMRA.

or quotation – or, indeed, any provision setting out how the default market value is to be determined if there have been no sales, purchases or quotations but, for whatever reason, the requirements described in the list above are not satisfied.

There is a further issue to be considered in relation to net value under the 2011 GMRA. Neither the definition of 'net value'[75] nor paragraph 10(f)(iii) sets out with any clarity the time at which the net value is to be determined. (In the 2000 GMRA, by contrast, paragraph 10(e)(ii) clearly stipulates that it is the net value as at the default valuation time which is to be used.)

Under the 2011 GMRA, however, in contrast to the 2000 GMRA, there is no need for a default valuation notice to be served before the default valuation time in order for the sale or purchase prices or quotations to be used to establish the default market value (see above).

---

75   Paragraph 10(e)(iii) of the 2011 GMRA.

Accounting

Andrew Spooner
Deloitte LLP

The key accounting question for sale and repurchase arrangements (or repos) and stock lending transactions involving the transfer of a financial instrument, from the perspective of the repo seller or stock lender (the 'transferor'), is whether the asset subject to the transfer is removed from the balance sheet and recognised in the balance sheet of the repo buyer or stock borrower (the 'transferee'). In accounting speak, the removal of an item from the balance sheet is referred to as 'derecognition' and the inclusion of an asset in the balance sheet is referred to as 'recognition'. These terms will be used throughout this chapter.

In the United Kingdom, the accounting requirements that apply to repos and stock lending will vary depending on the accounting framework applied by the reporting entity. This chapter summarises the applicable guidance on this topic in International Financial Reporting Standards (IFRS) and UK Generally Accepted Accounting Practice (UK GAAP). The concepts used in IFRS and UK GAAP in this area are broadly similar. This chapter does not cover US GAAP. It is of note that, even though the US and IFRS disclosure requirements for transactions that pass or fail the 'derecognition test' are the same, the test itself is not. Accordingly, the accounting for these transactions under US GAAP differs from IFRS and UK GAAP.

1. IFRS in the United Kingdom

Since 2005, companies incorporated in and whose shares are listed on a regulated market of the European Union or European Economic Area are required to apply IFRS in their consolidated financial statements[1] (ie, they cannot apply UK GAAP).

Each EU Member State may, if they wish, extend the requirement to apply IFRS to the consolidated financial statements of non-listed companies and to the separate (ie, company only) financial statements of reporting entities. In the United Kingdom, entities not required to apply IFRS by the EU IAS regulation are permitted, but not required, to apply IFRS. Consequently, it is possible that a UK-listed group will apply UK GAAP in the separate financial statements of the ultimate parent company and its subsidiaries but apply IFRS in the group financial statements. Conversely, it is possible for IFRS to be applied by all entities in a listed group (ie, that both the consolidated and separate financial statements of the UK parent and the separate financial statements of all its subsidiaries are prepared in accordance with IFRS, subject to any overseas subsidiaries being permitted to apply IFRS).

---

1   Article 4 of the IAS Regulation.

At the time of writing, UK GAAP is going through a period of significant change; for periods beginning on or after January 1 2015 a package of new standards ('new UK GAAP')[2] comes into force. This change will impact all but the smallest entities and, as new UK GAAP is available for early adoption, a wider range of alternative approaches to the derecognition of financial assets are currently available.

1.1 IFRS accounting requirements

The accounting standard relevant to the accounting for repos and stock lending is IAS 39 *Financial Instruments: Recognition and Measurement*. The International Accounting Standards Board (IASB) has been working for some time on replacing IAS 39 with a new standard, IFRS 9 *Financial Instruments*. The new standard was finalised and issued in July 2014. At the time of writing, IFRS 9 has not been endorsed for use in Europe. However, the introduction of IFRS 9 will not change the accounting requirements in this area for IFRS reporters as the requirements for derecognition in IAS 39 and IFRS 9 are the same.

The derecognition requirements of IAS 39 and IFRS 9 apply to financial instruments only. A repo or lending of a non-financial item (eg, property or inventory), will not be subject to the requirements of IAS 39 or IFRS 9 but will be subject to other requirements in IFRS, notably IAS 18 *Revenue* and IFRS 15 *Revenue from Contracts with Customers*.[3] This chapter focuses on the accounting for repos and lending of financial instruments only. It is of note that the definition of a financial instrument in IFRS is broad and, in practice, includes loans, bonds, most derivatives and equity securities, among other financial assets.

1.2 Principles of derecognition

A financial asset is derecognised (ie, removed from the balance sheet or 'statement of financial position' of the transferor), when, and only when, either the contractual rights to the asset's cash flows expire, or the asset is transferred and that transfer qualifies for derecognition.

For repos and stock lending the critical question is whether a transfer of the financial asset that is subject to the repo or stock lending arrangement leads to derecognition of the asset. To answer this question, IAS 39 and IFRS 9 apply a combination of two concepts:
- a 'risks and rewards' concept; and
- a control concept.

These concepts are reflected in a set of criteria – in the form of a decision tree – to be satisfied for the transferred financial asset to qualify for full or partial derecognition. Where these criteria are not met, the asset fails derecognition and continues to be recognised in full.

---

[2] FRS 100 *Application of Financial Reporting Requirements* and related standards, including FRS 101 *Reduced Disclosure Framework* and FRS 102 *The Financial Reporting Standard Applicable in the UK and Republic of Ireland*.

[3] IFRS 15 applies for annual accounting periods beginning on or after January 1 2017, although like IFRS 9, at the time of writing it has not been endorsed for use in Europe.

The risks and rewards test seeks to establish the extent to which, having transferred a financial asset, the transferor continues to be exposed to the risks of ownership of the asset and/or continues to enjoy the benefits that it generates. The control tests are designed to assess which entity, transferor or transferee, controls the asset (ie, which entity can direct how the benefits of that asset are realised).

The use of two, potentially conflicting, accounting concepts could lead to confusion in application. However, IAS 39 and IFRS 9 addresses this by providing a clear hierarchy for application of the two concepts. The risks and rewards tests are applied first, with the control tests used only where an entity has neither transferred substantially all, nor retained substantially all, of the risks and rewards of the asset.

Inherent in the derecognition model in IAS 39 and IFRS 9 is the notion of 'stickiness' (ie, it is more difficult to remove an asset from an entity's balance sheet than it is to recognise that asset initially). Derecognition cannot be achieved by mere transfer of legal title to a financial asset of another party. The substance of the arrangement must be assessed to determine whether the entity has transferred the economic exposure associated with the rights inherent in the asset (ie, its risks and rewards) and, additionally, in some cases, control of those rights.

1.3 Derecognition decision tree

Figure 1 on the next page illustrates the questions to be answered to determine whether a transferred asset is derecognised from the perspective of the transferor.

Step 1 – consolidation

The first step in the derecognition decision tree is relevant only if the reporting entity is determining the accounting for the arrangement in its consolidated financial statements, in which case the entity must first consolidate all its subsidiaries before progressing further down the decision tree. The entity's subsidiaries may include special purpose entities (SPEs), one of which may, in fact, be the entity that acquired the transferred asset. The requirements to consolidate subsidiaries are contained in IFRS 10 *Consolidated Financial Statements*. The requirements to consolidate subsidiaries under IFRS are not considered in this chapter.

The purpose of this first step is to ensure that, where the transferee is a subsidiary, the derecognition analysis is applied at the level of the group to which it belongs when consolidated financial statements are being prepared. This ensures that the derecognition analysis is determined from the perspective of the group, not from the perspective of the individual entity that transferred the asset to the transferee. The effect of this is that repos and stock lending agreements between two entities in the same group will generally lead to continued recognition of the transferred asset in the consolidated balance sheet. This could differ to the outcome in the separate financial statements of the transferor. This approach is supported by the broader consolidation principle that intercompany transactions between entities within a group are eliminated on consolidation for the purposes of preparation of consolidated financial statements.

Accounting

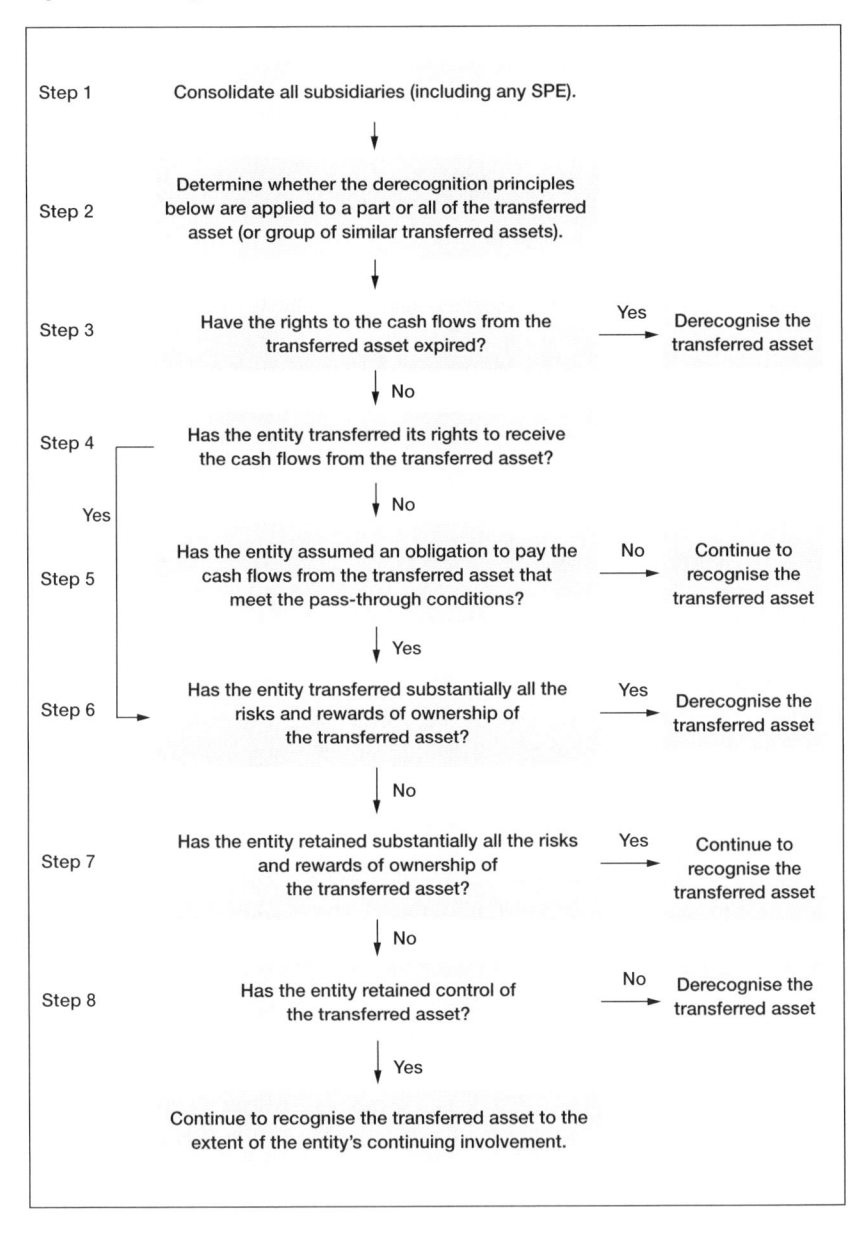

Figure 1: Derecognition decision tree

Step	Question/Action	Outcome
Step 1	Consolidate all subsidiaries (including any SPE).	
Step 2	Determine whether the derecognition principles below are applied to a part or all of the transferred asset (or group of similar transferred assets).	
Step 3	Have the rights to the cash flows from the transferred asset expired?	Yes → Derecognise the transferred asset
Step 4	Has the entity transferred its rights to receive the cash flows from the transferred asset?	Yes → go to Step 6
Step 5	Has the entity assumed an obligation to pay the cash flows from the transferred asset that meet the pass-through conditions?	No → Continue to recognise the transferred asset
Step 6	Has the entity transferred substantially all the risks and rewards of ownership of the transferred asset?	Yes → Derecognise the transferred asset
Step 7	Has the entity retained substantially all the risks and rewards of ownership of the transferred asset?	Yes → Continue to recognise the transferred asset
Step 8	Has the entity retained control of the transferred asset?	No → Derecognise the transferred asset
	Continue to recognise the transferred asset to the extent of the entity's continuing involvement.	

Step 2 – identify the asset subject to the transfer

To proceed with the derecognition analysis, it is necessary to determine what is the asset to which the next steps in the decision tree must be applied. IAS 39 provides detailed guidance on determining whether the asset subject to transfer is considered to be all or part of the cash flows of a financial instrument. In most repos and stock lending transactions the asset subject to transfer is all of the cash flows of the asset, not a portion. In practice, therefore, for repos and stock lending transactions, the next steps in the derecognition tree are applied to the financial asset in full.

Step 3 – determine whether the rights to the assets have expired
At its most basic, an asset ceases to be recognised in the balance sheet if the rights to cash flows of the asset cease to exist because they have expired. Examples include a bond maturing, or the unexercised expiry of a derivative purchased option.

As the rights to the cash flows of the asset subject to transfer in a repo or stock lending transaction do not normally expire at the date the asset is transferred, this step is easy to answer. The rights to the cash flows of the transferred asset still exist; the analysis therefore moves on to step 4.

Step 4 – transfer of the contractual rights to receive cash flows
Transfers for accounting purposes can occur in one of two ways. Either the contractual rights to receive the cash flows of the asset are transferred from the transferor to the transferee, or they are retained by the transferor but the transferor has agreed to pass the cash flows it receives from the asset to the transferee (without transferring the contractual rights to those cash flows). The latter approach is referred to as a 'pass-through' transaction. Whether the contractual rights to receive the cash flows have been transferred is a legal question.

With respect to repos and stock lending transactions, the transferee becomes the legal owner of the asset subject to the repo or stock lending arrangement, so that the contractual rights to receive the cash flows of the asset will have been transferred. Therefore, the derecognition analysis moves to step 6. As such, step 5, which assesses whether the pass-through test is met, is generally not relevant for repos and stock lending transactions.

Steps 6 and 7 – transfer or retention of risk and rewards
Steps 1 to 5 of the derecognition decision tree do not draw on the two key derecognition concepts: risks and rewards, and control. Steps 6 and 7, however, do draw on these concepts and they generally determine whether the asset subject to transfer in a repo or stock loan continues to be recognised on the transferor's balance sheet (ie, fails derecognition). These two steps focus on whether substantially all of the risks and rewards of ownership of the asset have been retained by the transferor, or have transferred to the transferee. The greater the risks and rewards retained, the greater is the likelihood of continued recognition. The degree to which risks and rewards have transferred and its effect on the accounting outcome is illustrated in Figure 2 on the next page.

When an entity transfers substantially all of the risks and rewards of ownership of a financial asset, the asset should be derecognised. The entity may have to recognise separately any rights and obligations created or retained in the transfer.

There is no 'bright line' in IAS 39 and IFRS 9 on what is meant by 'substantially all' of the risks and rewards of ownership of an asset. Therefore, a significant degree of judgment is required when applying the risks and rewards test.

Figure 2

Situation		Accounting treatment for transferor
Substantially all risks and rewards transferred		Derecognise transferred asset Recognise any new assets/liabilities
Neither retained nor transferred substantially all risks and rewards of ownership	Control no longer retained by transferor – transferee can unilaterally sell the transferred asset	
	Control retained by transferor – transferee cannot unilaterally sell the transferred asset	Recognise asset liability to the extent of continuing involvement
Substantially all risks and rewards retained		Continue to recognise transferred asset Proceeds from transfer are recognised as a financial liability

More risks and rewards transferred from the transferor to the transferee

There are other references in IAS 39 and IFRS 9 to yardsticks that need to be met for derecognition. For example, when comparing the original and revised terms of a modified financial liability to establish whether it has been substantially modified and should result in derecognition of the original liability and recognition of a new one, the terms are considered to be 'substantially different' if the present value of the cash flows under the new terms is at least 10% different from the discounted present value of the remaining cash flows of the original financial liability. While IAS 39 and IFRS 9 does not apply this 90% present value test to the derecognition of financial assets, it seems imprudent to conclude that substantially all of the risks and rewards of ownership of an asset have been transferred when computations show that the entity still retains more than 10% of the exposure to the variability in present value of the expected future cash flows after the transfer.

1.4 Examples of derecognition

IAS 39 and IFRS 9 provide three examples[4] of when a transferor has transferred substantially all of the risks and rewards of ownership, hence derecognition is required:

- an unconditional sale of a financial asset;
- a sale of a financial asset together with an option to repurchase the financial asset at its fair value at the time of repurchase; and
- a sale of a financial asset together with a put or call option that is deeply out of the money (ie, an option that is so far out of the money that it is highly unlikely to be in the money before expiry).

In the first example, it is clear that there has been a transfer of all the risks and rewards of ownership of the asset. In the second example, the entity has sold the asset and, although it can call the asset back, this can only be done at the fair market value of the asset at the time of reacquisition. The entity is in the same economic position as having sold the asset outright: if it went into the market to reacquire the asset it would be required to pay fair market value (ie, it has transferred the full price risk of the asset). In the third example, the option is highly unlikely, if ever, to be exercised (and has very little value at the date the asset is transferred) so IAS 39 and IFRS 9 deem the transferor to be in substantially the same economic position as having made an unconditional sale.

1.5 Examples of continued recognition

IAS 39 and IFRS 9 provide examples[5] of transfers where substantially all of the risks and rewards of ownership have been retained, hence derecognition is precluded:

- a sale and repurchase transaction where the repurchase price is a fixed price or the sale price plus a lender's return;
- a securities lending transaction;
- a sale of a financial asset together with a total return swap that transfers the market risk back to the transferor entity;
- a sale of a financial asset together with a deep in-the-money written put option or purchased call option (ie, an option that is so far in the money that it is highly unlikely to go out of the money before expiry); and
- a sale of short-term receivables in which the transferor entity guarantees to compensate the transferee for credit losses that are likely to occur.

IAS and IFRS note that fixed-price repos and stock lending transactions do not result in derecognition for the transferor where substantially all of the risks and rewards of ownership of the asset subject to the arrangement are retained. This will be the case where the asset sold is the same, or substantially the same, as the asset to be repurchased. Similarly, if the transferee has a right to return a different asset and that substitute asset is similar and of equal fair value at the repurchase date to the

---

4   See IAS 39:AG39, IFRS 9:B3.2.4.
5   See IAS 39:AG40, IFRS 9:B3.2.5.

original asset, the accounting treatment will be equivalent to that applicable to a repo requiring the same asset to be returned.

1.6 Applying the risks and rewards test to repos

In the case of a fixed-price repo, the transferor (repo seller) retains substantially all of the risks and rewards of ownership of the transferred asset through the obligation to reacquire the transferred asset at a fixed price in the future. Economically, the transferor has retained substantially all of the risks and rewards of ownership, therefore the transferred asset is not derecognised. The cash proceeds the transferor receives under the repo are recognised with a counter-entry to recognise a financial liability for the obligation to return the proceeds plus accrued interest back to the transferee at maturity of the repo. The presentation of the repo in the financial statements of the transferor follows the economic substance of the arrangement – a borrowing that is collateralised on the transferred asset. The inverse presentation applies for the transferee. The transferee does not recognise the asset subject to the transfer as substantially all of the risks and ownership of the asset are retained by the transferor. Hence, the proceeds paid to acquire the asset are recognised as a loan receivable due from the transferor that is collateralised on the asset that was received from the transferor.

In the case of a variable-price repo, where the repurchase price is equal to the future market value of the asset subject to the repo at the date of repurchase, the accounting treatment differs to that of a fixed-price repo. In this case, substantially all of the risks and rewards of ownership are transferred from the transferor to the transferee (since the transferor will repurchase the asset at its future market value, not at a fixed price so it has transferred the full price risk) and therefore the transferor derecognises the asset. Consequently, the transferor recognises the proceeds received, removes the asset from its balance sheet and recognises a gain or loss on disposal of the asset equal to the difference between the proceeds received (or receivable) and the carrying value of the asset transferred at the date of transfer. The inverse accounting applies for the transferee. The transferee recognises the asset transferred to it at the amount it pays (or is payable), being the fair value of the asset at the date of transfer. Consequently, the transferor or transferee do not present this as a collateralised lending or borrowing transaction as – for accounting purposes – the transaction is regarded as an outright sale with an obligation to repurchase at future market value, as opposed to a financing transaction.

In these two examples (the fixed-price repo and variable-price repo), steps 6 and 7 provide a clear answer regarding whether the asset subject to the arrangement is derecognised by the transferor or not. Consequently, no consideration is given to step 8, which assesses which entity controls the asset. Step 8 applies only where substantially all the risks and rewards of ownership are neither transferred nor retained by the transferor. This could be the case where the risks and rewards of ownership are effectively shared between the transferor and the transferee. An example is the transfer of a financial asset under the terms of which the transferor is obliged to buy the asset back at a fixed price if the market price is below a certain level at the repurchase date. From the transferor's perspective, the transaction is economically similar to a concurrent sale of an asset and sold put option at a fixed price over that asset; from the transferee's perspective, the transaction is economically similar to an asset purchase and purchased put option at a fixed price over the same asset. Where the deemed exercise price of the economic option is neither deeply in nor deeply out of the money, the risks and rewards of ownership of the transferred asset are shared between the transferor and the transferee (and therefore are neither substantially retained nor transferred by the transferor). In this situation the analysis moves to step 8.

1.7 Applying the risks and rewards test to stock lending

Stock lending that involves the transfer of a financial asset in exchange for the receipt of a fee by the transferor from the transferee during the period of the stock lend (with the transferee returning the financial asset to the transferor on maturity of the transaction) results in the retention by the transferor of substantially all of the risks and rewards of ownership of the asset. The asset subject to the stock loan is neither derecognised by the transferor nor recognised by the transferee. The accounting entries are generally limited to recognition of fee income by the transferor and fee expense by the transferee. The fee income and expense will generally be measured on an accruals basis evenly over the period of the stock loan. Further accounting entries may be required where the transferee (stock borrower) provides the transferor (stock lender) with cash or other collateral. Whether cash or other collateral is recognised by the transferor (and concurrently derecognised by the transferee) will depend on whether the transferor has unlimited access to that collateral.

In some cases, a transaction may be economically similar to a simultaneous stock loan and stock borrow over different securities transacted as a single arrangement (ie, an asset exchange for a specified period). At inception, the two parties exchange one non-cash financial asset for a different non-cash financial asset and at maturity the assets are returned. Throughout the arrangement the parties have access to the financial asset they received under the arrangement. As substantially all of the risks and rewards of ownership of the assets transferred (in both directions) by the respective transferors are retained, the transferors do not derecognise the asset they lend and do not recognise the asset they borrow. Like a conventional stock loan, any fee charged will be recognised as fee income or expense as appropriate by the two parties.

Step 8 – control

As discussed above, the control assessment is only relevant in those cases where the transferor neither retains nor transfers substantially all of the risks and rewards of ownership of an asset. In those cases, an assessment is required of whether the transferor has retained control of the asset. Control of the asset is considered from an economic but not necessarily a legal perspective. The transferor assesses its control of the asset by considering what the transferee can practically do with it. If the transferee has the practical ability to sell the asset in its entirety to a third party that is unrelated either to it or the transferor and is able to exercise that right unilaterally and without the imposition of additional restrictions on the transfer, the transferee controls the asset. Therefore, the transferor must have relinquished control.[6] One of the considerations in determining which party has control of the asset is whether the transferee can sell it without restrictions and has the practical ability to repurchase the asset in the market in the future if it needs to. That practical ability will depend on whether the transferred asset is readily available in the market.

Where it is deemed that the transferor no longer controls the asset, it will derecognise the asset in full and it will be recognised in full by the transferee.

Where control of the asset continues to be retained by the transferor, the accounting entries are more complex. The aim is to present in the balance sheet the exposure to the asset that the transferor has retained and to remove the amount of the exposure the transferor has transferred to the transferee. Inversely, the transferee must present the exposure to the asset it has taken on, and reflect the fact that some exposure still lies with the transferor. These complex accounting entries are referred to as 'continuing involvement accounting'. The requirements of continuing involvement accounting are beyond the scope of this chapter.

The following table gives examples of the accounting treatment of various repurchase arrangements under IAS 39 and IFRS 9.

Features	Applying derecognition in IAS 39 and IFRS 9
The repurchase price is an agreed price that is higher than the market value at the date of sale.	If the repurchase price results in a return for the transferee equivalent to that of a cash lender, then the transferor has not transferred, but has retained, substantially all of the risks and rewards of ownership of the asset. The return earned by the transferee is consistent with the economic substance of the arrangement being a collateralised cash lending for the transferee and a collateralised cash borrowing for the transferor.
The repurchase leg of the arrangement is an option for the transferor to repurchase the asset at a fixed price (where the call option is neither deeply in nor out of the money), and the asset is readily obtainable in the market.	The asset is derecognised. The transferor has neither transferred nor retained substantially all of the risks and rewards of ownership, but has lost control over the asset since the asset is readily obtainable in the market (ie, the transferee has the practical ability to sell the asset and, if necessary, source the asset again to settle the call option it has sold to the transferor). The transferor will recognise a stand-alone call option in its statement of financial position measured at fair value with gains or losses recognised in profit or loss.

continued on next page

---

6   IAS 39:23, IFRS 9:3.2.9.

Features	Applying derecognition in IAS 39 and IFRS 9
The repurchase leg of the arrangement is an option for the transferor to repurchase the asset at a fixed price (where the call option is neither deeply in nor out of the money), and the asset is not readily obtainable in the market.	The transferor has neither transferred nor retained substantially all of the risks and rewards of ownership but has retained control of the asset because the asset is not readily obtainable in the market (ie, the transferee does not have the practical ability to sell the asset and source the asset again). Hence, the transferor continues to recognise the asset to the extent of its continuing involvement.
The repurchase leg of the arrangement is an option for the transferee to require the transferor to repurchase the asset at a fixed price (where the put option is neither deeply in nor out of the money) and the asset is readily obtainable in the market.	The asset is derecognised. This is because the transferor has neither retained nor transferred substantially all of the risks and rewards of ownership, but has lost control over the asset because the asset is readily obtainable in the market (ie, the transferee has the practical ability to sell the asset). The transferor recognises a stand-alone put option in its statement of financial position measured at fair value with gains or losses recognised in profit or loss.
The repurchase leg of the arrangement is an option for the transferee to require the transferor to repurchase the asset at a fixed price (where the put option is neither deeply in nor out of the money) and the asset is not readily obtainable in the market.	The transferor has neither transferred nor retained substantially all of the risks and rewards of the asset and has retained control of the asset because the asset is not readily obtainable in the market (ie, the transferee does not have the practical ability to sell the asset). Hence it continues to recognise the asset to the extent of its continuing involvement.
The repurchase price, whether paid through a put, a call or a forward arrangement, is the market price at the time of repurchase.	The transferor has transferred substantially all of the risks and rewards of ownership of the asset because the transferor can only repurchase the asset at its fair market value. Hence, the asset is derecognised.
The asset repurchased is substantially the same as the asset that is transferred or the transferee can substitute the asset with one that is of similar or equal fair value.	The transferor retains substantially all the risks and rewards of ownership of the asset and, therefore, derecognition is precluded.

If, following the inception of the arrangement, whether a repo or a stock loan, cash collateral is paid or received as between the transferor and transferee, this will be recognised by the receiver (and derecognised by the payer) if the recipient of that cash has unlimited access to it. If the recipient's right to the cash is restricted (eg, the cash is available only to the recipient in the case of default under the arrangement), then the recipient will not recognise the cash until such time as default occurs. If the recipient's right to the cash is unlimited, then the recipient will recognise the cash and concurrently recognise a liability to return the cash to the payer. Similar principles apply in relation to non-cash collateral.

2. **UK GAAP**

UK GAAP has various strands and different entities may, or may be required to, apply different requirements. With respect to derecognition of financial assets, the first question to ask is which set of recognition and measurement requirements is applicable?

Most entities applying new UK GAAP[7] will have a choice between applying FRS 101 *Reduced Disclosure Framework* and FRS 102 *The Financial Reporting Standard Applicable in the UK and Republic of Ireland*. Entities reporting under FRS 101 will use the recognition and measurement requirements of the full EU-endorsed IFRS which currently include those of IAS 39. Entities reporting under FRS 102 may choose whether to apply the financial instruments recognition and measurement requirements of that standard,[8] or those of either IAS 39 or IFRS 9. Application of new UK GAAP is mandatory for accounting periods beginning on or after January 1 2015, but is available for early adoption.

Even before the publication of new UK GAAP, not all entities reporting under 'old' UK GAAP applied the same financial instrument recognition and measurement requirements. Some entities were required[9] to apply FRS 26 *Financial Instruments: Recognition and Measurement*, which is the UK GAAP equivalent of IAS 39. An entity that is not required to apply FRS 26 may choose to apply it if it so wishes.[10] 'Old' UK GAAP, apart from the Financial Reporting Standard for Smaller Entities (FRSSE), will cease to be available after the mandatory effective date of new UK GAAP.

With respect to derecognition of financial assets, the requirements of FRS 26, IAS 39 and IFRS 9 are the same. Therefore if an entity is applying

- 'old' UK GAAP including FRS 26;
- FRS 101;
- FRS 102 with the recognition and measurement provisions of IAS 39; or
- FRS 102 with the recognition and measurement provisions of IFRS 9

the derecognition requirements will be the same for IFRS. The remainder of this section will be applicable only if a reporting entity is applying either FRS 102 with Sections 11 and 12 in their entirety or 'old' UK GAAP excluding FRS 26.

---

7   See footnote 2 above.
8   Found in Section 11 *Basic Financial Instruments* and Section 12 *Other Financial Instrument Issues*.
9   FRS 26 is part of a wider package of accounting standards that must be applied at the same time. Application of FRS 26 under old UK GAAP is required for listed companies or entities preparing their financial statements in accordance with the UK Companies Act fair value accounting rules except for those entities applying the Financial Reporting Standard for Smaller Entities (FRSSE). The Companies Act fair value accounting rules are set out in the Large and Medium-sized Companies and Groups (Accounts and Reports) Regulations 2008 or the Large and Medium-sized Limited Liability Partnerships (Accounts) Regulations 2008.
10 Which includes FRS 23 *The Effects of Changes in Foreign Exchange Rates*, FRS 24 *Financial Reporting in Hyperinflationary Economies* and FRS 29 *Financial Instruments: Disclosures*.

2.1 Reporting entities applying Sections 11 and 12 of FRS 102

Section 11 of FRS 102 is relevant to the accounting for repos and stock lending. The requirements in Section 11 relating to the derecognition of financial assets are taken directly from the equivalent section of the IFRS for Small and Medium Entities (IFRS for SMEs). The IFRS for SMEs was published by the IASB in 2009 to provide an alternative framework to IFRS for entities that are eligible to apply it. Although generally based on IFRS principles, in developing the IFRS for SMEs the IASB sought to simplify some areas including the accounting for financial instruments.

The requirements of Section 11 are contained in just three paragraphs.[11] This means that many of the more specific requirements of IAS 39 and IFRS 9 are not replicated in Section 11. Although it may be appropriate to apply guidance from IAS 39 and IFRS 9 where it is illustrating a principle that is common to both IFRS and Section 11, care must be taken not to apply specific rules in IAS 39 and IFRS 9 that could be seen as restrictions on or deviations from those principles.

(a) Principles of derecognition

As under IFRS, the determination of whether a financial asset that is subject to a repo or stock lending arrangement should be derecognised depends on the application of both risks and rewards and control tests. The control test is applied only where an entity has retained some (but not all) significant risks of ownership. However, under Section 11, there is no concept of 'continuing involvement accounting'. The asset transferred either continues to be recognised or is derecognised in its entirety.

Where an entity either has transferred substantially all the risks and rewards of ownership, or has retained some – but not all – significant risks of ownership but has transferred control of the asset, the asset is derecognised and any rights and obligations retained or created in the transfer are recognised separately.

Where an entity has either retained substantially all the risks and rewards of ownership, or has retained some – but not all – significant risks of ownership and has retained control of the transferred asset, the asset continues to be recognised in its entirety (not just to the extent of the continuing involvement) and the entity recognises a financial liability for the consideration received.

The financial liability recognised for the consideration received will be accounted for as any other financial instrument within the scope of Sections 11 and 12. Accordingly, the accounting will depend on whether it is 'basic' or not. If non-basic, the liability will be measured at fair value through profit or loss. This is likely to be the case where repayment of the liability is related to the performance of the transferred asset that is not derecognised (eg, where an entity must pass on some of the cash flows on a financial asset only to the extent it receives them). Under IAS 39, an entity will not be required to measure the equivalent financial liability at fair value through profit or loss.

2.2 Reporting entities applying 'old' UK GAAP excluding FRS 26

FRS 5 *Reporting the Substance of Transactions* is the accounting standard in 'old' UK

---

[11] FRS 102:11.33–35.

Accounting

GAAP (other than FRS 26) that provides guidance relevant to the accounting for repos and stock lending. FRS 5 includes an Application Note B that specifically sets out the accounting treatment for repurchase arrangements. FRS 5 applies to a broad range of transactions, not solely those involving financial instruments. However, for the purposes of this chapter, only the application of FRS 5 to repurchase and stock lending arrangements involving the transfer of financial assets (not non-financial items) is considered.

(a)   *Principles of derecognition*

The basis for determining whether the transfer of a financial asset results in its derecognition from the transferor's balance sheet is an analysis, from the transferor's perspective, of whether there is a significant change in the exposure to the risks and rewards of the assets that is transferred as a result of the transaction. FRS 5[12] provides that where a transaction involving a previously recognised asset results in no significant change in the entity's rights or other access to benefits to that asset, or its exposure to the risks inherent in those benefits, the entire asset should continue to be recognised, stressing that where a transaction is – in substance – a financing transaction, it should be presented as such. Conversely, where all significant rights or other access to benefits and significant exposure to the risks inherent in those benefits relating to the asset are transferred, the entire asset ceases to be recognised by the transferor.[13]

FRS 5 includes a concept of 'linked presentation' which applies to certain non-recourse finance that is repayable only out of the proceeds of the asset transferred/financed. This chapter does not include the detailed criteria for linked presentation as it is unlikely that such an approach would be relevant for repos and stock lending arrangements since any repurchase features will breach one of the criteria for linked presentation, which is that "there is no provision whatsoever whereby the entity may either keep the item on repayment of the finance or reacquire it at any time".[14]

3. **FRS 5 Application Note B**

FRS 5 Application Note B specifically considers sale and repurchase agreements. It addresses two types of transaction:
- the sale and potential repurchase of an existing asset; and
- the future purchase of an asset that has been acquired on the entity's behalf by a third party.

There are three possible outcomes to a transaction under Application Note B:
- the substance is that of a secured loan requiring gross presentation of the original asset and treatment of receipts as a financial liability;
- the substance is that of an outright sale allowing derecognition of the original asset and treatment of receipts as proceeds of sale; or

---
12   FRS 5:21.
13   FRS 5:22.
14   FRS 5:26(b).

- the seller no longer has access to the original asset, but has a new asset. An example of this outcome would be the sale of an asset together with a call option to repurchase the asset at a fixed price in the future. Application Note B21 describes the appropriate accounting entries for this scenario – the seller would derecognise the asset, recognise a new asset (being the call option) and recognise a liability for any unconditional obligations. It would also be required to disclose information in its accounts about the main features of the arrangement.

Consistent with the approach taken in IAS 39 (and FRS 26), fixed-price repurchase arrangements will result in continued recognition of the asset transferred by the transferor (and no recognition by the transferee of the asset transferred). The proceeds the transferor receives on transfer are recognised as a borrowing as, in substance, the transaction is treated as a collateralised borrowing. This is because there is no significant change in exposure to risks and rewards from either the perspective of the transferor or the transferee. The transferee will account for the transaction as a collateralised lending. Correspondingly, consistent with the approach taken in IAS 39, IFRS 9 and FRS 26, a repurchase arrangement where the repurchase price is based on the future market price of the asset transferred at the repurchase date will result in derecognition of the asset by the transferor and its recognition by the transferee. This is because the risks and rewards of the asset have passed from the transferor to the transferee.

Although FRS 5 does not specifically refer to stock lending arrangements, the guidance on sale and repurchase arrangements is equally relevant. Where a stock loan leads to retention by the transferor of the risks and rewards of the financial instrument subject to the stock lending arrangement, the transferor (stock lender), will not derecognise the asset nor will it be recognised by the transferee (stock borrower).

4. Comparison of IFRS and UK GAAP

As explained above, some entities reporting under new UK GAAP may apply the recognition and measurement requirements of IAS 39 or IFRS 9. In addition, IAS 39 and IFRS 9 are the same as FRS 26 in 'old' UK GAAP with respect to the rules on derecognition of financial assets. However, it is still possible that entities reporting under FRS 102 (in accordance with the requirements of Sections 11 and 12) or 'old' UK GAAP excluding FRS 26, may reach the same accounting conclusion on a repo or stock lending transaction as under IFRS. This will be particularly true for repos and stock lending arrangements where the transferor (repo seller or stock lender) retains substantially all of the risks and rewards of ownership of the asset subject to transfer. Similarly, although there is little guidance on the accounting treatment for cash collateral, it is likely that this will be similar across the different accounting frameworks. Even though the standards differ – with IFRS being more prescriptive – all applicable standards have the concept of risks and rewards at their heart. As many repo and stock lending transactions are structured in such a way as to be financings in economic substance (ie, their objective is to limit economic exposure of the repo buyer and stock borrower to the transferred asset), the outcome under all applicable accounting standards will often be the same.

Differences in the accounting treatment for repo and stock lending transactions between IAS 39, FRS 26, IFRS 9 and FRS 5 or Section 11 of FRS 102 are more likely in the event of more esoteric transactions where the repo seller or stock lender neither transfers nor retains substantially all the risks and rewards of the transferred asset. In such cases, IFRS and UK GAAP that includes FRS 26, IAS 39 or IFRS 9 has more prescriptive guidance so will not necessarily result in the same accounting outcome achieved under FRS 102 (in accordance with the requirements of Sections 11 and 12) or 'old' UK GAAP excluding FRS 26. In such circumstances, the conclusion as to whether the transferred asset continues to be recognised or is derecognised under Section 11 is more likely to be consistent with 'old' UK GAAP excluding FRS 26 than with IFRS.

UK taxation of repo and stock lending transactions

Nicholas Noble
Fieldfisher

1. Introduction

1.1 Summary of tax issues

This introduction summarises some of the key tax issues which can arise in the context of both repo and stock lending transactions. These issues are then illustrated by reference to the specific tax treatment which applies in the United Kingdom to repos (Part 2) and stock lending (Part 3).

A repo transaction needs to be considered in the context of the following possible areas of taxation:

- repo interest – involving both the possible taxation of the income for the buyer and the deductibility of the expense for the seller as well as the possibility of there being an obligation to withhold tax from the payment by the seller, also, there is the possibility of repo interest being negative due to the special nature of the purchased securities;
- income on the purchased securities – here it is necessary to consider the tax treatment of the dividends (for equities) or coupons (for fixed-income securities) as well as the possible taxation of any manufactured payment relating to the real income and, again, whether the manufactured payment can be paid gross or whether an amount in respect of tax has to be deducted;
- interest on cash margin – the issues in 'repo interest' need to be considered also in the context of cash margin, bearing in mind that it could be either party posting margin in the form of cash and also that negative interest rates can apply to cash balances;
- income on margin securities – the issues in 'income on the purchased securities' need to be considered also in this context, bearing in mind that it could be either party posting margin securities;
- the sale and repurchase of securities – whether the sales are considered as a disposal giving rise to a capital gain (or conceivably loss) or otherwise crystallising a profit/loss for the seller (on the initial sale) or the buyer (on the subsequent repurchase);
- transfers of securities – whether these attract stamp duties and other transfer taxes;
- sales taxes such as VAT – whether any of the transactions or payments attract these taxes.

A stock lending transaction needs to be considered in the context of the following possible areas of taxation:
- the lending fee – involving both the possible taxation of the income for the lender and the deductibility of the expense for the borrower as well as the possibility of there being an obligation to withhold tax from the payment by the borrower;
- income on the loaned securities – here it is necessary to consider the tax treatment of the dividends (for equities) or coupons (for fixed-income securities) as well as the possible taxation of the manufactured payment relating to the real income and, again, whether the manufactured payment can be paid gross or whether an amount in respect of tax has to be deducted;
- interest on cash collateral – similar issues to those for 'repo interest' need to be considered also in this context, bearing in mind it could be either party posting collateral in the form of cash and also bearing in mind that cash balances can attract negative interest rates and that interest on cash collateral may be factored into the lending fee;
- income on collateral securities – the issues in 'income on the loaned securities' need to be considered also in this context, bearing in mind it could be either party posting securities as collateral;
- the transfer and redelivery of the loaned securities – whether they are considered as a disposal giving rise to a capital gain (or conceivably loss) or otherwise crystallising a profit/loss for the lender (on the initial transfer) or the borrower (on the subsequent redelivery);
- transfers of securities – whether these attract stamp duties and other transfer taxes;
- sales taxes such as VAT – whether any of the transactions or payments attract these taxes.

Each of the above tax issues has to be considered for both parties, which may well be subject to different tax regimes or jurisdictions. The position may be further complicated in that the jurisdiction of the issuer of the underlying debt or equity securities may introduce a further layer of tax treatment that may, in turn, affect the amount of the payment to be made under the repo or stock lending transaction.

While securities under repo and stock lending transactions are often substituted to avoid the problems that can arise in terms of income and manufactured payments, both repos and stock loans are still in many cases held over dividends/interest payment dates whether for commercial reasons or for tax reasons (eg, one holder may be able to avoid suffering an adverse tax treatment such as a withholding).

The introduction of tri-party agents and agent lenders into the structure can further complicate the tax issues as they typically share fees or make other charges to one or both of the parties to the transaction.

1.2 **Repo: general principles**
The detailed UK tax treatment of a repo is dealt with in Part 2 of this chapter.

As a general rule of thumb, it is desirable that:
- repo interest should be treated in the same way as interest payable on a cash loan for the seller and the buyer and in the context of withholdings, and the same for interest on cash margins;
- manufactured payments should be treated in the same way as the real dividends or interest of which they are representative and payments in respect of cash collateral should be treated as interest;
- there should be no withholdings from repo interest or manufactured payments;
- as the sale and repurchase is, from a financial perspective, effectively by way of security (and only expected to be temporary without the economic risk of ownership being transferred) the tax treatment would be not to treat the initial sale of the purchased securities as a disposal of them by the seller and not to consider the initial purchase as an acquisition by the buyer;
- given that the transfer of securities is only temporary and is not accompanied by the transfer of effective economic ownership, it should be expected that the transfers are not subject to taxes which can be imposed on outright sales for value;
- with the exception of the services that may be being provided by agents, there are no sales of goods or supplies of services which might be expected to attract sales taxes.

In the detailed description of the UK tax regime for repos in Part 2 below, we seek to identify whether the actual UK tax treatment follows the desired treatment described above.

1.3   **Stock lending: general principles**
The detailed UK tax treatment of stock lending transactions is contained in Part 3 of this chapter.

As a general rule of thumb, it is desirable that:
- manufactured payments should be treated in the same way as the real dividends or interest of which they are representative and the same for manufactured payments in respect of securities collateral;
- there should be no withholdings from manufactured payments;
- given that the transfer of the stock loan is only temporary, it should be expected that the transfers are not treated as sales and purchases and not subject to taxes which can be imposed on outright sales for value;
- with the exception of the services that may be provided by agents, there are no sales of goods or supplies of services which might be expected to attract sales tax;
- the lender should as far as possible be no worse off than if it had continued to hold the stock lent and should be better off by earning the stock lending fee;
- those stock lenders which are exempt (eg, registered pension schemes and charities) should as far as possible be exempt in respect of the stock lending fee.

In the detailed description of the UK tax regime for stock lending transactions in Part 3 below, we seek to identify whether the actual UK tax treatment follows the desired treatment above.

2. UK taxation of repo transactions

2.1 Introduction

This Part deals with the detailed UK taxation treatment of repo transactions. On April 6 2013 there were major changes in the taxation of repos for income tax purposes. These are now dealt with under the disguised interest provisions rather than under the special provisions in Sections 607–14 of the Income Tax Act (ITA) 2007. There was a consultation by HMRC in 2012 on the law relating to manufactured payments which concluded with HMRC producing the Summary Reponses on December 11 2012 together with draft legislation. This legislation is contained in Schedule 29 to the Finance Act (FA) 2013 and applies to dividend or interest payments made on or after January 1 2014.

This Part sets out the UK tax rules relating to repos as from January 1 2014. There are parallel income tax and corporation tax provisions and the format of this Part is to consider the income tax treatment first in a transaction between two income taxpayers and, after that, to look at the corporation tax treatment in a transaction between two corporation taxpayers and finally transactions combining the two. It should be borne in mind that the most likely combination for a repo is a transaction between two companies, one of which could be an income taxpayer (ie, not resident and not trading in the United Kingdom through a permanent establishment).

By the time you have finished reading this Part, you may feel just a touch of regret at what now seem like halcyon days when income and corporation tax rules relating to repos could almost all be found in or around Section 730A of the Income and Corporation Taxes Act (ICTA) 1988. In this brave new world of 2015 we have to get used to flitting between at least seven acts (two different Income Tax Acts, two different Corporation Tax Acts, the Taxation of Chargeable Gains Act 1992, the Value Added Tax Act 1994 and the FA 1986), constantly bearing in mind at least seven parallel tax worlds (income tax, corporation tax, tax on capital gains, VAT, stamp duty, stamp duty reserve tax and now, potentially, financial transaction tax). The responsibility for this rests partly with HMRC's (justified) frustration with the taxpayer avoidance schemes utilising repos and also partly with the tax simplification process which in this situation has produced amplification more than simplification.

Hopefully, however, this Part will prove helpful even if it only pulls together and explains the disparate and exotic places where the tax repo legislation can be found.

2.2 Repos/income tax provisions

Sections 381A–381E of the Income Tax (Trading and Other Income) Act (ITTOIA) 2005 (forming Chapter 2A Part 4) inserted by Schedule 12 to the FA 2013 set out the provisions relating to disguised interest. These provisions charge to income tax any return economically equivalent to interest in relation to a principal amount where a person is party to an arrangement which produces such a return.

There is such a return if (and only if):
- it is reasonable to assume that it is a return by reference to the time value of that amount of money; and
- it is a rate reasonably comparable to what is (in all the circumstances) a commercial rate of interest; and
- at the relevant time there is no practical likelihood that the return will cease to be produced in accordance with the arrangement unless the person by whom it falls to be produced is prevented (by reason of insolvency or otherwise) from producing it.

The reference to relevant time is the time when the person becomes a party to the arrangement or, if later, when the arrangement begins to produce a return for the person.

Tax is charged on the full amount of the return under Chapter 2A Part 4 of the ITTOIA 2005 arising in the tax year and the person liable is the person receiving or entitled to the return. There are provisions which seek to prevent double taxation. The disguised interest charge is a secondary charge in that it does not apply if the return is otherwise subject to income tax or would be but for an exemption. A claim can be made under Section 381D of the ITTOIA 2005 for one or more consequential adjustments if a tax other than income tax is charged in relation to the return which is charged under Chapter 2A.

The detailed mechanical provisions for repos contained in Sections 607–14 of the ITA 2007 have all been repealed with effect from April 6 2013.

The new disguised interest provisions can be seen to work to some extent as expected in the case of the following repo:

Example 1

Seller		Buyer
	Sale of securities →	
	← Purchase price £10m	
	← Repurchase of securities	
	Repurchase price of £10.4m →	

There is no interest or dividend payable on the securities sold during the life of the repo. In the case of example 1, the seller (ie, the borrower) sells the securities to the buyer (ie, the lender) for £10 million and repurchases them for £10.4 million with the £400,000 difference being equivalent to a rate of interest. The buyer will be taxed on the £400,000 return under Chapter 2A Part 4 of the ITTOIA 2005.

The points in the following paragraphs should be noted in relation to repos and income taxpayers.

Chapter 2A Part 4 of the ITTOIA 2005 taxes the buyer on the return equivalent to a rate of interest under the repo. It provides for no deduction for the seller in respect of the equivalent borrowing cost. If the seller is a trader acting in the course of his trade, he may obtain a trading expense on general principles subject to the usual conditions (eg, the seller is a financial trader). This absence of a deduction will presumably dissuade most income taxpayers from using repos as a means of borrowing since they will prefer to choose a method of financing which gives them a deduction for their borrowing costs. There should be excluded from such income taxpayers those who can obtain a trading expense (eg, a financial trader) or non-residents whether corporate or non-corporate who are not trading in the United Kingdom through a permanent establishment if they can obtain a deduction in their home jurisdiction.

Chapter 2A Part 4 of the ITTOIA 2005 does not deem the return equivalent to a rate of interest to be interest. There is no mechanism to require the deduction of UK tax from that return. Therefore, the income obtained in the case of a repo between income taxpayers can always be paid gross. A non-resident buyer (ie, lender) might like to enter into a repo with an income tax borrower since the return equivalent to the rate of interest can be obtained without the deduction of UK income tax at source. Section 811 of the ITA 2007 (individuals) and Section 815 of the ITA 2007 (companies) then provide that there can be no direct UK tax liability.

Buyers (ie, lenders) which are exempt from income tax (eg, registered pension schemes and charitable trusts) will want to be sure that the return equivalent to a rate of interest which they receive is exempt in their hands before they enter into a repo. Section 186(1)(a) of the FA 2004 exempts a registered pension scheme from income tax as regards income derived from investments or from deposits held for the purpose of the registered pension scheme. Section 186(3) of the FA 2004 extends the meaning of investments to include futures contracts and option contracts and income derived from investments includes income derived from such contracts. If the return equivalent to a rate of interest under Chapter 2A Part 4 of the ITTOIA 2005 is income derived from a futures contract or options contract, then the income tax exemption for registered pension schemes will apply. However, the wording of Chapter 2A Part 4 does not fall naturally within the exemption since the Chapter 2A return arises on an amount of notional principal not from any contracts. The application of the exemption may, in practice, be permitted by HMRC. It seems that a charitable trust will have no exemption from income tax in respect of a Chapter 2A return because the return will not fall within the definition of savings and investment income in Section 532 of the ITA 2007 or within any of the other income tax exemptions applicable to charitable trusts. A repo is also unlikely to be an approved charitable investment for a charitable trust so it is doubtful that the trust would enter into such a transaction.

It is necessary to consider the form of repo which is more like a stock loan. There may be a repo of a security which is sufficiently hard to obtain in the market so that the stock lending return which the seller obtains equals or exceeds the return equivalent to a rate of interest. Example 2 below considers a repo where the two returns are equal and example 3 considers a repo where the stock lending return is greater than the interest return and in each case there is no set-off.

Example 2

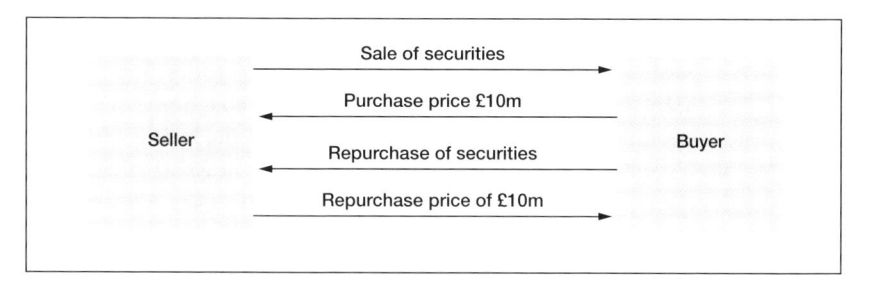

```
                    Sale of securities
                 ──────────────────────▶
                    Purchase price £10m
                 ◀──────────────────────
     Seller                                    Buyer
                   Repurchase of securities
                 ◀──────────────────────
                  Repurchase price of £10m
                 ──────────────────────▶
```

In example 2, the buyer obtains no return equivalent to a rate of interest because it has sacrificed it in order to borrow the securities during the life of the repo. It would seem that Chapter 2A would not apply.

Example 3

```
                    Sale of securities
                 ──────────────────────▶
                   Purchase price £10.1m
                 ◀──────────────────────
     Seller                                    Buyer
                   Repurchase of securities
                 ◀──────────────────────
                  Repurchase price of £10m
                 ──────────────────────▶
```

In example 3, the stock lending return exceeds the interest return so there is a net payment by the buyer (ie, the lender) to the seller (ie, the borrower). Chapter 2A again would not seem to apply because there is no return equivalent to a rate of interest. The profit of £100,000 which the seller obtains is more of a stock lending return which is different from a return equivalent to a rate of interest.

It is likely that a buyer would only enter into the transactions in examples 2 and 3 if he is a financial trader, in which case he will in any event be taxed on his accounting profit. The overall effect of the above will mean that income taxpayers should not enter into repos without at least considering their position carefully beforehand.

2.3 Repos/manufactured payments/income tax

It is then necessary to consider the manufactured payment provisions in relation to repos if there is a real dividend or real interest payable on the securities sold under the repo during the life of the repo and assuming that there is no substitution. Substitution means that the securities sold and on which a dividend or interest would become payable are handed back before the dividend/interest is payable and replaced by other securities on which no dividend/interest is payable during the life of the repo.

Sections 614ZA–614ZD of the ITA 2007 apply where there is a manufactured

payment relationship. There is such a relationship where all the following conditions A–C are satisfied.
- Condition A is that under any arrangement an amount is payable by or to a person or any other benefit is given by or to the person including the release of the whole or part of any liability to pay an amount.
- Condition B is that the arrangements relate to the transfer of securities.
- Condition C is that the amount or value of the other benefit is representative of a dividend or interest payment on the securities or will fall to be treated as representative of such a dividend or interest when it is paid or given.

Once all of conditions A–C are satisfied, the person who pays the manufactured dividend/interest obtains no tax deduction for the payment except where it is deductible as a trading expense (eg, he is a financial trader) (Section 614ZC). The recipient of the manufactured payment is treated as if he had received the real dividend/interest payment except where the recipient is a trader and the manufactured payment is brought in as part of his trading profits (Section 614ZD). The recipient is not entitled to a tax credit in the case of a manufactured dividend and is not entitled to double tax relief in respect of a manufactured dividend or interest. (The legislation refers to manufactured payments representative of or in respect of dividends or interest and so the references to manufactured dividends or manufactured interest are used as shorthand for these longer expressions.)

Example 4

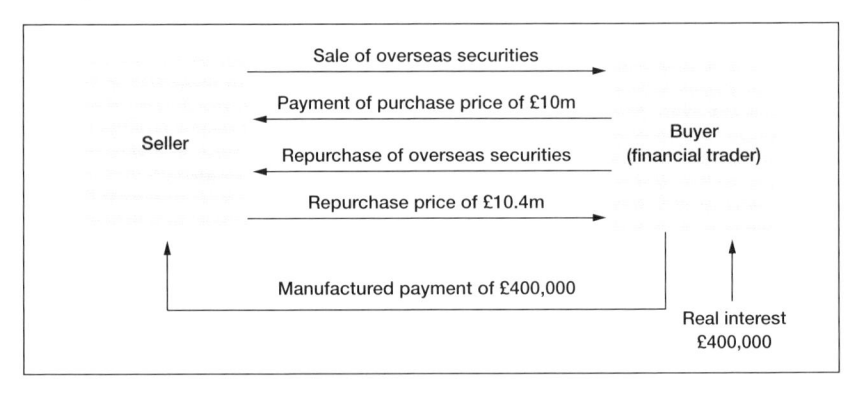

```
                    Sale of overseas securities
                    ─────────────────────────────►
                    Payment of purchase price of £10m
                    ◄─────────────────────────────
     Seller                                              Buyer
                    Repurchase of overseas securities    (financial trader)
                    ◄─────────────────────────────
                    Repurchase price of £10.4m
                    ─────────────────────────────►

                    Manufactured payment of £400,000
            ▲───────────────────────────────────┐
                                                │
                                                │ Real interest
                                                │ £400,000
```

The consequences of the repo in example 4 are the same as in example 1 except that the buyer receives the real dividend/interest and pays a manufactured dividend/interest to the seller. The buyer as a financial trader will be taxable on the real dividend/interest payment received but will obtain a deduction for the manufactured dividend/interest paid to the seller. The seller is taxed on the manufactured dividend/interest payment as if it were the real dividend/interest. The equivalent results would happen if the sale of the securities under the repo was a sale of UK equities and the buyer received the real dividend and passed it on as a manufactured dividend. In this and other examples the repo interest and the manufactured intererest are the same (ie, £400,000) but, in practice, these two amounts will almost always be different.

The buyer, when he manufactures the manufactured payment to the seller, has to consider whether it is necessary to deduct income tax from the manufactured payment, and, in particular, whether the manufactured payment is within the withholding provisions of Sections 918–21 of the ITA 2007. (Sections 922 to 925 have been repealed.) The deduction of UK income tax from manufactured payments is as follows. (It should be noted throughout this Part that HMRC does not regard manufactured payments as annual payments requiring the deduction of tax under, for example, Section 898 of the ITA 2007.):

- If there is a manufactured payment on UK shares (not being Real Estate Investment Trust (REIT) shares), there is no deduction since there is no provision requiring a deduction in these circumstances.
- If there is a manufactured payment on UK shares being REIT shares, then there is a deduction of the same amount as would have been deducted under Section 973 of the ITA 2007 (Section 918 of the ITA 2007).
- If the manufactured payment is on net paying UK securities, then there is a deduction of income tax at the basic rate (Section 919) because the payer is not a company.
- If the manufactured payment is on gross paying UK securities (eg, UK government bonds), then there is no deduction of income tax (Section 921).
- If there is a manufactured payment in respect of overseas shares or overseas bonds, there is no deduction of income tax since there is no provision requiring a deduction in these circumstances.

Example 5

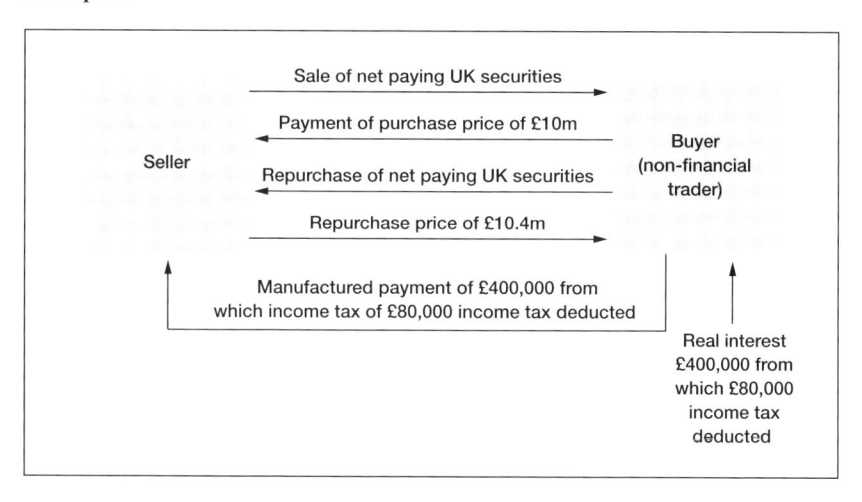

```
                Sale of net paying UK securities
              ─────────────────────────────────►
                Payment of purchase price of £10m
              ◄─────────────────────────────────
  Seller                                              Buyer
                Repurchase of net paying UK securities  (non-financial
              ◄─────────────────────────────────        trader)
                Repurchase price of £10.4m
              ─────────────────────────────────►

              Manufactured payment of £400,000 from
              which income tax of £80,000 income tax deducted

                                              Real interest
                                              £400,000 from
                                              which £80,000
                                              income tax
                                              deducted
```

The HMRC view is that manufactured payment provisions in Sections 614ZA–614ZD of the ITA 2007 do still apply, even in the case of example 6 where there is no provision for manufactured payments.

Example 6

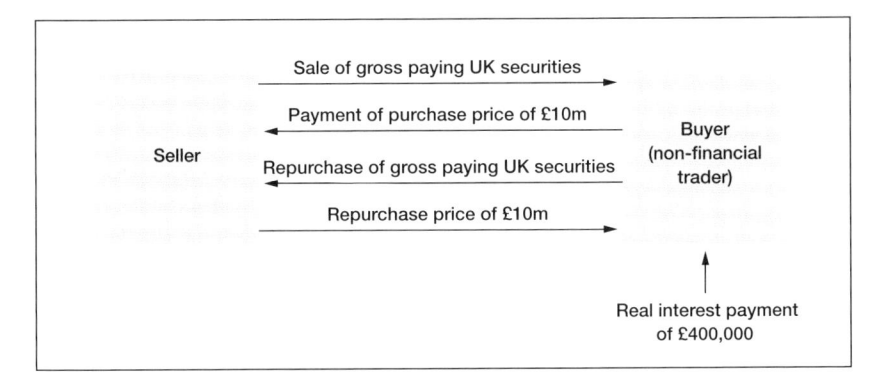

```
                Sale of gross paying UK securities
         ─────────────────────────────────────────▶
                Payment of purchase price of £10m
         ◀─────────────────────────────────────────
Seller                                                  Buyer
                Repurchase of gross paying UK securities  (non-financial
         ◀─────────────────────────────────────────      trader)
                Repurchase price of £10m
         ─────────────────────────────────────────▶

                                                    ▲
                                                    │
                                              Real interest payment
                                                  of £400,000
```

In the case of example 6, HMRC considers that conditions A–C are still satisfied. Even though no amount is payable, a benefit is given which is representative of a dividend or interest payment and this falls within conditions A–C and therefore there is a payment representative of interest for tax purposes within Sections 614ZA–614ZD of the ITA 2007.

2.4 Accrued income scheme

Sections 654 and 655 of the ITA 2007 contain provisions whereby, if there is a repo as defined in Section 654, the transfer of the securities and the transfer back of the securities is not subject to the accrued income scheme. There is a repo within Section 654 where:

- securities are transferred under an agreement to sell them; and
- the transferor or a person connected with him is required to buy back the securities under the agreement or a related agreement; or
- the transferor or a person connected with him is required to buy back the securities as the result of exercising an option acquired under the agreement or related agreement; or
- the transferor or person connected with him exercises an option to buy back the securities which option was acquired under the agreement or related agreement.

2.5 Repos/corporation tax provisions

The form of the corporation tax legislation for repos differs significantly from the income tax legislation in that the specific detailed legislation for repos remains in place and there is a specific deduction for the finance charge. Repos are divided into:

- creditor repos (Section 543 of the Corporation Tax Act (CTA) 2009);
- creditor quasi-repos (Section 544);
- debtor repos (Section 548);
- debtor quasi-repos (Section 549);
- non-standard repos (Section 555).

A creditor and a debtor repo are looking at the creditor and debtor relationships in respect of the repo. Each of these different provisions are considered in turn.

A creditor repo is where the buyer meets the following five conditions:
- condition A – there is an arrangement where the seller receives money or an asset from the buyer (the advance); and
- condition B – in accordance with generally accepted accounting practice (GAAP) the accounts for the buyer for the period in which the advance is made record a financial asset in respect of the advance; and
- condition C – under the arrangement the seller sells securities at any time to the buyer; and
- condition D – the arrangement makes provision conferring a right or imposing an obligation on the buyer to sell the same or similar securities at any subsequent time; and
- condition E – in accordance with GAAP the subsequent sale of the same or similar securities extinguishes the financial asset in respect of the advance in the accounts of the buyer.

Example 7

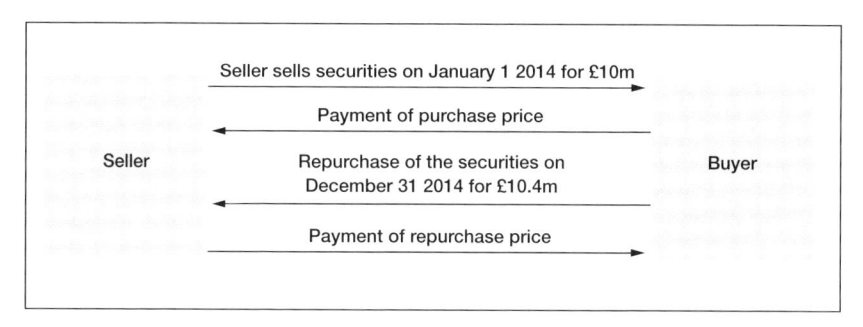

```
                 Seller sells securities on January 1 2014 for £10m
                 ──────────────────────────────────────────────────→
                           Payment of purchase price
                 ←──────────────────────────────────────────────────
     Seller                                                              Buyer
                      Repurchase of the securities on
                         December 31 2014 for £10.4m
                 ←──────────────────────────────────────────────────
                           Payment of repurchase price
                 ──────────────────────────────────────────────────→
```

The accounting entries for the buyer in accordance with GAAP are outlined below. In this and the following examples, there is an assumption that £0.4 million interest or other relevant amount of interest has accrued to the profit and loss account over the relevant period.

January 1 2014 making of advance	Dr financial asset £10 million Cr cash £10 million
December 31 2014 sale of securities	Dr cash £10.4 million Cr financial asset £10.4 million

The buyer does have a creditor repo because all of the conditions A–E in Section 543 of the CTA 2009 are satisfied.

A creditor quasi-repo is where the buyer does not have a creditor repo and where each of conditions A–E below are met:

- condition A – there is an arrangement where a person receives from the buyer any money or other asset (the advance); and
- condition B – in accordance with GAAP the accounts of the buyer for the period in which the advance is made record a financial asset in respect of the advance; and
- condition C – under that or any other arrangement a person sells securities to the buyer or any other person; and
- condition D – the arrangement or other arrangement makes provision conferring a right or imposing an obligation on the buyer to sell the securities or any other securities at any subsequent time or makes provision conferring such a right or imposing such an obligation on any other person and makes other relevant provision. There is other relevant provision if the arrangement makes provision for the receipt of money, securities or other assets from the buyer for the purpose of enabling the other person to make the subsequent sale or for the discharge of any liability to the buyer under the arrangement for that purpose; and
- condition E – in accordance with GAAP the subsequent sale of the securities or other securities by the buyer or the receipt of the assets from the buyer or the discharge of the liability to the buyer will extinguish the financial asset in respect of the advance recorded in the accounts of the buyer.

Example 8

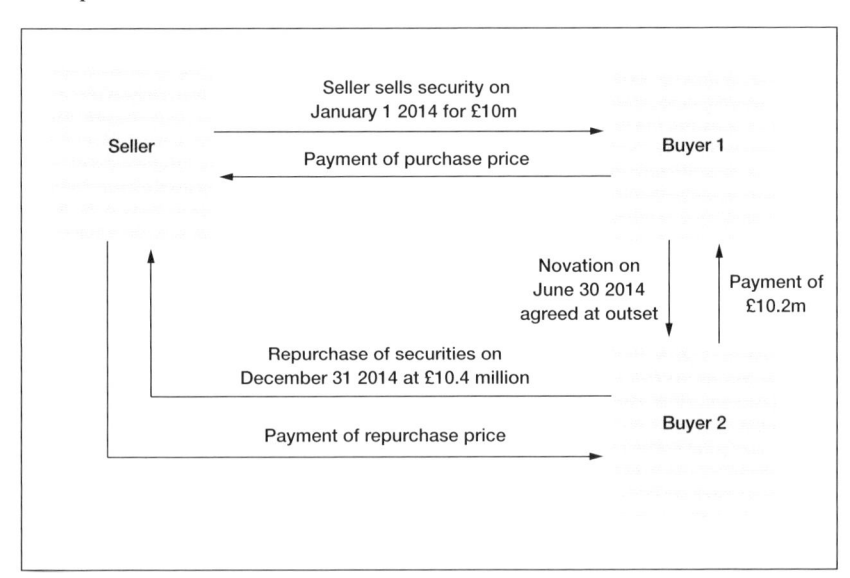

Example 8 is an example of a creditor quasi-repo where there is novation by the buyer. In words:
- the Seller sells securities to the Buyer 1 on January 1 2014 for £10 million;
- Buyer 1 novates its rights and obligations under the repo to Buyer 2 agreed at

the outset on June 30 2014 and Buyer 1 receives £10.2 million from Buyer 2;
- Buyer 2 sells the securities to the Seller on December 31 2014 for £10.4 million.

The accounting entries for Buyer 1 in accordance with GAAP are:

January 1 2014 making of advance	Dr financial asset £10 million Cr cash £10 million
June 30 2014 novation to Buyer 2	Dr cash £10.2 million Cr financial asset £10.2 million

Buyer 1 does not have a creditor repo because it does not meet conditions D and E of the creditor repo conditions. In particular, Buyer 1's financial asset is not extinguished by the sale of the securities. Buyer 1 does have a creditor quasi-repo because all of conditions A–E of Section 544 of the CTA 2009 are satisfied.

The accounting entries for Buyer 2 in accordance with GAAP are as follows:

June 30 2014 making of the advance	Dr financial asset £10.2 million Cr cash £10.2 million
December 31 2014 sale of the securities	Dr cash £10.4 million Cr financial asset £10.4 million

Buyer 2 does not have a creditor repo because conditions A, B and C of the creditor repo conditions are not met. Buyer 2 does have a creditor quasi-repo because all of the conditions A–E in Section 544 of the CTA 2009 are satisfied.

Where there is a creditor repo or a creditor quasi-repo, the Corporation Tax Acts for the purposes of corporation tax on income have effect as if any buyer did not hold the securities for any period during which the agreement is in force, and any buyer did not make in that period any payment representative of the income payable in respect of the securities (Section 545 of the CTA 2009). This restates the accounting treatment of a repo for a buyer. The buyer does not recognise the temporarily acquired asset on its balance sheet but instead recognises a financial asset of an advance to the seller. Equally, when a buyer receives a real dividend payment in respect of the securities and makes a manufactured payment in respect of that income, it will recognise in its profit and loss account neither the income it receives nor the corresponding manufactured payment. There are exceptions in Section 545(4)–(6).

Another effect of the creditor repo or a creditor quasi-repo is that the advance is treated as a money debt for the purposes of the loan relationship legislation where the money debt is owed by the seller to the buyer (Section 546). The arrangement is treated as a transaction for the lending of money and any amount which in accordance with GAAP is recognised in the accounts of the buyer as a finance return is treated as interest receivable under the money debt. The interest is treated as received at the earlier of the repurchase date or when it becomes clear that the repurchase will not take effect.

A debtor repo is one where the seller meets the following conditions A–E:
- condition A – there is an arrangement where the seller receives from the buyer any money or other asset (the advance); and
- condition B – in accordance with GAAP the accounts of the seller for the period in which the advance is received record a financial liability in respect of the advance; and
- condition C – under the arrangement the seller sells any securities at any time to the buyer; and
- condition D – the arrangement makes provision conferring a right or imposing an obligation on the seller to buy the securities or similar securities at any subsequent time; and
- condition E – in accordance with GAAP the subsequent repurchase of the securities or similar securities extinguishes the financial liability in respect of the advance recorded in the accounts of the seller.

Example 9
This is the same as example 7 above except it looks at the repo from the seller's (ie, the borrower's) perspective. The accounting entries for the seller in accordance with GAAP are:

January 1 2014 receipt of advance	Dr cash £10 million Cr financial liability £10 million
December 31 2014 repayment of advance	Dr financial liability £10.4 million Cr cash £10.4 million

It should be noted that the seller also has a debtor repo in the case of example 8 since the seller still meets each of conditions A–E for a debtor repo in Section 548 of the CTA 2009.

A debtor quasi-repo is where a seller does not have a debtor repo and where each of the conditions A–E below are met:
- condition A – the seller receives money or other asset (the advance) under an arrangement; and
- condition B – in accordance with GAAP the accounts of the seller for the period in which the advance is received record a financial liability in respect of the advance; and
- condition C – under that or any other arrangement the seller or any other person sells securities at any time; and
- condition D – the arrangement or other arrangement makes provision conferring a right or imposing an obligation on the seller to buy the securities

or other securities at any subsequent time or makes provision conferring such a right or imposing such an obligation on any other person and makes other relevant provision. There is other relevant provision if the arrangement makes provision for the receipt of any money or other asset from the seller under the arrangement for the purpose of enabling the other person to make the subsequent purchase or for the discharge of any liability to the seller under this arrangement; and

- condition E – in accordance with GAAP the subsequent buying of the securities by the seller or the receipt of the asset from the seller or the discharging of the liability to the seller under the arrangement or other arrangement would extinguish the financial liability in respect of the advance recorded in the accounts of the seller.

Example 10

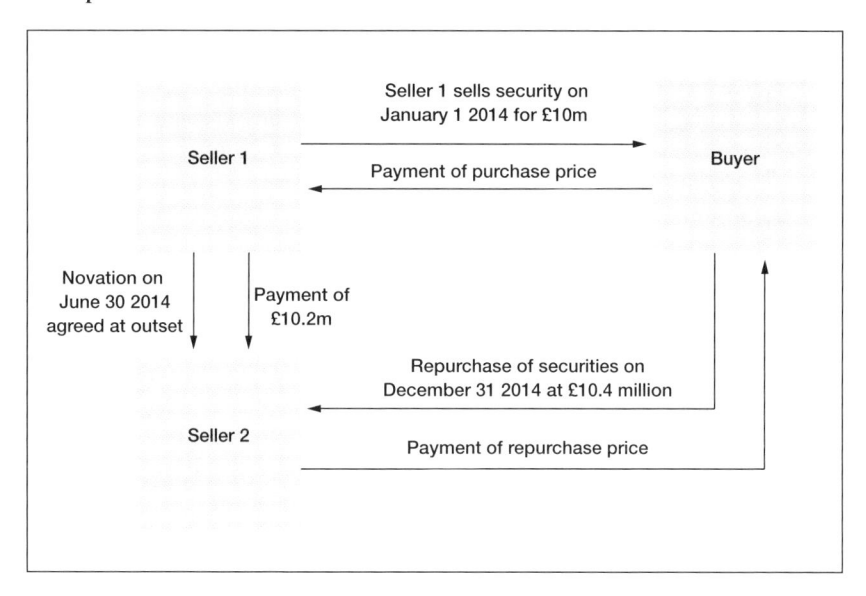

```
                    Seller 1 sells security on
                    January 1 2014 for £10m
    Seller 1  ─────────────────────────────>  Buyer
              <─────────────────────────────
                 Payment of purchase price

Novation on       │
June 30 2014      │  Payment of
agreed at outset  │    £10.2m
    │             │
    ▼             ▼
                    Repurchase of securities on
                    December 31 2014 at £10.4 million
    Seller 2  <─────────────────────────────
              ─────────────────────────────>
                 Payment of repurchase price
```

Example 10 is the reverse of example 8 above.

Example 10 is an example of a debtor quasi-repo. In words:
- Seller 1 sells securities to the Buyer on January 1 2014 for £10 million;
- Seller 1 novates on June 30 2014 its rights and obligations under the repo to Seller 2 agreed at the outset and Seller 1 pays Seller 2 £10.2 million;
- the Buyer sells the same or similar securities to Seller 2 on December 31 2014 for £10.4 million.

The accounting entries for Seller 1 in accordance with GAAP are:

January 1 2014 receipt of advance	Dr cash £10 million Cr financial liability £10 million
June 30 2014 novation payment to Seller 2	Dr financial liability £10.2 million Cr cash £10.2 million

Seller 1 does not have a debtor repo because it does not meet conditions D and E of the debtor repo conditions. In particular, Seller 1's financial liability is extinguished otherwise than by the purchase of the securities. Seller 1 does have a debtor quasi-repo because all the conditions A–E of Section 549 of the CTA 2009 are satisfied.

The accounting entries for Seller 2 in accordance with GAAP are:

June 30 2014 receipt of advance	Dr cash £10.2 million Cr financial liability £10.2 million
December 31 2014 purchase of securities	Dr financial liability £10.4 million Cr cash £10.4 million

Seller 2 does not have a debtor repo because it does not meet condition C (ie, it does not sell any securities to the Buyer). Seller 2 does have a debtor quasi-repo because all of conditions A–E in Section 549 of the CTA 2009 are satisfied.

Where there is a debtor repo or a debtor quasi-repo, the Corporation Tax Acts for the purpose of corporation tax on income for a seller have the effect as if the seller held the securities which are sold for the period while the arrangement is in force and the seller did not in that period receive amounts representative of the income payable on the securities (Section 550 of the CTA 2009). This is restating the accounting treatment of a seller in a financing repo. The seller will continue to recognise on its balance sheet the securities temporarily transferred on the basis that it retains the risks and rewards of price fluctuations. (The finance represented by the proceeds of sale are recorded in the seller's accounts as cash received and a liability whose amount will increase at a constant rate to reflect the implicit rate of interest with the 'interest' being debited as a finance charge in the profit and loss account on an accruals or amortised cost basis. Equally, the income on the securities will continue to be recognised in the seller's accounts as if the sale of the securities had not taken place.)

Another effect of the debtor repo or a debtor quasi-repo is that the advance is treated as a money debt for the purposes of the loan relationship legislation where the money debt is owed by the seller to the buyer. The arrangement is treated as a transaction for the lending of money and any amount which, in accordance with GAAP, is recorded as a finance charge in the accounts of the seller is treated both for the purposes of the loan relationship legislation and for the purposes of deduction of income tax (ie, Part 15 of the ITA 2007) as interest payable under the money debt (Section 551 of the CTA 2009). The interest is treated as paid at the earlier of the time when the repurchase takes place or the time when it becomes apparent that there will be no repurchase. It is in this context that it is necessary to decide whether the interest is short interest or annual interest. If it is short interest, it is not necessary to consider the deduction of UK tax at all. If the interest is annual interest, there is a deduction of UK tax unless there is a relief (eg, a nil or reduced rate of deduction by virtue of a double tax treaty).

There are adjustments for non-standard repos or where there is a redemption during the course of the repo.

2.6 Repo/manufactured payments/corporation tax

It is now necessary to consider the manufactured payments rules in relation to repos where all the parties are subject to corporation tax. The income tax rules on manufactured payments in Sections 614ZA–614ZD of the ITA 2007 and the income tax rules on the deduction of tax from manufactured payments in Sections 918–21 of the ITA 2007 have already been discussed in paragraph 2.3 above. There are corporation tax rules on manufactured payments representative of dividends (but not on interest) in Sections 814A–814D of the CTA 2010 parallel to the income tax rules in Sections 614ZA–614ZD of the ITA 2007. The operation of Sections 918–21 of the ITA 2007 in relation to corporation tax is discussed below.

In fact, in the case of repos between two corporation tax companies, the manufactured payment rules in Sections 814A–814D of the CTA 2010 drop away and do not apply because Section 545(2)(b) of the CTA 2009 (in the case of creditor repos and creditor quasi-repos) and Section 550(3) of the CTA 2009 (in the case of debtor repos and debtor quasi-repos) deem there to be no manufactured payment for the purpose of corporation tax on income.

Sections 545(2)(b) and 550(3)(b) of the CTA 2009 do not apply for the purposes of income tax.

The manufactured payments are not manufactured payments within Sections 614ZA–614ZD of the ITA 2007 which takes effect only for the purposes of income tax.

However, Section 925A of the ITA 2007 locks the buyer (ie, the lender) into the withholding provisions in Sections 918–21 – discussed immediately before example 5 above – where it makes a manufactured payment to the seller (ie, borrower). In the case of a repo between two companies within the charge to corporation tax, all manufactured payments can be made gross if:

- the manufactured payment is in respect of UK shares (not being REIT shares) – there is no deduction since there is no specific provision requiring a deduction in these circumstances;
- it is a manufactured payment in respect of UK shares being REIT shares – there is the same deduction as would have to be made under Section 973 of the ITA 2007 which in this case is nil (Sections 918(3) and 973 and Regulation 7(2) of SI 2006/2867);

- the manufactured payment is in respect of net paying UK securities – the deduction in this case is nil (Sections 919(4) and 933);
- the manufactured payment is in respect of gross paying UK securities (eg, UK government bonds) – there is no deduction of UK tax (Section 921);
- there is a manufactured payment in respect of overseas shares or overseas bonds – there is no deduction of UK tax since there is no specific provision requiring a deduction in these circumstances.

2.7 Accrued income scheme

The accrued income scheme does not apply for the purposes of corporation tax.

2.8 Mixed party repos

It is now necessary to reconsider the above in respect of mixed party repos (ie, where one party is an income taxpayer and the other is a corporation taxpayer). Part 2 has so far considered repo transactions and the making of manufactured payments where the parties to the repos are all subject to income tax or where the parties to the repos are all subject to corporation tax. This section looks at repos, first where the seller is a corporation taxpayer and the buyer is an income taxpayer and, second, where the seller is an income taxpayer and the buyer is a corporation taxpayer.

Where the seller is a corporation taxpayer and the buyer is an income taxpayer the effects are as follows.

The debtor repo provisions apply to the seller. This means it is deemed for the purposes of corporation tax on income to continue to own the securities which are the subject of the repo and not to receive the manufactured payment from the buyer (Section 550(3) of the CTA 2009) and it obtains a deduction for the deemed interest on the repo as if it were interest on a money debt which is a loan relationship (Section 551). The seller is taxed as if it received the real dividend if the repo crosses a dividend or coupon date.

The buyer is taxed on any return equivalent to a rate of interest under Sections 381A–381E of the ITTOIA 2005. If, for example, it is a registered pension scheme, it may obtain an income tax exemption for that return depending on whether or not the finance return is agreed to derive from a futures contract or options contract or any other investment (see paragraph 2.2 above). The buyer will receive any real dividend/interest on the securities which are the subject of the repo arising during the course of the repo and will be subject to income tax in the normal course on that dividend/interest. It will obtain no deduction for any manufactured payment it makes to the seller unless it is a financial trader. In an extreme case where the buyer is not exempt and it buys securities for 100, receives real interest of 5 and sells back for 99, the buyer might be taxed on disguised interest of 4 and on real interest of 5 with no deduction for the deemed manufactured payment. If the buyer is a registered pension scheme, it will be exempt from income tax in respect of the real dividend received under Section 186 of the FA 2004. It will obtain no deduction for the manufactured payment made to the seller but this is unlikely to matter since it will have been exempt on the real dividend/interest received. The buyer will have to deduct tax under Sections 918 and 919 of the ITA 2007 as appropriate. It will not be able to pay gross under any of the provisions in Chapter 11 Part 15 of the ITA 2007 because it is not a company.

Where the seller is an income taxpayer and the buyer is a corporation taxpayer, the tax effects are as follows.

The seller will obtain no tax deduction for the finance charge. He will be taxed in the normal way on any manufactured payment received under Sections 614ZA–614ZD of the ITA 2007 as if it was the real dividend/interest payment but will obtain no double tax relief except where the foreign tax is deducted from the manufactured payment. If the seller is a registered pension scheme, for example, it could obtain no deduction for the finance charge but this is unlikely to matter because it would have been unlikely to have any taxable income against which any deduction could be set. If the seller is a registered pension scheme, it will presumably be exempt on the manufactured payment it receives as if it would be on a payment of the real income. The seller is not required to deduct income tax from the finance charge because the finance charge, so far as it is concerned, is not interest.

The creditor repo provisions apply to the buyer. This means it is deemed for the purposes of corporation tax on income as not owning the securities which are the subject of the repo and as not making the manufactured payment to the seller (Section 545(2) of the CTA 2009). The buyer is taxed on the finance return as if it had been interest on a money debt. The buyer is not taxable on any real dividend/interest received on the securities which are the subject of the repo and obtains no deduction for the manufactured payment. The buyer will be subject to the deduction provisions of Sections 918 and 919 of the ITA 2007 in respect of any manufactured payment made as appropriate.

Therefore, the tax treatment of a repo with a mixture of income and corporation taxpayers involves piecing together the correct components from the tax analysis where both parties are subject to income tax or both parties are subject to corporation tax.

2.9 Capital gains tax/corporation tax on chargeable gains

This section of Part 2 examines the capital gains tax and corporation tax on chargeable gains provisions in relation to repos.

Section 263A of the Taxation of Chargeable Gains Act (TCGA) 1992 contains the capital gains provisions relating to repos. It previously piggy-backed on the definition of a repo in Section 607 of the ITA 2007 but, with the repeal of Section 607 by the FA 2013, it has been necessary to insert a self-standing definition of a repo in Section 263A and this has been achieved by Paragraph 9 of Schedule 12 to the FA 2013 which has inserted a new Section 263AA(A1).

Section 263A(A1) provides that there is a repo where:
- the seller has agreed to sell securities to the buyer; and
- the seller or a person connected with him:
  - is required to buy back the securities under the agreement or a related agreement; or
  - is required to buy back the securities as a result of an option acquired under the agreement or a related agreement; or

- exercises an option to buy back the securities which were acquired under the agreement or a related agreement.

There is a new Section 263AA which provides a series of definitions largely for the purposes of Section 263A(A1). Therefore, in particular, 'securities' (as defined in Section 263AA(8)) also includes 'similar securities' (as defined in Section 263AA(5) and (6)).

If the seller is subject to income tax (eg, an individual), it is likely that the securities which are the subject of the repo will be held by him as a capital asset so that the danger for him will be a charge to capital gains tax made on the disposal of securities when they are sold. This charge is removed by Section 263A of the TCGA 1992 which provides that the sale is disregarded for the purposes of capital gains tax where there is a repo within Section 263A(A1) and where there is an acquisition of securities by the buyer and a disposal by him to the seller. If at any time after the sale to the buyer it becomes apparent that the buyer will not dispose of the securities to the seller, the buyer is treated as acquiring the securities for a consideration equal to the market value at that time (Section 263A(1A)). If at any time after the sale it becomes apparent that the seller will not acquire the securities on a repurchase, the seller is treated as disposing of the securities for a consideration equal to their market value at that time (Section 263(1B)).

If the seller is subject to income tax but exempt (eg, a registered pension scheme or a charitable trust), then the seller is not concerned by capital gains tax because it will be exempt in respect of the capital gains arising on any disposal.

If the seller is subject to corporation tax and undertaking the repo as part of its financial trade, then it realises no profit on the sale because Sections 548 and 550 of the CTA 2009 deem there to be no transfer of the securities for the purposes of corporation tax on income and the securities will not be chargeable assets for capital gains purposes. This is also the effect of the accounting treatment for the seller. If the seller is not a financial trader but the securities are loan relationships, then again Sections 548 and 550 take effect so that no profit is realised on the sale of such a loan relationship and the capital gains regime will not be applicable. If the seller is not a financial trader and the securities are not loan relationships (eg, equities), then Section 263A of the TCGA 1992 does not apply but paragraph 6 of Schedule 13 to the FA 2007 applies so that the sale of the equities and their subsequent purchase are ignored for the purposes of corporation tax on chargeable gains. Paragraph 11 of Schedule 13 to the FA 2007 achieves the same for the buyer's purchase and subsequent resale of the equities.

Section 263A of the TCGA 1992 applies only to the securities which are subject to the repo. It does not apply to movements of collateral which are treated as a stock loan and are therefore dealt with in Part 3 of this chapter. Interest on cash collateral is similarly dealt with in Part 3 of this chapter.

2.10 **Value added tax**

In order to determine the correct VAT treatment of repos, it is helpful to consider first the VAT treatment of stock lending, where the view of HMRC is set out both in its public notice and internal guidance, and which has been considered in a VAT tribunal case.

HM Customs & Excise (as it then was) was originally of the view that:

In VAT terms, there are exempt supplies under VATA 1994 Sch 9 Group 5 item 6 in both directions. The exempt value of the supply by the lender is the open market value of the securities transferred to the borrower, plus any interest received or other payment in lieu of interest. The exempt value of the later supply by the borrower to the lender is the open market value of the equivalent securities, plus any fee charged for depositing a cash collateral" (Customs Notice 701/44 para 2.2).

However, in the case of *Scottish Eastern Investment Trust plc*, EDN/99/211 (VTD 16882), the VAT tribunal held that a stock loan should be treated as an exempt supply by the lender with a value equal only to the fee charged. This is reflected in HMRC's current published guidance (paragraph 6.3 of Notice 701/49/13 and VATFIN4450). The reasoning of the tribunal included the following (paragraph 22):

The Note, para 2.2., involves two artificialities. It states that the whole value of the shares the title to which is transferred is the consideration, although nothing is in fact paid; and also when the arrangement is unwound by the transfer of title to the equivalent stock to the lender again, the whole value of the stock transferred is the consideration. At best that appears unreal.

It is considered that this reasoning would not be applicable to a repo where the full purchase price of the securities is paid for the purchase and repurchase and it is understood that, on this basis, the practice is for the above not to apply to repos. In example 1 in paragraph 2.2 above, then, the seller will make an exempt supply valued at £10 million and the buyer will make an exempt supply valued at £10.4 million. If either party belongs outside of the European Union and the other party belongs in the United Kingdom, the party belonging in the United Kingdom will be able to recover related input VAT (Regulation 103 of the Value Added Tax Regulations 1995 (SI 1995/2518) and Article 3(a) of the Value Added Tax (Input Tax) (Specified Supplies) Order 1999 (SI 1999/3121)).

The VAT treatment of manufactured payments is more difficult to establish. There is a possible analogy with a stock loan where the lender receives interest on collateral provided by the borrower and makes a payment to the borrower. In this case, HMRC recognises a supply by the borrower (VATFIN4450). Arguably, the manufactured payment is consideration for a supply by the seller, although since the seller only makes a single supply to the buyer (ie, the sale of the securities) then the manufactured payment could only be additional consideration for that supply. This, then, will have limited effect on the seller's ability to recover input VAT if the seller operates a transaction count partial exemption method.

2.11 **Stamp duty and stamp duty reserve tax**

There are two parallel exemptions for stamp tax purposes, one for stamp duty in Section 80C of the FA 1986 and the other for stamp duty reserve tax (SDRT) in Section 89AA of the FA 1986. They are both cast in largely the same terms so that the two exemptions are dealt with together. It should be noted that these exemptions largely apply to only UK registered shares since the transfer of most loan capital is exempt under Section 79(4) of the FA 1986 and most shares of non-UK incorporated companies with no UK registers are usually outside the scope of UK stamp taxes.

Sections 80C and 89AA deal with arrangements where A has entered into an arrangement with B under which B is to transfer stock of a particular kind to A or its nominee and stock of the same kind and amount is to be transferred by A or its nominee to B or its nominee and where one of two sets of conditions is satisfied.

In the above situation there is no stamp duty chargeable on an instrument transferring stock from B to A or from A to B pursuant to the arrangements (Section 80C(2)) and no SDRT as regards an agreement to transfer chargeable securities from B to A or from A to B pursuant to the arrangements (Section 89AA(2)) provided that the relevant conditions below are met.

The first set of conditions for the stamp duty exemption is that A or B is authorised under the law of an EEA state to provide any of the investment services or activities listed in Section A2 or 3 of Annex 1 to Directive 2004/39/EC of the European Parliament and of the Council dated April 21 2004 (execution of orders on behalf of clients and dealing on own account) in relation to the stock of the kind concerned, whether or not A or B is authorised under the directive and the stock of the kind concerned is regularly traded on a regulated market. The first set of conditions for the SDRT exemption is the same as for the stamp duty exemption except that, in addition, the chargeable securities must be transferred to A or its nominee or to B or its nominee pursuant to the arrangements.

The second set of conditions for the purposes of the stamp duty exemption is that the arrangement is effected on a regulated market, a multilateral trading facility or a recognised foreign exchange and the stock of the kind concerned is regularly traded on that market, facility or exchange. The second set of conditions for the SDRT exemption is the same as for the stamp duty exemption except, in addition, the chargeable securities must be transferred to A or its nominee or to B or its nominee pursuant to the arrangements.

The two parallel exemptions for stamp duty and SDRT are framed so that they apply equally to the repo itself and to the movement of collateral.

2.12 **Financial transaction tax**

On February 14 2013 the European Commission produced a proposal for a council directive on a common system for a financial transaction tax (FTT) to be implemented under enhanced cooperation by 11 member states, namely Austria, Belgium, Estonia, France, Germany, Greece, Italy, Portugal, Slovakia, Slovenia and Spain.

Ten of the 11 member states subsequently issued a statement reiterating their commitment to FTT. They acknowledged that complex issues had arisen in the discussion of the technical, legal and economic dimensions of the tax and that more work was needed. They aimed to finalise 'viable solutions' by December 31 2014, taking into account concerns raised by non-participating member states. They agreed the following key elements:

- a step-by-step implementation with each step to be designed to take into consideration possible economic impacts;
- the first step should be to apply FTT to equities and some derivatives;
- the first step should be implemented no later than January 1 2016;

- participating member states should be free to apply FTT to other products from January 1 2016 in order to maintain existing taxes.

On January 21 2015 the French and Austrian finance ministers sent a joint letter to the other nine participating countries of the EU FTT coalition in order to relaunch the discussion on how the EU FTT could be designed and implemented.

They proposed to discuss the FTT on a wide base and at low rates.

They also proposed to create a secretariat chaired by one of the participating countries in order to prepare and debrief meetings with the technical support of the European Commission. The Austrian finance minister would have the permanent chairmanship of the group and the Portuguese finance minister would lead the technical work.

Following the above, on January 27 2015 10 countries of the EU FTT coalition (excluding Greece) released a joint statement officially supporting the initiative taken by France and Austria. They also reiterated their willingness to implement the tax on January 1 2016.

If FTT were adopted in its original form, then, subject to certain exemptions, the FTT would apply to financial transactions as defined including:
- purchases or sales of a wide range of financial instruments which is very broadly defined and includes shares, bonds, money marketing instruments and many other instruments;
- the conclusion of derivative contracts

(each a financial transaction).

FTT would be chargeable at rates to be determined by each participating member state but a rate must be set at least equal to 0.1% of the price paid or, if higher, the market value of the financial instruments, and 0.01% of the notional value of the derivative contract.

In order for FTT to apply to a particular financial transaction:
- at least one party would have to be established in a participating member state; and
- a financial institution established in a participating member state would have to be a party to that transaction.

A financial institution would be treated as established in a participating member state if the other party to the transaction was established in a participating member state or the financial instrument which is the subject of the financial transaction was issued within the participating member state.

The FTT would primarily be a tax levied on financial institutions (eg, banks, credit institutions and pension funds). However, such financial institutions may choose to transfer an FTT cost on to other persons. It should be noted that liability to FTT would be joint and several.

In the form of the original proposal for FTT, a 'repurchase agreement' and 'reverse repurchase agreement' were considered a financial transaction and therefore taxable once, at a minimum of 0.1% of the value of the collateral.

2.13 Base erosion and profit shifting

The OECD's base erosion and profit shifting (BEPS) work is addressing many issues and includes Action 2 which seeks to neutralise the effects of hybrid mismatch arrangements through recommendations for domestic rules and recommended changes to the Model Double Taxation Convention. The 'Action 2: 2014 Deliverable' (September 2014) notes that:

> *Furthermore there are a number of specific areas where the domestic rules in Part 1 may need to be further refined. This is the case for certain capital markets transactions (such as on-market stock lending and repos).*

The UK government issued a consultancy document entitled "Tackling aggressive tax planning: Implementing the agreed G20-OECD approach for addressing hybrid mismatch arrangements" in December 2014. The consultation period closed on February 11 2015 and a summary of responses is due to be published in the summer of 2015.

3. UK taxation of stock lending transactions

3.1 Introduction

Part 3 deals with the UK taxation of stock lending and manufactured payments made in relation to stock lending. There has been a change in the taxation of stock lending for income and corporation tax purposes with the deletion of Sections 565–614 of the ITA 2007 and Sections 780–814 of the CTA 2010 as from April 6 2013 or January 1 2014 together with all the stock lending provisions included in those sections. There was a consultation by HMRC on the law relating to manufactured dividends in 2012 ending with the HMRC publication of the Summary Responses on December 11 2012 together with draft legislation. This legislation is contained in Schedule 29 to the FA 2013, all taking effect in relation to payments representative of dividends or interest made on or after January 1 2014.

This Part sets out the UK tax rules relating to stock lending as from January 1 2014. It looks at stock lending where, for example, an institution lends in return for a stock lending fee one or more specified stocks to another party which may be shorting the stock. There will be the following transactions:

- the lender will lend the stock to the borrower;
- the borrower will provide securities collateral or cash collateral to the lender;
- the borrower will manufacture dividends/interest to the lender if the borrower receives the real dividends/interest on the borrowed stock during the life of the stock loan;
- the lender will make manufactured dividends/interest to the borrower in respect of securities collateral if the lender receives real dividends/interest on the securities collateral during the life of the stock loan or, alternatively, will pay the borrower interest in respect of any cash collateral;
- the borrower will pay the lender a stock lending fee or, alternatively, may charge the lender a reduced rate of interest in respect of the cash collateral.

The above list is illustrated diagrammatically in example 11 based on securities collateral and example 12 based on cash collateral.

Example 11

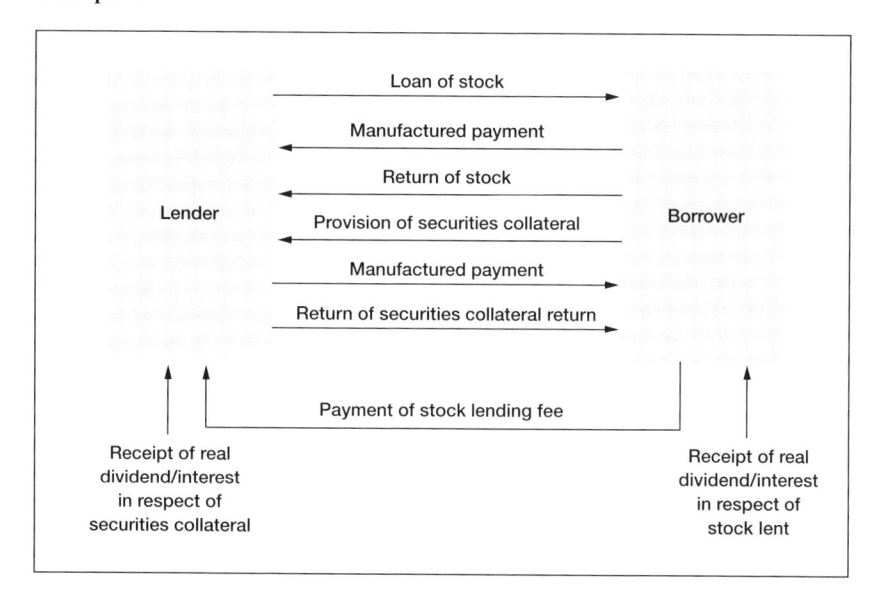

```
                    Loan of stock
                ─────────────────────►
                 Manufactured payment
                ◄─────────────────────
                    Return of stock
                ◄─────────────────────
  Lender       Provision of securities collateral      Borrower
                ◄─────────────────────
                 Manufactured payment
                ─────────────────────►
              Return of securities collateral return
                ─────────────────────►

              Payment of stock lending fee

  Receipt of real                              Receipt of real
  dividend/interest                            dividend/interest
  in respect of                                in respect of
  securities collateral                        stock lent
```

Example 12

```
                    Loan of stock
                ─────────────────────►
                 Manufactured payment
                ◄─────────────────────
                    Return of stock
                ◄─────────────────────
  Lender        Provision of cash collateral         Borrower
                ◄─────────────────────
                  Payment of interest
                ─────────────────────►
                  Cash collateral return
                ─────────────────────►

         Payment of stock lending fee (where applicable)

                                               Receipt of real
                                               dividend/interest
                                               in respect of
                                               stock lent
```

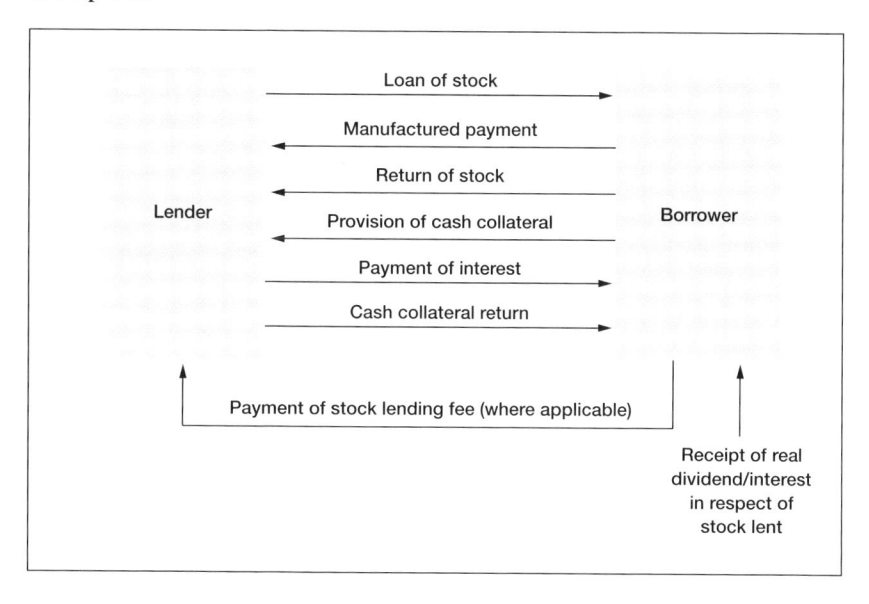

This Part considers stock loans by taking stock loans granted by four typical categories of institutional stock lenders as examples (ie, a registered pension scheme, an authorised investment fund, a charitable trust and an insurance company in respect of basic life assurance and general annuity business (BLAGAB)) to a borrower which is a financial trader within the charge to corporation tax. It deals with:

- the tax treatment of the manufactured payments in respect of the stock lent and on any securities collateral;
- the tax treatment of cash collateral and the payment of interest on the cash collateral;
- the tax treatment of the movements of securities in each direction whether in respect of the stock loan or the securities collateral;
- the tax treatment of the stock lending fee or reduced interest on cash collateral.

The entire panoply of stock lending provisions is dealt with under each category of institutional stock lender even though this involves repetition so that each category stands complete on its own. This Part assumes that the borrower is a financial trader within the charge to corporation tax. This is simpler than a frequent situation where the institutional lender lends through an agency stock lender and therefore where the institutional lender may not know who or what the real borrower is.

3.2   Registered pension schemes

(a)   Introduction

This section examines stock lending by a registered pension scheme, first with securities collateral and, secondly, with cash collateral examining each component set out in the final four bullet points of paragraph 3.1 above and assuming that the borrower is a financial trader within the charge to corporation tax.

(b)   Tax treatment of manufactured payments

The manufactured payments may go both ways. The borrower (financial trader) can make manufactured payments to the registered pension scheme in respect of the stock lent and the registered pension scheme can make manufactured payments to the borrower in respect of the securities collateral.

It is clear that all of conditions A–C in Section 614ZB of the ITA 2007 (which applies for income tax purposes) apply to manufactured payments on the stock lent and received by the registered pension scheme. Condition A is satisfied in that an amount is payable under arrangements. Condition B is satisfied in that the arrangements relate to a transfer of securities. Condition C is satisfied in that the amount in condition A is representative of a dividend or interest on securities.

The registered pension scheme is therefore treated as receiving the real dividend or interest payment on the securities lent (Section 614ZB(2)). The registered pension scheme is treated as receiving income derived from an investment and so obtains the income tax exemption under Section 186(1) of the FA 2004. This is the case even though, strictly speaking, it is arguable that the registered pension scheme has no investments since the legal and beneficial ownership of the stock lent lies with the borrower. The registered pension scheme will not obtain any tax credit or double tax relief. In particular, if the stock lent comprises overseas shares where, for example, the registered pension scheme could have obtained a nil rate of overseas withholding tax on the real dividend if it had held the overseas shares directly by virtue of the double tax treaty with that country, there is no formal pass-through of this benefit as there was under the old manufactured dividend legislation. This is because the formal pass-through should not be needed since the registered pension scheme should be able to obtain the manufactured payment without deduction.

It is also necessary to consider whether the borrower can pay the registered pension scheme the manufactured payment on the securities lent gross or net. It should be noted that throughout this Part HMRC does not regard manufactured payments as annual payments requiring the deduction of tax (eg, under Section 898 of the ITA 2007). It should also be noted that:
- if the stock lent is UK shares (not being REIT shares), the borrower can make the manufactured payment gross since there is no provision requiring a deduction;
- if the stock lent is UK REIT shares, there is the same deduction as would be made under Section 973 of the ITA 2007 which in this case is nil (Sections 918(3), and 973 and Regulation 7(4) and (5) of SI 2006/2867);
- if the manufactured payment is in respect of net paying UK securities, the deduction in this case is nil (Sections 919(4) and 936(2)(g));
- if the manufactured payment is in respect of gross paying UK securities (eg, UK government bonds), there is no deduction of UK tax (Section 921); and
- if there is a manufactured payment in respect of overseas shares or bonds, there is no deduction of UK tax since there is no provision requiring a deduction.

Section 614ZB of the ITA 2007 applies to the registered pension scheme in respect of manufactured payments it makes on securities collateral. The registered pension scheme obtains no deduction for the manufactured payment which it pays the borrower in respect of the securities collateral (Section 614ZC(2)). This does not adversely affect the registered pension scheme because it is exempt in respect of the real dividends or real interest it receives on the securities collateral.

The registered pension scheme can make the manufactured payment on the securities collateral gross or net depending upon the nature of the collateral:
- if the collateral is UK shares (not being REIT shares), there is no deduction since there is no provision requiring a deduction;
- if the collateral is UK REIT shares, then there is the deduction of the same amount as would have been deducted under Section 973 of the ITA 2007 which in this case is nil (Sections 918 and 973 and Regulation 7(2) of SI 2006/2867);
- if the collateral is net paying UK securities, there is a deduction of UK income tax at the basic rate (Section 919) because the registered pension scheme is not a company;
- if the collateral is gross paying UK securities (eg, UK government bonds), then there is no deduction of UK tax (Section 921); and
- if the collateral is overseas shares or bonds, there is no deduction of UK tax since there is no provision requiring a deduction.

(c) Tax treatment of cash collateral

The interest which the registered pension scheme pays on cash collateral is real interest (as opposed to the manufactured interest payable in respect of securities collateral consisting of bonds). The registered pension scheme can always pay interest on cash collateral gross because the registered pension scheme is not a company or local authority or partnership under Section 874(1)(a)–(c) of the ITA 2007 and the lender of the collateral is not a person whose usual place of abode is outside the United Kingdom within Section 874(1)(d).

(d) The tax treatment of the movement of securities in each direction

The only UK tax issues applying to the movement of the securities lent or the securities collateral are taxes on capital gains and stamp taxes.

A registered pension scheme is exempt from tax on capital gains on the disposal of investments held for the purposes of the scheme (Section 271(1A) of the TCGA 1992). However, there is no capital gain to which this exemption applies if there is no disposal as provided for stock loans falling within Section 263B of the TCGA 1992. Section 263B applies equally to the stock loan and to the provision and return of securities collateral. A stock lending arrangement is defined in Section 263B(1) as any arrangement between two persons (the borrower and the lender) under which the lender transfers securities to the borrower otherwise than by way of sale and a requirement is imposed on the borrower to transfer the securities back to the lender otherwise than by way of sale. Section 263B(2) then provides that disposals and acquisitions made in pursuance of any stock lending arrangement are disregarded for capital gains tax purposes. If, at any time, it becomes apparent that the requirement for the borrower to transfer the securities back to the lender will not be met, then the lender is deemed to make a disposal to the borrower at that time and the borrower is deemed to make an acquisition (Section 263B(4)).

There are two parallel exemptions for stamp tax purposes, one for stamp duty in Section 80C of the FA 1986 and the other for stamp duty reserve tax in Section 89AA of the FA 1986. They are both cast largely in the same terms so that the two exemptions are dealt with together. It should be noted that these exemptions are largely relevant to only UK registered shares since the transfer of most registered loan capital is exempt under Section 79(4) of the FA 1986 and most shares of non-UK incorporated companies with no UK register are usually outside the scope of UK stamp taxes.

Sections 80C and 89AA deal with the situation where A has entered into an arrangement with B under which B is to transfer stock of a particular kind to A or its nominee and stock of the same kind and amount is to be transferred by A or its nominee to B or its nominee and where one of two sets of conditions is satisfied.

In the above situation, subject to all the conditions there is no stamp duty charge for an instrument transferring stock from B to A or back from A to B pursuant to the arrangement (Section 80C(2)) and no stamp duty reserve tax as regards the agreement to transfer chargeable securities from B to A or back from A to B pursuant to the arrangement (Section 89AA(2)). There is, however, no exemption unless the arrangement is such as is entered into by persons dealing with each other at arm's length and all benefits or risks arising from fluctuations in the market value of the stock before the transfer back to B must lie with B.

The first set of conditions for the stamp duty exemption is that A or B is authorised under the law of an EEA state to provide any of the investment services or activities listed in Section A2 or 3 of Annex 1 to Directive 2004/39/EC of the European Parliament and of the Council dated April 21 2004 (execution of orders on behalf of clients and dealing on own account) in relation to the stock of the kind concerned, whether or not A or B is authorised under the directive and the stock of the kind concerned is regularly traded on a regulated market. The first set of conditions for the stamp duty reserve tax exemption is the same as for the stamp duty exemption except that, in addition, the chargeable securities must be transferred to A or its nominee or to B or its nominee pursuant to the arrangement.

The second set of conditions for the purposes of the stamp duty exemption is that the arrangement is effected on a regulated market, a multilateral trading facility or a recognised foreign exchange and stock of the kind that is regularly traded on that market, facility or exchange. The second set of conditions for the stamp duty reserve tax exemption is the same as for the stamp duty exemption except, in addition, the chargeable securities must be transferred to A or its nominee or to B or its nominee pursuant to the arrangement. An arrangement is regarded as effected on a regulated market, multilateral trading facility or recognised foreign exchange if it is subject to the rules of that market, facility or exchange and it is reported to the market, facility or exchange in accordance with the rules of the market, facility or exchange.

The two parallel exemptions for stamp duty and stamp duty reserve tax apply to the movement of the stock lent and to the movement of collateral, both of which are regarded as stock loans. Therefore, the parties which are B or A will vary depending upon whether one is looking at the stock loan or the provision of collateral.

(e) **Financial transaction tax**

On February 14 2013 the European Commission produced a proposal for a council directive on a common system for a financial transaction tax (FTT) to be implemented under enhanced cooperation by 11 member states, namely Austria, Belgium, Estonia, France, Germany, Greece, Italy, Portugal, Slovakia, Slovenia and Spain.

Ten of the 11 member states subsequently issued a statement reiterating their commitment to FTT. They acknowledged that complex issues had arisen in the discussion of the technical, legal and economic dimensions of the tax and more work was needed. They aimed to finalise 'viable solutions' by December 31 2014, taking into account concerns raised by non-participating member states. They agreed the following key elements:
- a step-by-step implementation with each step to be designed to take into consideration possible economic impacts;
- the first step should be to apply FTT to equities and some derivatives;
- the first step should be implemented no later than January 1 2016;

- participating member states should be free to apply FTT to other products from January 1 2016 in order to maintain existing taxes.

On January 21 2015 the French and Austrian finance ministers sent a joint letter to the other nine participating countries of the EU FTT coalition to relaunch the discussion on how the EU FTT could be designed and implemented.

They proposed to discuss the FTT on a wide base and at low rates.

They also proposed to create a secretariat chaired by one of the participating countries in order to prepare and debrief meetings with the technical support of the European Commission. The Austrian finance minister would have the permanent chairmanship of the group and the Portuguese finance minister would lead the technical work.

Following the above, on January 27 2015 10 countries of the EU FTT coalition (excluding Greece) released a joint statement to officially support the initiative taken by France and Austria. They also reiterated their willingness to implement the tax on January 1 2016.

If FTT were adopted in its original form, then, subject to certain exemptions, the FTT would apply to financial transactions as defined including:
- purchases or sales of a wide range of financial instruments which is very broadly defined and includes shares, bonds, money marketing instruments and many other instruments;
- the conclusion of derivative contracts

(each a financial transaction).

FTT would be chargeable at rates to be determined by each participating member state but a rate must be set at least equal to 0.1% of the price paid or, if higher, the market value of the financial instruments, and 0.01% of the notional value of the derivative contract.

In order for FTT to apply to a particular financial transaction:
- at least one party would have to be established in a participating member state; and
- a financial institution established in a participating member state would have to be a party to that transaction.

A financial institution would be treated as established in a participating member state if the other party to the transaction was established in a participating member state or the financial instrument which was the subject of the financial transaction was issued within the participating member state.

The FTT would primarily be a tax levied on financial institutions (eg, banks, credit institutions and pension funds). However, such financial institutions may choose to transfer an FTT cost on to other persons. It should be noted that liability to FTT would be joint and several.

In the form of the original proposal for FTT, a 'securities lending and borrowing agreement' was considered a financial transaction and therefore taxable once, at a minimum of 0.1% of the value of the collateral.

(f)   VAT

In *Scottish Eastern Investment Trust plc,* EDN/99/211 (VTD 16882), the VAT tribunal held that a stock loan should be treated as an exempt supply by the lender with a value equal only to the fee charged. This is reflected in HMRC's current published guidance (paragraph 6.3 of Notice 701/49/13 and VATFIN4450).

If the borrower belongs outside of the European Union and the lender belongs in the United Kingdom, the lender will be able to recover related input VAT (Regulation 103 of the Value Added Tax Regulations 1995 (SI 1995/2518) and Article 3(a) of the Value Added Tax (Input Tax) (Specified Supplies) Order 1999 (SI 1999/3121)).

Where the lender receives interest on collateral provided by the borrower, HMRC recognises a further exempt supply by the lender. Where the lender then makes a payment to the borrower in respect of such interest, HMRC recognises an exempt supply by the borrower (VATFIN4450). This may reduce the borrower's recoverable input VAT depending upon the particular partial exemption method adopted.

In contrast, dividends received by the lender in respect of securities collateral will be outside the scope of VAT, although it is arguable that manufactured payments give rise to exempt supplies by the recipient.

VATFIN4450 also confirms that if the borrower defaults, any cash collateral retained by the lender is compensation and outside the scope of VAT; and that any part of the collateral returned to the defaulting borrower is also outside the scope of VAT on the basis of not being consideration for any supply.

(g)   Tax treatment of stock lending fees

A relevant stock lending fee received by a registered pension scheme and derived from investments of the scheme is exempt from income tax unless the fee is derived from an investment in a property LLP (Section 186 of the FA 2004; Section 129B of the ICTA 1988 and paragraph 4103040 of the HMRC Registered Pension Scheme Manual). A relevant stock lending fee in relation to an investment means any amount that is in the nature of a fee which is payable in connection with the stock lending arrangement relating to investments that, but for any transfer under the arrangement, would be investments held for the purposes of the registered pension scheme. The meaning of a stock lending arrangement is the same meaning as in Section 263B of the TCGA 1992. A registered pension scheme is therefore more concerned that a stock loan should fall within Section 263B in order to obtain the income tax exemption on the stock lending fee than to ensure that there is no disposal for capital gains purposes where, if there was a disposal, the registered pension scheme would be exempt from tax on capital gains.

3.3   Authorised investment funds

(a)   Introduction

This section examines stock lending by an authorised investment fund (AIF) within the meaning of the Authorised Investment Funds (Tax) Regulations 2006 (SI 2006 964), first with securities collateral and, secondly, with cash collateral examining each component set out in the final four bullet points of paragraph 3.1 above, assuming that the borrower is a financial trader within the charge to corporation tax. The principal differences for AIFs as compared with registered pension schemes is that AIFs are within the charge to corporation tax so they fall within a separate sequence of corporation tax provisions as opposed to the sequence of income tax provisions applying to registered pension schemes.

(b) *Tax treatment of manufactured payments*
The manufactured payments between the AIF and the borrower may go both ways. The borrower (ie, the financial trader) can make manufactured payments to the AIF in respect of the stock lent and the AIF can make manufactured payments to the borrower in respect of the securities collateral.

In the context of an AIF, Section 614ZB of the ITA 2007 (which applies for the purposes of income tax) is not relevant. Instead, Sections 814A–814D of the CTA 2010 apply but only in respect of stock loans of shares and manufactured dividends on shares. It is clear that all of conditions A–C in Section 814B of the CTA 2010 apply to manufactured payments on the stock lent and received by the AIF where the stock loan comprises shares. Condition A is satisfied in that an amount is payable under arrangements. Condition B is satisfied in that the arrangements relate to the transfer of shares in a company. Condition C is satisfied in that the amount referred to in condition A is an amount representative of a dividend on shares.

The AIF is therefore treated as receiving the real dividend on the shares lent (Section 814D(2) of the CTA 2010). The AIF will not obtain any tax credit or double tax relief in respect of the manufactured dividend (Section 814D(8) and (5) of the CTA 2009). The AIF should, however, obtain the exemption from corporation tax in respect of the manufactured dividend on, for example, shares of a UK resident company (not being an REIT) in the same way as for a real dividend (Section 931D of the CTA 2009). An AIF is not a small company (Section 931S of the CTA 2009). A manufactured dividend should fall within the exempt class in Section 931F of the CTA 2009 (ie, a distribution in respect of ordinary shares which are not redeemable). The AIF would be taxable on a manufactured dividend on REIT shares as it would be taxed on a real REIT dividend.

The loan relationship provisions parallel to Sections 814A–814D of the CTA 2010 are contained in Sections 539–41 of the CTA 2009. (Section 541 of the CTA 2010 is now redundant because it applies for the purposes of Section 812 of the CTA 2010 which has been repealed from January 1 2014. It may be that Section 541 of the CTA 2010 will be repealed in due course.) A manufactured interest payment falls within these sections if it satisfies conditions A and B in Section 539 of the CTA 2009 which are equivalent to conditions A–C in Section 814B of the CTA 2010 for manufactured dividends on shares. Condition A is that an amount is payable by or to the AIF under any arrangement and the arrangement relates to the transfer of an asset representing a loan relationship. Condition B is that the amount in condition A is representative of interest under a loan relationship. The loan relationship legislation then applies to the AIF as if the manufactured interest is payable on a loan by the AIF and the manufactured interest relationship is the loan relationship under which the real interest is paid. Therefore, the AIF is taxable under the loan relationship legislation in respect of the manufactured interest payment made to it by the borrower.

It is then necessary to consider whether or not the borrower can pay the AIF the manufactured payment on securities lent gross:
- if the stock lent is UK shares (not being REIT shares) the borrower can make manufactured payment gross since there is no provision requiring a deduction;
- if the stock lent is UK REIT shares, there is the same deduction that would be made under Section 973 of the ITA 2007 which in this case is nil (Sections 918(3) and 973 of the ITA 2007 and Regulation 7(2) of SI 2006/2867);
- if the manufactured payment is in respect of net paying UK securities, the deduction in this case is nil (Sections 919(4) and 933);
- if the manufactured payment is in respect of gross paying UK securities (eg, UK government bonds), there is no deduction of UK tax (Section 921);
- if there is a manufactured payment in respect of overseas shares or bonds, there is no deduction of UK tax since there is no provision requiring a deduction.

Sections 814A–814D of the CTA 2010 and Sections 539–41 of the CTA 2009 apply equally to the AIF in respect of manufactured payments made by the AIF on share collateral and bond collateral respectively. The AIF obtains no deduction for any manufactured dividend paid to the borrower on share collateral (with the exception of a manufactured dividend on REIT shares) but this does not adversely affect it because it should be exempt in respect of the real dividend it receives on share collateral under Section 931D of the CTA 2009. In the case of REIT share collateral where the AIF is taxable on receipt of the real REIT dividend on the REIT shares, the AIF can obtain a deduction when it pays a manufactured dividend in respect of such shares because the AIF is carrying on an investment business (Section 814C(4) and (5) of the ITA 2007). In contrast, the AIF is taxable under the loan relationship legislation in respect of the real interest it obtains on any bond collateral but it can obtain a deduction for the manufactured interest payment made to the borrower under Section 540(1) of the CTA 2009 if these amounts are recognised in the AIF's income statement.

The AIF can then make the manufactured payments in respect of the securities collateral gross or net depending upon the nature of the collateral:
- if the collateral is UK shares (not being REIT shares) there is no deduction since there is no provision requiring a deduction;
- if the collateral is UK REIT shares, then there is the same deduction as would be made under Section 973 of the ITA 2007 which in this case is nil (Sections 918(3), 973 and Regulation 7(2) of SI 2006/2867);
- if the manufactured payment is in respect of net paying securities then the deduction in this case is nil (Sections 919(4) and 933);
- it the manufactured payment is in respect of gross paying UK securities (eg, UK government bonds) there is no deduction of UK tax (Section 921);
- if there is a manufactured payment in respect of overseas shares or bonds, there is no deduction of UK tax since there is no provision requiring a deduction.

(c) **Tax treatment of interest on cash collateral**
The interest which the AIF pays on cash collateral is real interest. The AIF is a company within Section 874(1)(a) of the ITA 2007 but it has an obligation to only deduct tax at the basic rate on annual interest. Interest payable on cash collateral in respect of a stock loan will be short interest if the cash collateral will be outstanding for less than one year and the stock loan is self-standing and does not form part of other arrangements. If the interest on cash collateral is ever annual interest, then the AIF should be able to pay the interest on the cash collateral to the borrower assumed in this Part (ie, a financial trader) gross either as a UK resident company within Section 933 of the ITA 2007 or as a non-resident company within the charge to corporation tax under Section 934.

(d) **Tax treatment of the movement of securities in each direction**
The only UK tax issues applying to the movement of the securities lent or the securities collateral are tax on capital gains and stamp taxes.

An AIF is exempt from tax on capital gains (Section 100(1) of the TCGA 1992). However, there is no capital gain to which the exemption applies if there is no disposal as provided for a stock loan within Section 263B of the TCGA 1992. Section 263B applies equally to the stock loan and to the provision and return of collateral. A stock lending arrangement is defined in Section 263B(1) as any arrangement between two persons (the borrower and the lender) under which the lender transfers securities to the borrower otherwise than by way of sale and a requirement is imposed on the borrower to transfer the securities back to the lender otherwise than by way of sale. Section 263B(2) then provides that disposals and acquisitions made in pursuance of any stock lending arrangement are disregarded for capital gains tax purposes. If, at any time, it becomes apparent that the requirement for the borrower to transfer the securities back to the lender will not be met, then the lender is deemed to make a disposal to the borrower at that time and the borrower is deemed to make an acquisition (Section 263B(4)). The above does not apply to stock loans of loan relationships. If a capital profit, gain or loss were recognised in the AIF's accounts, this would be taxed under Section 332 of the CTA 2009 but this would be prevented from happening to an AIF by virtue of Regulation 10 of SI 2006/964. However, an AIF should not realise any profit or loss in respect of movements in value of a bond lent or in respect of bond collateral. The former never leaves the AIF's balance sheet under the statement of recommended practice and the latter never enters the AIF's balance sheet with the result that there should be no profit or loss recognised from movements in value of the bond itself (as opposed to amounts in respect of which manufactured interest, the stock lending fee or real interest which it is understood do appear in the AIF's income statement).

There are two parallel exemptions for stamp tax purposes, one for stamp duty in Section 80C of the FA 1986 and the other for stamp duty reserve tax in Section 89AA of the FA 1986. They are both cast largely in the same terms so that the two exemptions are dealt with together. It should be noted that these exemptions are largely relevant to only UK registered shares since the transfer of most registered loan capital is exempt under Section 79(4) of the FA 1986 and most shares of non-UK incorporated companies with no UK register are usually outside the scope of UK stamp taxes.

Sections 80C and 89AA deal with the situation where A has entered into an arrangement with B under which B is to transfer stock of a particular kind to A or its nominee and stock of the same kind and amount is to be transferred by A or its nominee to B or its nominee and where one of two sets of conditions is satisfied.

In the above situation and subject to all the conditions, there is no stamp duty charge for an instrument transferring stock from B to A or back from A to B pursuant to the arrangement (Section 80C(2)) and no stamp duty reserve tax as regards the agreement to transfer chargeable securities from B to A or back from A to B pursuant to the arrangement (Section 89AA(2)). There is, however, no exemption unless the arrangement is such as is entered into by persons dealing with each other at arm's length and all benefits or risks arising from fluctuations in the market value of the stock before the transfer back to B must lie with B.

The first set of conditions for the stamp duty exemption is that A or B is authorised under the law of an EEA state to provide any of the investment services or activities listed in Section A2 or 3 of Annex 1 to Directive 2004/39/EC of the European Parliament and of the Council dated April 21 2004 (execution of orders on behalf of clients and dealing on own account) in relation to the stock of the kind concerned, whether or not A or B is authorised under the directive and the stock of the kind concerned is regularly traded on a regulated market. The first set of conditions for the stamp duty reserve tax exemption is the same as for the stamp duty exemption except that, in addition, the chargeable securities must be transferred to A or its nominee or to B or its nominee pursuant to the arrangement.

The second set of conditions for the purposes of the stamp duty exemption is that the arrangement is effected on a regulated market, a multilateral trading facility or a recognised foreign exchange and stock of the kind that is regularly traded on that market, facility or exchange. The second set of conditions for the stamp duty reserve tax exemption is the same as for the stamp duty exemption except, in addition, the chargeable securities must be transferred to A or its nominee or to B or its nominee pursuant to the arrangements. An arrangement is regarded as effected on a regulated market, multilateral trading facility or recognised foreign exchange if it is subject to the rules of that market, facility or exchange and it is reported to the market, facility or exchange in accordance with the rules of the market, facility or exchange.

The two parallel exemptions for stamp duty and stamp duty reserve tax apply to the movement of the stock lent and to the movement of collateral, both of which are regarded as stock loans. Therefore, the parties which are B or A will vary depending on whether one is looking at the stock loan or the provision of collateral.

(e) *Financial transaction tax*

On February 14 2013 the European Commission produced a proposal for a council directive on a common system for a financial transaction tax (FTT) to be implemented under enhanced cooperation by 11 member states, namely Austria, Belgium, Estonia, France, Germany, Greece, Italy, Portugal, Slovakia, Slovenia and Spain.

Ten of the 11 member states subsequently issued a statement reiterating their

commitment to FTT. They acknowledged that complex issues had arisen in the discussion of the technical, legal and economic dimensions of the tax and more work was needed. They aimed to finalise 'viable solutions' by December 31 2014, taking into account concerns raised by non-participating member states. They agreed the following key elements:
- a step-by-step implementation with each step to be designed to take into consideration possible economic impacts;
- the first step should be to apply FTT to equities and some derivatives;
- the first step should be implemented no later than January 1 2016;
- participating member states should be free to apply FTT to other products from January 1 2016 in order to maintain existing taxes.

On January 21 2015 the French and Austrian finance ministers sent a joint letter to the other nine participating countries of the EU FTT coalition in order to relaunch the discussion on how the EU FTT could be designed and implemented.

They proposed to discuss the FTT on a wide base and at low rates.

They also proposed to create a secretariat chaired by one of the participating countries in order to prepare and debrief meetings with the technical support of the European Commission. The Austrian finance minister would have the permanent chairmanship of the group and the Portuguese finance minister would lead the technical work.

Following the above, on January 27 2015 10 countries of the EU FTT coalition (excluding Greece) released a joint statement to officially support the initiative taken by France and Austria. They also reiterated their willingness to implement the tax on January 1 2016.

If FTT were adopted in its original form, then, subject to certain exemptions, the FTT would apply to financial transactions as defined including:
- purchases or sales of a wide range of financial instruments which is very broadly defined and includes shares, bonds, money marketing instruments and many other instruments;
- the conclusion of derivative contracts

(each a financial transaction).

FTT would be chargeable at rates to be determined by each participating member state but a rate must be set at least equal to 0.1% of the price paid or, if higher, the market value of the financial instruments, and 0.01% of the notional value of the derivative contract.

In order for FTT to apply to a particular financial transaction:
- at least one party would have to be established in a participating member state; and
- a financial institution established in a participating member state would have to be a party to that transaction.

A financial institution would be treated as established in a participating member state if the other party to the transaction was established in a participating member state or the financial instrument which was the subject of the financial transaction was issued within the participating member state.

The FTT would primarily be a tax levied on financial institutions (eg, banks, credit institutions and pension funds). However, such financial institutions may choose to transfer an FTT cost on to other persons. It should be noted that liability to FTT would be joint and several.

In the form of the original proposal for FTT, a 'securities lending and borrowing agreement' was considered a financial transaction and therefore taxable once, at a minimum of 0.1% of the value of the collateral.

(f) **VAT**

In *Scottish Eastern Investment Trust plc*, EDN/99/211 (VTD 16882), the VAT tribunal held that a stock loan should be treated as an exempt supply by the lender with a value equal only to the fee charged. This is reflected in HMRC's current published guidance (paragraph 6.3 of Notice 701/49/13 and VATFIN4450).

If the borrower belongs outside of the European Union and the lender belongs in the United Kingdom, the lender will be able to recover related input VAT (Regulation 103 of the Value Added Tax Regulations 1995 (SI 1995/2518) and Article 3(a) of the Value Added Tax (Input Tax) (Specified Supplies) Order 1999 (SI 1999/3121)).

Where the lender receives interest on collateral provided by the borrower, HMRC recognises a further exempt supply by the lender. Where the lender then makes a payment to the borrower in respect of such interest, HMRC recognises an exempt supply by the borrower (VATFIN4450). This may reduce the borrower's recoverable input VAT depending on the particular partial exemption method adopted.

In contrast, dividends received by the lender in respect of securities collateral will be outside the scope of VAT, although it is arguable that manufactured payments give rise to exempt supplies by the recipient.

VATFIN4450 also confirms that if the borrower defaults, any cash collateral retained by the lender is compensation and outside the scope of VAT; and that any part of the collateral returned to the defaulting borrower is also outside the scope of VAT on the basis of not being consideration for any supply.

(g) *Tax treatment of the stock lending fee*

HMRC has always considered that pension schemes, before they obtained the exemption from income tax in respect of stock lending fees contained in Section 129B of the ICTA 1988, were taxable on stock lending fees under what was then Schedule D Case VI (ie, income not otherwise chargeable to tax) and not as income from a trade under Schedule D Case I. AIFs have no special exemption from corporation tax in respect of stock lending fees and it is therefore considered that an AIF is taxable on a stock lending fee in respect of a loan on shares under Section 979 of the CTA 2009 (charge to tax on income not otherwise charged). The stock lending fee is not made an exempt capital gain by Regulation 14E of SI 2006/964 since it appears in the income line in its statement of total return for an accounting period and not under net capital gains/losses. The stock lending fee is not a profit from a trade unless otherwise the AIF is considered to be trading. The stock lending fee in respect of a stock loan of a bond will be a profit arising from a loan relationship and so will be taxed under the loan relationship legislation.

3.4 Charitable trusts

(a) Introduction
Institutional stock lenders which are charities are divided between charitable trusts subject to the income tax regime and obtaining income tax exemptions and charitable companies which are subject to the corporation tax regime and obtaining corporation tax exemptions. This section examines stock lending by a charitable trust (falling within the definition in paragraph 1 of Schedule 6 to the FA 2010) first with securities collateral and, secondly, with cash collateral examining each component set out in the final four bullet points of paragraph 3.1 above assuming that the borrower is a financial trader within the charge to corporation tax.

(b) Tax treatment of manufactured payments
The manufactured payments may go both ways. The borrower (the financial trader) can make manufactured payments to the charitable trust in respect of the stock lent and the charitable trust can make manufactured payments to the borrower in respect of any securities collateral.

It is clear that all of conditions A–C in Section 614ZB of the ITA 2007 (which applies for income tax purposes) apply to manufactured payments on the stock lent and received by the charitable trust. Condition A is satisfied in that an amount is payable under any arrangements. Condition B is satisfied in that the arrangements relate to a transfer of securities. Condition C is satisfied in that the amount in condition A is representative of a dividend or interest on the securities.

The charitable trust is therefore treated as receiving the real dividend or interest payment on the securities lent (Section 614ZD(2)). The relevant income tax exemption for a charitable trust is contained in Section 532 of the ITA 2007. Section 532(1) provides that income within Section 532(2) is not taken into account in calculating the total income of the charitable trust if it is income of a charitable trust and it was required under any trust deed to be applied for charitable purposes only. Income within Section 532(2) includes interest, dividends of a UK resident company and dividends of a non-UK resident company. There is no limitation as there is for a registered pension scheme that the income must be derived from an investment. There is, however, a parallel issue. A charitable trust can have its income tax exemption limited by Section 540 if it incurs non-charitable expenditure. Section 543(1)(i) provides that the amount which a charitable trust invests in an investment which is not an approved charitable investment is non-charitable expenditure. Section 558 lists approved charitable investments. HMRC has confirmed that one can look through to the stock lent in relation to identifying the investment and the stock loan is not a loan within type 12 in Section 558. The charitable trust is therefore exempt under Section 532 in respect of the manufactured dividend or interest payment which it receives from the borrower assuming that there is no limitation under Section 540. The charitable trust will not obtain any tax credit or double tax relief.

It is necessary to consider whether the borrower can pay the charitable trust the manufactured payments on the stock lent gross or net:
- if stock lent is UK shares (not being REIT shares) the borrower can make the manufactured payment gross since there is no provision for the deduction of tax;
- if the stock lent is UK REIT shares, there is the same deduction as would be made under Section 973 which in this case is nil (Sections 918(3) and 973 and Regulation 7(3)(d) of SI 2006/2867);
- if the manufactured payment is in respect of net paying UK securities, the deduction in this case is nil (Sections 919(4) and 936(2)(d));
- if the manufactured payment is in respect of gross paying UK securities (eg, UK government bonds) there is no deduction of UK tax (Section 921); and
- if there is a manufactured payment in respect of overseas shares or bonds, there is no deduction of UK tax since there is no provision for the deduction of tax.

Section 614ZB of the ITA 2007 equally applies to the charitable trust in respect of manufactured payments it makes on the securities collateral (although as will be seen later, it is usually preferable for a charitable trust to take cash collateral). The charitable trust cannot claim a deduction for the manufactured payment which it pays the borrower in respect of securities collateral (Section 614ZC(2)). This does not adversely affect the charitable trust because it is exempt in respect of the real dividend or interest it receives on the securities collateral. The charitable trust will, however, wish to ensure that the security chosen for the collateral is an approved charitable investment.

The charitable trust can make a manufactured payment on the securities collateral gross or not depending on the nature of the collateral:
- if the collateral is UK shares (not being REIT shares) there is no deduction since there is no provision for the deduction of tax;
- if the collateral is UK REIT shares, then there is a deduction of the same amount as would have been deducted under Section 973 which in this case is nil (Sections 918 and 973 and Regulation 7(2) of SI 2006/2867);
- if the collateral is net paying UK securities, there is a deduction to UK tax at the basic rate (Section 919) because the charitable trust is not a company;
- if the collateral is gross paying UK securities (eg, UK government bonds) then there is no deduction of UK income tax (Section 921); and
- if the collateral is overseas shares or bonds, then there is no deduction of income tax since there is no provision for the deduction of tax.

(c) *Tax treatment of interest on cash collateral*
The interest which the charitable trust pays on cash collateral is real interest. The charitable trust can always pay interest on the cash collateral gross because the charitable trust is not a company or local authority or partnership under Section 874(1)(a)–(c) of the ITA 2007 and the lender of the collateral is not a person whose usual place of abode is outside the United Kingdom within Section 874(1)(d). Interest on cash collateral is considered further at 'the tax treatment of the stock lending fee' in sub-paragraph (g) below.

(d) ***The tax treatment of the movement of securities in each direction***
The only UK tax issues applying to the movement of the securities lent on the securities collateral are taxes on capital gains and stamp taxes.

The charitable trust is exempt from tax on capital gains if the capital gains belong to the charitable trust and are applicable and applied for charitable purposes only (Section 256 of the TCGA 1992). There is a similar limitation on exemption as for the exemption from income tax on income if the charitable trust has non-charitable expenditure. However, there is no capital gain to which the exemption can apply if there is no disposal as provided for stock loans falling within Section 263B of the TCGA 1992. Section 263B applies equally to the stock loan and to the provision and return of securities collateral. A stock lending arrangement is defined in Section 263B(1) as any arrangement between two persons (a borrower and a lender) under which the lender transfers securities to the borrower otherwise than by way of sale and a requirement is imposed on the borrower to transfer those securities back to the lender otherwise than by way of sale. Section 263B(2) then provides that disposals and acquisitions made in pursuance of any stock lending arrangements are disregarded for capital gains tax purposes. If, at any time, it becomes clear that the requirement for the borrower to transfer the securities back to the lender will not be met, then the lender is deemed to make a disposal to the borrower at that time and the borrower is deemed to make an acquisition (Section 263B(4)).

There are two parallel exemptions for stamp taxes, one for stamp duty in Section 80C of the FA 1986 and the other for stamp duty reserve tax in Section 89AA of the FA 1986. They are both cast largely in the same terms so that the two exemptions are dealt with together. It should be noted that these exemptions largely apply to only UK registered shares since the transfer of most registered loan capital is exempt under Section 79(4) and most shares of non-UK incorporated companies with no UK register are usually outside the scope of UK stamp taxes.

Sections 80C and 89AA deal with the situation where A has entered into an arrangement with B under which B is to transfer stock of a particular kind to A or its nominee and stock of the same kind and amount is to be transferred by A or its nominee to B or its nominee where one of two sets of conditions is satisfied.

In the above situation and subject to all the conditions, there is no stamp duty charge for an instrument transferring stock from B to A or back from A to B pursuant to the arrangement (Section 80C(2)) and no stamp duty reserve tax as regards the agreement to transfer chargeable securities from B to A or back from A to B pursuant to the arrangement (Section 89AA(2)). There is, however, no exemption unless the arrangement is such as is entered into by persons dealing with each other at arm's length and all benefits or risks arising from fluctuations in the market value of the stock before the transfer back to B must lie with B.

The first set of conditions for the stamp duty exemption is that A or B is authorised under the law of an EEA state to provide any of the investment services or activities listed in Section A2 or 3 of Annex 1 to Directive 2004/39/EC of the European Parliament and of the Council dated April 21 2004 (execution of orders on behalf of clients and dealing on own account) in relation to the stock of the kind concerned, whether or not A or B is authorised under the directive and the stock of the kind concerned is regularly traded on a regulated market. The first set of conditions for the stamp duty reserve tax exemption is the same as for the stamp duty exemption except that, in addition, the chargeable securities must be transferred to A or its nominee or to B or its nominee pursuant to the arrangement.

The second set of conditions for the purposes of the stamp duty exemption is that the arrangement is effected on a regulated market, a multilateral trading facility or a recognised foreign exchange and stock of the kind that is regularly traded on that market, facility or exchange. The second set of conditions for the stamp duty reserve tax exemption is the same as for the stamp duty exemption except, in addition, the chargeable securities must be transferred to A or its nominee or to B or its nominee pursuant to the arrangement. An arrangement is regarded as effected on a regulated market, multilateral trading facility or recognised foreign exchange if it is subject to the rules of that market, facility or exchange and it is reported to the market, facility or exchange in accordance with the rules of the market, facility or exchange.

The two parallel exemptions for stamp duty and stamp duty reserve tax apply to the movement of the stock lent and to the movement of collateral, both of which are regarded as stock loans. Therefore, the parties which are B or A vary depending on whether one is looking at the stock loan or the provision of collateral.

(e) *Financial transaction tax*

On February 14 2013 the European Commission produced a proposal for a council directive on a common system for a financial transaction tax (FTT) to be implemented under enhanced cooperation by 11 member states, namely Austria, Belgium, Estonia, France, Germany, Greece, Italy, Portugal, Slovakia, Slovenia and Spain.

Ten of the 11 member states subsequently issued a statement reiterating their commitment to FTT. They acknowledged that complex issues had arisen in the discussion of the technical, legal and economic dimensions of the tax and more work was needed. They aimed to finalise 'viable solutions' by December 31 2014, taking into account concerns raised by non-participating member states. They agreed the following key elements:
- a step-by-step implementation with each step to be designed to take into consideration possible economic impacts;
- the first step should be to apply FTT to equities and some derivatives;
- the first step should be implemented no later than January 1 2016;
- participating member states should be free to apply FTT to other products from January 1 2016 in order to maintain existing taxes.

On January 21 2015 the French and Austrian finance ministers sent a joint letter to the other nine participating countries of the EU FTT coalition in order to relaunch the discussion on how the EU FTT could be designed and implemented.

They proposed to discuss the FTT on a wide base and at low rates. They also proposed to create a secretariat chaired by one of the participating countries in order to prepare and debrief meetings with the technical support of the European

Commission. The Austrian finance minister would have the permanent chairmanship of the group and the Portuguese finance minister would lead the technical work.

Following the above, on 27 January 2015 10 countries of the EU FTT coalition (excluding Greece) released a joint statement to officially support the initiative taken by France and Austria. They also reiterated their willingness to implement the tax on January 1 2016.

If FTT were adopted in its original form, then, subject to certain exemptions, the FTT would apply to financial transactions as defined including:
- purchases or sales of a wide range of financial instruments which is very broadly defined and includes shares, bonds, money marketing instruments and many other instruments;
- the conclusion of derivative contracts

(each a financial transaction).

FTT would be chargeable at rates to be determined by each participating member state but a rate must be set at least equal to 0.1% of the price paid or, if higher, the market value of the financial instruments, and 0.01% of the notional value of the derivative contract.

In order for FTT to apply to a particular financial transaction:
- at least one party would have to be established in a participating member state; and
- a financial institution established in a participating member state would have to be a party to that transaction.

A financial institution would be treated as established in a participating member state if the other party to the transaction was established in a participating member state, or the financial instrument which was the subject of the financial transaction was issued within the participating member state.

The FTT would primarily be a tax levied on financial institutions (eg, banks, credit institutions and pension funds). However, such financial institutions may choose to transfer an FTT cost on to other persons. It should be noted that liability to FTT would be joint and several.

In the form of the original proposal for FTT, a 'securities lending and borrowing agreement' was considered a financial transaction and therefore taxable once, at a minimum of 0.1% of the value of the collateral.

(f)   VAT

In *Scottish Eastern Investment Trust plc*, EDN/99/211 (VTD 16882), the VAT tribunal held that a stock loan should be treated as an exempt supply by the lender with a value equal only to the fee charged. This is reflected in HMRC's current published guidance (paragraph 6.3 of Notice 701/49/13 and VATFIN4450).

If the borrower belongs outside of the European Union and the lender belongs in the United Kingdom, the lender will be able to recover related input VAT (Regulation 103 of the Value Added Tax Regulations 1995 (SI 1995/2518) and Article 3(a) of the Value Added Tax (Input Tax) (Specified Supplies) Order 1999 (SI 1999/3121)).

Where the lender receives interest on collateral provided by the borrower, HMRC recognises a further exempt supply by the lender. Where the lender then makes a payment to the borrower in respect of such interest, HMRC recognises an exempt supply by the borrower (VATFIN4450). This may reduce the borrower's recoverable input VAT depending upon the particular partial exemption method adopted.

In contrast, dividends received by the lender in respect of securities collateral will be outside the scope of VAT, although it is arguable that manufactured payments give rise to exempt supplies by the recipient.

VATFIN4450 also confirms that if the borrower defaults, any cash collateral retained by the lender is compensation and outside the scope of VAT; and that any part of the collateral returned to the defaulting borrower is also outside the scope of VAT on the basis of not being consideration for any supply.

(g) *The tax treatment of the stock lending fee*

The practice has been for a charitable trust not to take securities collateral but to take cash collateral, keep some of the interest on the cash collateral and pay a reduced amount of interest on the cash collateral. The interest retained equates to what would have been the stock lending fee. There will then be no stock lending fee and the interest on the cash collateral retained in effect compensates the charitable trust in lieu of the stock lending fee.

The origin of the above is that the charitable trust is exempt from income tax on interest on cash collateral with any exemption on the stock lending fee being more problematic. It has already been mentioned that the stock lending fee is taxable as income under what was previously Schedule D Case VI (see paragraph 3.2(g) above) and now income not otherwise charged (Section 687 of the ITTOIA 2005). Charitable trusts do have an exemption from income tax in respect of such income under Section 527 of the ITA 2007 but this is restricted by conditions A and B in Section 527(3) and (4). In particular, condition A is only met if the charitable trust's trading income and miscellaneous income for the tax year either is an amount not exceeding or is not expected to exceed the requisite limit which cannot be above £50,000 (Section 528(6)(b)). It is therefore less problematic for the charitable trust to keep some or all of the interest on the cash collateral in respect of which there is no such limitation and this has been accepted in the past by HMRC. It was not possible for the charitable trust to keep the real interest/dividend on securities collateral without paying a manufactured dividend because it was deemed to make a manufactured dividend under what was Section 596 of the ITA 2007.

The law has changed in that Section 596 has been repealed as from January 1 2014 and there are new disguised interest provisions both for the purposes of income tax and corporation tax. It is considered, however, that the arrangement is still effective for a charitable trust. Sections 614ZA–614ZD of the ITA 2007 cannot apply to a payment of real interest on cash collateral. There is also no disguised interest because a stock lending fee is different to a return equivalent to a rate of interest.

3.5 Insurance companies in respect of BLAGAB

(a) Introduction

This section examines stock lending by an insurance company in respect of basic life assurance and general annuity business (BLAGAB) (taxable on the I minus E basis contained within Sections 55–149 of the FA 2012). It looks first at stock lending with securities collateral and second at stock lending with cash collateral, examining each component set out in the final bullet points of paragraph 3.1 above and assuming that the borrower is a financial trader within the charge to corporation tax.

(b) Tax treatment of manufactured payments

The manufactured payments can go both ways. The borrower (a financial trader) may make manufactured payments to the insurance company in respect of BLAGAB (insurance company) in respect of the stock lent and the insurance company may make manufactured payments to the borrower in respect of any securities collateral.

In the context of an insurance company, Section 614ZB of the ITA 2007 (which applies for the purposes of income tax) will not apply. Instead, Sections 814A–814D of the CTA 2010 apply but only in respect of stock loans of shares and manufactured dividends in respect of shares. It is clear that all of conditions A–C in Section 814B of the CTA 2010 apply to manufactured payments on the stock lent and received by the insurance company. Condition A is satisfied in that an amount is payable under arrangements. Condition B is satisfied in that the arrangements relate to a transfer of shares in a company. Condition C is satisfied in that there is an amount representative of a dividend on the shares.

The insurance company is therefore treated as receiving the real dividend on the shares lent (Section 814D(2) of the CTA 2010). The insurance company will not obtain any tax credit or double tax relief in respect of the manufactured dividend (Section 814D(8) and (5)). The insurance company should, however, obtain the exemption from corporation tax in respect of the manufactured dividend on, for example, shares of a UK resident company (not being an REIT) in the same way as for a real dividend (Section 931D of the CTA 2009). The insurance company will not normally be a small company (Section 931S of the CTA 2009). The manufactured dividend should fall within the exempt class in Section 931F of the CTA 2009 (ie, a distribution in respect of shares which are ordinary shares and which are not redeemable). The insurance company would be taxable on a manufactured dividend in respect of REIT shares as it would be taxed on a real REIT dividend.

The loan relationship provisions parallel to Sections 814A–814B of the CTA 2010 are contained in Sections 539–41 of the CTA 2009. (The same comments regarding Section 541 of the CTA 2009 apply as are made at paragraph 3.3(b)). The manufactured interest payment falls within these sections if it satisfies conditions A and B in Section 539 of the CTA 2009 which are equivalent to conditions A–C in Section 814B of the CTA 2010 for manufactured dividends on shares. Condition A is that an amount is payable by the insurance company under any arrangement and the arrangement relates to a transfer of an asset representing a loan relationship. Condition B is that the amount in condition A is representative of interest under a loan relationship. The loan relationship legislation then applies to the insurance company as if the manufactured interest were payable on a loan by the insurance company and the manufactured interest relationship is the loan relationship under which the real interest is paid. Therefore the insurance company is taxable under the loan relationship legislation in respect of the manufactured interest payment from the borrower.

It is then necessary to consider whether or not the borrower can pay the insurance company the manufactured payment on the securities lent gross:

- if the stock lent is UK shares (not being REIT shares) the borrower can make the manufactured payment gross since there is no provision requiring a deduction;
- if the stock lent is UK REIT shares, there is the same deduction to be made under Section 973 of the ITA 2007 which in this case is nil (Sections 918(3), 973 and Regulation 7(2) of SI 2006/2867);
- if the manufactured payment is in respect of net paying UK securities, the deduction in this case is nil (Sections 919(4) and 933);
- if the manufactured payment is in respect of gross paying UK securities (eg, UK government bonds), there is no deduction to UK tax (Section 921);
- if there is a manufactured payment in respect of overseas shares or bonds, there is no deduction to UK tax since there is no provision requiring a deduction.

Sections 814A–814D of the CTA 2010 and Sections 539–41 of the CTA 2009 apply equally to the insurance company in respect of manufactured payments made by the insurance company on share collateral and bond collateral respectively. The insurance company obtains no deduction for any manufactured dividend (with the exception of a manufactured dividend on REIT shares) paid to the borrower on share collateral but this does not adversely affect the insurance company because it should be exempt in respect of the real dividends received on the share collateral under Section 931D of the CTA 2009. The one exception relates to dividends on REIT shares which the insurance company receives and on which it is taxable. In this case the insurance company does obtain a deduction for the manufactured dividend it pays on the REIT shares by virtue of Section 814C(6) and (7) of the CTA 2010. In the case of REIT share collateral where the insurance company is taxable on the real dividend on the shares, the insurance company can obtain a deduction when it pays the manufactured dividend in respect of such shares as a deemed BLAGAB management expense under Section 76 of the FA 2012. The insurance company is taxed under loan relationship legislation in respect of the real interest it obtains on any bond collateral but it can obtain a deduction for the manufactured interest payment under Section 540(1) of the CTA 2009 if these amounts are recognised in its accounts.

The insurance company can then make manufactured payments on the securities collateral gross or net depending upon the nature of the collateral:

- if the collateral is UK shares (not being REIT shares) there is no deduction since there is no provision requiring a deduction;
- if the collateral is UK REIT shares then there is the same deduction that would

have been made under Section 973 of the ITA 2007 which in this case is nil (Sections 918(3) and 973 and Regulation 7(2) of SI 2006/2867);
- if the manufactured payment is in respect of net paying UK securities, the deduction in this case is nil (Sections 919(4) and 933);
- if the manufactured payment is in respect of gross paying UK securities (eg, UK government bonds), then there is no deduction to UK tax (Section 921 of the ITA 2007);
- if there is a manufactured payment in respect of overseas shares or bonds, there is no deduction to UK tax since there is no provision requiring a deduction.

(c) *Tax treatment of interest on cash collateral*
The interest which the insurance company pays on cash collateral is real interest. The insurance company is a company within Section 874(1)(a) of the ITA 2007 but it only has an obligation to deduct tax at the basic rate on annual interest. Interest payable on cash collateral in respect of the stock loan will be short interest where the cash collateral will be outstanding for less than one year and the stock loan is self-standing and does not form part of other arrangements. If the interest on cash collateral is annual interest, then the insurance company should be able to pay the interest to the borrower gross either as a UK resident company within Section 933 of the ITA 2007 or as a non-resident company within the charge to corporation tax under Section 934.

(d) *The tax treatment of the movement of securities in each direction*
The only UK tax issues applying to movement of the securities lent and the securities collateral are tax on capital gains and stamp taxes. The insurance company suffers no tax on capital gains in respect of the stock lent where the terms of Section 263B of the TCGA 1985 provide that there is no disposal. Section 263B applies equally to the stock loan and the provision and return of collateral. A stock lending arrangement is defined in Section 263B(1) as any arrangement between two persons (the borrower and the lender) in which the lender transfers securities to the borrower otherwise than by way of sale and a requirement is imposed on the borrower to transfer those securities back to the lender otherwise than by way of sale. Section 263B(2) then provides that disposals and acquisitions made in pursuance of any stock lending arrangement are disregarded for capital gains tax purposes. If at any time it becomes apparent that the requirement for the borrower to transfer the securities back to the lender will not be met then the lender is deemed to make a disposal to the borrower at that time and the borrower is deemed to make an acquisition (Section 263B(4)). The above does not apply to stock loans of loan relationships which are within the income and not a capital gains regime. An insurance company should not realise any profit or loss in respect of movements in value of a bond lent or in respect of bond collateral in its accounts. (If it did so, these would be taxable under Section 332 of the CTA 2009.) The former never leaves the insurance company's balance sheet and the latter never enters the insurance company's balance sheet with the result that there should be no profit or loss recognised from movements in value of the bond itself (as opposed to amounts in respect of income from manufactured interest, the

stock lending fee or real interest to the extent these are recognised in its accounts).

There are two parallel exemptions for stamp taxes, one for stamp duty in Section 80C of the FA 1986 and the other for the standard reserve tax in Section 89AA of the FA 1986. They are both cast largely in the same terms so that the two exemptions are dealt with together. Each one of these exemptions largely only applies to UK registered shares since the transfer of most registered loan capital is exempt under Section 79(4) and most shares of non-UK incorporated companies with no UK register are usually outside the scope of UK stamp taxes.

Sections 80C and 89AA deal with the situation where A has entered into an arrangement with B under which B is to transfer stock of a particular kind to A or its nominee and stock of the same kind and amount is to be transferred by A or its nominee to B or its nominee and where one of two sets of conditions is satisfied.

In the above situation, subject to all the conditions there is no stamp duty charge for an instrument transferring stock from B to A or back from A to B pursuant to the arrangement (Section 80C(2)) and no stamp duty reserve tax as regards the agreement to transfer chargeable securities from B to A or back from A to B pursuant to the arrangement (Section 89AA(2)). There is, however, no exemption unless the arrangement is such as is entered into by persons dealing with each other at arm's length and all benefits or risks arising from fluctuations in the market value of the stock before the transfer back to B must lie with B.

The first set of conditions for the stamp duty exemption is that A or B is authorised under the law of an EEA state to provide any of the investment services or activities listed in Section A2 or 3 of Annex 1 to Directive 2004/39/EC of the European Parliament and of the Council dated April 21 2004 (execution of orders on behalf of clients and dealing on own account) in relation to the stock of the kind concerned, whether or not A or B is authorised under the directive and the stock of the kind concerned is regularly traded on a regulated market. The first set of conditions for the stamp duty reserve tax exemption is the same as for the stamp duty exemption except that, in addition, the chargeable securities must be transferred to A or its nominee or to B or its nominee pursuant to the arrangement.

The second set of conditions for the purposes of the stamp duty exemption is that the arrangement is effected on a regulated market, a multilateral trading facility or a recognised foreign exchange and stock of the kind that is regularly traded on that market, facility or exchange. The second set of conditions for the stamp duty reserve tax exemption is the same as for the stamp duty exemption except, in addition, the chargeable securities must be transferred to A or its nominee or to B or its nominee pursuant to the arrangements. An arrangement is regarded as effected on a regulated market, multilateral trading facility or recognised foreign exchange if it is subject to the rules of that market, facility or exchange and it is reported to the market, facility or exchange in accordance with the rules of the market, facility or exchange.

The two parallel exemptions for stamp duty and stamp duty reserve tax apply to the movement of the stock lent and to the movement of collateral, both of which are regarded as stock loans. Therefore, the parties which are B or A will vary depending on whether one is looking at the stock loan or the provision of collateral.

(e) Financial transaction tax

On February 14 2013 the European Commission produced a proposal for a council directive on a common system for a financial transaction tax (FTT) to be implemented under enhanced cooperation by 11 member states, namely Austria, Belgium, Estonia, France, Germany, Greece, Italy, Portugal, Slovakia, Slovenia and Spain.

Ten of the 11 member states subsequently issued a statement reiterating their commitment to FTT. They acknowledged that complex issues had arisen in the discussion of the technical, legal and economic dimensions of the tax and more work was needed. They aimed to finalise 'viable solutions' by December 31 2014, taking into account concerns raised by non-participating member states. They agreed the following key elements:

- a step-by-step implementation with each step to be designed to take into consideration possible economic impacts;
- the first step should be to apply FTT to equities and some derivatives;
- the first step should be implemented no later than January 1 2016;
- participating member states should be free to apply FTT to other products from January 1 2016 in order to maintain existing taxes.

On January 21 2015 the French and Austrian finance ministers sent a joint letter to the other nine participating countries of the EU FTT coalition in order to relaunch the discussion on how the EU FTT could be designed and implemented.

They proposed to discuss the FTT on a wide base and at low rates.

They also proposed to create a secretariat chaired by one of the participating countries in order to prepare and debrief meetings with the technical support of the European Commission. The Austrian finance minister would have the permanent chairmanship of the group and the Portuguese finance minister would lead the technical work.

Following the above, on January 27 2015 10 countries of the EU FTT coalition (excluding Greece) released a joint statement to officially support the initiative taken by France and Austria. They also reiterated their willingness to implement the tax on January 1 2016.

If FTT were adopted in its original form, then, subject to certain exemptions, the FTT would apply to financial transactions as defined including:

- purchases or sales of a wide range of financial instruments which is very broadly defined and includes shares, bonds, money marketing instruments and many other instruments;
- the conclusion of derivative contracts

(each a financial transaction).

FTT would be chargeable at rates to be determined by each participating member state but a rate must be set at least equal to 0.1% of the price paid or, if higher, the market value of the financial instruments, and 0.01% of the notional value of the derivative contract .

In order for FTT to apply to a particular financial transaction:

- at least one party would have to be established in a participating member state; and
- a financial institution established in a participating member state would have to be a party to that transaction.

A financial institution would be treated as established in a participating member state if the other party to the transaction was established in a participating member state or the financial instrument which was the subject to the financial transaction was issued within the participating member state.

The FTT would primarily be a tax levied on financial institutions (eg banks, credit institutions and pension funds). However, such financial institutions may choose to transfer an FTT cost on to other persons. It should be noted that liability to FTT would be joint and several.

In the form of the original proposal for FTT, a 'securities lending and borrowing agreement' was considered a financial transaction and therefore taxable once, at a minimum of 0.1% of the value of the collateral.

(f)   VAT

In *Scottish Eastern Investment Trust plc*, EDN/99/211 (VTD 16882), the VAT tribunal held that a stock loan should be treated as an exempt supply by the lender with a value equal only to the fee charged. This is reflected in HMRC's current published guidance (paragraph 6.3 of Notice 701/49/13 and VATFIN4450).

If the borrower belongs outside of the European Union and the lender belongs in the United Kingdom, the lender will be able to recover related input VAT (Regulation 103 of the Value Added Tax Regulations 1995 (SI 1995/2518) and Article 3(a) of the Value Added Tax (Input Tax) (Specified Supplies) Order 1999 (SI 1999/3121)).

Where the lender receives interest on collateral provided by the borrower, HMRC recognises a further exempt supply by the lender. Where the lender then makes a payment to the borrower in respect of such interest, HMRC recognises an exempt supply by the borrower (VATFIN4450). This may reduce the borrower's recoverable input VAT depending on the particular partial exemption method adopted.

In contrast, dividends received by the lender in respect of securities collateral will be outside the scope of VAT, although it is arguable that manufactured payments give rise to exempt supplies by the recipient.

VATFIN4450 also confirms that if the borrower defaults, any cash collateral retained by the lender is compensation and outside the scope of VAT; and that any part of the collateral returned to the defaulting borrower is also outside the scope of VAT on the basis of not being consideration for any supply.

(g)   *Tax treatment of stock lending fee*

HMRC had always considered that pension schemes, before they obtained the exemption from income tax in respect of stock lending fees contained in Section 129B of the ICTA 1998, were taxable on stock lending fees under what was then Schedule D Case VI and not as income from a trade under Schedule D Case I. An insurance company has no special exemption from corporation tax in respect of stock lending fees and it is therefore considered that an insurance company is taxable on a stock lending fee in respect of a stock loan of shares and income. A stock lending fee in respect of a stock loan of a bond will be for a profit arising from a loan relationship and so will be taxed under the loan relationship legislation.

3.6   Tax position of the borrower

(a)   Corporation tax treatment
This Part has indicated how the borrower of stock, which is a financial trader within the charge to corporation tax, should treat manufactured payments to the lender in the case of four different categories of institutional lender.

It is necessary to deal with the borrower's own corporation tax position. The financial trader will be subject to corporation tax on any real dividend obtained on shares borrowed to the extent these are recognised in its profit and loss accounts (Section 931W(1)(b) of the CTA 2009 and Section 46 of the CTA 2009). It will equally obtain a deduction for the corresponding manufactured dividend paid to the lender by virtue of Section 814C(3) of the ITA 2007 to the extent to which it is allowed a deduction from its trading profits under Part 3 of the CTA 2009 and such deduction is recognised in its profit and loss account. The financial trader will also be subject to corporation tax under the loan relationship legislation in respect of any interest received on bonds borrowed as a trading credit and will equally obtain a deduction for the corresponding manufactured interest payment under Section 540(1) of the CTA 2009 as a trading debit to the extent to which these are recognised in its profit and loss account.

The financial trader will not need Section 263B of the TCGA 1992 in order for there to be no disposal for the purposes of tax on capital gains since all the transactions will take place as part of a financial trade. The profit or loss of the financial trade from the stock lending transaction will be determined by the financial trader's accounting profit and loss account and it would not normally have any profit or loss from movements in value of the stock borrowed or the securities collateral since these would normally not be recognised in its accounts. If the stock borrowed is used, for example, to settle a short sale, the financial trader will recognise an unrealised profit or loss on the short position if this crosses an accounting year end, and be taxed on the fair value movement.

(b)   Stamp duty and stamp duty reserve tax
The financial trader will be able to rely on Section 80C of the FA 1986 and Section 89AA of the FA 1986 in order to have an exemption from stamp duty and stamp duty reserve tax in respect of the acquisition of the stock borrowed and the return of any collateral. It would not seek to obtain exemption from stamp duty under, for example, Section 80A of the FA 1986 (sales to intermediaries) because such intermediary relief requires a sale and there is no sale in the context of a stock loan or the provision or return of collateral. The same comments regarding stamp duty and stamp duty reserve tax apply to the financial trader as to the stock lender.

(c) Financial transaction tax

On February 14 2013 the European Commission produced a proposal for a council directive on a common system for a financial transaction tax (FTT) to be implemented under enhanced cooperation by 11 member states, namely Austria, Belgium, Estonia, France, Germany, Greece, Italy, Portugal, Slovakia, Slovenia and Spain.

Ten of the 11 member states subsequently issued a statement reiterating their commitment to FTT. They acknowledged that complex issues had arisen in the discussion of the technical, legal and economic dimensions of the tax and more work was needed. They aimed to finalise 'viable solutions' by December 31 2014, taking into account concerns raised by non-participating member states. They agreed the following key elements:

- a step-by-step implementation with each step to be designed to take into consideration possible economic impacts;
- the first step should be to apply FTT to equities and some derivatives;
- the first step should be implemented no later than January 1 2016;
- participating member states should be free to apply FTT to other products from January 1 2016 in order to maintain existing taxes.

On 21 January 2015 the French and Austrian finance ministers sent a joint letter to the other nine participating countries of the EU FTT coalition in order to relaunch the discussion on how the EU FTT could be designed and implemented.

They proposed to discuss the FTT on a wide base and at low rates.

They also proposed to create a secretariat chaired by one of the participating countries in order to prepare and debrief meetings with the technical support of the European Commission. The Austrian finance minister would have the permanent chairmanship of the group and the Portuguese finance minister would lead the technical work.

Following the above, on January 27 2015 10 countries of the EU FTT coalition (excluding Greece) released a joint statement to officially support the initiative taken by France and Austria. They also reiterated their willingness to implement the tax on January 1 2016.

If FTT were adopted in its original form, then, subject to certain exemptions, the FTT would apply to financial transactions as defined including:

- purchases or sales of a wide range of financial instruments which is very broadly defined and includes shares, bonds, money marketing instruments and many other instruments;
- the conclusion of derivative contracts

(each a financial transaction).

FTT would be chargeable at rates to be determined by each participating member state but a rate must be set at least equal to 0.1% of the price paid or, if higher, the market value of the financial instruments, and 0.01% of the notional value of the derivative contract.

In order for FTT to apply to a particular financial transaction:

- at least one party would have to be established in a participating member state; and
- a financial institution established in a participating member state would have to be a party to that transaction.

A financial institution would be treated as established in a participating member state if the other party to the transaction was established in a participating member state or the financial instrument which was the subject of the financial transaction was issued within the participating member state.

The FTT would primarily be a tax levied on financial institutions (eg, banks, credit institutions and pension funds). However, such financial institutions may choose to transfer an FTT cost on to other persons. It should be noted that liability to FTT would be joint and several.

In the form of the original proposal for FTT, a 'securities lending and borrowing agreement' was considered a financial transaction and therefore taxable once, at a minimum of 0.1% of the value of the collateral.

(d) **VAT**

In *Scottish Eastern Investment Trust plc*, EDN/99/211 (VTD 16882), the VAT tribunal held that a stock loan should be treated as an exempt supply by the lender with a value equal only to the fee charged. This is reflected in HMRC's current published guidance (paragraph 6.3 of Notice 701/49/13 and VATFIN4450).

If the borrower belongs outside of the European Union and the lender belongs in the United Kingdom, the lender will be able to recover related input VAT (Regulation 103 of the Value Added Tax Regulations 1995 (SI 1995/2518) and Article 3(a) of the Value Added Tax (Input Tax) (Specified Supplies) Order 1999 (SI 1999/3121)).

Where the lender receives interest on collateral provided by the borrower, HMRC recognises a further exempt supply by the lender. Where the lender then makes a payment to the borrower in respect of such interest, HMRC recognises an exempt supply by the borrower (VATFIN4450). This may reduce the borrower's recoverable input VAT depending upon the particular partial exemption method adopted.

In contrast, dividends received by the lender in respect of securities collateral will be outside the scope of VAT, although it is arguable that manufactured payments give rise to exempt supplies by the recipient.

VATFIN4450 also confirms that if the borrower defaults, any cash collateral retained by the lender is compensation and outside the scope of VAT; and that any part of the collateral returned to the defaulting borrower is also outside the scope of VAT on the basis of not being consideration for any supply.

3.7 **Base erosion and profit shifting**

The OECD's base erosion and profit shifting (BEPS) work is addressing many issues and includes Action 2 which seeks to neutralise the effects of hybrid mismatch arrangements through recommendations for domestic rules and recommended changes to the Model Double Taxation Convention. The 'Action 2: 2014 Deliverable' (September 2014) notes that:

Furthermore there are a number of specific areas where the domestic rules in Part 1 may need to be further refined. This is the case for certain capital markets transactions (such as on-market stock lending and repos).

The UK government issued a consultancy document entitled "Tackling aggressive tax planning: implementing the agreed G20-OECD approach for addressing hybrid mismatch arrangements" in December 2014. The consultation period closed on February 11 2015 and a summary of responses is due to be published in the summer of 2015.

4. Conclusion

This ends the extended journey through the UK tax legislation as it deals with repos and stock loans. It is surprising that such day-to-day transactions require such detailed legislation in such disparate places but, dear reader, whatever you do please do not ask for the legislation to be simplified.

The author would like to especially thank Nick Beecham for his contribution of the VAT portions of this chapter and also those very helpful persons who have given comments on earlier drafts of this chapter and, in particular, Geoff Pennells and Jorge Morley-Smith (in respect of AIFs in Part 3). Any errors are the author's.

Appendices

TBMA/ISMA —————— 254
**– Global Master
Repurchase Agreement
(2000 version)**
A facsimile of the Global Master Repurchase Agreement (2000 version) reproduced by kind permission of the Securities Industry and Financial Markets Association and the International Capital Market Association.

SIFMA/ICMA —————— 289
**– Global Master
Repurchase Agreement
(2011 version)**
A facsimile of the Global Master Repurchase Agreement (2011 version) reproduced by kind permission of the Securities Industry and Financial Markets Association and the International Capital Market Association.

ISLA —————— 325
**Global Master
Securities
Lending Agreement (2010 version)**
A facsimile of the Global Master Securities Lending Agreement (2010 version) and related Tax Addenda reproduced by kind permission of the International Securities Lending Association.

ISLA —————— 365
**Global Master Securities
Lending Agreement – 2014 UK
Tax Addendum**
Reproduced by kind permission as aforesaid.

ISLA —————— 371
**Global Master Securities
Lending Agreement – 2014 US
Tax Addendum**
Reproduced by kind permission as aforesaid.

Appendices

The Bond Market Association
New York • Washington • London
www.bondmarkets.com

International Securities Market Association
Rigistrasse 60, P.O. Box, CH-8033, Zürich
www.isma.org

2000 VERSION

TBMA/ISMA

GLOBAL MASTER REPURCHASE AGREEMENT

Dated as of _____

Between:

_____ ("Party A")

and

_____ ("Party B")

1. **Applicability**

(a) From time to time the parties hereto may enter into transactions in which one party, acting through a Designated Office, ("Seller") agrees to sell to the other, acting through a Designated Office, ("Buyer") securities and financial instruments ("Securities") (subject to paragraph 1(c), other than equities and Net Paying Securities) against the payment of the purchase price by Buyer to Seller, with a simultaneous agreement by Buyer to sell to Seller Securities equivalent to such Securities at a date certain or on demand against the payment of the repurchase price by Seller to Buyer.

(b) Each such transaction (which may be a repurchase transaction ("Repurchase Transaction") or a buy and sell back transaction ("Buy/Sell Back Transaction")) shall be referred to herein as a "Transaction" and shall be governed by this Agreement, including any supplemental terms or conditions contained in Annex I hereto, unless otherwise agreed in writing.

October 2000

254

(c) If this Agreement may be applied to -

    (i) Buy/Sell Back Transactions, this shall be specified in Annex I hereto, and the provisions of the Buy/Sell Back Annex shall apply to such Buy/Sell Back Transactions;

    (ii) Net Paying Securities, this shall be specified in Annex I hereto and the provisions of Annex I, paragraph 1(b) shall apply to Transactions involving Net Paying Securities.

(d) If Transactions are to be effected under this Agreement by either party as an agent, this shall be specified in Annex I hereto, and the provisions of the Agency Annex shall apply to such Agency Transactions.

2. Definitions

(a) "Act of Insolvency" shall occur with respect to any party hereto upon -

    (i) its making a general assignment for the benefit of, entering into a reorganisation, arrangement, or composition with creditors; or

    (ii) its admitting in writing that it is unable to pay its debts as they become due; or

    (iii) its seeking, consenting to or acquiescing in the appointment of any trustee, administrator, receiver or liquidator or analogous officer of it or any material part of its property; or

    (iv) the presentation or filing of a petition in respect of it (other than by the counterparty to this Agreement in respect of any obligation under this Agreement) in any court or before any agency alleging or for the bankruptcy, winding-up or insolvency of such party (or any analogous proceeding) or seeking any reorganisation, arrangement, composition, re-adjustment, administration, liquidation, dissolution or similar relief under any present or future statute, law or regulation, such petition (except in the case of a petition for winding-up or any analogous proceeding, in respect of which no such 30 day period shall apply) not having been stayed or dismissed within 30 days of its filing; or

    (v) the appointment of a receiver, administrator, liquidator or trustee or analogous officer of such party or over all or any material part of such party's property; or

    (vi) the convening of any meeting of its creditors for the purposes of considering a voluntary arrangement as referred to in section 3 of the Insolvency Act 1986 (or any analogous proceeding);

(b) "Agency Transaction", the meaning specified in paragraph 1 of the Agency Annex;

(c) "Appropriate Market", the meaning specified in paragraph 10;

(d) "Base Currency", the currency indicated in Annex I hereto;

(e) "Business Day" -

    (i) in relation to the settlement of any Transaction which is to be settled through Clearstream or Euroclear, a day on which Clearstream or, as the case may be, Euroclear is open to settle business in the currency in which the Purchase Price and the Repurchase Price are denominated;

    (ii) in relation to the settlement of any Transaction which is to be settled through a settlement system other than Clearstream or Euroclear, a day on which that settlement system is open to settle such Transaction;

    (iii) in relation to any delivery of Securities not falling within (i) or (ii) above, a day on which banks are open for business in the place where delivery of the relevant Securities is to be effected; and

    (iv) in relation to any obligation to make a payment not falling within (i) or (ii) above, a day other than a Saturday or a Sunday on which banks are open for business in the principal financial centre of the country of which the currency in which the payment is denominated is the official currency and, if different, in the place where any account designated by the parties for the making or receipt of the payment is situated (or, in the case of a payment in euro, a day on which TARGET operates);

(f) "Cash Margin", a cash sum paid to Buyer or Seller in accordance with paragraph 4;

(g) "Clearstream", Clearstream Banking, société anonyme, (previously Cedelbank) or any successor thereto;

(h) "Confirmation", the meaning specified in paragraph 3(b);

(i) "Contractual Currency", the meaning specified in paragraph 7(a);

(j) "Defaulting Party", the meaning specified in paragraph 10;

(k) "Default Market Value", the meaning specified in paragraph 10;

(l) "Default Notice", a written notice served by the non-Defaulting Party on the Defaulting Party under paragraph 10 stating that an event shall be treated as an Event of Default for the purposes of this Agreement;

(m) "Default Valuation Notice", the meaning specified in paragraph 10;

(n) "Default Valuation Time", the meaning specified in paragraph 10;

(o) "Deliverable Securities", the meaning specified in paragraph 10;

(p) "Designated Office", with respect to a party, a branch or office of that party which is specified as such in Annex I hereto or such other branch or office as may be agreed to by the parties;

(q) "Distributions", the meaning specified in sub-paragraph (w) below;

(r) "Equivalent Margin Securities", Securities equivalent to Securities previously transferred as Margin Securities;

(s) "Equivalent Securities", with respect to a Transaction, Securities equivalent to Purchased Securities under that Transaction. If and to the extent that such Purchased Securities have been redeemed, the expression shall mean a sum of money equivalent to the proceeds of the redemption;

(t) Securities are "equivalent to" other Securities for the purposes of this Agreement if they are: (i) of the same issuer; (ii) part of the same issue; and (iii) of an identical type, nominal value, description and (except where otherwise stated) amount as those other Securities, provided that -

   (A) Securities will be equivalent to other Securities notwithstanding that those Securities have been redenominated into euro or that the nominal value of those Securities has changed in connection with such redenomination; and

   (B) where Securities have been converted, subdivided or consolidated or have become the subject of a takeover or the holders of Securities have become entitled to receive or acquire other Securities or other property or the Securities have become subject to any similar event, the expression "equivalent to" shall mean Securities equivalent to (as defined in the provisions of this definition preceding the proviso) the original Securities together with or replaced by a sum of money or Securities or other property equivalent to (as so defined) that receivable by holders of such original Securities resulting from such event;

(u) "Euroclear", Morgan Guaranty Trust Company of New York, Brussels office, as operator of the Euroclear System or any successor thereto;

(v) "Event of Default", the meaning specified in paragraph 10;

(w) "Income", with respect to any Security at any time, all interest, dividends or other distributions thereon, but excluding distributions which are a payment or repayment of principal in respect of the relevant securities ("Distributions");

(x) "Income Payment Date", with respect to any Securities, the date on which Income is paid in respect of such Securities or, in the case of registered Securities, the date by reference to which particular registered holders are identified as being entitled to payment of Income;

(y) "LIBOR", in relation to any sum in any currency, the one month London Inter Bank Offered Rate in respect of that currency as quoted on page 3750 on the Bridge

Telerate Service (or such other page as may replace page 3750 on that service) as of 11:00 a.m., London time, on the date on which it is to be determined;

(z) "Margin Ratio", with respect to a Transaction, the Market Value of the Purchased Securities at the time when the Transaction was entered into divided by the Purchase Price (and so that, where a Transaction relates to Securities of different descriptions and the Purchase Price is apportioned by the parties among Purchased Securities of each such description, a separate Margin Ratio shall apply in respect of Securities of each such description), or such other proportion as the parties may agree with respect to that Transaction;

(aa) "Margin Securities", in relation to a Margin Transfer, Securities reasonably acceptable to the party calling for such Margin Transfer;

(bb) "Margin Transfer", any, or any combination of, the payment or repayment of Cash Margin and the transfer of Margin Securities or Equivalent Margin Securities;

(cc) "Market Value", with respect to any Securities as of any time on any date, the price for such Securities at such time on such date obtained from a generally recognised source agreed to by the parties (and where different prices are obtained for different delivery dates, the price so obtainable for the earliest available such delivery date) (provided that the price of Securities that are suspended shall (for the purposes of paragraph 4) be nil unless the parties otherwise agree and (for all other purposes) shall be the price of those Securities as of close of business on the dealing day in the relevant market last preceding the date of suspension) plus the aggregate amount of Income which, as of such date, has accrued but not yet been paid in respect of the Securities to the extent not included in such price as of such date, and for these purposes any sum in a currency other than the Contractual Currency for the Transaction in question shall be converted into such Contractual Currency at the Spot Rate prevailing at the relevant time;

(dd) "Net Exposure", the meaning specified in paragraph 4(c);

(ee) the "Net Margin" provided to a party at any time, the excess (if any) at that time of (i) the sum of the amount of Cash Margin paid to that party (including accrued interest on such Cash Margin which has not been paid to the other party) and the Market Value of Margin Securities transferred to that party under paragraph 4(a) (excluding any Cash Margin which has been repaid to the other party and any Margin Securities in respect of which Equivalent Margin Securities have been transferred to the other party) over (ii) the sum of the amount of Cash Margin paid to the other party (including accrued interest on such Cash Margin which has not been paid by the other party) and the Market Value of Margin Securities transferred to the other party under paragraph 4(a) (excluding any Cash Margin which has been repaid by the other party and any Margin Securities in respect of which Equivalent Margin Securities have been transferred by the other party) and for this purpose any amounts not denominated in the Base Currency shall be converted into the Base Currency at the Spot Rate prevailing at the relevant time;

(ff) "Net Paying Securities", Securities which are of a kind such that, were they to be the subject of a Transaction to which paragraph 5 applies, any payment made by Buyer under paragraph 5 would be one in respect of which either Buyer would or might be required to make a withholding or deduction for or on account of taxes or duties or Seller might be required to make or account for a payment for or on account of taxes or duties (in each case other than tax on overall net income) by reference to such payment;

(gg) "Net Value", the meaning specified in paragraph 10;

(hh) "New Purchased Securities", the meaning specified in paragraph 8(a);

(ii) "Price Differential", with respect to any Transaction as of any date, the aggregate amount obtained by daily application of the Pricing Rate for such Transaction to the Purchase Price for such Transaction (on a 360 day basis or 365 day basis in accordance with the applicable ISMA convention, unless otherwise agreed between the parties for the Transaction), for the actual number of days during the period commencing on (and including) the Purchase Date for such Transaction and ending on (but excluding) the date of calculation or, if earlier, the Repurchase Date;

(jj) "Pricing Rate", with respect to any Transaction, the per annum percentage rate for calculation of the Price Differential agreed to by Buyer and Seller in relation to that Transaction;

(kk) "Purchase Date", with respect to any Transaction, the date on which Purchased Securities are to be sold by Seller to Buyer in relation to that Transaction;

(ll) "Purchase Price", on the Purchase Date, the price at which Purchased Securities are sold or are to be sold by Seller to Buyer;

(mm) "Purchased Securities", with respect to any Transaction, the Securities sold or to be sold by Seller to Buyer under that Transaction, and any New Purchased Securities transferred by Seller to Buyer under paragraph 8 in respect of that Transaction;

(nn) "Receivable Securities", the meaning specified in paragraph 10;

(oo) "Repurchase Date", with respect to any Transaction, the date on which Buyer is to sell Equivalent Securities to Seller in relation to that Transaction;

(pp) "Repurchase Price", with respect to any Transaction and as of any date, the sum of the Purchase Price and the Price Differential as of such date;

(qq) "Special Default Notice", the meaning specified in paragraph 14;

October 2000

Appendices

(rr) "Spot Rate", where an amount in one currency is to be converted into a second currency on any date, unless the parties otherwise agree, the spot rate of exchange quoted by Barclays Bank PLC in the London inter-bank market for the sale by it of such second currency against a purchase by it of such first currency;

(ss) "TARGET", the Trans-European Automated Real-time Gross Settlement Express Transfer System;

(tt) "Term", with respect to any Transaction, the interval of time commencing with the Purchase Date and ending with the Repurchase Date;

(uu) "Termination", with respect to any Transaction, refers to the requirement with respect to such Transaction for Buyer to sell Equivalent Securities against payment by Seller of the Repurchase Price in accordance with paragraph 3(f), and reference to a Transaction having a "fixed term" or being "terminable upon demand" shall be construed accordingly;

(vv) "Transaction Costs", the meaning specified in paragraph 10;

(ww) "Transaction Exposure", with respect to any Transaction at any time during the period from the Purchase Date to the Repurchase Date (or, if later, the date on which Equivalent Securities are delivered to Seller or the Transaction is terminated under paragraph 10(g) or 10(h)), the difference between (i) the Repurchase Price at such time multiplied by the applicable Margin Ratio (or, where the Transaction relates to Securities of more than one description to which different Margin Ratios apply, the amount produced by multiplying the Repurchase Price attributable to Equivalent Securities of each such description by the applicable Margin Ratio and aggregating the resulting amounts, the Repurchase Price being for this purpose attributed to Equivalent Securities of each such description in the same proportions as those in which the Purchase Price was apportioned among the Purchased Securities) and (ii) the Market Value of Equivalent Securities at such time. If (i) is greater than (ii), Buyer has a Transaction Exposure for that Transaction equal to that excess. If (ii) is greater than (i), Seller has a Transaction Exposure for that Transaction equal to that excess; and

(xx) except in paragraphs 14(b)(i) and 18, references in this Agreement to "written" communications and communications "in writing" include communications made through any electronic system agreed between the parties which is capable of reproducing such communication in hard copy form.

3. **Initiation; Confirmation; Termination**

(a) A Transaction may be entered into orally or in writing at the initiation of either Buyer or Seller.

(b) Upon agreeing to enter into a Transaction hereunder Buyer or Seller (or both), as shall have been agreed, shall promptly deliver to the other party written confirmation

October 2000

of such Transaction (a "Confirmation").

The Confirmation shall describe the Purchased Securities (including CUSIP or ISIN or other identifying number or numbers, if any), identify Buyer and Seller and set forth -

(i) the Purchase Date;

(ii) the Purchase Price;

(iii) the Repurchase Date, unless the Transaction is to be terminable on demand (in which case the Confirmation shall state that it is terminable on demand);

(iv) the Pricing Rate applicable to the Transaction;

(v) in respect of each party the details of the bank account[s] to which payments to be made hereunder are to be credited;

(vi) where the Buy/Sell Back Annex applies, whether the Transaction is a Repurchase Transaction or a Buy/Sell Back Transaction;

(vii) where the Agency Annex applies, whether the Transaction is an Agency Transaction and, if so, the identity of the party which is acting as agent and the name, code or identifier of the Principal; and

(viii) any additional terms or conditions of the Transaction;

and may be in the form of Annex II hereto or may be in any other form to which the parties agree.

The Confirmation relating to a Transaction shall, together with this Agreement, constitute prima facie evidence of the terms agreed between Buyer and Seller for that Transaction, unless objection is made with respect to the Confirmation promptly after receipt thereof. In the event of any conflict between the terms of such Confirmation and this Agreement, the Confirmation shall prevail in respect of that Transaction and those terms only.

(c) On the Purchase Date for a Transaction, Seller shall transfer the Purchased Securities to Buyer or its agent against the payment of the Purchase Price by Buyer.

(d) Termination of a Transaction will be effected, in the case of on demand Transactions, on the date specified for Termination in such demand, and, in the case of fixed term Transactions, on the date fixed for Termination.

(e) In the case of on demand Transactions, demand for Termination shall be made by Buyer or Seller, by telephone or otherwise, and shall provide for Termination to occur after not less than the minimum period as is customarily required for the settlement or delivery of money or Equivalent Securities of the relevant kind.

(f) On the Repurchase Date, Buyer shall transfer to Seller or its agent Equivalent

Securities against the payment of the Repurchase Price by Seller (less any amount then payable and unpaid by Buyer to Seller pursuant to paragraph 5).

4. **Margin Maintenance**

(a) If at any time either party has a Net Exposure in respect of the other party it may by notice to the other party require the other party to make a Margin Transfer to it of an aggregate amount or value at least equal to that Net Exposure.

(b) A notice under sub-paragraph (a) above may be given orally or in writing.

(c) For the purposes of this Agreement a party has a Net Exposure in respect of the other party if the aggregate of all the first party's Transaction Exposures plus any amount payable to the first party under paragraph 5 but unpaid less the amount of any Net Margin provided to the first party exceeds the aggregate of all the other party's Transaction Exposures plus any amount payable to the other party under paragraph 5 but unpaid less the amount of any Net Margin provided to the other party; and the amount of the Net Exposure is the amount of the excess. For this purpose any amounts not denominated in the Base Currency shall be converted into the Base Currency at the Spot Rate prevailing at the relevant time.

(d) To the extent that a party calling for a Margin Transfer has previously paid Cash Margin which has not been repaid or delivered Margin Securities in respect of which Equivalent Margin Securities have not been delivered to it, that party shall be entitled to require that such Margin Transfer be satisfied first by the repayment of such Cash Margin or the delivery of Equivalent Margin Securities but, subject to this, the composition of a Margin Transfer shall be at the option of the party making such Margin Transfer.

(e) Any Cash Margin transferred shall be in the Base Currency or such other currency as the parties may agree.

(f) A payment of Cash Margin shall give rise to a debt owing from the party receiving such payment to the party making such payment. Such debt shall bear interest at such rate, payable at such times, as may be specified in Annex I hereto in respect of the relevant currency or otherwise agreed between the parties, and shall be repayable subject to the terms of this Agreement.

(g) Where Seller or Buyer becomes obliged under sub-paragraph (a) above to make a Margin Transfer, it shall transfer Cash Margin or Margin Securities or Equivalent Margin Securities within the minimum period specified in Annex I hereto or, if no period is there specified, such minimum period as is customarily required for the settlement or delivery of money, Margin Securities or Equivalent Margin Securities of the relevant kind.

(h) The parties may agree that, with respect to any Transaction, the provisions of sub-paragraphs (a) to (g) above shall not apply but instead that margin may be provided

October 2000

separately in respect of that Transaction in which case -

- (i) that Transaction shall not be taken into account when calculating whether either party has a Net Exposure;

- (ii) margin shall be provided in respect of that Transaction in such manner as the parties may agree; and

- (iii) margin provided in respect of that Transaction shall not be taken into account for the purposes of sub-paragraphs (a) to (g) above.

(i) The parties may agree that any Net Exposure which may arise shall be eliminated not by Margin Transfers under the preceding provisions of this paragraph but by the repricing of Transactions under sub-paragraph (j) below, the adjustment of Transactions under sub-paragraph (k) below or a combination of both these methods.

(j) Where the parties agree that a Transaction is to be repriced under this sub-paragraph, such repricing shall be effected as follows -

- (i) the Repurchase Date under the relevant Transaction (the "Original Transaction") shall be deemed to occur on the date on which the repricing is to be effected (the "Repricing Date");

- (ii) the parties shall be deemed to have entered into a new Transaction (the "Repriced Transaction") on the terms set out in (iii) to (vi) below;

- (iii) the Purchased Securities under the Repriced Transaction shall be Securities equivalent to the Purchased Securities under the Original Transaction;

- (iv) the Purchase Date under the Repriced Transaction shall be the Repricing Date;

- (v) the Purchase Price under the Repriced Transaction shall be such amount as shall, when multiplied by the Margin Ratio applicable to the Original Transaction, be equal to the Market Value of such Securities on the Repricing Date;

- (vi) the Repurchase Date, the Pricing Rate, the Margin Ratio and, subject as aforesaid, the other terms of the Repriced Transaction shall be identical to those of the Original Transaction;

- (vii) the obligations of the parties with respect to the delivery of the Purchased Securities and the payment of the Purchase Price under the Repriced Transaction shall be set off against their obligations with respect to the delivery of Equivalent Securities and payment of the Repurchase Price under the Original Transaction and accordingly only a net cash sum shall be paid by one party to the other. Such net cash sum shall be paid within the period specified in sub-paragraph (g) above.

Appendices

(k) The adjustment of a Transaction (the "Original Transaction") under this sub-paragraph shall be effected by the parties agreeing that on the date on which the adjustment is to be made (the "Adjustment Date") the Original Transaction shall be terminated and they shall enter into a new Transaction (the "Replacement Transaction") in accordance with the following provisions -

(i) the Original Transaction shall be terminated on the Adjustment Date on such terms as the parties shall agree on or before the Adjustment Date;

(ii) the Purchased Securities under the Replacement Transaction shall be such Securities as the parties shall agree on or before the Adjustment Date (being Securities the aggregate Market Value of which at the Adjustment Date is substantially equal to the Repurchase Price under the Original Transaction at the Adjustment Date multiplied by the Margin Ratio applicable to the Original Transaction);

(iii) the Purchase Date under the Replacement Transaction shall be the Adjustment Date;

(iv) the other terms of the Replacement Transaction shall be such as the parties shall agree on or before the Adjustment Date; and

(v) the obligations of the parties with respect to payment and delivery of Securities on the Adjustment Date under the Original Transaction and the Replacement Transaction shall be settled in accordance with paragraph 6 within the minimum period specified in sub-paragraph (g) above.

5. **Income Payments**

Unless otherwise agreed -

(i) where the Term of a particular Transaction extends over an Income Payment Date in respect of any Securities subject to that Transaction, Buyer shall on the date such Income is paid by the issuer transfer to or credit to the account of Seller an amount equal to (and in the same currency as) the amount paid by the issuer;

(ii) where Margin Securities are transferred from one party ("the first party") to the other party ("the second party") and an Income Payment Date in respect of such Securities occurs before Equivalent Margin Securities are transferred by the second party to the first party, the second party shall on the date such Income is paid by the issuer transfer to or credit to the account of the first party an amount equal to (and in the same currency as) the amount paid by the issuer;

and for the avoidance of doubt references in this paragraph to the amount of any Income paid by the issuer of any Securities shall be to an amount paid without any

October 2000

withholding or deduction for or on account of taxes or duties notwithstanding that a payment of such Income made in certain circumstances may be subject to such a withholding or deduction.

6. **Payment and Transfer**

(a) Unless otherwise agreed, all money paid hereunder shall be in immediately available freely convertible funds of the relevant currency. All Securities to be transferred hereunder (i) shall be in suitable form for transfer and shall be accompanied by duly executed instruments of transfer or assignment in blank (where required for transfer) and such other documentation as the transferee may reasonably request, or (ii) shall be transferred through the book entry system of Euroclear or Clearstream, or (iii) shall be transferred through any other agreed securities clearance system or (iv) shall be transferred by any other method mutually acceptable to Seller and Buyer.

(b) Unless otherwise agreed, all money payable by one party to the other in respect of any Transaction shall be paid free and clear of, and without withholding or deduction for, any taxes or duties of whatsoever nature imposed, levied, collected, withheld or assessed by any authority having power to tax, unless the withholding or deduction of such taxes or duties is required by law. In that event, unless otherwise agreed, the paying party shall pay such additional amounts as will result in the net amounts receivable by the other party (after taking account of such withholding or deduction) being equal to such amounts as would have been received by it had no such taxes or duties been required to be withheld or deducted.

(c) Unless otherwise agreed in writing between the parties, under each Transaction transfer of Purchased Securities by Seller and payment of Purchase Price by Buyer against the transfer of such Purchased Securities shall be made simultaneously and transfer of Equivalent Securities by Buyer and payment of Repurchase Price payable by Seller against the transfer of such Equivalent Securities shall be made simultaneously.

(d) Subject to and without prejudice to the provisions of sub-paragraph 6(c), either party may from time to time in accordance with market practice and in recognition of the practical difficulties in arranging simultaneous delivery of Securities and money waive in relation to any Transaction its rights under this Agreement to receive simultaneous transfer and/or payment provided that transfer and/or payment shall, notwithstanding such waiver, be made on the same day and provided also that no such waiver in respect of one Transaction shall affect or bind it in respect of any other Transaction.

(e) The parties shall execute and deliver all necessary documents and take all necessary steps to procure that all right, title and interest in any Purchased Securities, any Equivalent Securities, any Margin Securities and any Equivalent Margin Securities shall pass to the party to which transfer is being made upon transfer of the same in accordance with this Agreement, free from all liens, claims, charges and encumbrances.

Appendices

(f) Notwithstanding the use of expressions such as "*Repurchase Date*", "*Repurchase Price*", "*margin*", "*Net Margin*", "*Margin Ratio*" and "*substitution*", which are used to reflect terminology used in the market for transactions of the kind provided for in this Agreement, all right, title and interest in and to Securities and money transferred or paid under this Agreement shall pass to the transferee upon transfer or payment, the obligation of the party receiving Purchased Securities or Margin Securities being an obligation to transfer Equivalent Securities or Equivalent Margin Securities.

(g) Time shall be of the essence in this Agreement.

(h) Subject to paragraph 10, all amounts in the same currency payable by each party to the other under any Transaction or otherwise under this Agreement on the same date shall be combined in a single calculation of a net sum payable by one party to the other and the obligation to pay that sum shall be the only obligation of either party in respect of those amounts.

(i) Subject to paragraph 10, all Securities of the same issue, denomination, currency and series, transferable by each party to the other under any Transaction or hereunder on the same date shall be combined in a single calculation of a net quantity of Securities transferable by one party to the other and the obligation to transfer the net quantity of Securities shall be the only obligation of either party in respect of the Securities so transferable and receivable.

(j) If the parties have specified in Annex I hereto that this paragraph 6(j) shall apply, each obligation of a party under this Agreement (other than an obligation arising under paragraph 10) is subject to the condition precedent that none of those events specified in paragraph 10(a) which are identified in Annex I hereto for the purposes of this paragraph 6(j) (being events which, upon the serving of a Default Notice, would be an Event of Default with respect to the other party) shall have occurred and be continuing with respect to the other party.

7. **Contractual Currency**

(a) All the payments made in respect of the Purchase Price or the Repurchase Price of any Transaction shall be made in the currency of the Purchase Price (the "Contractual Currency") save as provided in paragraph 10(c)(ii). Notwithstanding the foregoing, the payee of any money may, at its option, accept tender thereof in any other currency, provided, however, that, to the extent permitted by applicable law, the obligation of the payer to pay such money will be discharged only to the extent of the amount of the Contractual Currency that such payee may, consistent with normal banking procedures, purchase with such other currency (after deduction of any premium and costs of exchange) for delivery within the customary delivery period for spot transactions in respect of the relevant currency.

(b) If for any reason the amount in the Contractual Currency received by a party, including amounts received after conversion of any recovery under any judgment or

October 2000

(c)   order expressed in a currency other than the Contractual Currency, falls short of the amount in the Contractual Currency due and payable, the party required to make the payment will, as a separate and independent obligation, to the extent permitted by applicable law, immediately transfer such additional amount in the Contractual Currency as may be necessary to compensate for the shortfall.

(c)   If for any reason the amount in the Contractual Currency received by a party exceeds the amount of the Contractual Currency due and payable, the party receiving the transfer will refund promptly the amount of such excess.

8. **Substitution**

(a)   A Transaction may at any time between the Purchase Date and Repurchase Date, if Seller so requests and Buyer so agrees, be varied by the transfer by Buyer to Seller of Securities equivalent to the Purchased Securities, or to such of the Purchased Securities as shall be agreed, in exchange for the transfer by Seller to Buyer of other Securities of such amount and description as shall be agreed ("New Purchased Securities") (being Securities having a Market Value at the date of the variation at least equal to the Market Value of the Equivalent Securities transferred to Seller).

(b)   Any variation under sub-paragraph (a) above shall be effected, subject to paragraph 6(d), by the simultaneous transfer of the Equivalent Securities and New Purchased Securities concerned.

(c)   A Transaction which is varied under sub-paragraph (a) above shall thereafter continue in effect as though the Purchased Securities under that Transaction consisted of or included the New Purchased Securities instead of the Securities in respect of which Equivalent Securities have been transferred to Seller.

(d)   Where either party has transferred Margin Securities to the other party it may at any time before Equivalent Margin Securities are transferred to it under paragraph 4 request the other party to transfer Equivalent Margin Securities to it in exchange for the transfer to the other party of new Margin Securities having a Market Value at the time of transfer at least equal to that of such Equivalent Margin Securities. If the other party agrees to the request, the exchange shall be effected, subject to paragraph 6(d), by the simultaneous transfer of the Equivalent Margin Securities and new Margin Securities concerned. Where either or both of such transfers is or are effected through a settlement system in circumstances which under the rules and procedures of that settlement system give rise to a payment by or for the account of one party to or for the account of the other party, the parties shall cause such payment or payments to be made outside that settlement system, for value the same day as the payments made through that settlement system, as shall ensure that the exchange of Equivalent Margin Securities and new Margin Securities effected under this sub-paragraph does not give rise to any net payment of cash by either party to the other.

9. **Representations**

    Each party represents and warrants to the other that -

    (a) it is duly authorised to execute and deliver this Agreement, to enter into the Transactions contemplated hereunder and to perform its obligations hereunder and thereunder and has taken all necessary action to authorise such execution, delivery and performance;

    (b) it will engage in this Agreement and the Transactions contemplated hereunder (other than Agency Transactions) as principal;

    (c) the person signing this Agreement on its behalf is, and any person representing it in entering into a Transaction will be, duly authorised to do so on its behalf;

    (d) it has obtained all authorisations of any governmental or regulatory body required in connection with this Agreement and the Transactions contemplated hereunder and such authorisations are in full force and effect;

    (e) the execution, delivery and performance of this Agreement and the Transactions contemplated hereunder will not violate any law, ordinance, charter, by-law or rule applicable to it or any agreement by which it is bound or by which any of its assets are affected;

    (f) it has satisfied itself and will continue to satisfy itself as to the tax implications of the Transactions contemplated hereunder;

    (g) in connection with this Agreement and each Transaction -

       (i) unless there is a written agreement with the other party to the contrary, it is not relying on any advice (whether written or oral) of the other party, other than the representations expressly set out in this Agreement;

       (ii) it has made and will make its own decisions regarding the entering into of any Transaction based upon its own judgment and upon advice from such professional advisers as it has deemed it necessary to consult;

       (iii) it understands the terms, conditions and risks of each Transaction and is willing to assume (financially and otherwise) those risks; and

    (h) at the time of transfer to the other party of any Securities it will have the full and unqualified right to make such transfer and that upon such transfer of Securities the other party will receive all right, title and interest in and to those Securities free of any lien, claim, charge or encumbrance.

    On the date on which any Transaction is entered into pursuant hereto, and on each day on which Securities, Equivalent Securities, Margin Securities or Equivalent Margin Securities are to be transferred under any Transaction, Buyer and Seller shall each be deemed to repeat all the foregoing representations. For the avoidance of doubt and notwithstanding any arrangements which Seller or Buyer may have with any third party, each party will be liable as a principal for its obligations under this Agreement and each Transaction.

10. **Events of Default**

(a) If any of the following events (each an "Event of Default") occurs in relation to either party (the "Defaulting Party", the other party being the "non-Defaulting Party") whether acting as Seller or Buyer -

(i) Buyer fails to pay the Purchase Price upon the applicable Purchase Date or Seller fails to pay the Repurchase Price upon the applicable Repurchase Date, and the non-Defaulting Party serves a Default Notice on the Defaulting Party; or

(ii) if the parties have specified in Annex I hereto that this sub-paragraph shall apply, Seller fails to deliver Purchased Securities on the Purchase Date or Buyer fails to deliver Equivalent Securities on the Repurchase Date, and the non-Defaulting Party serves a Default Notice on the Defaulting Party; or

(iii) Seller or Buyer fails to pay when due any sum payable under sub-paragraph (g) or (h) below, and the non-Defaulting Party serves a Default Notice on the Defaulting Party; or

(iv) Seller or Buyer fails to comply with paragraph 4 and the non-Defaulting Party serves a Default Notice on the Defaulting Party; or

(v) Seller or Buyer fails to comply with paragraph 5 and the non-Defaulting Party serves a Default Notice on the Defaulting Party; or

(vi) an Act of Insolvency occurs with respect to Seller or Buyer and (except in the case of an Act of Insolvency which is the presentation of a petition for winding-up or any analogous proceeding or the appointment of a liquidator or analogous officer of the Defaulting Party in which case no such notice shall be required) the non-Defaulting Party serves a Default Notice on the Defaulting Party; or

(vii) any representations made by Seller or Buyer are incorrect or untrue in any material respect when made or repeated or deemed to have been made or repeated, and the non-Defaulting Party serves a Default Notice on the Defaulting Party; or

(viii) Seller or Buyer admits to the other that it is unable to, or intends not to, perform any of its obligations hereunder and/or in respect of any Transaction and the non-Defaulting Party serves a Default Notice on the Defaulting Party; or

Appendices

THE BOND MARKET ASSOCIATION

ISMA

(ix) Seller or Buyer is suspended or expelled from membership of or participation in any securities exchange or association or other self regulating organisation, or suspended from dealing in securities by any government agency, or any of the assets of either Seller or Buyer or the assets of investors held by, or to the order of, Seller or Buyer are transferred or ordered to be transferred to a trustee by a regulatory authority pursuant to any securities regulating legislation and the non-Defaulting Party serves a Default Notice on the Defaulting Party; or

(x) Seller or Buyer fails to perform any other of its obligations hereunder and does not remedy such failure within 30 days after notice is given by the non-Defaulting Party requiring it to do so, and the non-Defaulting Party serves a Default Notice on the Defaulting Party;

then sub-paragraphs (b) to (f) below shall apply.

(b) The Repurchase Date for each Transaction hereunder shall be deemed immediately to occur and, subject to the following provisions, all Cash Margin (including interest accrued) shall be immediately repayable and Equivalent Margin Securities shall be immediately deliverable (and so that, where this sub-paragraph applies, performance of the respective obligations of the parties with respect to the delivery of Securities, the payment of the Repurchase Prices for any Equivalent Securities and the repayment of any Cash Margin shall be effected only in accordance with the provisions of sub-paragraph (c) below).

(c) (i) The Default Market Values of the Equivalent Securities and any Equivalent Margin Securities to be transferred, the amount of any Cash Margin (including the amount of interest accrued) to be transferred and the Repurchase Prices to be paid by each party shall be established by the non-Defaulting Party for all Transactions as at the Repurchase Date; and

(ii) on the basis of the sums so established, an account shall be taken (as at the Repurchase Date) of what is due from each party to the other under this Agreement (on the basis that each party's claim against the other in respect of the transfer to it of Equivalent Securities or Equivalent Margin Securities under this Agreement equals the Default Market Value therefor) and the sums due from one party shall be set off against the sums due from the other and only the balance of the account shall be payable (by the party having the claim valued at the lower amount pursuant to the foregoing) and such balance shall be due and payable on the next following Business Day. For the purposes of this calculation, all sums not denominated in the Base Currency shall be converted into the Base Currency on the relevant date at the Spot Rate prevailing at the relevant time.

(d) For the purposes of this Agreement, the "Default Market Value" of any Equivalent Securities or Equivalent Margin Securities shall be determined in accordance with sub-paragraph (e) below, and for this purpose -

(i) the "Appropriate Market" means, in relation to Securities of any description, the market which is the most appropriate market for Securities of that description, as determined by the non-Defaulting Party;

(ii) the "Default Valuation Time" means, in relation to an Event of Default, the close of business in the Appropriate Market on the fifth dealing day after the day on which that Event of Default occurs or, where that Event of Default is the occurrence of an Act of Insolvency in respect of which under paragraph 10(a) no notice is required from the non-Defaulting Party in order for such event to constitute an Event of Default, the close of business on the fifth dealing day after the day on which the non-Defaulting Party first became aware of the occurrence of such Event of Default;

(iii) "Deliverable Securities" means Equivalent Securities or Equivalent Margin Securities to be delivered by the Defaulting Party;

(iv) "Net Value" means at any time, in relation to any Deliverable Securities or Receivable Securities, the amount which, in the reasonable opinion of the non-Defaulting Party, represents their fair market value, having regard to such pricing sources and methods (which may include, without limitation, available prices for Securities with similar maturities, terms and credit characteristics as the relevant Equivalent Securities or Equivalent Margin Securities) as the non-Defaulting Party considers appropriate, less, in the case of Receivable Securities, or plus, in the case of Deliverable Securities, all Transaction Costs which would be incurred in connection with the purchase or sale of such Securities;

(v) "Receivable Securities" means Equivalent Securities or Equivalent Margin Securities to be delivered to the Defaulting Party; and

(vi) "Transaction Costs" in relation to any transaction contemplated in paragraph 10(d) or (e) means the reasonable costs, commission, fees and expenses (including any mark-up or mark-down) that would be incurred in connection with the purchase of Deliverable Securities or sale of Receivable Securities, calculated on the assumption that the aggregate thereof is the least that could reasonably be expected to be paid in order to carry out the transaction;

(e) (i) If between the occurrence of the relevant Event of Default and the Default Valuation Time the non-Defaulting Party gives to the Defaulting Party a written notice (a "Default Valuation Notice") which –

(A) states that, since the occurrence of the relevant Event of Default, the non-Defaulting Party has sold, in the case of Receivable Securities, or purchased, in the case of Deliverable Securities, Securities which form part of the same issue and are of an identical type and description as those Equivalent Securities or Equivalent Margin Securities, and that the non-Defaulting Party elects to treat as the Default Market Value -

(aa) in the case of Receivable Securities, the net proceeds of such sale after deducting all reasonable costs, fees and expenses incurred in connection therewith (provided that, where the Securities sold are not identical in amount to the Equivalent Securities or Equivalent Margin Securities, the non-Defaulting Party may either (x) elect to treat such net proceeds of sale divided by the amount of Securities sold and multiplied by the amount of the Equivalent Securities or Equivalent Margin Securities as the Default Market Value or (y) elect to treat such net proceeds of sale of the Equivalent Securities or Equivalent Margin Securities actually sold as the Default Market Value of that proportion of the Equivalent Securities or Equivalent Margin Securities, and, in the case of (y), the Default Market Value of the balance of the Equivalent Securities or Equivalent Margin Securities shall be determined separately in accordance with the provisions of this paragraph 10(e) and accordingly may be the subject of a separate notice (or notices) under this paragraph 10(e)(i)); or

(bb) in the case of Deliverable Securities, the aggregate cost of such purchase, including all reasonable costs, fees and expenses incurred in connection therewith (provided that, where the Securities purchased are not identical in amount to the Equivalent Securities or Equivalent Margin Securities, the non-Defaulting Party may either (x) elect to treat such aggregate cost divided by the amount of Securities sold and multiplied by the amount of the Equivalent Securities or Equivalent Margin Securities as the Default Market Value or (y) elect to treat the aggregate cost of purchasing the Equivalent Securities or Equivalent Margin Securities actually purchased as the Default Market Value of that proportion of the Equivalent Securities or Equivalent Margin Securities, and, in the case of (y), the Default Market Value of the balance of the Equivalent Securities or Equivalent Margin Securities shall be determined separately in accordance with the provisions of this paragraph 10(e) and accordingly may be the subject of a separate notice (or notices) under this paragraph 10(e)(i));

(B) states that the non-Defaulting Party has received, in the case of Deliverable Securities, offer quotations or, in the case of Receivable

Securities, bid quotations in respect of Securities of the relevant description from two or more market makers or regular dealers in the Appropriate Market in a commercially reasonable size (as determined by the non-Defaulting Party) and specifies -

(aa) the price or prices quoted by each of them for, in the case of Deliverable Securities, the sale by the relevant market marker or dealer of such Securities or, in the case of Receivable Securities, the purchase by the relevant market maker or dealer of such Securities;

(bb) the Transaction Costs which would be incurred in connection with such a transaction; and

(cc) that the non-Defaulting Party elects to treat the price so quoted (or, where more than one price is so quoted, the arithmetic mean of the prices so quoted), after deducting, in the case of Receivable Securities, or adding, in the case of Deliverable Securities, such Transaction Costs, as the Default Market Value of the relevant Equivalent Securities or Equivalent Margin Securities; or

(C) states –

(aa) that either (x) acting in good faith, the non-Defaulting Party has endeavoured but been unable to sell or purchase Securities in accordance with sub-paragraph (i)(A) above or to obtain quotations in accordance with sub-paragraph (i)(B) above (or both) or (y) the non-Defaulting Party has determined that it would not be commercially reasonable to obtain such quotations, or that it would not be commercially reasonable to use any quotations which it has obtained under sub-paragraph (i)(B) above; and

(bb) that the non-Defaulting Party has determined the Net Value of the relevant Equivalent Securities or Equivalent Margin Securities (which shall be specified) and that the non-Defaulting Party elects to treat such Net Value as the Default Market Value of the relevant Equivalent Securities or Equivalent Margin Securities,

then the Default Market Value of the relevant Equivalent Securities or Equivalent Margin Securities shall be an amount equal to the Default Market Value specified in accordance with (A), (B)(cc) or, as the case may be, (C)(bb) above.

Appendices

(ii) If by the Default Valuation Time the non-Defaulting Party has not given a Default Valuation Notice, the Default Market Value of the relevant Equivalent Securities or Equivalent Margin Securities shall be an amount equal to their Net Value at the Default Valuation Time; provided that, if at the Default Valuation Time the non-Defaulting Party reasonably determines that, owing to circumstances affecting the market in the Equivalent Securities or Equivalent Margin Securities in question, it is not possible for the non-Defaulting Party to determine a Net Value of such Equivalent Securities or Equivalent Margin Securities which is commercially reasonable, the Default Market Value of such Equivalent Securities or Equivalent Margin Securities shall be an amount equal to their Net Value as determined by the non-Defaulting Party as soon as reasonably practicable after the Default Valuation Time.

(f) The Defaulting Party shall be liable to the non-Defaulting Party for the amount of all reasonable legal and other professional expenses incurred by the non-Defaulting Party in connection with or as a consequence of an Event of Default, together with interest thereon at LIBOR or, in the case of an expense attributable to a particular Transaction, the Pricing Rate for the relevant Transaction if that Pricing Rate is greater than LIBOR.

(g) If Seller fails to deliver Purchased Securities to Buyer on the applicable Purchase Date Buyer may -

(i) if it has paid the Purchase Price to Seller, require Seller immediately to repay the sum so paid;

(ii) if Buyer has a Transaction Exposure to Seller in respect of the relevant Transaction, require Seller from time to time to pay Cash Margin at least equal to such Transaction Exposure;

(iii) at any time while such failure continues, terminate the Transaction by giving written notice to Seller. On such termination the obligations of Seller and Buyer with respect to delivery of Purchased Securities and Equivalent Securities shall terminate and Seller shall pay to Buyer an amount equal to the excess of the Repurchase Price at the date of Termination over the Purchase Price.

(h) If Buyer fails to deliver Equivalent Securities to Seller on the applicable Repurchase Date Seller may -

(i) if it has paid the Repurchase Price to Buyer, require Buyer immediately to repay the sum so paid;

(ii) if Seller has a Transaction Exposure to Buyer in respect of the relevant Transaction, require Buyer from time to time to pay Cash Margin at least equal to such Transaction Exposure;

October 2000

(iii) at any time while such failure continues, by written notice to Buyer declare that that Transaction (but only that Transaction) shall be terminated immediately in accordance with sub-paragraph (c) above (disregarding for this purpose references in that sub-paragraph to transfer of Cash Margin and delivery of Equivalent Margin Securities and as if references to the Repurchase Date were to the date on which notice was given under this sub-paragraph).

(i) The provisions of this Agreement constitute a complete statement of the remedies available to each party in respect of any Event of Default.

(j) Subject to paragraph 10(k), neither party may claim any sum by way of consequential loss or damage in the event of a failure by the other party to perform any of its obligations under this Agreement.

(k) (i) Subject to sub-paragraph (ii) below, if as a result of a Transaction terminating before its agreed Repurchase Date under paragraphs 10(b), 10(g)(iii) or 10(h)(iii), the non-Defaulting Party, in the case of paragraph 10(b), Buyer, in the case of paragraph 10(g)(iii), or Seller, in the case of paragraph 10(h)(iii), (in each case the "first party") incurs any loss or expense in entering into replacement transactions, the other party shall be required to pay to the first party the amount determined by the first party in good faith to be equal to the loss or expense incurred in connection with such replacement transactions (including all fees, costs and other expenses) less the amount of any profit or gain made by that party in connection with such replacement transactions; provided that if that calculation results in a negative number, an amount equal to that number shall be payable by the first party to the other party.

(ii) If the first party reasonably decides, instead of entering into such replacement transactions, to replace or unwind any hedging transactions which the first party entered into in connection with the Transaction so terminating, or to enter into any replacement hedging transactions, the other party shall be required to pay to the first party the amount determined by the first party in good faith to be equal to the loss or expense incurred in connection with entering into such replacement or unwinding (including all fees, costs and other expenses) less the amount of any profit or gain made by that party in connection with such replacement or unwinding; provided that if that calculation results in a negative number, an amount equal to that number shall be payable by the first party to the other party.

(l) Each party shall immediately notify the other if an Event of Default, or an event which, upon the serving of a Default Notice, would be an Event of Default, occurs in relation to it.

Appendices

11. **Tax Event**

(a) This paragraph shall apply if either party notifies the other that -

   (i) any action taken by a taxing authority or brought in a court of competent jurisdiction (regardless of whether such action is taken or brought with respect to a party to this Agreement); or

   (ii) a change in the fiscal or regulatory regime (including, but not limited to, a change in law or in the general interpretation of law but excluding any change in any rate of tax),

   has or will, in the notifying party's reasonable opinion, have a material adverse effect on that party in the context of a Transaction.

(b) If so requested by the other party, the notifying party will furnish the other with an opinion of a suitably qualified adviser that an event referred to in sub-paragraph (a)(i) or (ii) above has occurred and affects the notifying party.

(c) Where this paragraph applies, the party giving the notice referred to in sub-paragraph (a) may, subject to sub-paragraph (d) below, terminate the Transaction with effect from a date specified in the notice, not being earlier (unless so agreed by the other party) than 30 days after the date of the notice, by nominating that date as the Repurchase Date.

(d) If the party receiving the notice referred to in sub-paragraph (a) so elects, it may override that notice by giving a counter-notice to the other party. If a counter-notice is given, the party which gives the counter-notice will be deemed to have agreed to indemnify the other party against the adverse effect referred to in sub-paragraph (a) so far as relates to the relevant Transaction and the original Repurchase Date will continue to apply.

(e) Where a Transaction is terminated as described in this paragraph, the party which has given the notice to terminate shall indemnify the other party against any reasonable legal and other professional expenses incurred by the other party by reason of the termination, but the other party may not claim any sum by way of consequential loss or damage in respect of a termination in accordance with this paragraph.

(f) This paragraph is without prejudice to paragraph 6(b) (obligation to pay additional amounts if withholding or deduction required); but an obligation to pay such additional amounts may, where appropriate, be a circumstance which causes this paragraph to apply.

12. **Interest**

   To the extent permitted by applicable law, if any sum of money payable hereunder or under any Transaction is not paid when due, interest shall accrue on the unpaid sum as a separate debt at the greater of the Pricing Rate for the Transaction to which such sum relates (where such sum is referable to a Transaction) and LIBOR on a 360 day basis or 365 day basis in accordance with the applicable ISMA convention, for the actual number of days during the period from and including the date on which payment was due to, but excluding, the date of payment.

13. **Single Agreement**

    Each party acknowledges that, and has entered into this Agreement and will enter into each Transaction hereunder in consideration of and in reliance upon the fact that all Transactions hereunder constitute a single business and contractual relationship and are made in consideration of each other. Accordingly, each party agrees (i) to perform all of its obligations in respect of each Transaction hereunder, and that a default in the performance of any such obligations shall constitute a default by it in respect of all Transactions hereunder, and (ii) that payments, deliveries and other transfers made by either of them in respect of any Transaction shall be deemed to have been made in consideration of payments, deliveries and other transfers in respect of any other Transactions hereunder.

14. **Notices and Other Communications**

    (a) Any notice or other communication to be given under this Agreement -

        (i)   shall be in the English language, and except where expressly otherwise provided in this Agreement, shall be in writing;

        (ii) may be given in any manner described in sub-paragraphs (b) and (c) below;

        (iii) shall be sent to the party to whom it is to be given at the address or number, or in accordance with the electronic messaging details, set out in Annex I hereto.

    (b) Subject to sub-paragraph (c) below, any such notice or other communication shall be effective -

        (i)   if in writing and delivered in person or by courier, at the time when it is delivered;

        (ii) if sent by telex, at the time when the recipient's answerback is received;

        (iii) if sent by facsimile transmission, at the time when the transmission is received by a responsible employee of the recipient in legible form (it being agreed that the burden of proving receipt will be on the sender and will not be met by a transmission report generated by the sender's facsimile machine);

        (iv) if sent by certified or registered mail (airmail, if overseas) or the equivalent (return receipt requested), at the time when that mail is delivered or its delivery is attempted;

(v) if sent by electronic messaging system, at the time that electronic message is received;

except that any notice or communication which is received, or delivery of which is attempted, after close of business on the date of receipt or attempted delivery or on a day which is not a day on which commercial banks are open for business in the place where that notice or other communication is to be given shall be treated as given at the opening of business on the next following day which is such a day.

(c) If -

(i) there occurs in relation to either party an event which, upon the service of a Default Notice, would be an Event of Default; and

(ii) the non-Defaulting Party, having made all practicable efforts to do so, including having attempted to use at least two of the methods specified in sub-paragraph (b)(ii), (iii) or (v), has been unable to serve a Default Notice by one of the methods specified in those sub-paragraphs (or such of those methods as are normally used by the non-Defaulting Party when communicating with the Defaulting Party),

the non-Defaulting Party may sign a written notice (a "Special Default Notice") which -

(aa) specifies the relevant event referred to in paragraph 10(a) which has occurred in relation to the Defaulting Party;

(bb) states that the non-Defaulting Party, having made all practicable efforts to do so, including having attempted to use at least two of the methods specified in sub-paragraph (b)(ii), (iii) or (v), has been unable to serve a Default Notice by one of the methods specified in those sub-paragraphs (or such of those methods as are normally used by the non-Defaulting Party when communicating with the Defaulting Party);

(cc) specifies the date on which, and the time at which, the Special Default Notice is signed by the non-Defaulting Party; and

(dd) states that the event specified in accordance with sub-paragraph (aa) above shall be treated as an Event of Default with effect from the date and time so specified.

On the signature of a Special Default Notice the relevant event shall be treated with effect from the date and time so specified as an Event of Default in relation to the Defaulting Party, and accordingly references in paragraph 10 to a Default Notice shall be treated as including a Special Default Notice. A Special Default Notice shall be given to the Defaulting Party as soon as practicable after it is signed.

(d) Either party may by notice to the other change the address, telex or facsimile number or electronic messaging system details at which notices or other communications are to be given to it.

15. **Entire Agreement; Severability**

    This Agreement shall supersede any existing agreements between the parties containing general terms and conditions for Transactions. Each provision and agreement herein shall be treated as separate from any other provision or agreement herein and shall be enforceable notwithstanding the unenforceability of any such other provision or agreement.

16. **Non-assignability; Termination**

(a) Subject to sub-paragraph (b) below, neither party may assign, charge or otherwise deal with (including without limitation any dealing with any interest in or the creation of any interest in) its rights or obligations under this Agreement or under any Transaction without the prior written consent of the other party. Subject to the foregoing, this Agreement and any Transactions shall be binding upon and shall inure to the benefit of the parties and their respective successors and assigns.

(b) Sub-paragraph (a) above shall not preclude a party from assigning, charging or otherwise dealing with all or any part of its interest in any sum payable to it under paragraph 10(c) or (f) above.

(c) Either party may terminate this Agreement by giving written notice to the other, except that this Agreement shall, notwithstanding such notice, remain applicable to any Transactions then outstanding.

(d) All remedies hereunder shall survive Termination in respect of the relevant Transaction and termination of this Agreement.

(e) The participation of any additional member State of the European Union in economic and monetary union after 1 January 1999 shall not have the effect of altering any term of the Agreement or any Transaction, nor give a party the right unilaterally to alter or terminate the Agreement or any Transaction.

17. **Governing Law**

    This Agreement shall be governed by and construed in accordance with the laws of England. Buyer and Seller hereby irrevocably submit for all purposes of or in connection with this Agreement and each Transaction to the jurisdiction of the Courts of England.

    Party A hereby appoints the person identified in Annex I hereto as its agent to receive on its behalf service of process in such courts. If such agent ceases to be its agent,

Party A shall promptly appoint, and notify Party B of the identity of, a new agent in England.

Party B hereby appoints the person identified in Annex I hereto as its agent to receive on its behalf service of process in such courts. If such agent ceases to be its agent, Party B shall promptly appoint, and notify Party A of the identity of, a new agent in England.

Each party shall deliver to the other, within 30 days of the date of this Agreement in the case of the appointment of a person identified in Annex I or of the date of the appointment of the relevant agent in any other case, evidence of the acceptance by the agent appointed by it pursuant to this paragraph of such appointment.

Nothing in this paragraph shall limit the right of any party to take proceedings in the courts of any other country of competent jurisdiction.

18. **No Waivers, etc.**

    No express or implied waiver of any Event of Default by either party shall constitute a waiver of any other Event of Default and no exercise of any remedy hereunder by any party shall constitute a waiver of its right to exercise any other remedy hereunder. No modification or waiver of any provision of this Agreement and no consent by any party to a departure herefrom shall be effective unless and until such modification, waiver or consent shall be in writing and duly executed by both of the parties hereto. Without limitation on any of the foregoing, the failure to give a notice pursuant to paragraph 4(a) hereof will not constitute a waiver of any right to do so at a later date.

19. **Waiver of Immunity**

    Each party hereto hereby waives, to the fullest extent permitted by applicable law, all immunity (whether on the basis of sovereignty or otherwise) from jurisdiction, attachment (both before and after judgment) and execution to which it might otherwise be entitled in any action or proceeding in the Courts of England or of any other country or jurisdiction, relating in any way to this Agreement or any Transaction, and agrees that it will not raise, claim or cause to be pleaded any such immunity at or in respect of any such action or proceeding.

20. **Recording**

    The parties agree that each may electronically record all telephone conversations between them.

21. **Third Party Rights**

    No person shall have any right to enforce any provision of this Agreement under the Contracts (Rights of Third Parties) Act 1999.

October 2000

[Name of Party]	[Name of Party]
By_____	By_____
Title_____	Title_____
Date_____	Date_____

ANNEX I

Supplemental Terms or Conditions

Paragraph references are to paragraphs in the Agreement.

1. The following elections shall apply -

[(a)] paragraph 1(c)(i). Buy/Sell Back Transactions [may/may not] be effected under this Agreement, and accordingly the Buy/Sell Back Annex [shall/shall not] apply.]*

[(b)] paragraph 1(c)(ii). Transactions in Net Paying Securities [may/may not] be effected under this Agreement, and accordingly the provisions of sub-paragraphs (i) and (ii) below [shall/shall not] apply.

  (i) The phrase "other than equities and Net Paying Securities" shall be replaced by the phrase "other than equities".

  (ii) In the Buy/Sell Back Annex the following words shall be added to the end of the definition of the expression "IR": "and for the avoidance of doubt the reference to the amount of Income for these purposes shall be to an amount paid without withholding or deduction for or on account of taxes or duties notwithstanding that a payment of such Income made in certain circumstances may be subject to such a withholding or deduction".]*

[(c)] paragraph 1(d). Agency Transactions [may/may not] be effected under this Agreement, and accordingly the Agency Annex [shall/shall not] apply.]*

(d) paragraph 2(d). The Base Currency shall be: _____.

(e) paragraph 2(p). [list Buyer's and Seller's Designated Offices]

(f) paragraph 2(cc). The pricing source for calculation of Market Value shall be: _____.

(g) paragraph 2(rr). Spot rate to be: _____.

(h) paragraph 3(b). [Seller/Buyer/both Seller and Buyer]* to deliver Confirmation.

(i) paragraph 4(f). Interest rate on Cash Margin to be [ ]% for _____ currency.
[ ]% for _____ currency.

Interest to be payable [payment intervals and dates].

(j) paragraph 4(g). Delivery period for margin calls to be: _____.

* Delete as appropriate

October 2000

[(k)] paragraph 6(j). Paragraph 6(j) shall apply and the events specified in paragraph 10(a) identified for the purposes of paragraph 6(j) shall be those set out in sub paragraphs [   ] of paragraph 10(a) of the Agreement.]*

[(l)] paragraph 10(a)(ii). Paragraph 10(a)(ii) shall apply.]*

(m) paragraph 14. For the purposes of paragraph 14 of this Agreement -

    (i) Address for notices and other communications for Party A -

        Address:
        Attention:
        Telephone:
        Facsimile:
        Telex:
        Answerback:
        Other:

    (ii) Address for notices and other communications for Party B -

        Address:
        Attention:
        Telephone:
        Facsimile:
        Telex:
        Answerback:
        Other:

[(n)] paragraph 17. For the purposes of paragraph 17 of this Agreement -

    (i) Party A appoints [   ] as its agent for service of process;

    (ii) Party B appoints [   ] as its agent for service of process.]*

* Delete as appropriate

Appendices

2. The following supplemental terms and conditions shall apply -

[Existing Transactions

(a) The parties agree that this Agreement shall apply to all transactions which are subject to the PSA/ISMA Global Master Repurchase Agreement between them dated _____ and which are outstanding as at the date of this Agreement so that such transactions shall be treated as if they had been entered into under this Agreement, and the terms of such transactions are amended accordingly with effect from the date of this Agreement.]*

[Forward Transactions

(b) The parties agree that Forward Transactions (as defined in sub-paragraph (i)(A) below) may be effected under this Agreement and accordingly the provisions of sub-paragraphs (i) to (iv) below shall apply.

  (i) The following definitions shall apply -

    (A) "Forward Transaction", a Transaction in respect of which the Purchase Date is at least [three] Business Days after the date on which the Transaction was entered into and has not yet occurred;

    (B) "Forward Repricing Date", with respect to any Forward Transaction the date which is such number of Business Days before the Purchase Date as is equal to the minimum period for the delivery of margin applicable under paragraph 4(g).

  (ii) The Confirmation relating to any Forward Transaction may describe the Purchased Securities by reference to a type or class of Securities, which, without limitation, may be identified by issuer or class of issuers and a maturity or range of maturities. Where this paragraph applies, the parties shall agree the actual Purchased Securities not less than two Business Days before the Purchase Date and Buyer or Seller (or both), as shall have been agreed, shall promptly deliver to the other party a Confirmation which shall describe such Purchased Securities.

  (iii) At any time between the Forward Repricing Date and the Purchase Date for any Forward Transaction the parties may agree either –

    (A) to adjust the Purchase Price under that Forward Transaction; or

    (B) to adjust the number of Purchased Securities to be sold by Seller to Buyer under that Forward Transaction.

* Delete as appropriate

October 2000

(iv) Where the parties agree to an adjustment under paragraph (iii) above, Buyer or Seller (or both), as shall have been agreed, shall promptly deliver to the other party a Confirmation of the Forward Transaction, as adjusted under paragraph (iii) above.

(c) Where the parties agree that this paragraph shall apply, paragraphs 2 and 4 of the Agreement are amended as follows.

(i) Paragraph 2(ww) is deleted and replaced by the following -

"(ww) "Transaction Exposure" means -

(i) with respect to any Forward Transaction at any time between the Forward Repricing Date and the Purchase Date, the difference between (A) the Market Value of the Purchased Securities at the relevant time and (B) the Purchase Price;

(ii) with respect to any Transaction at any time during the period (if any) from the Purchase Date to the date on which the Purchased Securities are delivered to Buyer or, if earlier, the date on which the Transaction is terminated under paragraph 10(g), the difference between (A) the Market Value of the Purchased Securities at the relevant time and (B) the Repurchase Price at the relevant time;

(iii) with respect to any Transaction at any time during the period from the Purchase Date (or, if later, the date on which the Purchased Securities are delivered to Buyer or the Transaction is terminated under paragraph 10(g)) to the Repurchase Date (or, if later, the date on which Equivalent Securities are delivered to Seller or the Transaction is terminated under paragraph 10(h)), the difference between (A) the Repurchase Price at the relevant time multiplied by the applicable Margin Ratio (or, where the Transaction relates to Securities of more than one description to which different Margin Ratios apply, the amount produced by multiplying the Repurchase Price attributable to Equivalent Securities of each such description by the applicable Margin Ratio and aggregating the resulting amounts, the Repurchase Price being for this purpose attributed to Equivalent Securities of each such description in the same proportions as those in which the Purchase Price was apportioned among the Purchased Securities) and (B) the Market Value of Equivalent Securities at the relevant time.

In each case, if (A) is greater than (B), Buyer has a Transaction Exposure for that Transaction equal to the excess, and if (B) is greater than (A), Seller has a Transaction Exposure to Buyer equal to the excess."

(ii) In paragraph 4(c) -

(aa) the words "any amount payable to the first party under paragraph 5 but unpaid" are deleted and replaced by "any amount which will become payable to the first party under paragraph 5 during the period after the time at which the calculation is made which is equal to the minimum period for the delivery of margin applicable under paragraph 4(g) or which is payable to the first party under paragraph 5 but unpaid"; and

(bb) the words "any amount payable to the other party under paragraph 5 but unpaid" are deleted and replaced by "any amount which will become payable to the other party under paragraph 5 during the period after the time at which the calculation is made which is equal to the minimum period for the delivery of margin applicable under paragraph 4(g) or which is payable to the other party under paragraph 5 but unpaid".]*

* Delete as appropriate

October 2000

ANNEX II

Form of Confirmation

To: _____

From: _____

Date: _____

Subject: [Repurchase][Buy/Sell Back]* Transaction
            (Reference Number:)

Dear Sirs,

The purpose of this [letter]/[facsimile]//[telex], a "Confirmation" for the purposes of the Agreement, is to set forth the terms and conditions of the above repurchase transaction entered into between us on the Contract Date referred to below.

This Confirmation supplements and forms part of, and is subject to, the Global Master Repurchase Agreement as entered into between us as of [ ] as the same may be amended from time to time (the "Agreement"). All provisions contained in the Agreement govern this Confirmation except as expressly modified below. Words and phrases defined in the Agreement and used in this Confirmation shall have the same meaning herein as in the Agreement.

1. Contract Date:

2. Purchased Securities [state type[s] and nominal value[s]]:

3. CUSIP, ISIN or other identifying number[s]:

4. Buyer:

5. Seller:

6. Purchase Date:

7. Purchase Price:

8. Contractual Currency:

[9. Repurchase Date]:*

[10. Terminable on demand]:*

11. Pricing Rate:

---

* Delete as appropriate

[12]. Sell Back Price:]*

13. Buyer's Bank Account[s] Details:

14. Seller's Bank Account[s] Details:

[15. The Transaction is an Agency Transaction. [Name of Agent] is acting as agent for [name or identifier of Principal]]:*

[16. Additional Terms]:*

Yours faithfully,

* Delete as appropriate

sifma

Securities Industry and Financial Markets Association
New York • Washington
www.sifma.org

ICMA
International Capital Market Association

International Capital Market Association
Talacker 29, 8001 Zurich, Switzerland
www.icmagroup.org

2011 version

Global Master Repurchase Agreement

Dated as of _____

Between:

_____ ("Party A")

and

_____ ("Party B")

1. **Applicability**

   (a) From time to time the parties hereto may enter into transactions in which one party, acting through a Designated Office, ("Seller") agrees to sell to the other, acting through a Designated Office, ("Buyer") securities or other financial instruments ("Securities") (subject to paragraph 1(c), other than equities and Net Paying Securities) against the payment of the purchase price by Buyer to Seller, with a simultaneous agreement by Buyer to sell to Seller Securities equivalent to such Securities at a date certain or on demand against the payment of the repurchase price by Seller to Buyer.

   (b) Each such transaction (which may be a repurchase transaction ("Repurchase Transaction") or a buy and sell back transaction ("Buy/Sell Back Transaction")) shall be referred to herein as a "Transaction" and shall be governed by this Agreement, including any supplemental terms or conditions contained in Annex I and any annex specified in Annex I, unless otherwise agreed in writing.

   (c) If this Agreement may be applied to -

   (i) Buy/Sell Back Transactions, this shall be specified in Annex I hereto, and the provisions of the Buy/Sell Back Annex shall apply to such Buy/Sell Back Transactions;

April 2011

(ii) Net Paying Securities, this shall be specified in Annex I hereto and the provisions of Annex I, paragraph 1(b) shall apply to Transactions involving Net Paying Securities.

2. **Definitions**

(a) "Act of Insolvency" shall occur with respect to any party hereto upon -

(i) its making a general assignment for the benefit of, or entering into a reorganisation, arrangement, or composition with, creditors; or

(ii) a secured party taking possession of, or carrying out other enforcement measures in relation to, all or substantially all assets of such party, provided the relevant process is not dismissed, discharged, stayed or restrained within 15 days; or

(iii) its becoming insolvent or becoming unable to pay its debts as they become due or failing or admitting in writing its inability generally to pay its debts as they become due; or

(iv) its seeking, consenting to or acquiescing in the appointment of any trustee, administrator, receiver or liquidator or analogous officer of it or any material part of its property; or

(v) the presentation or filing of a petition in respect of it (other than by the other party to this Agreement in respect of any obligation under this Agreement) in any court or before any agency or the commencement of any proceeding by any Competent Authority alleging or for the bankruptcy, winding-up or insolvency of such party (or any analogous proceeding) or seeking any reorganisation, arrangement, composition, re-adjustment, administration, liquidation, dissolution or similar relief under any present or future statute, law or regulation, such petition not having been stayed or dismissed within 15 days of its filing (except in the case of a petition presented by a Competent Authority or for winding-up or any analogous proceeding, in respect of which no such 15 day period shall apply); or

(vi) the appointment of a receiver, administrator, liquidator, conservator, custodian or trustee or analogous officer of such party or over all or any material part of such party's property; or

(vii) the convening of any meeting of its creditors for the purpose of considering a voluntary arrangement as referred to in section 3 of the Insolvency Act 1986 (or any analogous proceeding);

(b) "Agency Transaction", the meaning specified in paragraph 1 of the Agency Annex to this Agreement as published by ICMA;

(c) "Applicable Rate", in relation to any sum in any currency:

April 2011

(i) for the purposes of paragraph 10, the rate selected in a commercially reasonable manner by the non-Defaulting Party;

(ii) for any other purpose, the rate agreed by the parties acting in a commercially reasonable manner;

(d) "Appropriate Market", the meaning specified in paragraph 10;

(e) "Base Currency", the currency indicated in Annex I;

(f) "Business Day" means -

(i) in relation to the settlement of a Transaction or delivery of Securities under this Agreement through a settlement system, a day on which that settlement system is open for business;

(ii) in relation to the settlement of a Transaction or delivery of Securities under this Agreement otherwise than through a settlement system, a day on which banks are open for business in the place where the relevant Securities are to be delivered and, if different, the place in which the relevant payment is to be made; and

(iii) in relation to the payment of any amount under this Agreement not falling within (i) or (ii) above, a day other than a Saturday or a Sunday on which banks are open for business in the principal financial centre of the country of which the currency in which the payment is denominated is the official currency and, if different, in the place where any account designated by the parties for the making or receipt of the payment is situated (or, in the case of a payment in euro, a day on which TARGET2 operates).

(g) "Cash Equivalent Amount" has the meaning given in paragraph 4(h);

(h) "Cash Margin", a cash sum paid or to be paid to Buyer or Seller in accordance with paragraph 4;

(i) "Competent Authority", a regulator, supervisor or any similar official with primary insolvency, rehabilitative or regulatory jurisdiction over a party in the jurisdiction of its incorporation or establishment or the jurisdiction of its head office;

(j) "Confirmation", the meaning specified in paragraph 3(b);

(k) "Contractual Currency", the meaning specified in paragraph 7(a);

(l) "Defaulting Party", the meaning specified in paragraph 10;

(m) "Default Market Value", the meaning specified in paragraph 10;

(n) "Default Notice", a written notice served by the non-Defaulting Party on the Defaulting Party under paragraph 10(b) designating a day as an Early Termination Date;

(o) "Deliverable Securities", the meaning specified in paragraph 10;

(p) "Designated Office", a branch or office which is specified as such in Annex I or such other branch or office as may be agreed in writing by the parties;

(q) "Distribution(s)", the meaning specified in sub-paragraph (y) below;

(r) "Early Termination Date", the date designated as such in a Default Notice or as otherwise determined in accordance with paragraph 10(b);

(s) "Electronic Messaging System", an electronic system for communication capable of reproducing communication in hard copy form, including email;

(t) "Equivalent Margin Securities", Securities equivalent to Securities previously transferred as Margin Securities;

(u) "Equivalent Securities", with respect to a Transaction, Securities equivalent to Purchased Securities under that Transaction. If and to the extent that such Purchased Securities have been redeemed, the expression shall mean a sum of money equivalent to the proceeds of the redemption (other than Distributions);

(v) Securities are "equivalent to" other Securities for the purposes of this Agreement if they are: (i) of the same issuer; (ii) part of the same issue; and (iii) of an identical type, nominal value, description and (except where otherwise stated) amount as those other Securities, provided that -

   (A) Securities will be equivalent to other Securities notwithstanding that those Securities have been redenominated into euro or that the nominal value of those Securities has changed in connection with such redenomination; and

   (B) where Securities have been converted, subdivided or consolidated or have become the subject of a takeover or the holders of Securities have become entitled to receive or acquire other Securities or other property or the Securities have become subject to any similar event other than a Distribution, the expression "equivalent to" shall mean Securities equivalent to (as defined in the provisions of this definition preceding the proviso) the original Securities together with or replaced by a sum of money or Securities or other property equivalent to (as so defined) that receivable by holders of such original Securities resulting from such event;

(w) "Event of Default", the meaning specified in paragraph 10;

(x) "Forward Transaction", the meaning specified in paragraph 2(c)(i) of Annex I;

(y) "Income", with respect to any Security at any time, all interest, dividends or other distributions thereon, including distributions which are a payment or repayment of principal in respect of the relevant securities ("Distribution(s)");

(z) "Income Payment Date", with respect to any Securities, the date on which Income is

April 2011

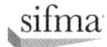

paid in respect of such Securities or, in the case of registered Securities, the date by reference to which particular registered holders are identified as being entitled to payment of Income;

(aa) "Margin Percentage", with respect to any Margin Securities or Equivalent Margin Securities, the percentage, if any, agreed by the parties acting in a commercially reasonable manner;

(bb) "Margin Ratio", with respect to a Transaction, the Market Value of the Purchased Securities at the time when the Transaction was entered into divided by the Purchase Price (and so that, where a Transaction relates to Securities of different descriptions and the Purchase Price is apportioned by the parties among Purchased Securities of each such description, a separate Margin Ratio shall apply in respect of Securities of each such description), or such other proportion as the parties may agree with respect to that Transaction;

(cc) "Margin Securities", in relation to a Margin Transfer, Securities of the type and value (having applied Margin Percentage, if any) reasonably acceptable to the party calling for such Margin Transfer;

(dd) "Margin Transfer", any, or any combination of, the payment or repayment of Cash Margin and the transfer of Margin Securities or Equivalent Margin Securities;

(ee) "Market Value", with respect to any Securities as of any time on any date, the price for such Securities (after having applied the Margin Percentage, if any, in the case of Margin Securities) at such time on such date obtained from a generally recognised source agreed by the parties or as otherwise agreed by the parties (and where different prices are obtained for different delivery dates, the price so obtainable for the earliest available such delivery date) having regard to market practice for valuing Securities of the type in question plus the aggregate amount of Income which, as at such date, has accrued but not yet been paid in respect of the Securities to the extent not included in such price as of such date, and for these purposes any sum in a currency other than the Contractual Currency for the Transaction in question shall be converted into such Contractual Currency at the Spot Rate prevailing at the time of the determination;

(ff) "Net Exposure", the meaning specified in paragraph 4(c);

(gg) the "Net Margin" provided to a party at any time, the excess (if any) at that time of (i) the sum of the amount of Cash Margin paid to that party (including accrued interest on such Cash Margin which has not been paid to the other party) and the Market Value of Margin Securities transferred to that party under paragraph 4(a) (excluding any Cash Margin which has been repaid to the other party and any Margin Securities in respect of which Equivalent Margin Securities have been transferred or a Cash Equivalent Amount has been paid to the other party) over (ii) the sum of the amount of Cash Margin paid to the other party (including accrued interest on such Cash Margin which has not been paid by the other party) and the Market Value of Margin Securities transferred to the other party under paragraph 4(a) (excluding any Cash Margin which has been repaid by the other party and any Margin Securities in respect of which Equivalent Margin Securities have been transferred or a Cash Equivalent Amount has been paid by the other party) and for this purpose any amounts not denominated in the Base Currency shall be converted into the Base Currency at the Spot Rate prevailing at the time of the determination;

(hh) "Net Paying Securities", Securities which are of a kind such that, were they to be the subject of a Transaction to which paragraph 5 applies, any payment made by Buyer under paragraph 5 would be one in respect of which either Buyer would or might be required to make a withholding or deduction for or on account of taxes or duties or Seller might be required to make or account for a payment for or on account of taxes or duties (in each case other than tax on overall net income) by reference to such payment;

(ii) "Net Value", the meaning specified in paragraph 10;

(jj) "New Purchased Securities", the meaning specified in paragraph 8(a);

(kk) "Price Differential", with respect to any Transaction as of any date, the aggregate amount obtained by daily application of the Pricing Rate for such Transaction to the Purchase Price for such Transaction (on a 360 day, 365 day or other day basis in accordance with the applicable market convention, unless otherwise agreed between the parties for the Transaction) for the actual number of days during the period commencing on (and including) the Purchase Date for such Transaction and ending on (but excluding) the date of calculation or, if earlier, the Repurchase Date;

(ll) "Pricing Rate", with respect to any Transaction, the per annum percentage rate for calculation of the Price Differential agreed to by Buyer and Seller in relation to that Transaction;

(mm) "Purchase Date", with respect to any Transaction, the date on which Purchased Securities are to be sold by Seller to Buyer in relation to that Transaction;

(nn) "Purchase Price", on the Purchase Date, the price at which Purchased Securities are sold or are to be sold by Seller to Buyer;

(oo) "Purchased Securities", with respect to any Transaction, the Securities sold or to be sold by Seller to Buyer under that Transaction, and any New Purchased Securities transferred by Seller to Buyer under paragraph 8 in respect of that Transaction;

(pp) "Receivable Securities", the meaning specified in paragraph 10;

(qq) "Repurchase Date", with respect to any Transaction, the date on which Buyer is to sell Equivalent Securities to Seller in relation to that Transaction;

(rr) "Repurchase Price", with respect to any Transaction and as of any date, the sum of the Purchase Price and the Price Differential as of such date;

April 2011

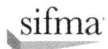

(ss) "Spot Rate", where an amount in one currency is to be converted into a second currency on any date, unless the parties otherwise agree

   (i) for the purposes of paragraph 10, the spot rate of exchange obtained by reference to a pricing source or quoted by a bank, in each case specified by the non-Defaulting Party, in the London inter-bank market for the purchase of the second currency with the first currency at such dates and times determined by the non-Defaulting Party; and

   (ii) for any other purpose, the latest available spot rate of exchange obtained by reference to a pricing source or quoted by a bank, in each case agreed by the parties (or in the absence of such agreement, specified by Buyer), in the London inter-bank market for the purchase of the second currency with the first currency on the day on which the calculation is to be made or, if that day is not a day on which banks are open for business in London, the spot rate of exchange quoted at close of business in London on the immediately preceding day in London on which such a quotation was available;

(tt) "TARGET2", the Second Generation Trans-European Automated Real-time Gross Settlement Express Transfer System, or any other system that replaces it;

(uu) "Term", with respect to any Transaction, the interval of time commencing with the Purchase Date and ending with the Repurchase Date;

(vv) "Termination", with respect to any Transaction, refers to the requirement with respect to such Transaction for Buyer to sell Equivalent Securities against payment by Seller of the Repurchase Price in accordance with paragraph 3(f), and reference to a Transaction having a "fixed term" or being "terminable upon demand" shall be construed accordingly;

(ww) "Transaction Costs", the meaning specified in paragraph 10;

(xx) "Transaction Exposure", with respect to any Transaction at any time during the period from the Purchase Date to the Repurchase Date (or, if later, the date on which Equivalent Securities are delivered to Seller or the Transaction is terminated under paragraph 10(h) or 10(i)) the amount "E" determined in accordance with (A) or (B) below as specified in Annex I (or as agreed by the parties with respect to particular transactions):

   (A) the result of formula $E = (R \times MR) - MV$, where:

   R = the Repurchase Price at such time

   MR = the applicable Margin Ratio

   MV = the Market Value of Equivalent Securities at such time

   and so that where the Transaction relates to Securities of more than one description or to which different Margin Ratios apply, E shall be determined by multiplying the Repurchase Price attributable to Equivalent Securities of each such description by the applicable Margin Ratio and aggregating the results and for this purpose the Repurchase Price shall be attributed to Equivalent Securities of each such description in the same proportions as those in which the Purchase Price was apportioned among the Purchased Securities.

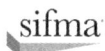

If E is greater than zero, Buyer has a Transaction Exposure equal to E and if E is less than zero, Seller has a Transaction Exposure equal to the absolute value of E; provided that E shall not be greater than the amount of the Repurchase Price on the date of the determination; or

(B) the result of the formula $E = R - V$, where:

R = the Repurchase Price at such time

V = the Adjusted Value of Equivalent Securities at such time or, where a Transaction relates to Securities of more than one description or to which different haircuts apply, the sum of the Adjusted Values of the Securities of each such description.

For this purpose the "Adjusted Value" of any Securities is their value determined on the basis of the formula, $(MV(1 - H))$, where:

MV = the Market Value of Equivalent Securities at such time

H = the "haircut" for the relevant Securities, if any, as agreed by the parties from time to time, being a discount from the Market Value of the Securities.

If E is greater than zero, Buyer has a Transaction Exposure equal to E and if E is less than zero, Seller has a Transaction Exposure equal to the absolute value of E; and

(yy) except in paragraphs 14(b)(i) and 18, references in this Agreement to "written" communications and communications "in writing" include communications made through any Electronic Messaging System agreed between the parties.

3. **Initiation; Confirmation; Termination**

(a) A Transaction may be entered into orally or in writing at the initiation of either Buyer or Seller.

(b) Upon agreeing to enter into a Transaction hereunder Buyer or Seller (or both), as shall have been agreed, shall promptly deliver to the other party written confirmation of such Transaction (a "Confirmation").

The Confirmation shall describe the Purchased Securities (including CUSIP or ISIN or other identifying number or numbers, if any), identify Buyer and Seller and set forth -

(i)   the Purchase Date;

(ii) the Purchase Price;

(iii) the Repurchase Date, unless the Transaction is to be terminable on demand (in which case the Confirmation shall state that it is terminable on demand);

(iv) the Pricing Rate applicable to the Transaction;

(v)   in respect of each party the details of the bank account(s) to which payments to be made hereunder are to be credited;

(vi) where the Buy/Sell Back Annex applies, whether the Transaction is a Repurchase Transaction or a Buy/Sell Back Transaction;

(vii) where the Agency Annex applies, whether the Transaction is an Agency Transaction and, if so, the identity of the party which is acting as agent and the name, code or identifier of the Principal; and

(viii) any additional terms or conditions of the Transaction;

and may be in the form of Annex II or may be in any other form to which the parties agree.

The Confirmation relating to a Transaction shall, together with this Agreement, constitute prima facie evidence of the terms agreed between Buyer and Seller for that Transaction, unless objection is made with respect to the Confirmation promptly after receipt thereof. In the event of any conflict between the terms of such Confirmation and this Agreement, the Confirmation shall prevail in respect of that Transaction and those terms only.

(c) On the Purchase Date for a Transaction, Seller shall transfer the Purchased Securities to Buyer or its agent against the payment of the Purchase Price by Buyer in accordance with paragraph 6(c).

(d) Termination of a Transaction will be effected, in the case of on demand Transactions, on the date specified for Termination in such demand, and, in the case of fixed term Transactions, on the date fixed for Termination.

(e) In the case of on demand Transactions, demand for Termination shall be made by Buyer or Seller, by telephone or otherwise, and shall provide for Termination to occur after not less than the minimum period as is customarily required for the settlement or delivery of money or Equivalent Securities of the relevant kind.

(f) On the Repurchase Date, Buyer shall transfer to Seller or its agent Equivalent Securities against the payment of the Repurchase Price by Seller (less any amount then payable and unpaid by Buyer to Seller pursuant to paragraph 5).

4. **Margin Maintenance**

(a) If at any time either party has a Net Exposure in respect of the other party it may by notice to the other party require the other party to make a Margin Transfer to it of an aggregate amount or value at least equal to that Net Exposure.

(b) A notice under sub-paragraph (a) above may be given orally or in writing.

(c) For the purposes of this Agreement a party has a Net Exposure in respect of the other party if the aggregate of all the first party's Transaction Exposures plus any amount payable to the first party under paragraph 5 but unpaid less the amount of any Net Margin provided to the first party exceeds the aggregate of all the other party's Transaction Exposures plus any amount payable to the other party under paragraph 5 but unpaid less the amount of any Net Margin provided to the other party; and the amount of the Net Exposure is the amount of the excess. For this purpose any amounts not denominated in the Base Currency shall be converted into the Base Currency at the Spot Rate prevailing at the relevant time.

(d) To the extent that a party calling for a Margin Transfer has previously paid Cash Margin which has not been repaid or delivered Margin Securities in respect of which Equivalent Margin Securities have not been delivered to it or a Cash Equivalent Amount has not been paid, that party shall be entitled to require that such Margin Transfer be satisfied first by the repayment of such Cash Margin or the delivery of Equivalent Margin Securities but, subject to this, the composition of a Margin Transfer shall be at the option of the party making such Margin Transfer.

(e) Any Cash Margin transferred shall be in the Base Currency or such other currency as the parties may agree.

(f) A payment of Cash Margin shall give rise to a debt owing from the party receiving such payment to the party making such payment. Such debt shall bear interest at such rate, payable at such times, as may be specified in Annex I in respect of the relevant currency or otherwise agreed between the parties, and shall be repayable subject to the terms of this Agreement.

(g) Where Seller or Buyer becomes obliged under sub-paragraph (a) above to make a Margin Transfer, it shall transfer Cash Margin or Margin Securities or Equivalent Margin Securities within the minimum period specified in Annex I or, if no period is there specified, such minimum period as is customarily required for the settlement or delivery of money, Margin Securities or Equivalent Margin Securities of the relevant kind.

(h) Where a party (the "Transferor") becomes obliged to transfer Equivalent Margin Securities and, having made all reasonable efforts to do so, is, for any reason relating to the Securities or the clearing system through which the Securities are to be transferred, unable to transfer Equivalent Margin Securities then

   (i) the Transferor shall immediately pay to the other party Cash Margin at least equal to the Market Value of such Equivalent Margin Securities (and, unless the parties otherwise agree, such Cash Margin shall not bear interest in accordance with paragraph 4(f)); and

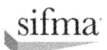

(ii) if the failure is continuing for two Business Days or more the other party may by notice to the Transferor require the Transferor to pay an amount (the "Cash Equivalent Amount") equal to the Default Market Value of the Equivalent Margin Securities determined by the other party in accordance with paragraph 10(f) which shall apply on the basis that references to the non-Defaulting Party were to the other party and references to the Early Termination Date were to the date on which notice under this paragraph is effective.

(i) The parties may agree that, with respect to any Transaction, the provisions of sub-paragraphs (a) to (h) above shall not apply but instead that margin may be provided separately in respect of that Transaction in which case -

(i) that Transaction shall not be taken into account when calculating whether either party has a Net Exposure;

(ii) margin shall be provided in respect of that Transaction in such manner as the parties may agree; and

(iii) margin provided in respect of that Transaction shall not be taken into account for the purposes of sub-paragraphs (a) to (h) above.

(j) The parties may agree that any Net Exposure which may arise shall be eliminated not by Margin Transfers under the preceding provisions of this paragraph but by the repricing of Transactions under sub-paragraph (k) below, the adjustment of Transactions under sub-paragraph (l) below or a combination of both these methods.

(k) Where the parties agree that a Transaction is to be repriced under this sub-paragraph, such repricing shall be effected as follows -

(i) the Repurchase Date under the relevant Transaction (the "Original Transaction") shall be deemed to occur on the date on which the repricing is to be effected (the "Repricing Date");

(ii) the parties shall be deemed to have entered into a new Transaction (the "Repriced Transaction") on the terms set out in (iii) to (vi) below;

(iii) the Purchased Securities under the Repriced Transaction shall be Securities equivalent to the Purchased Securities under the Original Transaction;

(iv) the Purchase Date under the Repriced Transaction shall be the Repricing Date;

(v) the Purchase Price under the Repriced Transaction shall be such amount as shall, when multiplied by the Margin Ratio applicable to the Original Transaction, be equal to the Market Value of such Securities on the Repricing Date;

(vi) the Repurchase Date, the Pricing Rate, the Margin Ratio and, subject as aforesaid, the other terms of the Repriced Transaction shall be identical to those of the Original Transaction;

(vii) the obligations of the parties with respect to the delivery of the Purchased Securities and the payment of the Purchase Price under the Repriced Transaction shall be set off against their obligations with respect to the delivery of Equivalent Securities and payment of the Repurchase Price under the Original Transaction and accordingly only a net cash sum shall be paid by one party to the other. Such net cash sum shall be paid within the minimum period specified in sub-paragraph (g) above.

(I) The adjustment of a Transaction (the "Original Transaction") under this sub-paragraph shall be effected by the parties agreeing that on the date on which the adjustment is to be made (the "Adjustment Date") the Original Transaction shall be terminated and they shall enter into a new Transaction (the "Replacement Transaction") in accordance with the following provisions -

(i) the Original Transaction shall be terminated on the Adjustment Date on such terms as the parties shall agree on or before the Adjustment Date;

(ii) the Purchased Securities under the Replacement Transaction shall be such Securities as the parties shall agree on or before the Adjustment Date (being Securities the aggregate Market Value of which at the Adjustment Date is substantially equal to the Repurchase Price under the Original Transaction at the Adjustment Date multiplied by the Margin Ratio applicable to the Original Transaction);

(iii) the Purchase Date under the Replacement Transaction shall be the Adjustment Date;

(iv) the other terms of the Replacement Transaction shall be such as the parties shall agree on or before the Adjustment Date; and

(v) the obligations of the parties with respect to payment and delivery of Securities on the Adjustment Date under the Original Transaction and the Replacement Transaction shall be settled in accordance with paragraph 6 within the minimum period specified in sub-paragraph (g) above.

5. **Income Payments**

Unless otherwise agreed -

(a) where: (i) the Term of a particular Transaction extends over an Income Payment Date in respect of any Securities subject to that Transaction; or (ii) an Income Payment Date in respect of any such Securities occurs after the Repurchase Date but before Equivalent Securities have been delivered to Seller or, if earlier, the occurrence of an Early Termination Date or the termination of the Transaction under paragraph 10(i) then Buyer shall on the date such Income is paid by the issuer transfer to or credit to the account of Seller an amount equal to (and in the same currency as) the amount paid by the issuer;

(b) where Margin Securities are transferred from one party ("the first party") to the other party ("the second party") and an Income Payment Date in respect of such Securities occurs before Equivalent Margin Securities are transferred or a Cash Equivalent Amount is paid by the second party to the first party, the second party shall on the date such Income is paid by the issuer transfer to or credit to the account of the first party an amount equal to (and in the same currency as) the amount paid by the issuer;

and for the avoidance of doubt references in this paragraph to the amount of any Income paid by the issuer of any Securities shall be to an amount paid without any withholding or deduction for or on account of taxes or duties notwithstanding that a payment of such Income made in certain circumstances may be subject to such a withholding or deduction.

6. **Payment and Transfer**

(a) Unless otherwise agreed, all money paid hereunder shall be in immediately available freely convertible funds of the relevant currency. All Securities to be transferred hereunder (i) shall be in suitable form for transfer and shall be accompanied by duly executed instruments of transfer or assignment in blank (where required for transfer) and such other documentation as the transferee may reasonably request, or (ii) shall be transferred through any agreed book entry or other securities clearance system or (iii) shall be transferred by any other method mutually acceptable to Seller and Buyer.

(b) Unless otherwise agreed, all money payable by one party to the other in respect of any Transaction shall be paid free and clear of, and without withholding or deduction for, any taxes or duties of whatsoever nature imposed, levied, collected, withheld or assessed by any authority having power to tax, unless the withholding or deduction of such taxes or duties is required by law. In that event, unless otherwise agreed, the paying party shall pay such additional amounts as will result in the net amounts receivable by the other party (after taking account of such withholding or deduction) being equal to such amounts as would have been received by it had no such taxes or duties been required to be withheld or deducted.

(c) Unless otherwise agreed in writing between the parties, under each Transaction transfer of Purchased Securities by Seller and payment of Purchase Price by Buyer against the transfer of such Purchased Securities shall be made simultaneously and transfer of Equivalent Securities by Buyer and payment of Repurchase Price payable by Seller against the transfer of such Equivalent Securities shall be made simultaneously.

(d) Subject to and without prejudice to the provisions of sub-paragraph 6(c), either party may from time to time in accordance with market practice and in recognition of the practical difficulties in arranging simultaneous delivery of Securities and money waive in relation to any Transaction its rights under this Agreement to receive simultaneous transfer and/or payment provided that transfer and/or payment shall, notwithstanding such waiver, be made on the same day and provided also that no such waiver in respect of one Transaction shall affect or bind it in respect of any other Transaction.

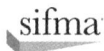

(e) The parties shall execute and deliver all necessary documents and take all necessary steps to procure that all right, title and interest in any Purchased Securities, any Equivalent Securities, any Margin Securities and any Equivalent Margin Securities shall pass to the party to which transfer is being made upon transfer of the same in accordance with this Agreement, free from all liens (other than a lien granted to the operator of the clearance system through which the Securities are transferred), claims, charges and encumbrances.

(f) Notwithstanding the use of expressions such as "Repurchase Date", "Repurchase Price", "margin", "Net Margin", "Margin Ratio" and "substitution", which are used to reflect terminology used in the market for transactions of the kind provided for in this Agreement, all right, title and interest in and to Securities and money transferred or paid under this Agreement shall pass to the transferee upon transfer or payment, the obligation of the party receiving Purchased Securities or Margin Securities being an obligation to transfer Equivalent Securities or Equivalent Margin Securities.

(g) Time shall be of the essence in this Agreement.

(h) Subject to paragraph 10, all amounts in the same currency payable by each party to the other under any Transaction or otherwise under this Agreement on the same date shall be combined in a single calculation of a net sum payable by one party to the other and the obligation to pay that sum shall be the only obligation of either party in respect of those amounts.

(i) Subject to paragraph 10, all Securities of the same issue, denomination, currency and series, transferable by each party to the other under any Transaction or hereunder on the same date shall be combined in a single calculation of a net quantity of Securities transferable by one party to the other and the obligation to transfer the net quantity of Securities shall be the only obligation of either party in respect of the Securities so transferable and receivable.

(j) If the parties have specified in Annex I that this paragraph 6(j) shall apply, each obligation of a party under this Agreement (the "first party") (other than an obligation arising under paragraph 10) is subject to the condition precedent that none of the events specified in paragraph 10(a) (Events of Default) shall have occurred and be continuing with respect to the other party.

7. **Contractual Currency**

(a) All the payments made in respect of the Purchase Price or the Repurchase Price of any Transaction shall be made in the currency of the Purchase Price (the "Contractual Currency") save as provided in paragraph 10(d)(ii). Notwithstanding the foregoing, the

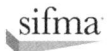

(b) If for any reason the amount in the Contractual Currency received by a party, including amounts received after conversion of any recovery under any judgment or order expressed in a currency other than the Contractual Currency, falls short of the amount in the Contractual Currency due and payable, the party required to make the payment will, as a separate and independent obligation, to the extent permitted by applicable law, immediately transfer such additional amount in the Contractual Currency as may be necessary to compensate for the shortfall.

(c) If for any reason the amount in the Contractual Currency received by a party exceeds the amount of the Contractual Currency due and payable, the party receiving the transfer will refund promptly the amount of such excess.

8. **Substitution**

(a) A Transaction may at any time between the Purchase Date and Repurchase Date, if Seller so requests and Buyer so agrees, be varied by the transfer by Buyer to Seller of Securities equivalent to the Purchased Securities, or to such of the Purchased Securities as shall be agreed, in exchange for the transfer by Seller to Buyer of other Securities of such amount and description as shall be agreed ("New Purchased Securities") (being Securities having a Market Value at the date of the variation at least equal to the Market Value of the Equivalent Securities transferred to Seller).

(b) Any variation under sub-paragraph (a) above shall be effected, subject to paragraph 6(d), by the simultaneous transfer of the Equivalent Securities and New Purchased Securities concerned.

(c) A Transaction which is varied under sub-paragraph (a) above shall thereafter continue in effect as though the Purchased Securities under that Transaction consisted of or included the New Purchased Securities instead of the Securities in respect of which Equivalent Securities have been transferred to Seller.

(d) Where either party has transferred Margin Securities to the other party it may at any time before Equivalent Margin Securities are transferred to it under paragraph 4 request the other party to transfer Equivalent Margin Securities to it in exchange for the transfer to the other party of new Margin Securities having a Market Value at the time at which the exchange is agreed at least equal to that of such Equivalent Margin Securities. If the other party agrees to the request, the exchange shall be effected, subject to paragraph 6(d), by the simultaneous transfer of the Equivalent Margin Securities and new Margin Securities concerned. Where either or both of such

April 2011

transfers is or are effected through a settlement system in circumstances which under the rules and procedures of that settlement system give rise to a payment by or for the account of one party to or for the account of the other party, the parties shall cause such payment or payments to be made outside that settlement system, for value the same day as the payments made through that settlement system, as shall ensure that the exchange of Equivalent Margin Securities and new Margin Securities effected under this sub-paragraph does not give rise to any net payment of cash by either party to the other.

9. **Representations**

Each party represents and warrants to the other that -

(a) it is duly authorised to execute and deliver this Agreement, to enter into the Transactions contemplated hereunder and to perform its obligations hereunder and thereunder and has taken all necessary action to authorise such execution, delivery and performance;

(b) it will engage in this Agreement and the Transactions contemplated hereunder (other than Agency Transactions) as principal;

(c) the person signing this Agreement on its behalf is, and any person representing it in entering into a Transaction will be, duly authorised to do so on its behalf;

(d) it has obtained all authorisations of any governmental or regulatory body required in connection with this Agreement and the Transactions contemplated hereunder and such authorisations are in full force and effect;

(e) the execution, delivery and performance of this Agreement and the Transactions contemplated hereunder will not violate any law, ordinance, charter, by-law or rule applicable to it or any agreement by which it is bound or by which any of its assets are affected;

(f) it has satisfied itself and will continue to satisfy itself as to the tax implications of the Transactions contemplated hereunder;

(g) in connection with this Agreement and each Transaction -

(i) unless there is a written agreement with the other party to the contrary, it is not relying on any advice (whether written or oral) of the other party, other than the representations expressly set out in this Agreement;

(ii) it has made and will make its own decisions regarding the entering into of any Transaction based upon its own judgment and upon advice from such professional advisers as it has deemed it necessary to consult;

(iii) it understands the terms, conditions and risks of each Transaction and is willing to assume (financially and otherwise) those risks; and

Appendices

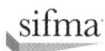

(h) at the time of transfer to the other party of any Securities it will have the full and unqualified right to make such transfer and that upon such transfer of Securities the other party will receive all right, title and interest in and to those Securities free of any lien (other than a lien granted to the operator of the clearance system through which the Securities are transferred), claim, charge or encumbrance.

On the date on which any Transaction is entered into pursuant hereto, and on each day on which Securities, Equivalent Securities, Margin Securities or Equivalent Margin Securities are to be transferred under any Transaction, Buyer and Seller shall each be deemed to repeat all the foregoing representations. For the avoidance of doubt and notwithstanding any arrangements which Seller or Buyer may have with any third party, each party will be liable as a principal for its obligations under this Agreement and each Transaction.

10. **Events of Default**

(a) If any of the following events (each an "Event of Default") occurs in relation to either party (the "Defaulting Party", the other party being the "non-Defaulting Party") whether acting as Seller or Buyer -

   (i) Buyer fails to pay the Purchase Price upon the applicable Purchase Date or Seller fails to pay the Repurchase Price upon the applicable Repurchase Date; or

   (ii) if the parties have specified in Annex I that this sub-paragraph shall apply, Seller fails to deliver Purchased Securities on the Purchase Date or Buyer fails to deliver Equivalent Securities on the Repurchase Date, in either case within the standard settlement time for delivery of the Securities concerned; or

   (iii) Seller or Buyer fails to pay when due any sum payable under sub-paragraph (h) or (i) below; or

   (iv) Seller or Buyer fails to:

      (A) make a Margin Transfer within the minimum period in accordance with paragraph 4(g) or, in the case of an obligation to deliver Equivalent Margin Securities, either to deliver the relevant Equivalent Margin Securities or to pay Cash Margin in accordance with paragraph 4(h)(i) or to pay the Cash Equivalent Amount in accordance with paragraph 4(h)(ii);

      (B) where paragraph 4(i) applies, to provide margin in accordance with that paragraph; or

      (C) to pay any amount or to transfer any Securities in accordance with paragraphs 4(k) or (l); or

   (v) Seller or Buyer fails to comply with paragraph 5; or

   (vi) an Act of Insolvency occurs with respect to Seller or Buyer; or

(vii) any representations made by Seller or Buyer are incorrect or untrue in any material respect when made or repeated or deemed to have been made or repeated; or

(viii) Seller or Buyer admits to the other that it is unable to, or intends not to, perform any of its obligations hereunder or in respect of any Transaction; or

(ix) Seller or Buyer being declared in default or being suspended or expelled from membership of or participation in, any securities exchange or suspended or prohibited from dealing in securities by any Competent Authority, in each case on the grounds that it has failed to meet any requirements relating to financial resources or credit rating; or

(x) Seller or Buyer fails to perform any other of its obligations hereunder and does not remedy such failure within 30 days after notice is given by the non-Defaulting Party requiring it to do so,

then sub-paragraphs (b) to (g) below shall apply.

(b) If at any time an Event of Default has occurred and is continuing the non-Defaulting Party may, by not more than 20 days' notice to the Defaulting Party specifying the relevant Event of Default, designate a day not earlier than the day such notice is effective as an Early Termination Date in respect of all outstanding Transactions. If, however, "Automatic Early Termination" is specified in Annex I with respect to the Defaulting Party, then an Early Termination Date in respect of all outstanding Transactions will occur at the time immediately preceding the occurrence with respect to the Defaulting Party of an Act of Insolvency which is the presentation of a petition for winding-up or any analogous proceeding or the appointment of a liquidator or analogous officer of the Defaulting Party.

(c) If an Early Termination Date occurs, the Repurchase Date for each Transaction hereunder shall be deemed to occur on the Early Termination Date and, subject to the following provisions, all Cash Margin (including interest accrued) shall be repayable and Equivalent Margin Securities shall be deliverable and Cash Equivalent Amounts shall be payable, in each case on the Early Termination Date (and so that, where this sub-paragraph applies, performance of the respective obligations of the parties with respect to the delivery of Securities, the payment of the Repurchase Prices for any Equivalent Securities, the repayment of any Cash Margin and the payment of Cash Equivalent Amounts shall be effected only in accordance with the provisions of sub-paragraph (d) below).

(d) (i) The Default Market Values of the Equivalent Securities and any Equivalent Margin Securities to be transferred, the amount of any Cash Margin (including the amount of interest accrued) to be transferred and the Repurchase Prices and Cash Equivalent Amounts to be paid by each party shall be established by the non-Defaulting Party for all Transactions as at the Early Termination Date;

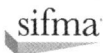

(ii) on the basis of the sums so established, an account shall be taken (as at the Early Termination Date) of what is due from each party to the other under this Agreement (on the basis that each party's claim against the other in respect of the transfer to it of Equivalent Securities or Equivalent Margin Securities under this Agreement equals the Default Market Value therefor and including amounts payable under paragraphs 10(g) and 12) and the sums due from one party shall be set off against the sums due from the other and only the balance of the account shall be payable (by the party having the claim valued at the lower amount pursuant to the foregoing). For the purposes of this calculation, all sums not denominated in the Base Currency shall be converted into the Base Currency at the Spot Rate; and

(iii) as soon as reasonably practicable after effecting the calculation above, the non-Defaulting Party shall provide to the Defaulting Party a statement showing in reasonable detail such calculations and specifying the balance payable by one party to the other and such balance shall be due and payable on the Business Day following the date of such statement provided that, to the extent permitted by applicable law, interest shall accrue on such amount on a 360 day, 365 day or other day basis in accordance with the applicable market convention (or as otherwise agreed by the parties), for the actual number of days during the period from and including the Early Termination Date to, but excluding, the date of payment.

(e) For the purposes of this Agreement, the "Default Market Value" of any Equivalent Securities or Equivalent Margin Securities shall be determined by the non-Defaulting Party on or as soon as reasonably practicable after the Early Termination Date in accordance with sub-paragraph (f) below, and for this purpose -

(i) the "Appropriate Market" means, in relation to Securities of any description, the market which is the most appropriate market for Securities of that description, as determined by the non-Defaulting Party;

(ii) "Deliverable Securities" means Equivalent Securities or Equivalent Margin Securities to be delivered by the Defaulting Party;

(iii) "Net Value" means at any time, in relation to any Deliverable Securities or Receivable Securities, the amount which, in the reasonable opinion of the non-Defaulting Party, represents their fair market value, having regard to such pricing sources (including trading prices) and methods (which may include, without limitation, available prices for Securities with similar maturities, terms and credit characteristics as the relevant Equivalent Securities or Equivalent Margin Securities) as the non-Defaulting Party considers appropriate, less, in the case of Receivable Securities, or plus, in the case of Deliverable Securities, all Transaction Costs which would be incurred or reasonably anticipated in connection with the purchase or sale of such Securities;

(iv) "Receivable Securities" means Equivalent Securities or Equivalent Margin Securities to be delivered to the Defaulting Party; and

(v) "Transaction Costs" in relation to any transaction contemplated in paragraph 10(e) or (f) means the reasonable costs, commissions, fees and expenses (including any mark-up or mark-down or premium paid for guaranteed delivery) incurred or reasonably anticipated in connection with the purchase of Deliverable Securities or sale of Receivable Securities, calculated on the assumption that the aggregate thereof is the least that could reasonably be expected to be paid in order to carry out the transaction.

(f) If -

(i) on or about the Early Termination Date the non-Defaulting Party has sold, in the case of Receivable Securities, or purchased, in the case of Deliverable Securities, Securities which form part of the same issue and are of an identical type and description as those Equivalent Securities or Equivalent Margin Securities (regardless as to whether or not such sales or purchases have settled), the non-Defaulting Party may elect to treat as the Default Market Value -

(A) in the case of Receivable Securities, the net proceeds of such sale after deducting all reasonable costs, commissions, fees and expenses incurred in connection therewith (provided that, where the Securities sold are not identical in amount to the Equivalent Securities or Equivalent Margin Securities, the non-Defaulting Party may, acting in good faith, either (x) elect to treat such net proceeds of sale divided by the amount of Securities sold and multiplied by the amount of the Equivalent Securities or Equivalent Margin Securities as the Default Market Value or (y) elect to treat such net proceeds of sale of the Equivalent Securities or Equivalent Margin Securities actually sold as the Default Market Value of that proportion of the Equivalent Securities or Equivalent Margin Securities, and, in the case of (y), the Default Market Value of the balance of the Equivalent Securities or Equivalent Margin Securities shall be determined separately in accordance with the provisions of this paragraph 10(f)); or

(B) in the case of Deliverable Securities, the aggregate cost of such purchase, including all reasonable costs, commissions, fees and expenses incurred in connection therewith (provided that, where the Securities purchased are not identical in amount to the Equivalent Securities or Equivalent Margin Securities, the non-Defaulting Party may, acting in good faith, either (x) elect to treat such aggregate cost divided by the amount of Securities sold and multiplied by the amount of the Equivalent Securities or Equivalent Margin Securities as the Default Market Value or (y) elect to treat the aggregate cost of purchasing the Equivalent Securities or Equivalent Margin Securities actually purchased as the Default Market Value of that proportion of the Equivalent Securities or Equivalent Margin Securities, and, in the case of (y), the Default Market Value of the balance of the Equivalent Securities or Equivalent Margin Securities shall be determined separately in accordance with the provisions of this paragraph 10(f));

(ii) on or about the Early Termination Date the non-Defaulting Party has received, in the case of Deliverable Securities, offer quotations or, in the case of Receivable Securities, bid quotations in respect of Securities of the relevant description from two or more market makers or regular dealers in the Appropriate Market in a commercially reasonable size, using pricing methodology which is customary for the relevant type of security (as determined by the non-Defaulting Party) the non-Defaulting Party may elect to treat as the Default Market Value of such Securities -

(A) the price quoted (or where a price is quoted by two or more market makers, the arithmetic mean of such prices) by each of them for, in the case of Deliverable Securities, the sale by the relevant market maker or dealer of such Securities or, in the case of Receivable Securities, the purchase by the relevant market maker or dealer of such Securities provided that such price or prices quoted may be adjusted in a commercially reasonable manner by the non-Defaulting Party (x) to reflect accrued but unpaid coupons not reflected in the price or prices quoted in respect of such securities and (y) in respect of any Pool Factor Affected Security, to reflect the realisable value of such Security, taking into consideration the Pool Factor Distortion (and for this purpose, "Pool Factor Affected Security" means a security other than an equity security in respect of which the decimal value of the outstanding principal divided by the original principal balance of such Security is less than one (as indicated by any pool factor applicable to such security), such circumstance a "Pool Factor Distortion");

(B) after deducting, in the case of Receivable Securities, or adding, in the case of Deliverable Securities the Transaction Costs which would be incurred or reasonably anticipated in connection with such a transaction; or

(iii) if, acting in good faith the non-Defaulting Party either -

(A) has endeavoured but been unable to sell or purchase Securities in accordance with sub-paragraph (i) above or to obtain quotations in accordance with sub-paragraph (ii) above (or both); or

(B) has determined that it would not be commercially reasonable to sell or purchase Securities at the prices bid or offered or to obtain such quotations, or that it would not be commercially reasonable to use any quotations which it has obtained under sub-paragraph (ii) above, the non-Defaulting Party may determine the Net Value of the relevant Equivalent Securities or Equivalent Margin Securities (which shall be specified) and may treat such Net Value as the Default Market Value of the relevant Equivalent Securities or Equivalent Margin Securities.

(g) The Defaulting Party shall be liable to the non-Defaulting Party for the amount of all reasonable and legal and other professional expenses incurred by the non-Defaulting Party in connection with or as a consequence of an Event of Default, together with interest thereon at the Applicable Rate or, in the case of an expense attributable to a particular Transaction, the Pricing Rate for the relevant Transaction if that Pricing Rate is greater than the Applicable Rate.

(h) If Seller fails to deliver Purchased Securities to Buyer on the applicable Purchase Date Buyer may -

(i) if it has paid the Purchase Price to Seller, require Seller immediately to repay the sum so paid;

(ii) if Buyer has a Transaction Exposure to Seller in respect of the relevant Transaction, require Seller from time to time to pay Cash Margin at least equal to such Transaction Exposure;

(iii) at any time while such failure continues, terminate the Transaction by giving written notice to Seller. On such termination the obligations of Seller and Buyer with respect to delivery of Purchased Securities and Equivalent Securities shall terminate and Seller shall pay to Buyer an amount equal to the excess of the Repurchase Price at the date of Termination over the Purchase Price.

(i) If Buyer fails to deliver some or all Equivalent Securities to Seller on the applicable Repurchase Date Seller may -

(i) if it has paid the Repurchase Price to Buyer, require Buyer immediately to repay the sum so paid;

(ii) if Seller has a Transaction Exposure to Buyer in respect of the relevant Transaction, require Buyer from time to time to pay Cash Margin at least equal to such Transaction Exposure;

(iii) at any time while such failure continues, by written notice to Buyer declare that that Transaction or part of that Transaction corresponding to the Equivalent Securities that have not been delivered (but only that Transaction or part of Transaction) shall be terminated immediately in accordance with sub-paragraph (c) above (disregarding for this purpose references in that sub-paragraph to transfer of Cash Margin, delivery of Equivalent Margin Securities and payment of Cash Equivalent Amount and as if references to the Repurchase Date were to the date on which notice was given under this sub-paragraph).

(j) The provisions of this Agreement constitute a complete statement of the remedies available to each party in respect of any Event of Default.

(k) Subject to paragraph 10(l), neither party may claim any sum by way of consequential loss or damage in the event of a failure by the other party to perform any of its obligations under this Agreement.

(l) (i) Subject to sub-paragraph (ii) below, if as a result of a Transaction terminating before its agreed Repurchase Date or a Forward Transaction terminating before its Purchase Date under paragraphs 10(b), 10(h)(iii) or 10(i)(iii), the non-Defaulting Party, in the case of paragraph 10(b), Buyer, in the case of paragraph 10(h)(iii), or Seller, in the case of paragraph 10(i)(iii), (in each case the "first party") incurs any loss or expense in entering into replacement transactions or in otherwise hedging its exposure arising in connection with a Transaction so terminating, the other party shall be required to pay to the first party the amount determined by the first party in good faith and without double counting to be equal to the loss or expense incurred in connection with such replacement transactions or hedging (including all fees, costs and other expenses) less the amount of any profit or gain made by that party in connection with such replacement transactions or hedging; provided that if that calculation results in a negative number, an amount equal to that number shall be payable by the first party to the other party.

(ii) If the first party reasonably decides, instead of entering into such replacement transactions, to replace or unwind any hedging transactions which the first party entered into in connection with the Transaction so terminating, or to enter into any replacement hedging transactions, the other party shall be required to pay to the first party the amount determined by the first party in good faith to be equal to the loss or expense incurred in connection with entering into such replacement or unwinding (including all fees, costs and other expenses) less the amount of any profit or gain made by that party in connection with such replacement or unwinding; provided that if that calculation results in a negative number, an amount equal to that number shall be payable by the first party to the other party.

(m) Each party shall immediately notify the other if an Event of Default, or an event which, upon the service of a notice or the lapse of time, or both, would be an Event of Default, occurs in relation to it.

(n) Any amount payable to one party (the Payee) by the other party (the Payer) under paragraph 10(d) may, at the option of the non-Defaulting Party, be reduced by its set off against any amount payable (whether at such time or in the future or upon the occurrence of a contingency) by the Payee to the Payer (irrespective of the currency, place of payment or booking office of the obligation) under any other agreement between the Payee and the Payer or instrument or undertaking issued or executed by one party to, or in favour of, the other party. If an obligation is unascertained, the non-Defaulting Party may in good faith estimate that obligation and set off in respect of the

April 2011

estimate, subject to accounting to the other party when the obligation is ascertained. Nothing in this paragraph shall be effective to create a charge or other security interest. This paragraph shall be without prejudice and in addition to any right of set off, combination of accounts, lien or other right to which any party is at any time otherwise entitled (whether by operation of law, contract or otherwise).

11. **Tax Event**

(a) This paragraph shall apply if either party notifies the other that -

    (i) any action taken by a taxing authority or brought in a court of competent jurisdiction (regardless of whether such action is taken or brought with respect to a party to this Agreement); or

    (ii) a change in the fiscal or regulatory regime (including, but not limited to, a change in law or in the general interpretation of law but excluding any change in any rate of tax),

has or will, in the notifying party's reasonable opinion, have a material adverse effect on that party in the context of a Transaction.

(b) If so requested by the other party, the notifying party will furnish the other with an opinion of a suitably qualified adviser that an event referred to in sub-paragraph (a)(i) or (ii) above has occurred and affects the notifying party.

(c) Where this paragraph applies, the party giving the notice referred to in sub-paragraph (a) may, subject to sub-paragraph (d) below, terminate the Transaction with effect from a date specified in the notice, not being earlier (unless so agreed by the other party) than 30 days after the date of the notice, by nominating that date as the Repurchase Date.

(d) If the party receiving the notice referred to in sub-paragraph (a) so elects, it may override that notice by giving a counter-notice to the other party. If a counter-notice is given, the party which gives the counter-notice will be deemed to have agreed to indemnify the other party against the adverse effect referred to in sub-paragraph (a) so far as relates to the relevant Transaction and the original Repurchase Date will continue to apply.

(e) Where a Transaction is terminated as described in this paragraph, the party which has given the notice to terminate shall indemnify the other party against any reasonable legal and other professional expenses incurred by the other party by reason of the termination, but the other party may not claim any sum by way of consequential loss or damage in respect of a termination in accordance with this paragraph.

(f) This paragraph is without prejudice to paragraph 6(b) (obligation to pay additional amounts if withholding or deduction required); but an obligation to pay such additional amounts may, where appropriate, be a circumstance which causes this paragraph to apply.

April 2011

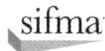

12. **Interest**

    To the extent permitted by applicable law, if any sum of money payable hereunder or under any Transaction is not paid when due, interest shall accrue on the unpaid sum as a separate debt at the greater of the Pricing Rate for the Transaction to which such sum relates (where such sum is referable to a Transaction) and Applicable Rate on a 360 day basis or 365 day basis in accordance with the applicable market convention (or as otherwise agreed by the parties), for the actual number of days during the period from and including the date on which payment was due to, but excluding, the date of payment.

13. **Single Agreement**

    Each party acknowledges that, and has entered into this Agreement and will enter into each Transaction hereunder in consideration of and in reliance upon the fact that all Transactions hereunder constitute a single business and contractual relationship and are made in consideration of each other. Accordingly, each party agrees (i) to perform all of its obligations in respect of each Transaction hereunder, and that a default in the performance of any such obligations shall constitute a default by it in respect of all Transactions hereunder, and (ii) that payments, deliveries and other transfers made by either of them in respect of any Transaction shall be deemed to have been made in consideration of payments, deliveries and other transfers in respect of any other Transactions hereunder.

14. **Notices and Other Communications**

    (a) Any notice or other communication to be given under this Agreement -

      (i) shall be in the English language, and except where expressly otherwise provided in this Agreement, shall be in writing;

      (ii) may be given in any manner described in sub-paragraphs (b) and (c) below;

      (iii) shall be sent to the party to whom it is to be given at the address or number, or in accordance with the electronic messaging details, set out in Annex I.

    (b) Subject to sub-paragraph (c) below, any such notice or other communication shall be effective -

      (i) if in writing and delivered in person or by courier, on the date when it is delivered;

      (ii) if sent by facsimile transmission, on the date when the transmission is received by a responsible employee of the recipient in legible form (it being agreed that the burden of proving receipt will be on the sender and will not be met by a transmission report generated by the sender's facsimile machine);

      (iii) if sent by certified or registered mail (airmail, if overseas) or the equivalent (return receipt requested), on the date that mail is delivered or its delivery is attempted; or

(iv) if sent by Electronic Messaging System, on the date that electronic message is received;

except that any notice or communication which is received, or delivery of which is attempted, after close of business on the date of receipt or attempted delivery or on a day which is not a day on which commercial banks are open for business in the place where that notice or other communication is to be given shall be treated as given at the opening of business on the next following day which is such a day.

(c) If -

(i) there occurs in relation to either party an Event of Default; and

(ii) the non-Defaulting Party, having made all practicable efforts to do so, including having attempted to use at least two of the methods specified in sub-paragraph (b)(ii), (iii) or (iv) above, has been unable to serve a Default Notice by one of the methods specified in those sub-paragraphs (or such of those methods as are normally used by the non-Defaulting Party when communicating with the Defaulting Party),

the non-Defaulting Party may sign a written notice (a "Special Default Notice") which -

(A) specifies the relevant event referred to in paragraph 10(a) which has occurred in relation to the Defaulting Party;

(B) specifies the Early Termination Date designated in the Default Notice;

(C) states that the non-Defaulting Party, having made all practicable efforts to do so, including having attempted to use at least two of the methods specified in sub-paragraph (b)(ii), (iii) or (iv) above, has been unable to serve a Default Notice by one of the methods specified in those sub-paragraphs (or such of those methods as are normally used by the non-Defaulting Party when communicating with the Defaulting Party); and

(D) specifies the date on which, and the time at which, the Special Default Notice is signed by the non-Defaulting Party.

On the signature of a Special Default Notice the Early Termination Date shall occur as designated in the Default Notice. A Special Default Notice shall be given to the Defaulting Party as soon as practicable after it is signed.

(d) Either party may by notice to the other change the address or facsimile number or Electronic Messaging System details at which notices or other communications are to be given to it.

15. **Entire Agreement; Severability**

This Agreement shall supersede any existing agreements between the parties containing general terms and conditions for Transactions. Each provision and agreement herein shall be treated as separate from any other provision or agreement herein and shall be enforceable notwithstanding the unenforceability of any such other provision or agreement.

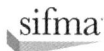

16. **Non-assignability; Termination**

(a) Subject to sub-paragraph (b) below, neither party may assign, charge or otherwise deal with (including without limitation any dealing with any interest in or the creation of any interest in) its rights or obligations under this Agreement or under any Transaction without the prior written consent of the other party. Subject to the foregoing, this Agreement and any Transactions shall be binding upon and shall inure to the benefit of the parties and their respective successors and assigns.

(b) Sub-paragraph (a) above shall not preclude a party from assigning, charging or otherwise dealing with all or any part of its interest in any sum payable to it under paragraph 10(c) or (g) above.

(c) Either party may terminate this Agreement by giving written notice to the other, except that this Agreement shall, notwithstanding such notice, remain applicable to any Transactions then outstanding.

(d) All remedies hereunder shall survive Termination in respect of the relevant Transaction and termination of this Agreement.

(e) The participation of any additional member State of the European Union in economic and monetary union after 1 January 1999 shall not have the effect of altering any term of the Agreement or any Transaction, nor give a party the right unilaterally to alter or terminate the Agreement or any Transaction.

17. **Governing Law**

This Agreement and any non-contractual obligations arising out of or in connection with this Agreement shall be governed by, and interpreted in accordance with, the laws of England.

The English courts shall have exclusive jurisdiction in relation to all disputes (including claims for set-off and counterclaims) arising out of or in connection with this Agreement including, without limitation disputes arising out of or in connection with: (i) the creation, validity, effect, interpretation, performance or non-performance of, or the legal relationships established by, this Agreement; and (ii) any non-contractual obligations arising out of or in connection with this Agreement. For such purposes, Buyer and Seller hereby irrevocably submit to the jurisdiction of the English courts and waive any objection to the exercise of such jurisdiction.

Party A hereby appoints the person identified in Annex I as its agent to receive on its behalf service of process in such courts. If such agent ceases to be its agent, Party A shall promptly appoint, and notify Party B of the identity of, a new agent in England. If

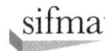

Party A fails to appoint such an agent, Party A agrees that Party B shall be entitled to appoint one on behalf of Party A at the expense of Party A.

Party B hereby appoints the person identified in Annex I as its agent to receive on its behalf service of process in such courts. If such agent ceases to be its agent, Party B shall promptly appoint, and notify Party A of the identity of, a new agent in England. If Party B fails to appoint such an agent, Party B agrees that Party A shall be entitled to appoint one on behalf of Party B at the expense of Party B.

Each party shall deliver to the other, within 30 days of the date of this Agreement in the case of the appointment of a person identified in Annex I or of the date of the appointment of the relevant agent in any other case, evidence of the acceptance by the agent appointed by it pursuant to this paragraph of such appointment.

18. **No Waivers, etc.**

No express or implied waiver of any Event of Default by either party shall constitute a waiver of any other Event of Default and no exercise of any remedy hereunder by any party shall constitute a waiver of its right to exercise any other remedy hereunder. No modification or waiver of any provision of this Agreement and no consent by any party to a departure herefrom shall be effective unless and until such modification, waiver or consent shall be in writing and duly executed by both of the parties hereto. Without limitation on any of the foregoing, the failure to give a notice pursuant to paragraph 4(a) hereof will not constitute a waiver of any right to do so at a later date.

19. **Waiver of Immunity**

Each party hereto hereby waives, to the fullest extent permitted by applicable law, all immunity (whether on the basis of sovereignty or otherwise) from jurisdiction, attachment (both before and after judgment) and execution to which it might otherwise be entitled in any action or proceeding in the Courts of England or of any other country or jurisdiction, relating in any way to this Agreement or any Transaction, and agrees that it will not raise, claim or cause to be pleaded any such immunity at or in respect of any such action or proceeding.

20. **Recording**

The parties agree that each may electronically record all telephone conversations between them.

21. **Third Party Rights**

No person shall have any right to enforce any provision of this Agreement under the Contracts (Rights of Third Parties) Act 1999.

April 2011

Appendices

[Name of Party]	[Name of Party]
By _____	By _____
Title _____	Title _____
Date _____	Date _____

Appendices

ANNEX I

Supplemental Terms or Conditions

Paragraph references are to paragraphs in the Agreement.

1. The following elections shall apply -

[(a) paragraph 1(c)(i). Buy/Sell Back Transactions [may/may not] be effected under this Agreement, and accordingly the Buy/Sell Back Annex [shall/shall not] apply.]*

[(b) paragraph 1(c)(ii). Transactions in Net Paying Securities [may/may not] be effected under this Agreement, and accordingly the following provisions [shall/shall not] apply.

   (i) The phrase "other than equities and Net Paying Securities" shall be replaced by the phrase "other than equities".

   (ii) In the Buy/Sell Back Annex the following words shall be added to the end of the definition of the expression "IR": "and for the avoidance of doubt the reference to the amount of Income for these purposes shall be to an amount paid without withholding or deduction for or on account of taxes or duties notwithstanding that a payment of such Income made in certain circumstances may be subject to such a withholding or deduction".]*

[(c) Agency Transactions [may/may not] be effected under this Agreement, and accordingly the Agency Annex [shall/shall not] apply.]*

[(d) The following Annex(es) shall apply in respect of specified Transactions -

   for _____ Transactions, the _____ annex shall apply,

   for _____ Transactions, the _____ annex shall apply.]*

(e) paragraph 2(e). The Base Currency shall be: _____.

(f) paragraph 2(p). [list Buyer's and Seller's Designated Offices]

_____

_____

(g) paragraph 2(xx): Transaction Exposure method [A]* [B]*

(h) paragraph 3(b). [Seller/Buyer/both Seller and Buyer]* to deliver Confirmation.

---

* Delete as appropriate

April 2011   - 30 -

(i) paragraph 4(f). Interest rate on Cash Margin to be _____% for _____ currency.
_____% for _____ currency.

Interest to be payable [payment intervals and dates] _____.

(j) paragraph 4(g). Delivery period for margin calls to be: _____.

[(k) paragraph 6(j). Paragraph 6(j) shall apply.]*

[(l) paragraph 10(a)(ii). Paragraph 10(a)(ii) shall apply.]*

[(m) paragraph 10(b). Automatic Early Termination shall apply with respect to [Party A] [Party B]]*

(n) paragraph 14. For the purposes of paragraph 14 of this Agreement -

    (i) Address for notices and other communications for Party A -

        Address: _____
        Attention: _____
        Telephone: _____
        Facsimile: _____
        Electronic Messaging System: _____
        Answerback: _____
        Other:

    (ii) Address for notices and other communications for Party B -

        Address: _____
        Attention: _____
        Telephone: _____
        Facsimile: _____
        Electronic Messaging System: _____
        Answerback: _____
        Other:

* Delete as appropriate

[(o) paragraph 17. For the purposes of paragraph 17 of this Agreement -

    (i) Party A appoints _____ as its agent for service of process;

    (ii) Party B appoints _____ as its agent for service of process.]*

2. The following supplemental terms and conditions shall apply -

[Existing Transactions

(a) The parties agree that this Agreement shall apply to all transactions which are subject to the Global Master Repurchase Agreement between them dated _____ and which are outstanding as at the date of this Agreement so that such transactions shall be treated as if they had been entered into under this Agreement, and the terms of such transactions are amended accordingly with effect from the date of this Agreement.]*

[Negative rate transactions

(b) In the case of Transactions in which the Pricing Rate will be negative, the parties agree that if Seller fails to deliver the Purchased Securities on the Purchase Date then -

    (i) Buyer may by notice to Seller terminate the Transaction (and may continue to do so for every day that Seller fails to deliver the Purchased Securities); and

    (ii) for every day that Seller fails to deliver the Purchased Securities the Pricing Rate shall be zero.]*

[Forward Transactions

(c) The parties agree that Forward Transactions (as defined in sub-paragraph (i)(A) below) may be effected under this Agreement and accordingly the provisions of sub-paragraphs (i) to (iv) below shall apply.

    (i) The following definitions shall apply -

        (A) "Forward Transaction", a Transaction in respect of which the Purchase Date is at least [three] Business Days after the date on which the Transaction was entered into and has not yet occurred;

        (B) "Forward Repricing Date", with respect to any Forward Transaction the date which is such number of Business Days before the Purchase Date as

* Delete as appropriate

April 2011

is equal to the minimum period for the delivery of margin applicable under paragraph 4(g).

(ii) The Confirmation relating to any Forward Transaction may describe the Purchased Securities by reference to a type or class of Securities, which, without limitation, may be identified by issuer or class of issuers and a maturity or range of maturities. Where this paragraph applies, the parties shall agree the actual Purchased Securities not less than two Business Days before the Purchase Date and Buyer or Seller (or both), as shall have been agreed, shall promptly deliver to the other party a Confirmation which shall describe such Purchased Securities.

(iii) At any time between the Forward Repricing Date and the Purchase Date for any Forward Transaction the parties may agree either -

(A) to adjust the Purchase Price under that Forward Transaction; or

(B) to adjust the number of Purchased Securities to be sold by Seller to Buyer under that Forward Transaction.

(iv) Where the parties agree to an adjustment under paragraph (iii) above, Buyer or Seller (or both), as shall have been agreed, shall promptly deliver to the other party a Confirmation of the Forward Transaction, as adjusted under paragraph (iii) above.

(d) Where the parties agree that this paragraph shall apply, paragraphs 2 and 4 of the Agreement are amended as follows.

(i) Paragraph 2(xx) is deleted and replaced by the following -

"(xx) "Transaction Exposure" means -

(i) with respect to any Forward Transaction at any time between the Forward Repricing Date and the Purchase Date, the difference between (A) the Market Value of the Purchased Securities at the relevant time and (B) the Purchase Price;

(ii) with respect to any Transaction at any time during the period (if any) from the Purchase Date to the date on which the Purchased Securities are delivered to Buyer or, if earlier, the date on which the Transaction is terminated under paragraph 10(h), the difference between (A) the Market Value of the Purchased Securities at the relevant time and (B) the Repurchase Price at the relevant time;

(iii) with respect to any Transaction at any time during the period from the Purchase Date (or, if later, the date on which the Purchased Securities are delivered to Buyer or the Transaction is terminated under paragraph 10(h)) to the Repurchase Date (or, if later, the date on which Equivalent Securities are delivered to Seller or the Transaction is terminated under paragraph 10(i)), the difference between (A) the Repurchase Price at the relevant time multiplied by the applicable Margin Ratio (or, where the Transaction relates to Securities of more than one description to which different Margin Ratios apply, the amount produced by multiplying the Repurchase Price attributable to Equivalent Securities of each such description by the applicable Margin Ratio and aggregating the resulting amounts, the Repurchase Price being for this purpose attributed to Equivalent Securities of each such description in the same proportions as those in which the Purchase Price was apportioned among the Purchased Securities) and (B) the Market Value of Equivalent Securities at the relevant time.

In each case, if (A) is greater than (B), Buyer has a Transaction Exposure for that Transaction equal to the excess, and if (B) is greater than (A), Seller has a Transaction Exposure to Buyer equal to the excess."

(ii) In paragraph 4(c) -

(aa) the words "any amount payable to the first party under paragraph 5 but unpaid" are deleted and replaced by "any amount which will become payable to the first party under paragraph 5 during the period after the time at which the calculation is made which is equal to the minimum period for the delivery of margin applicable under paragraph 4(g) or which is payable to the first party under paragraph 5 but unpaid"; and

(bb) the words "any amount payable to the other party under paragraph 5 but unpaid" are deleted and replaced by "any amount which will become payable to the other party under paragraph 5 during the period after the time at which the calculation is made which is equal to the minimum period for the delivery of margin applicable under paragraph 4(g) or which is payable to the other party under paragraph 5 but unpaid".]*

---

* Delete as appropriate

sifma   **ICMA** International Capital Market Association

ANNEX II

Form of Confirmation

To: _____

From: _____

Date: _____

Subject: [Repurchase] [Buy/Sell Back]*   Transaction
           (Reference Number: _____)

Dear Sirs,

The purpose of this [letter] [facsimile], a "Confirmation" for the purposes of the Agreement, is to set forth the terms and conditions of the above repurchase transaction entered into between us on the Contract Date referred to below.

This Confirmation supplements and forms part of, and is subject to, the Global Master Repurchase Agreement as entered into between us as of _____ as the same may be amended from time to time (the "Agreement"). All provisions contained in the Agreement govern this Confirmation except as expressly modified below. Words and phrases defined in the Agreement and used in this Confirmation shall have the same meaning herein as in the Agreement.

1. Contract Date: _____

2. Purchased Securities [state type[s] and nominal value[s]]:
   _____

3. CUSIP, ISIN or other identifying number[s]: _____

4. Buyer: _____

5. Seller: _____

6. Purchase Date: _____

7. Purchase Price: _____

8. Contractual Currency: _____

[9. Repurchase Date]:* _____

[10. Terminable on demand]:* _____

* Delete as appropriate

April 2011

Appendices

sifma   ICMA
                                                   International Capital Market Association

11. Pricing Rate: _____

[12. Sell Back Price]:* _____

13. Buyer's Bank Account[s] Details:

14. Seller's Bank Account[s] Details:

[15. The Transaction is an Agency Transaction.   [Name of Agent]   is   acting
     as agent for   [name or identifier of Principal]   ]:*

[16. Additional Terms]:*

Yours faithfully,

_____

* Delete as appropriate

VERSION: JANUARY 2010

ISLA
INTERNATIONAL
SECURITIES
LENDING
ASSOCIATION

GLOBAL MASTER SECURITIES LENDING AGREEMENT

FRESHFIELDS BRUCKHAUS DERINGER

CONTENTS

CLAUSE		PAGE
1.	APPLICABILITY	3
2.	INTERPRETATION	3
3.	LOANS OF SECURITIES	9
4.	DELIVERY	9
5.	COLLATERAL	10
6.	DISTRIBUTIONS AND CORPORATE ACTIONS	13
7.	RATES APPLICABLE TO LOANED SECURITIES AND CASH COLLATERAL	15
8.	DELIVERY OF EQUIVALENT SECURITIES	16
9.	FAILURE TO DELIVER	17
10.	EVENTS OF DEFAULT	18
11.	CONSEQUENCES OF AN EVENT OF DEFAULT	19
12.	TAXES	23
13.	LENDER'S WARRANTIES	25
14.	BORROWER'S WARRANTIES	25
15.	INTEREST ON OUTSTANDING PAYMENTS	25
16.	TERMINATION OF THIS AGREEMENT	26
17.	SINGLE AGREEMENT	26
18.	SEVERANCE	26
19.	SPECIFIC PERFORMANCE	26
20.	NOTICES	26
21.	ASSIGNMENT	27
22.	NON-WAIVER	27
23.	GOVERNING LAW AND JURISDICTION	27
24.	TIME	28
25.	RECORDING	28
26.	WAIVER OF IMMUNITY	28
27.	MISCELLANEOUS	28
SCHEDULE		31
AGENCY ANNEX		34
ADDENDUM FOR POOLED PRINCIPAL AGENCY LOANS		37

AGREEMENT

BETWEEN:

    (***Party A***) a company incorporated under the laws of acting through one or more Designated Offices; and

    (***Party B***) a company incorporated under the laws of acting through one or more Designated Offices.

1. APPLICABILITY

1.1 From time to time the Parties acting through one or more Designated Offices may enter into transactions in which one party (***Lender***) will transfer to the other (***Borrower***) securities and financial instruments (***Securities***) against the transfer of Collateral (as defined in paragraph 2) with a simultaneous agreement by Borrower to transfer to Lender Securities equivalent to such Securities on a fixed date or on demand against the transfer to Borrower by Lender of assets equivalent to such Collateral.

1.2 Each such transaction shall be referred to in this Agreement as a ***Loan*** and shall be governed by the terms of this Agreement, including the supplemental terms and conditions contained in the Schedule and any Addenda or Annexes attached hereto, unless otherwise agreed in writing. In the event of any inconsistency between the provisions of an Addendum or Annex and this Agreement, the provisions of such Addendum or Annex shall prevail unless the Parties otherwise agree.

1.3 Either Party may perform its obligations under this Agreement either directly or through a Nominee.

2. INTERPRETATION

2.1 In this Agreement:

Act of Insolvency means in relation to either Party:

(a) its making a general assignment for the benefit of, or entering into a reorganisation, arrangement, or composition with creditors; or

(b) its stating in writing that it is unable to pay its debts as they become due; or

(c) its seeking, consenting to or acquiescing in the appointment of any trustee, administrator, receiver or liquidator or analogous officer of it or any material part of its property; or

(d) the presentation or filing of a petition in respect of it (other than by the other Party to this Agreement in respect of any obligation under this Agreement) in any court or before any agency alleging or for the bankruptcy, winding-up or insolvency of such Party (or any analogous proceeding) or seeking any reorganisation, arrangement, composition, re-adjustment, administration, liquidation, dissolution or similar relief under any present or future statute, law or regulation, such petition not having been stayed or dismissed within 30 days of its filing (except in the case of a petition for winding-up or any analogous proceeding in respect of which no such 30 day period shall apply); or

(e) the appointment of a receiver, administrator, liquidator or trustee or analogous officer of such Party over all or any material part of such Party's property; or

(f) the convening of any meeting of its creditors for the purpose of considering a voluntary arrangement as referred to in Section 3 of the Insolvency Act 1986 (or any analogous proceeding);

Agency Annex means the Annex to this Agreement published by the International Securities Lending Association and providing for Lender to act as agent for a third party in respect of one or more Loans;

Alternative Collateral means Collateral having a Market Value equal to the Collateral delivered pursuant to paragraph 5 and provided by way of substitution in accordance with the provisions of paragraph 5.3;

Applicable Law means the laws, rules and regulations (including double taxation conventions) of any relevant jurisdiction, including published practice of any government or other taxing authority in connection with such laws, rules and regulations;

Automatic Early Termination has the meaning given in paragraph 10.1(d);

Base Currency means the currency indicated in paragraph 2 of the Schedule;

Business Day means:

(a) in relation to Delivery in respect of any Loan, a day other than a Saturday or a Sunday on which banks and securities markets are open for business generally in the place(s) where the relevant Securities, Equivalent Securities, Collateral or Equivalent Collateral are to be delivered;

(b) in relation to any payments under this Agreement, a day other than a Saturday or a Sunday on which banks are open for business generally in the principal financial centre of the country of which the currency in which the payment is denominated is the official currency and, if different, in the place where any account designated by the Parties for the making or receipt of the payment is situated (or, in the case of a payment in euro, a day on which TARGET operates);

(c) in relation to a notice or other communication served under this Agreement, any day other than a Saturday or a Sunday on which banks are open for business generally in the place designated for delivery in accordance with paragraph 3 of the Schedule; and

(d) in any other case, a day other than a Saturday or a Sunday on which banks are open for business generally in each place stated in paragraph 6 of the Schedule;

Buy-In means any arrangement under which, in the event of a seller or transferor failing to deliver securities to the buyer or transferee, the buyer or transferee of such securities is entitled under the terms of such arrangement to buy or otherwise acquire securities equivalent to such securities and to recover the cost of so doing from the seller or transferor;

Cash Collateral means Collateral taking the form of a transfer of currency;

Close of Business means the time at which the relevant banks, securities settlement systems or depositaries close in the business centre in which payment is to be made or Securities or Collateral is to be delivered;

Collateral means such securities or financial instruments or transfers of currency as are referred to in the table set out under paragraph 1 of the Schedule as being acceptable or any combination thereof as agreed between the Parties in relation to any particular Loan and which are delivered by Borrower to Lender in accordance with this Agreement and shall include Alternative Collateral;

Defaulting Party has the meaning given in paragraph 10;

Delivery in relation to any Securities or Collateral or Equivalent Securities or Equivalent Collateral comprising Securities means:

(a) in the case of Securities held by a Nominee or within a clearing or settlement system, the crediting of such Securities to an account of the Borrower or Lender, as the case may be, or as it shall direct, or,

(b) in the case of Securities otherwise held, the delivery to Borrower or Lender, as the case may be, or as the transferee shall direct of the relevant instruments of transfer, or

(c) by such other means as may be agreed,

and **deliver** shall be construed accordingly;

Designated Office means the branch or office of a Party which is specified as such in paragraph 6 of the Schedule or such other branch or office as may be agreed to in writing by the Parties;

Equivalent or **equivalent to** in relation to any Loaned Securities or Collateral (whether Cash Collateral or Non-Cash Collateral) provided under this Agreement means Securities or other property, of an identical type, nominal value, description and amount to particular Loaned Securities or Collateral (as the case may be) so provided. If and to the extent that such Loaned Securities or Collateral (as the case may be) consists of Securities that are partly paid or have been converted, subdivided, consolidated, made the subject of a takeover, rights of pre-emption, rights to receive securities or a certificate which may at a future date be exchanged for Securities, the expression shall include such Securities or other assets to which Lender or Borrower (as the case may be) is entitled following the occurrence of the relevant event, and, if appropriate, the giving of the relevant notice in accordance with paragraph 6.7 and provided that Lender or Borrower (as the case may be) has paid to the other Party all and any sums due in respect thereof. In the event that such Loaned Securities or Collateral (as the case may be) have been redeemed, are partly paid, are the subject of a capitalisation issue or are subject to an event similar to any of the foregoing events described in this paragraph, the expression shall have the following meanings:

Appendices

(a) in the case of redemption, a sum of money equivalent to the proceeds of the redemption;

(b) in the case of a call on partly-paid Securities, Securities equivalent to the relevant Loaned Securities or Collateral, as the case may be, provided that Lender shall have paid Borrower, in respect of Loaned Securities, and Borrower shall have paid to Lender, in respect of Collateral, an amount of money equal to the sum due in respect of the call;

(c) in the case of a capitalisation issue, Securities equivalent to the relevant Loaned Securities or Collateral, as the case may be, together with the securities allotted by way of bonus thereon;

(d) in the case of any event similar to any of the foregoing events described in this paragraph, Securities equivalent to the Loaned Securities or the relevant Collateral, as the case may be, together with or replaced by a sum of money or Securities or other property equivalent to that received in respect of such Loaned Securities or Collateral, as the case may be, resulting from such event;

Income means any interest, dividends or other distributions of any kind whatsoever with respect to any Securities or Collateral;

Income Record Date, with respect to any Securities or Collateral, means the date by reference to which holders of such Securities or Collateral are identified as being entitled to payment of Income;

Letter of Credit means an irrevocable, non-negotiable letter of credit in a form, and from a bank, acceptable to Lender;

Loaned Securities means Securities which are the subject of an outstanding Loan;

Margin has the meaning specified in paragraph 1 of the Schedule with reference to the table set out therein;

Market Value means:

(a) in relation to the valuation of Securities, Equivalent Securities, Collateral or Equivalent Collateral (other than Cash Collateral or a Letter of Credit):

(i) such price as is equal to the market quotation for the mid price of such Securities, Equivalent Securities, Collateral and/or Equivalent Collateral as derived from a reputable pricing information service reasonably chosen in good faith by Lender; or

(ii) if unavailable the market value thereof as derived from the mid price or rate bid by a reputable dealer for the relevant instrument reasonably chosen in good faith by Lender,

in each case at Close of Business on the previous Business Day, or as specified in the Schedule, unless agreed otherwise or, at the option of either Party where in its reasonable opinion there has been an exceptional movement in the price of the asset in question since such time, the latest available price, plus (in each case):

Appendices

        (iii)   the aggregate amount of Income which has accrued but not yet been paid in respect of the Securities, Equivalent Securities, Collateral or Equivalent Collateral concerned to the extent not included in such price,

provided that the price of Securities, Equivalent Securities, Collateral or Equivalent Collateral that are suspended or that cannot legally be transferred or that are transferred or required to be transferred to a government, trustee or third party (whether by reason of nationalisation, expropriation or otherwise) shall for all purposes be a commercially reasonable price agreed between the Parties, or absent agreement, be a price provided by a third party dealer agreed between the Parties, or if the Parties do not agree a third party dealer then a price based on quotations provided by the Reference Dealers. If more than three quotations are provided, the Market Value will be the arithmetic mean of the prices, without regard to the quotations having the highest and lowest prices. If three quotations are provided, the Market Value will be the quotation remaining after disregarding the highest and lowest quotations. For this purpose, if more than one quotation has the same highest or lowest price, then one of such quotations shall be disregarded. If fewer than three quotations are provided, the Market Value of the relevant Securities, Equivalent Securities, Collateral or Equivalent Collateral shall be determined by the Party making the determination of Market Value acting reasonably;

(b)   in relation to a Letter of Credit the face or stated amount of such Letter of Credit; and

(c)   in relation to Cash Collateral the amount of the currency concerned;

Nominee means a nominee or agent appointed by either Party to accept delivery of, hold or deliver Securities, Equivalent Securities, Collateral and/or Equivalent Collateral or to receive or make payments on its behalf;

Non-Cash Collateral means Collateral other than Cash Collateral;

Non-Defaulting Party has the meaning given in paragraph 10;

Notification Time means the time specified in paragraph 1.5 of the Schedule;

Parties means Lender and Borrower and ***Party*** shall be construed accordingly;

Posted Collateral has the meaning given in paragraph 5.4;

Reference Dealers means, in relation to any Securities, Equivalent Securities, Collateral or Equivalent Collateral, four leading dealers in the relevant securities selected by the Party making the determination of Market Value in good faith;

Required Collateral Value has the meaning given in paragraph 5.4;

Sales Tax means value added tax and any other Tax of a similar nature (including, without limitation, any sales tax of any relevant jurisdiction);

Settlement Date means the date upon which Securities are due to be transferred to Borrower in accordance with this Agreement,

Stamp Tax means any stamp, transfer, registration, documentation or similar Tax; and

Tax means any present or future tax, levy, impost, duty, charge, assessment or fee of any nature (including interest, penalties and additions thereto) imposed by any government or other taxing authority in respect of any transaction effected pursuant to or contemplated by, or any payment under or in respect of, this Agreement.

2.2 **Headings**

All headings appear for convenience only and shall not affect the interpretation of this Agreement.

2.3 **Market terminology**

Notwithstanding the use of expressions such as "borrow", "lend", "Collateral", "Margin" etc. which are used to reflect terminology used in the market for transactions of the kind provided for in this Agreement, title to Securities "borrowed" or "lent" and "Collateral" provided in accordance with this Agreement shall pass from one Party to another as provided for in this Agreement, the Party obtaining such title being obliged to deliver Equivalent Securities or Equivalent Collateral as the case may be.

2.4 **Currency conversions**

Subject to paragraph 11, for the purposes of determining any prices, sums or values (including Market Value and Required Collateral Value) prices, sums or values stated in currencies other than the Base Currency shall be converted into the Base Currency at the latest available spot rate of exchange quoted by a bank selected by Lender (or if an Event of Default has occurred in relation to Lender, by Borrower) in the London inter-bank market for the purchase of the Base Currency with the currency concerned on the day on which the calculation is to be made or, if that day is not a Business Day, the spot rate of exchange quoted at Close of Business on the immediately preceding Business Day on which such a quotation was available.

2.5 The Parties confirm that introduction of and/or substitution (in place of an existing currency) of a new currency as the lawful currency of a country shall not have the effect of altering, or discharging, or excusing performance under, any term of the Agreement or any Loan thereunder, nor give a Party the right unilaterally to alter or terminate the Agreement or any Loan thereunder. Securities will for the purposes of this Agreement be regarded as equivalent to other securities notwithstanding that as a result of such introduction and/or substitution those securities have been redenominated into the new currency or the nominal value of the securities has changed in connection with such redenomination.

2.6 **Modifications etc. to legislation**

Any reference in this Agreement to an act, regulation or other legislation shall include a reference to any statutory modification or re-enactment thereof for the time being in force.

3. LOANS OF SECURITIES

Lender will lend Securities to Borrower, and Borrower will borrow Securities from Lender in accordance with the terms and conditions of this Agreement. The terms of each Loan shall be agreed prior to the commencement of the relevant Loan either orally or in writing (including any agreed form of electronic communication) and confirmed in such form and on such basis as shall be agreed between the Parties. Unless otherwise agreed, any confirmation produced by a Party shall not supersede or prevail over the prior oral, written or electronic communication (as the case may be).

4. DELIVERY

4.1 Delivery of Securities on commencement of Loan

Lender shall procure the Delivery of Securities to Borrower or deliver such Securities in accordance with this Agreement and the terms of the relevant Loan.

4.2 Requirements to effect Delivery

The Parties shall execute and deliver all necessary documents and give all necessary instructions to procure that all right, title and interest in:

(a) any Securities borrowed pursuant to paragraph 3;

(b) any Equivalent Securities delivered pursuant to paragraph 8;

(c) any Collateral delivered pursuant to paragraph 5;

(d) any Equivalent Collateral delivered pursuant to paragraphs 5 or 8;

shall pass from one Party to the other subject to the terms and conditions set out in this Agreement, on delivery of the same in accordance with this Agreement with full title guarantee, free from all liens, charges and encumbrances. In the case of Securities, Collateral, Equivalent Securities or Equivalent Collateral title to which is registered in a computer-based system which provides for the recording and transfer of title to the same by way of book entries, delivery and transfer of title shall take place in accordance with the rules and procedures of such system as in force from time to time. The Party acquiring such right, title and interest shall have no obligation to return or deliver any of the assets so acquired but, in so far as any Securities are borrowed by or any Collateral is delivered to such Party, such Party shall be obliged, subject to the terms of this Agreement, to deliver Equivalent Securities or Equivalent Collateral as appropriate.

4.3 Deliveries to be simultaneous unless otherwise agreed

Where under the terms of this Agreement a Party is not obliged to make a Delivery unless simultaneously a Delivery is made to it, subject to and without prejudice to its rights under paragraph 8.6, such Party may from time to time in accordance with market practice and in recognition of the practical difficulties in arranging simultaneous delivery of Securities, Collateral and cash transfers, waive its right under this Agreement in respect of simultaneous delivery and/or payment provided that no such waiver (whether by course of conduct or otherwise) in respect of one transaction shall bind it in respect of any other transaction.

Appendices

4.4 **Deliveries of Income**

In respect of Income being paid in relation to any Loaned Securities or Collateral, Borrower (in the case of Income being paid in respect of Loaned Securities) and Lender (in the case of Income being paid in respect of Collateral) shall provide to the other Party, as the case may be, any endorsements or assignments as shall be customary and appropriate to effect, in accordance with paragraph 6, the payment or delivery of money or property in respect of such Income to Lender, irrespective of whether Borrower received such endorsements or assignments in respect of any Loaned Securities, or to Borrower, irrespective of whether Lender received such endorsements or assignments in respect of any Collateral.

5. COLLATERAL

5.1 **Delivery of Collateral on commencement of Loan**

Subject to the other provisions of this paragraph 5, Borrower undertakes to deliver to or deposit with Lender (or in accordance with Lender's instructions) Collateral simultaneously with Delivery of the Securities to which the Loan relates and in any event no later than Close of Business on the Settlement Date.

5.2 **Deliveries through securities settlement systems generating automatic payments**

Unless otherwise agreed between the Parties, where any Securities, Equivalent Securities, Collateral or Equivalent Collateral (in the form of securities) are transferred through a book entry transfer or settlement system which automatically generates a payment or delivery, or obligation to pay or deliver, against the transfer of such securities, then.

(a) such automatically generated payment, delivery or obligation shall be treated as a payment or delivery by the transferee to the transferor, and except to the extent that it is applied to discharge an obligation of the transferee to effect payment or delivery, such payment or delivery, or obligation to pay or deliver, shall be deemed to be a transfer of Collateral or delivery of Equivalent Collateral, as the case may be, made by the transferee until such time as the Collateral or Equivalent Collateral is substituted with other Collateral or Equivalent Collateral if an obligation to deliver other Collateral or deliver Equivalent Collateral existed immediately prior to the transfer of Securities, Equivalent Securities, Collateral or Equivalent Collateral; and

(b) the Party receiving such substituted Collateral or Equivalent Collateral, or if no obligation to deliver other Collateral or redeliver Equivalent Collateral existed immediately prior to the transfer of Securities, Equivalent Securities, Collateral or Equivalent Collateral, the Party receiving the deemed transfer of Collateral or Delivery of Equivalent Collateral, as the case may be, shall cause to be made to the other Party for value the same day either, where such transfer is a payment, an irrevocable payment in the amount of such transfer or, where such transfer is a Delivery, an irrevocable Delivery of securities (or other property, as the case may be) equivalent to such property.

5.3 **Substitutions of Collateral**

Borrower may from time to time call for the repayment of Cash Collateral or the Delivery of Collateral equivalent to any Collateral delivered to Lender prior to the date on which the same would otherwise have been repayable or deliverable provided that at or prior to the time of such repayment or Delivery Borrower shall have delivered Alternative Collateral acceptable to Lender and Borrower is in compliance with paragraph 5.4 or paragraph 5.5, as applicable.

5.4 **Marking to Market of Collateral during the currency of a Loan on aggregated basis**

Unless paragraph 1.3 of the Schedule indicates that paragraph 5.5 shall apply in lieu of this paragraph 5.4, or unless otherwise agreed between the Parties:

(a) the aggregate Market Value of the Collateral delivered to or deposited with Lender (excluding any Equivalent Collateral repaid or delivered under paragraphs 5.4(b) or 5.5(b) (as the case may be)) (*Posted Collateral*) in respect of all Loans outstanding under this Agreement shall equal the aggregate of the Market Value of Securities equivalent to the Loaned Securities and the applicable Margin (the *Required Collateral Value*) in respect of such Loans;

(b) if at any time on any Business Day the aggregate Market Value of the Posted Collateral in respect of all Loans outstanding under this Agreement together with: (i) all amounts due and payable by the Lender under this Agreement but which are unpaid; and (ii) if agreed between the parties and if the Income Record Date has occurred in respect of any Non-Cash Collateral, the amount or Market Value of Income payable in respect of such Non-Cash Collateral exceeds the aggregate of the Required Collateral Values in respect of such Loans together with: (i) all amounts due and payable by the Borrower under this Agreement but which are unpaid; and (ii) if agreed between the parties and if the Income Record Date has occurred in respect of any securities equivalent to Loaned Securities, the amount or Market Value of Income payable in respect of such Equivalent Securities, Lender shall (on demand) repay and/or deliver, as the case may be, to Borrower such Equivalent Collateral as will eliminate the excess;

(c) if at any time on any Business Day the aggregate Market Value of the Posted Collateral in respect of all Loans outstanding under this Agreement together with: (i) all amounts due and payable by the Lender under this Agreement but which are unpaid; and (ii) if agreed between the parties and if the Income Record Date has occurred in respect of any Non-Cash Collateral, the amount or Market Value of Income payable in respect of such Non-Cash Collateral falls below the aggregate of Required Collateral Values in respect of all such Loans together with: (i) all amounts due and payable by the Borrower under this Agreement but which are unpaid; and (ii) if agreed between the parties and if the Income Record Date has occurred in respect of Securities equivalent to any Loaned Securities, the amount or Market Value of Income payable in respect of such Equivalent Securities, Borrower shall (on demand) provide such further Collateral to Lender as will eliminate the deficiency;

Appendices

(d) where a Party acts as both Lender and Borrower under this Agreement, the provisions of paragraphs 5.4(b) and 5.4(c) shall apply separately (and without duplication) in respect of Loans entered into by that Party as Lender and Loans entered into by that Party as Borrower.

5.5 **Marking to Market of Collateral during the currency of a Loan on a Loan by Loan basis**

If paragraph 1.3 of the Schedule indicates this paragraph 5.5 shall apply in lieu of paragraph 5.4, the Posted Collateral in respect of any Loan shall bear from day to day and at any time the same proportion to the Market Value of Securities equivalent to the Loaned Securities as the Posted Collateral bore at the commencement of such Loan. Accordingly:

(a) the Market Value of the Posted Collateral to be delivered or deposited while the Loan continues shall be equal to the Required Collateral Value;

(b) if at any time on any Business Day the Market Value of the Posted Collateral in respect of any Loan together with: (i) all amounts due and payable by the Lender in respect of that Loan but which are unpaid; and (ii) if agreed between the parties and if the Income Record Date has occurred in respect of any Non-Cash Collateral, the amount or Market Value of Income payable in respect of such Non-Cash Collateral exceeds the Required Collateral Value in respect of such Loan together with: (i) all amounts due and payable by the Borrower in respect of that Loan; and (ii) if agreed between the parties and if the Income Record Date has occurred in respect of Securities equivalent to any Loaned Securities, the amount or Market Value of Income payable in respect of such Equivalent Securities, Lender shall (on demand) repay and/or deliver, as the case may be, to Borrower such Equivalent Collateral as will eliminate the excess; and

(c) if at any time on any Business Day the Market Value of the Posted Collateral together with: (i) all amounts due any payable by the Lender in respect of that Loan; and (ii) if agreed between the parties and if the Income Record Date has occurred in respect of any Non-Cash Collateral, the amount or Market Value of Income payable in respect of such Non-Cash Collateral falls below the Required Collateral Value together with: (i) all amounts due and payable by the Borrower in respect of that Loan; and (ii) if agreed between the parties and if the Income Record Date has occurred in respect of Securities equivalent to any Loaned Securities, the amount or Market Value of Income payable in respect of such Equivalent Securities, Borrower shall (on demand) provide such further Collateral to Lender as will eliminate the deficiency.

5.6 **Requirements to deliver excess Collateral**

Where paragraph 5.4 applies, unless paragraph 1.4 of the Schedule indicates that this paragraph 5.6 does not apply, if a Party (the *first Party*) would, but for this paragraph 5.6, be required under paragraph 5.4 to provide further Collateral or deliver Equivalent Collateral in circumstances where the other Party (the *second Party*) would, but for this paragraph 5.6, also be required to or provide Collateral or deliver Equivalent Collateral under paragraph 5.4, then the Market Value of the Collateral or Equivalent Collateral deliverable by the first Party (*X*) shall be set off against the Market Value of the Collateral or Equivalent Collateral deliverable by the second

Party (*Y*) and the only obligation of the Parties under paragraph 5.4 shall be, where X exceeds Y, an obligation of the first Party, or where Y exceeds X, an obligation of the second Party to repay and/or (as the case may be) deliver Equivalent Collateral or to deliver further Collateral having a Market Value equal to the difference between X and Y.

5.7 Where Equivalent Collateral is repaid or delivered (as the case may be) or further Collateral is provided by a Party under paragraph 5.6, the Parties shall agree to which Loan or Loans such repayment, delivery or further provision is to be attributed and failing agreement it shall be attributed, as determined by the Party making such repayment, delivery or further provision to the earliest outstanding Loan and, in the case of a repayment or delivery up to the point at which the Market Value of Collateral in respect of such Loan equals the Required Collateral Value in respect of such Loan, and then to the next earliest outstanding Loan up to the similar point and so on.

5.8 **Timing of repayments of excess Collateral or deliveries of further Collateral**

Where any Equivalent Collateral falls to be repaid or delivered (as the case may be) or further Collateral is to be provided under this paragraph 5, unless otherwise provided or agreed between the Parties, if the relevant demand is received by the Notification Time specified in paragraph 1.5 of the Schedule, then the delivery shall be made not later than the Close of Business on the same Business Day; if a demand is received after the Notification Time, then the relevant delivery shall be made not later than the Close of Business on the next Business Day after the date such demand is received.

5.9 **Substitutions and extensions of Letters of Credit**

Where Collateral is a Letter of Credit, Lender may by notice to Borrower require that Borrower, on the third Business Day following the date of delivery of such notice (or by such other time as the Parties may agree), substitute Collateral consisting of cash or other Collateral acceptable to Lender for the Letter of Credit. Prior to the expiration of any Letter of Credit supporting Borrower's obligations hereunder, Borrower shall, no later than 10.30 a.m. UK time on the second Business Day prior to the date such Letter of Credit expires (or by such other time as the Parties may agree), obtain an extension of the expiration of such Letter of Credit or replace such Letter of Credit by providing Lender with a substitute Letter of Credit in an amount at least equal to the amount of the Letter of Credit for which it is substituted.

6. **DISTRIBUTIONS AND CORPORATE ACTIONS**

6.1 In this paragraph 6, references to an amount of Income *received* by any Party in respect of any Loaned Securities or Non-Cash Collateral shall be to an amount received from the issuer after any applicable withholding or deduction for or on account of Tax.

6.2 **Manufactured payments in respect of Loaned Securities**

Where the term of a Loan extends over an Income Record Date in respect of any Loaned Securities, Borrower shall, on the date such Income is paid by the issuer, or on such other date as the Parties may from time to time agree, pay or deliver to Lender such sum of money or property as is agreed between the Parties or, failing such agreement, a sum of money or property equivalent to (and in the same currency as) the type and amount of such Income that would be received by Lender in respect of such Loaned Securities assuming such Securities were not loaned to Borrower and were retained by Lender on the Income Record Date.

6.3 **Manufactured payments in respect of Non-Cash Collateral**

Where Non-Cash Collateral is delivered by Borrower to Lender and an Income Record Date in respect of such Non-Cash Collateral occurs before Equivalent Collateral is delivered by Lender to Borrower, Lender shall on the date such Income is paid, or on such other date as the Parties may from time to time agree, pay or deliver to Borrower a sum of money or property as is agreed between the Parties or, failing such agreement, a sum of money or property equivalent to (and in the same currency as) the type and amount of such Income that would be received by Lender in respect of such Non-Cash Collateral assuming Lender:

(a) retained the Non-Cash Collateral on the Income Record Date; and

(b) is not entitled to any credit, benefit or other relief in respect of Tax under any Applicable Law.

6.4 **Indemnity for failure to redeliver Equivalent Non-Cash Collateral**

Unless paragraph 1.6 of the Schedule indicates that this paragraph does not apply, where:

(a) prior to any Income Record Date in relation to Non-Cash Collateral, Borrower has in accordance with paragraph 5.3 called for the Delivery of Equivalent Non-Cash Collateral;

(b) Borrower has given notice of such call to Lender so as to be effective, at the latest, five hours before the Close of Business on the last Business Day on which Lender would customarily be required to initiate settlement of the Non-Cash Collateral to enable settlement to take place on the Business Day immediately preceding the relevant Income Record Date;

(c) Borrower has provided reasonable details to Lender of the Non-Cash Collateral, the relevant Income Record Date and the proposed Alternative Collateral;

(d) Lender, acting reasonably, has determined that such Alternative Collateral is acceptable to it and Borrower shall have delivered or delivers such Alternative Collateral to Lender; and

(e) Lender has failed to make reasonable efforts to transfer Equivalent Non-Cash Collateral to Borrower prior to such Income Record Date,

Lender shall indemnify Borrower in respect of any cost, loss or damage (excluding any indirect or consequential loss or damage or any amount otherwise compensated by Lender, including pursuant to paragraphs 6.3 and/or 9.3) suffered by Borrower that it would not have suffered had the relevant Equivalent Non-Cash Collateral been transferred to Borrower prior to such Income Record Date.

6.5 Income in the form of Securities

Where Income, in the form of securities, is paid in relation to any Loaned Securities or Collateral, such securities shall be added to such Loaned Securities or Collateral (and shall constitute Loaned Securities or Collateral, as the case may be, and be part of the relevant Loan) and will not be delivered to Lender, in the case of Loaned Securities, or to Borrower, in the case of Collateral, until the end of the relevant Loan, provided that the Lender or Borrower (as the case may be) fulfils its obligations under paragraph 5.4 or 5.5 (as applicable) with respect to the additional Loaned Securities or Collateral, as the case may be.

6.6 Exercise of voting rights

Where any voting rights fall to be exercised in relation to any Loaned Securities or Collateral, neither Borrower, in the case of Equivalent Securities, nor Lender, in the case of Equivalent Collateral, shall have any obligation to arrange for voting rights of that kind to be exercised in accordance with the instructions of the other Party in relation to the Securities borrowed by it or transferred to it by way of Collateral, as the case may be, unless otherwise agreed between the Parties.

6.7 Corporate actions

Where, in respect of any Loaned Securities or any Collateral, any rights relating to conversion, sub-division, consolidation, pre-emption, rights arising under a takeover offer, rights to receive securities or a certificate which may at a future date be exchanged for securities or other rights, including those requiring election by the holder for the time being of such Securities or Collateral, become exercisable prior to the delivery of Equivalent Securities or Equivalent Collateral, then Lender or Borrower, as the case may be, may, within a reasonable time before the latest time for the exercise of the right or option give written notice to the other Party that on delivery of Equivalent Securities or Equivalent Collateral, as the case may be, it wishes to receive Equivalent Securities or Equivalent Collateral in such form as will arise if the right is exercised or, in the case of a right which may be exercised in more than one manner, is exercised as is specified in such written notice.

7. RATES APPLICABLE TO LOANED SECURITIES AND CASH COLLATERAL

7.1 Rates in respect of Loaned Securities

In respect of each Loan, Borrower shall pay to Lender, in the manner prescribed in sub-paragraph 7.3, sums calculated by applying such rate as shall be agreed between the Parties from time to time to the daily Market Value of the Loaned Securities.

7.2 Rates in respect of Cash Collateral

Where Cash Collateral is deposited with Lender in respect of any Loan, Lender shall pay to Borrower, in the manner prescribed in paragraph 7.3, sums calculated by applying such rates as shall be agreed between the Parties from time to time to the amount of such Cash Collateral. Any such payment due to Borrower may be set-off against any payment due to Lender pursuant to paragraph 7.1.

7.3 Payment of rates

In respect of each Loan, the payments referred to in paragraph 7.1 and 7.2 shall accrue daily in respect of the period commencing on and inclusive of the Settlement Date and terminating on and exclusive of the Business Day upon which Equivalent Securities are delivered or Cash Collateral is repaid. Unless otherwise agreed, the sums so accruing in respect of each calendar month shall be paid in arrears by the relevant Party not later than the Business Day which is the tenth Business Day after the last Business Day of the calendar month to which such payments relate or such other date as the Parties shall from time to time agree.

8. DELIVERY OF EQUIVALENT SECURITIES

8.1 Lender's right to terminate a Loan

Subject to paragraph 11 and the terms of the relevant Loan, Lender shall be entitled to terminate a Loan and to call for the delivery of all or any Equivalent Securities at any time by giving notice on any Business Day of not less than the standard settlement time for such Equivalent Securities on the exchange or in the clearing organisation through which the Loaned Securities were originally delivered. Borrower shall deliver such Equivalent Securities not later than the expiry of such notice in accordance with Lender's instructions.

8.2 Borrower's right to terminate a Loan

Subject to the terms of the relevant Loan, Borrower shall be entitled at any time to terminate a Loan and to deliver all and any Equivalent Securities due and outstanding to Lender in accordance with Lender's instructions and Lender shall accept such delivery.

8.3 Delivery of Equivalent Securities on termination of a Loan

Borrower shall procure the Delivery of Equivalent Securities to Lender or deliver Equivalent Securities in accordance with this Agreement and the terms of the relevant Loan on termination of the Loan. For the avoidance of doubt any reference in this Agreement or in any other agreement or communication between the Parties (howsoever expressed) to an obligation to deliver or account for or act in relation to Loaned Securities shall accordingly be construed as a reference to an obligation to deliver or account for or act in relation to Equivalent Securities.

8.4 Delivery of Equivalent Collateral on termination of a Loan

On the date and time that Equivalent Securities are required to be delivered by Borrower on the termination of a Loan, Lender shall simultaneously (subject to paragraph 5.4 if applicable) repay to Borrower any Cash Collateral or, as the case may be, deliver Collateral equivalent to the Collateral provided by Borrower pursuant to paragraph 5 in respect of such Loan. For the avoidance of doubt any reference in this Agreement or in any other agreement or communication between the Parties (however expressed) to an obligation to deliver or account for or act in relation to Collateral shall accordingly be construed as a reference to an obligation to deliver or account for or act in relation to Equivalent Collateral.

8.5 Delivery of Letters of Credit

Where a Letter of Credit is provided by way of Collateral, the obligation to deliver Equivalent Collateral is satisfied by Lender delivering for cancellation the Letter of Credit so provided, or where the Letter of Credit is provided in respect of more than one Loan, by Lender consenting to a reduction in the value of the Letter of Credit.

8.6 **Delivery obligations to be reciprocal**

Neither Party shall be obliged to make delivery (or make a payment as the case may be) to the other unless it is satisfied that the other Party will make such delivery (or make an appropriate payment as the case may be) to it. If it is not so satisfied (whether because an Event of Default has occurred in respect of the other Party or otherwise) it shall notify the other Party and unless that other Party has made arrangements which are sufficient to assure full delivery (or the appropriate payment as the case may be) to the notifying Party, the notifying Party shall (provided it is itself in a position, and willing, to perform its own obligations) be entitled to withhold delivery (or payment, as the case may be) to the other Party until such arrangements to assure full delivery (or the appropriate payment as the case may be) are made.

9. FAILURE TO DELIVER

9.1 **Borrower's failure to deliver Equivalent Securities**

If Borrower fails to deliver Equivalent Securities in accordance with paragraph 8.3 Lender may:

(a) elect to continue the Loan (which, for the avoidance of doubt, shall continue to be taken into account for the purposes of paragraph 5.4 or 5.5 as applicable); or

(b) at any time while such failure continues, by written notice to Borrower declare that that Loan (but only that Loan) shall be terminated immediately in accordance with paragraph 11.2 as if (i) an Event of Default had occurred in relation to the Borrower, (ii) references to the Termination Date were to the date on which notice was given under this sub-paragraph, and (iii) the Loan were the only Loan outstanding. For the avoidance of doubt, any such failure shall not constitute an Event of Default (including under paragraph 10.1(i)) unless the Parties otherwise agree.

9.2 **Lender's failure to deliver Equivalent Collateral**

If Lender fails to deliver Equivalent Collateral comprising Non-Cash Collateral in accordance with paragraph 8.4 or 8.5, Borrower may:

(a) elect to continue the Loan (which, for the avoidance of doubt, shall continue to be taken into account for the purposes of paragraph 5.4 or 5.5 as applicable); or

(b) at any time while such failure continues, by written notice to Lender declare that that Loan (but only that Loan) shall be terminated immediately in accordance with paragraph 11.2 as if (i) an Event of Default had occurred in relation to the Lender, (ii) references to the Termination Date were to the date on which notice was given under this sub-paragraph, and (iii) the Loan were the only Loan outstanding. For the avoidance of doubt, any such failure shall not constitute an Event of Default (including under paragraph 10.1(i)) unless the Parties otherwise agree.

9.3 **Failure by either Party to deliver**

Where a Party (the *Transferor*) fails to deliver Equivalent Securities or Equivalent Collateral by the time required under this Agreement or within such other period as may be agreed between the Transferor and the other Party (the *Transferee*) and the Transferee:

(a) incurs interest, overdraft or similar costs and expenses; or

(b) incurs costs and expenses as a direct result of a Buy-in exercised against it by a third party,

then the Transferor agrees to pay within one Business Day of a demand from the Transferee and hold harmless the Transferee with respect to all reasonable costs and expenses listed in sub-paragraphs (a) and (b) above properly incurred which arise directly from such failure other than (i) such costs and expenses which arise from the negligence or wilful default of the Transferee and (ii) any indirect or consequential losses.

10. **EVENTS OF DEFAULT**

10.1 Each of the following events occurring and continuing in relation to either Party (the *Defaulting Party*, the other Party being the *Non-Defaulting Party*) shall be an Event of Default but only (subject to sub-paragraph 10.1(d)) where the Non-Defaulting Party serves written notice on the Defaulting Party.

(a) Borrower or Lender failing to pay or repay Cash Collateral or to deliver Collateral on commencement of the Loan under paragraph 5.1 or to deliver further Collateral under paragraph 5.4 or 5.5;

(b) Lender or Borrower failing to comply with its obligations under paragraph 6.2 or 6.3 upon the due date and not remedying such failure within three Business Days after the Non-Defaulting Party serves written notice requiring it to remedy such failure;

(c) Lender or Borrower failing to pay any sum due under paragraph 9.1(b), 9.2(b) or 9.3 upon the due date;

(d) an Act of Insolvency occurring with respect to Lender or Borrower, provided that, where the Parties have specified in paragraph 5 of the Schedule that Automatic Early Termination shall apply, an Act of Insolvency which is the presentation of a petition for winding up or any analogous proceeding or the appointment of a liquidator or analogous officer of the Defaulting Party shall not require the Non-Defaulting Party to serve written notice on the Defaulting Party (*Automatic Early Termination*);

(e) any warranty made by Lender or Borrower in paragraph 13 or paragraphs 14(a) to 14(d) being incorrect or untrue in any material respect when made or repeated or deemed to have been made or repeated;

(f) Lender or Borrower admitting to the other that it is unable to, or it intends not to, perform any of its obligations under this Agreement and/or in respect of any Loan where such failure to perform would with the service of notice or lapse of time constitute an Event of Default;

(g) all or any material part of the assets of Lender or Borrower being transferred or ordered to be transferred to a trustee (or a person exercising similar functions) by a regulatory authority pursuant to any legislation;

(h) Lender (if applicable) or Borrower being declared in default or being suspended or expelled from membership of or participation in, any securities exchange or suspended or prohibited from dealing in securities by any regulatory authority, in each case on the grounds that it has failed to meet any requirements relating to financial resources or credit rating; or

(i) Lender or Borrower failing to perform any other of its obligations under this Agreement and not remedying such failure within 30 days after the Non-Defaulting Party serves written notice requiring it to remedy such failure.

10.2 Each Party shall notify the other (in writing) if an Event of Default or an event which, with the passage of time and/or upon the serving of a written notice as referred to above, would be an Event of Default, occurs in relation to it.

10.3 The provisions of this Agreement constitute a complete statement of the remedies available to each Party in respect of any Event of Default.

10.4 Subject to paragraphs 9 and 11, neither Party may claim any sum by way of consequential loss or damage in the event of failure by the other Party to perform any of its obligations under this Agreement.

11. CONSEQUENCES OF AN EVENT OF DEFAULT

11.1 If an Event of Default occurs in relation to either Party then paragraphs 11.2 to 11.7 below shall apply.

11.2 The Parties' delivery and payment obligations (and any other obligations they have under this Agreement) shall be accelerated so as to require performance thereof at the time such Event of Default occurs (the date of which shall be the *Termination Date*) so that performance of such delivery and payment obligations shall be effected only in accordance with the following provisions.

(a) The Default Market Value of the Equivalent Securities and Equivalent Non-Cash Collateral to be delivered and the amount of any Cash Collateral (including sums accrued) to be repaid and any other cash (including interest accrued) to be paid by each Party shall be established by the Non-Defaulting Party in accordance with paragraph 11.4 and deemed as at the Termination Date.

(b) On the basis of the sums so established, an account shall be taken (as at the Termination Date) of what is due from each Party to the other under this Agreement (on the basis that each Party's claim against the other in respect of delivery of Equivalent Securities or Equivalent Non-Cash Collateral equal to

Appendices

the Default Market Value thereof) and the sums due from one Party shall be set off against the sums due from the other and only the balance of the account shall be payable (by the Party having the claim valued at the lower amount pursuant to the foregoing) and such balance shall be payable on the next following Business Day after such account has been taken and such sums have been set off in accordance with this paragraph. For the purposes of this calculation, any sum not denominated in the Base Currency shall be converted into the Base Currency at the spot rate prevailing at such dates and times determined by the Non-Defaulting Party acting reasonably.

(c) If the balance under sub-paragraph (b) above is payable by the Non-Defaulting Party and the Non-Defaulting Party had delivered to the Defaulting Party a Letter of Credit, the Defaulting Party shall draw on the Letter of Credit to the extent of the balance due and shall subsequently deliver for cancellation the Letter of Credit so provided.

(d) If the balance under sub-paragraph (b) above is payable by the Defaulting Party and the Defaulting Party had delivered to the Non-Defaulting Party a Letter of Credit, the Non-Defaulting Party shall draw on the Letter of Credit to the extent of the balance due and shall subsequently deliver for cancellation the Letter of Credit so provided.

(e) In all other circumstances, where a Letter of Credit has been provided to a Party, such Party shall deliver for cancellation the Letter of Credit so provided.

11.3 For the purposes of this Agreement, the **Default Market Value** of any Equivalent Collateral in the form of a Letter of Credit shall be zero and of any Equivalent Securities or any other Equivalent Non-Cash Collateral shall be determined in accordance with paragraphs 11.4 to 11.6 below, and for this purpose:

(a) the **Appropriate Market** means, in relation to securities of any description, the market which is the most appropriate market for securities of that description, as determined by the Non-Defaulting Party;

(b) the **Default Valuation Time** means, in relation to an Event of Default, the close of business in the Appropriate Market on the fifth dealing day after the day on which that Event of Default occurs or, where that Event of Default is the occurrence of an Act of Insolvency in respect of which under paragraph 10.1(d) no notice is required from the Non-Defaulting Party in order for such event to constitute an Event of Default, the close of business on the fifth dealing day after the day on which the Non-Defaulting Party first became aware of the occurrence of such Event of Default;

(c) **Deliverable Securities** means Equivalent Securities or Equivalent Non-Cash Collateral to be delivered by the Defaulting Party;

(d) **Net Value** means at any time, in relation to any Deliverable Securities or Receivable Securities, the amount which, in the reasonable opinion of the Non-Defaulting Party, represents their fair market value, having regard to such pricing sources and methods (which may include, without limitation, available prices for securities with similar maturities, terms and credit characteristics as the relevant Equivalent Securities or Equivalent Collateral)

Appendices

as the Non-Defaulting Party considers appropriate, less, in the case of Receivable Securities, or plus, in the case of Deliverable Securities, all Transaction Costs incurred or reasonably anticipated in connection with the purchase or sale of such securities;

(e) **Receivable Securities** means Equivalent Securities or Equivalent Non-Cash Collateral to be delivered to the Defaulting Party; and

(f) **Transaction Costs** in relation to any transaction contemplated in paragraph 11.4 or 11.5 means the reasonable costs, commissions (including internal commissions), fees and expenses (including any mark-up or mark-down or premium paid for guaranteed delivery) incurred or reasonably anticipated in connection with the purchase of Deliverable Securities or sale of Receivable Securities, calculated on the assumption that the aggregate thereof is the least that could reasonably be expected to be paid in order to carry out the transaction.

11.4 If between the Termination Date and the Default Valuation Time:

(a) the Non-Defaulting Party has sold, in the case of Receivable Securities, or purchased, in the case of Deliverable Securities, securities which form part of the same issue and are of an identical type and description as those Equivalent Securities or that Equivalent Collateral, (and regardless as to whether or not such sales or purchases have settled) the Non-Defaulting Party may elect to treat as the Default Market Value:

(i) in the case of Receivable Securities, the net proceeds of such sale after deducting all Transaction Costs; provided that, where the securities sold are not identical in amount to the Equivalent Securities or Equivalent Collateral, the Non-Defaulting Party may, acting in good faith, either (A) elect to treat such net proceeds of sale divided by the amount of securities sold and multiplied by the amount of the Equivalent Securities or Equivalent Collateral as the Default Market Value or (B) elect to treat such net proceeds of sale of the Equivalent Securities or Equivalent Collateral actually sold as the Default Market Value of that proportion of the Equivalent Securities or Equivalent Collateral, and, in the case of (B), the Default Market Value of the balance of the Equivalent Securities or Equivalent Collateral shall be determined separately in accordance with the provisions of this paragraph 11.4; or

(ii) in the case of Deliverable Securities, the aggregate cost of such purchase, including all Transaction Costs; provided that, where the securities purchased are not identical in amount to the Equivalent Securities or Equivalent Collateral, the Non-Defaulting Party may, acting in good faith, either (A) elect to treat such aggregate cost divided by the amount of securities purchased and multiplied by the amount of the Equivalent Securities or Equivalent Collateral as the Default Market Value or (B) elect to treat the aggregate cost of purchasing the Equivalent Securities or Equivalent Collateral actually purchased as the Default Market Value of that proportion of the Equivalent Securities or Equivalent Collateral, and, in the case of (B), the Default Market Value of the balance of the Equivalent Securities or Equivalent Collateral shall be determined separately in accordance with the provisions of this paragraph 11.4;

(b) the Non-Defaulting Party has received, in the case of Deliverable Securities, offer quotations or, in the case of Receivable Securities, bid quotations in respect of securities of the relevant description from two or more market makers or regular dealers in the Appropriate Market in a commercially reasonable size (as determined by the Non-Defaulting Party) the Non-Defaulting Party may elect to treat as the Default Market Value of the relevant Equivalent Securities or Equivalent Collateral:

(i) the price quoted (or where more than one price is so quoted, the arithmetic mean of the prices so quoted) by each of them for, in the case of Deliverable Securities, the sale by the relevant market marker or dealer of such securities or, in the case of Receivable Securities, the purchase by the relevant market maker or dealer of such securities, provided that such price or prices quoted may be adjusted in a commercially reasonable manner by the Non-Defaulting Party to reflect accrued but unpaid coupons not reflected in the price or prices quoted in respect of such Securities;

(ii) after deducting, in the case of Receivable Securities or adding in the case of Deliverable Securities the Transaction Costs which would be incurred or reasonably anticipated in connection with such transaction.

11.5 If, acting in good faith, either (A) the Non-Defaulting Party has endeavoured but been unable to sell or purchase securities in accordance with paragraph 11.4(a) above or to obtain quotations in accordance with paragraph 11.4(b) above (or both) or (B) the Non-Defaulting Party has determined that it would not be commercially reasonable to sell or purchase securities at the prices bid or offered or to obtain such quotations, or that it would not be commercially reasonable to use any quotations which it has obtained under paragraph 11.4(b) above the Non-Defaulting Party may determine the Net Value of the relevant Equivalent Securities or Equivalent Collateral (which shall be specified) and the Non-Defaulting Party may elect to treat such Net Value as the Default Market Value of the relevant Equivalent Securities or Equivalent Collateral.

11.6 To the extent that the Non-Defaulting Party has not determined the Default Market Value in accordance with paragraph 11.4, the Default Market Value of the relevant Equivalent Securities or Equivalent Collateral shall be an amount equal to their Net Value at the Default Valuation Time; provided that, if at the Default Valuation Time the Non-Defaulting Party reasonably determines that, owing to circumstances affecting the market in the Equivalent Securities or Equivalent Collateral in question, it is not reasonably practicable for the Non-Defaulting Party to determine a Net Value of such Equivalent Securities or Equivalent Collateral which is commercially reasonable (by reason of lack of tradable prices or otherwise), the Default Market Value of such Equivalent Securities or Equivalent Collateral shall be an amount equal to their Net Value as determined by the Non-Defaulting Party as soon as reasonably practicable after the Default Valuation Time.

Appendices

Other costs, expenses and interest payable in consequence of an Event of Default

11.7 The Defaulting Party shall be liable to the Non-Defaulting Party for the amount of all reasonable legal and other professional expenses incurred by the Non-Defaulting Party in connection with or as a consequence of an Event of Default, together with interest thereon at such rate as is agreed by the Parties and specified in paragraph 10 of the Schedule or, failing such agreement, the overnight London Inter Bank Offered Rate as quoted on a reputable financial information service (***LIBOR***) as at 11.00 a.m., London time, on the date on which it is to be determined or, in the case of an expense attributable to a particular transaction and, where the Parties have previously agreed a rate of interest for the transaction, that rate of interest if it is greater than LIBOR. Interest will accrue daily on a compound basis.

Set-off

11.8 Any amount payable to one Party (the ***Payee***) by the other Party (the ***Payer***) under paragraph 11.2(b) may, at the option of the Non-Defaulting Party, be reduced by its set-off against any amount payable (whether at such time or in the future or upon the occurrence of a contingency) by the Payee to the Payer (irrespective of the currency, place of payment or booking office of the obligation) under any other agreement between the Payee and the Payer or instrument or undertaking issued or executed by one Party to, or in favour of, the other Party. If an obligation is unascertained, the Non-Defaulting Party may in good faith estimate that obligation and set off in respect of the estimate, subject to accounting to the other Party when the obligation is ascertained. Nothing in this paragraph shall be effective to create a charge or other security interest. This paragraph shall be without prejudice and in addition to any right of set-off, combination of accounts, lien or other right to which any Party is at any time otherwise entitled (whether by operation of law, contract or otherwise).

12. TAXES

Withholding, gross-up and provision of information

12.1 All payments under this Agreement shall be made without any deduction or withholding for or on account of any Tax unless such deduction or withholding is required by any Applicable Law.

12.2 Except as otherwise agreed, if the paying Party is so required to deduct or withhold, then that Party (***Payer***) shall:

(a) promptly notify the other Party (***Recipient***) of such requirement;

(b) pay or otherwise account for the full amount required to be deducted or withheld to the relevant authority;

(c) upon written demand of Recipient, forward to Recipient documentation reasonably acceptable to Recipient, evidencing such payment to such authorities; and

(d) other than in respect of any payment made by Lender to Borrower under paragraph 6.3, pay to Recipient, in addition to the payment to which Recipient is otherwise entitled under this Agreement, such additional amount as is necessary to ensure that the amount actually received by Recipient (after taking account of such withholding or deduction) will equal the amount Recipient would have received had no such deduction or withholding been required; provided Payer will not be required to pay any additional amount to Recipient under this sub-paragraph (d) to the extent it would not be required to be paid but for the failure by Recipient to comply with or perform any obligation under paragraph 12.3.

12.3 Each Party agrees that it will upon written demand of the other Party deliver to such other Party (or to any government or other taxing authority as such other Party directs), any form or document and provide such other cooperation or assistance as may (in either case) reasonably be required in order to allow such other Party to make a payment under this Agreement without any deduction or withholding for or on account of any Tax or with such deduction or withholding at a reduced rate (so long as the completion, execution or submission of such form or document, or the provision of such cooperation or assistance, would not materially prejudice the legal or commercial position of the Party in receipt of such demand). Any such form or document shall be accurate and completed in a manner reasonably satisfactory to such other Party and shall be executed and delivered with any reasonably required certification by such date as is agreed between the Parties or, failing such agreement, as soon as reasonably practicable.

Stamp Tax

12.4 Unless otherwise agreed, Borrower hereby undertakes promptly to pay and account for any Stamp Tax chargeable in connection with any transaction effected pursuant to or contemplated by this Agreement (other than any Stamp Tax that would not be chargeable but for Lender's failure to comply with its obligations under this Agreement).

12.5 Borrower shall indemnify and keep indemnified Lender against any liability arising as a result of Borrower's failure to comply with its obligations under paragraph 12.4.

Sales Tax

12.6 All sums payable by one Party to another under this Agreement are exclusive of any Sales Tax chargeable on any supply to which such sums relate and an amount equal to such Sales Tax shall in each case be paid by the Party making such payment on receipt of an appropriate Sales Tax invoice.

Retrospective changes in law

12.7 Unless otherwise agreed, amounts payable by one Party to another under this Agreement shall be determined by reference to Applicable Law as at the date of the relevant payment and no adjustment shall be made to amounts paid under this Agreement as a result of:

(a) any retrospective change in Applicable Law which is announced or enacted after the date of the relevant payment; or

(b) any decision of a court of competent jurisdiction which is made after the date of the relevant payment (other than where such decision results from an action taken with respect to this Agreement or amounts paid or payable under this Agreement).

13. **LENDER'S WARRANTIES**

    Each Party hereby warrants and undertakes to the other on a continuing basis to the intent that such warranties shall survive the completion of any transaction contemplated herein that, where acting as a Lender:

    (a) it is duly authorised and empowered to perform its duties and obligations under this Agreement;

    (b) it is not restricted under the terms of its constitution or in any other manner from lending Securities in accordance with this Agreement or from otherwise performing its obligations hereunder;

    (c) it is absolutely entitled to pass full legal and beneficial ownership of all Securities provided by it hereunder to Borrower free from all liens, charges and encumbrances; and

    (d) it is acting as principal in respect of this Agreement, other than in respect of an Agency Loan.

14. **BORROWER'S WARRANTIES**

    Each Party hereby warrants and undertakes to the other on a continuing basis to the intent that such warranties shall survive the completion of any transaction contemplated herein that, where acting as a Borrower:

    (a) it has all necessary licences and approvals, and is duly authorised and empowered, to perform its duties and obligations under this Agreement and will do nothing prejudicial to the continuation of such authorisation, licences or approvals;

    (b) it is not restricted under the terms of its constitution or in any other manner from borrowing Securities in accordance with this Agreement or from otherwise performing its obligations hereunder;

    (c) it is absolutely entitled to pass full legal and beneficial ownership of all Collateral provided by it hereunder to Lender free from all liens, charges and encumbrances;

    (d) it is acting as principal in respect of this Agreement; and

    (e) it is not entering into a Loan for the primary purpose of obtaining or exercising voting rights in respect of the Loaned Securities.

15. **INTEREST ON OUTSTANDING PAYMENTS**

    In the event of either Party failing to remit sums in accordance with this Agreement such Party hereby undertakes to pay to the other Party upon demand interest (before as well as after judgment) on the net balance due and outstanding, for the period commencing on and inclusive of the original due date for payment to (but excluding) the date of actual payment, in the same currency as the principal sum and at the rate referred to in paragraph 11.7. Interest will accrue daily on a compound basis and will be calculated according to the actual number of days elapsed. No interest shall be payable under this paragraph in respect of any day on which one Party endeavours to make a payment to the other Party but the other Party is unable to receive it.

16. TERMINATION OF THIS AGREEMENT

Each Party shall have the right to terminate this Agreement by giving not less than 15 Business Days' notice in writing to the other Party (which notice shall specify the date of termination) subject to an obligation to ensure that all Loans which have been entered into but not discharged at the time such notice is given are duly discharged in accordance with this Agreement.

17. SINGLE AGREEMENT

Each Party acknowledges that, and has entered into this Agreement and will enter into each Loan in consideration of and in reliance upon the fact that, all Loans constitute a single business and contractual relationship and are made in consideration of each other. Accordingly, each Party agrees:

(a) to perform all of its obligations in respect of each Loan, and that a default in the performance of any such obligations shall constitute a default by it in respect of all Loans, subject always to the other provisions of the Agreement; and

(b) that payments, deliveries and other transfers made by either of them in respect of any Loan shall be deemed to have been made in consideration of payments, deliveries and other transfers in respect of any other Loan.

18. SEVERANCE

If any provision of this Agreement is declared by any judicial or other competent authority to be void or otherwise unenforceable, that provision shall be severed from the Agreement and the remaining provisions of this Agreement shall remain in full force and effect. The Agreement shall, however, thereafter be amended by the Parties in such reasonable manner so as to achieve as far as possible, without illegality, the intention of the Parties with respect to that severed provision.

19. SPECIFIC PERFORMANCE

Each Party agrees that in relation to legal proceedings it will not seek specific performance of the other Party's obligation to deliver Securities, Equivalent Securities, Collateral or Equivalent Collateral but without prejudice to any other rights it may have.

20. NOTICES

20.1 Any notice or other communication in respect of this Agreement may be given in any manner set forth below to the address or number or in accordance with the electronic messaging system details set out in paragraph 6 of the Schedule and will be deemed effective as indicated:

(a) if in writing and delivered in person or by courier, on the date it is delivered;

(b) if sent by facsimile transmission, on the date that transmission is received by a responsible employee of the recipient in legible form (it being agreed that the burden of proving receipt will be on the sender and will not be met by a transmission report generated by the sender's facsimile machine);

(c) if sent by certified or registered mail (airmail, if overseas) or the equivalent (return receipt requested), on the date that mail is delivered or its delivery is attempted; or

(d) if sent by electronic messaging system, on the date that electronic message is received,

unless the date of that delivery (or attempted delivery) or the receipt, as applicable, is not a Business Day or that communication is delivered (or attempted) or received, as applicable, after the Close of Business on a Business Day, in which case that communication shall be deemed given and effective on the first following day that is a Business Day.

20.2 Either Party may by notice to the other change the address or facsimile number or electronic messaging system details at which notices or other communications are to be given to it.

21. ASSIGNMENT

21.1 Subject to paragraph 21.2, neither Party may charge, assign or otherwise deal with all or any of its rights or obligations hereunder without the prior consent of the other Party.

21.2 Paragraph 21.1 shall not preclude a party from charging, assigning or otherwise dealing with all or any part of its interest in any sum payable to it under paragraph 11.2(b) or 11.7.

22. NON-WAIVER

No failure or delay by either Party (whether by course of conduct or otherwise) to exercise any right, power or privilege hereunder shall operate as a waiver thereof nor shall any single or partial exercise of any right, power or privilege preclude any other or further exercise thereof or the exercise of any other right, power or privilege as herein provided.

23. GOVERNING LAW AND JURISDICTION

23.1 This Agreement and any non-contractual obligations arising out of or in connection with this Agreement shall be governed by, and shall be construed in accordance with, English law.

23.2 The courts of England have exclusive jurisdiction to hear and decide any suit, action or proceedings, and to settle any disputes or any non-contractual obligation which may arise out of or in connection with this Agreement (respectively, **Proceedings** and **Disputes**) and, for these purposes, each Party irrevocably submits to the jurisdiction of the courts of England.

Appendices

23.3 Each Party irrevocably waives any objection which it might at any time have to the courts of England being nominated as the forum to hear and decide any Proceedings and to settle any Disputes and agrees not to claim that the courts of England are not a convenient or appropriate forum.

23.4 Each Party hereby respectively appoints the person identified in paragraph 7 of the Schedule pertaining to the relevant Party as its agent to receive on its behalf service of process in the courts of England. If such an agent ceases to be an agent of a Party, the relevant Party shall promptly appoint, and notify the other Party of the identity of its new agent in England.

24. TIME

Time shall be of the essence of the Agreement.

25. RECORDING

The Parties agree that each may record all telephone conversations between them.

26. WAIVER OF IMMUNITY

Each Party hereby waives all immunity (whether on the basis of sovereignty or otherwise) from jurisdiction, attachment (both before and after judgement) and execution to which it might otherwise be entitled in any action or proceeding in the courts of England or of any other country or jurisdiction relating in any way to this Agreement and agrees that it will not raise, claim or cause to be pleaded any such immunity at or in respect of any such action or proceeding.

27. MISCELLANEOUS

27.1 This Agreement constitutes the entire agreement and understanding of the Parties with respect to its subject matter and supersedes all oral communication and prior writings with respect thereto.

27.2 The Party (the **Relevant Party**) who has prepared the text of this Agreement for execution (as indicated in paragraph 9 of the Schedule) warrants and undertakes to the other Party that such text conforms exactly to the text of the standard form Global Master Securities Lending Agreement (2010 version) posted by the International Securities Lending Association on its website except as notified by the Relevant Party to the other Party in writing prior to the execution of this Agreement.

27.3 Unless otherwise provided for in this Agreement, no amendment in respect of this Agreement will be effective unless in writing (including a writing evidenced by a facsimile transmission) and executed by each of the Parties or confirmed by an exchange of telexes or electronic messages on an electronic messaging system.

27.4 The Parties agree that where paragraph 11 of the Schedule indicates that this paragraph 27.4 applies, this Agreement shall apply to all loans which are outstanding as at the date of this Agreement and which are subject to the securities lending agreement or agreements specified in paragraph 11 of the Schedule, and such Loans shall be treated as if they had been entered into under this Agreement, and the terms of such loans are amended accordingly with effect from the date of this Agreement.

27.5 The Parties agree that where paragraph 12 of the Schedule indicates that this paragraph 27.5 applies, each may use the services of a third party vendor to automate the processing of Loans under this Agreement and that any data relating to such Loans received from the other Party may be disclosed to such third party vendors.

27.6 The obligations of the Parties under this Agreement will survive the termination of any Loan.

27.7 The warranties contained in paragraphs 13, 14 and 27.2 and in the Agency Annex will survive termination of this Agreement for so long as any obligations of either of the Parties pursuant to this Agreement remain outstanding.

27.8 Except as provided in this Agreement, the rights, powers, remedies and privileges provided in this Agreement are cumulative and not exclusive of any rights, powers, remedies and privileges provided by law.

27.9 This Agreement (and each amendment in respect of it) may be executed and delivered in counterparts (including by facsimile transmission), each of which will be deemed an original.

27.10 A person who is not a party to this Agreement has no right under the Contracts (Rights of Third Parties) Act 1999 to enforce any terms of this Agreement, but this does not affect any right or remedy of a third party which exists or is available apart from that Act.

Appendices

EXECUTED by the **PARTIES**

SIGNED by)
)
duly authorised for and)
on behalf of)

SIGNED by)
)
duly authorised for and)
on behalf of)

SCHEDULE

1. COLLATERAL

1.1 The securities, financial instruments and deposits of currency set out in the table below with a cross marked next to them are acceptable forms of Collateral under this Agreement.

1.2 Unless otherwise agreed between the Parties, the Market Value of the Collateral delivered pursuant to paragraph 5 by Borrower to Lender under the terms and conditions of this Agreement shall on each Business Day represent not less than the Market Value of the Loaned Securities together with the percentage contained in the row of the table below corresponding to the particular form of Collateral, referred to in this Agreement as the *Margin*.

Security/Financial Instrument/ Deposit of Currency	Mark "X" if acceptable form of Collateral	Margin (%)

1.3 Basis of Margin Maintenance:

Paragraph 5.4 (aggregation) shall not apply[*] ☐

Paragraph 5.4 (aggregation) applies unless the box is ticked.

1.4 Paragraph 5.6 (netting of obligations to deliver
Collateral and redeliver Equivalent Collateral) shall not apply[*] ☐

Paragraph 5.6 (netting) applies unless the box is ticked

1.5 For the purposes of Paragraph 5.8, Notification Time means by ☐ , London time.

1.6 Paragraph 6.4 (indemnity for failure to redeliver
Equivalent Non-Cash Collateral) shall not apply[*] ☐

Paragraph 6.4 (indemnity for failure to redeliver Equivalent Non-Cash Collateral) applies unless the box is ticked.

---

[*] Delete as appropriate.

[*] Delete as appropriate.

[*] Delete as appropriate.

Appendices

2. BASE CURRENCY

The Base Currency applicable to this Agreement is   provided that if that currency ceases to be freely convertible the Base Currency shall be [US Dollars] [Euro] [specify other currency]*

3. PLACES OF BUSINESS

(See definition of Business Day.)

4. MARKET VALUE

(See definition of Market Value.)

5. EVENTS OF DEFAULT

Automatic Early Termination shall apply in respect of Party A ☐

Automatic Early Termination shall apply in respect of Party B ☐

6. DESIGNATED OFFICE AND ADDRESS FOR NOTICES

(a) **Designated office of Party A**:

Address for notices or communications to Party A:

Address:

Attention:

Facsimile No:

Telephone No:

Electronic Messaging System Details:

(b) **Designated office of Party B**:

Address for notices or communications to Party B:

Address:

Attention:

Facsimile No:

Telephone No:

Electronic Messaging System Details:

7. (a) **Agent of Party A for Service of Process**

Name:

Address:

(b) **Agent of Party B for Service of Process**

Name:

Address:

8. **AGENCY**

– Party A [may][will always]* act as agent ☐

– Party B [may][will always]* act as agent ☐

– The Addendum for Pooled Principal Transactions may apply to Party A ☐

– The Addendum for Pooled Principal Transactions may apply to Party B ☐

9. **PARTY PREPARING THIS AGREEMENT**

Party A ☐

Party B ☐

10. **DEFAULT INTEREST**

Rate of default interest:

11. **EXISTING LOANS**

Paragraph 27.4 applies* ☐

[Overseas Securities Lenders Agreement dated   ]*

[Global Master Securities Lending Agreements dated   ]*

12. **AUTOMATION**

Paragraph 27.5 applies* ☐

* Delete as appropriate.

Appendices

AGENCY ANNEX

1. **TRANSACTIONS ENTERED INTO AS AGENT**

1.1 **Power for Lender to enter into Loans as agent**

Subject to the following provisions of this paragraph, Lender may enter into Loans as agent (in such capacity, the *Agent*) for a third person (a *Principal*), whether as custodian or investment manager or otherwise (a Loan so entered into being referred to in this paragraph as an *Agency Loan*).

If the Lender has indicated in paragraph 8 of the Schedule that it may act as Agent, it must identify each Loan in respect of which it acts as Agent as an Agency Loan at the time it is entered into. If the Lender has indicated in paragraph 8 of the Schedule that it will always act as Agent, it need not identify each Loan as an Agency Loan.

1.2 **[Pooled Principal transactions**

The Lender may enter into an Agency Loan on behalf of more than [one] Principal and accordingly the addendum hereto for pooled principal transactions shall apply.][*]

1.3 **Conditions for Agency Loan**

A Lender may enter into an Agency Loan if, but only if:

(a) it provides to Borrower, prior to effecting any Agency Loan, such information in its possession necessary to complete all required fields in the format generally used in the industry, or as otherwise agreed by Agent and Borrower (*Agreed Format*), and will use its best efforts to provide to Borrower any optional information that may be requested by the Borrower for the purpose of identifying such Principal (all such information being the *Principal Information*). Agent represents and warrants that the Principal Information is true and accurate to the best of its knowledge and has been provided to it by Principal;

(b) it enters into that Loan on behalf of a single Principal whose identity is disclosed to Borrower (whether by name or by reference to a code or identifier which the Parties have agreed will be used to refer to a specified Principal) either at the time when it enters into the Loan or before the Close of Business on the next Business Day after the date on which Loaned Securities are transferred to the Borrower in the Agreed Format or as otherwise agreed between the Parties; and

(c) it has at the time when the Loan is entered into actual authority to enter into the Loan and to perform on behalf of that Principal all of that Principal's obligations under the agreement referred to in paragraph 1.5(b) below.

Agent agrees that it will not effect any Loan with Borrower on behalf of any Principal unless Borrower has notified Agent of Borrower's approval of such Principal, and has not notified Agent that it has withdrawn such approval (such Principal, an *Approved Principal*), with both such notifications in the Agreed Format.

---

[*] Delete as appropriate.

Borrower acknowledges that Agent shall not have any obligation to provide it with confidential information regarding the financial status of its Principals; Agent agrees, however, that it will assist Borrower in obtaining from Agent's Principals such information regarding the financial status of such Principals as Borrower may reasonably request.

1.4 **Notification by Agent of certain events affecting any Principal**

Agent undertakes that, if it enters as agent into an Agency Loan, forthwith upon becoming aware:

(a) of any event which constitutes an Act of Insolvency with respect to the relevant Principal; or

(b) of any breach of any of the warranties given in paragraph 1.6 below or of any event or circumstance which results in any such warranty being untrue if repeated by reference to the then current facts,

it will inform Borrower of that fact and will, if so required by Borrower, furnish it with such additional information as it may reasonably request to the extent that such information is readily obtainable by Agent.

1.5 **Status of Agency Loan**

(a) Each Agency Loan shall be a transaction between the relevant Principal and Borrower and no person other than the relevant Principal and Borrower shall be a party to or have any rights or obligations under an Agency Loan. Without limiting the foregoing, Agent shall not be liable as principal for the performance of an Agency Loan, but this is without prejudice to any liability of Agent under any other provision of this Annex; and

(b) all the provisions of the Agreement shall apply separately as between Borrower and each Principal for whom the Agent has entered into an Agency Loan or Agency Loans as if each such Principal were a party to a separate agreement with Borrower in all respects identical with this Agreement other than this Annex and as if the Principal were Lender in respect of that agreement; provided that

(i) if there occurs in relation to the Agent an Event of Default or an event which would constitute an Event of Default if Borrower served written notice under any sub-clause of paragraph 10 of the Agreement, Borrower shall be entitled by giving written notice to the Principal (which notice shall be validly given if given in accordance with paragraph 20 of the Agreement) to declare that by reason of that event an Event of Default is to be treated as occurring in relation to the Principal. If Borrower gives such a notice then an Event of Default shall be treated as occurring in relation to the Principal at the time when the notice is deemed to be given; and

(ii) if the Principal is neither incorporated in nor has established a place of business in Great Britain, the Principal shall for the purposes of the agreement referred to in paragraph 1.5(b) above be deemed to have appointed as its agent to receive on its behalf service of process in the courts of England the Agent, or if the Agent is neither incorporated nor has established a place of business in Great Britain, the person appointed by the Agent for the purposes of this Agreement, or such other person as the Principal may from time to time specify in a written notice given to the other Party.

If Lender has indicated in paragraph 6 of the Schedule that it may enter into Loans as agent, the foregoing provisions of this paragraph do not affect the operation of the Agreement as between Borrower and Lender in respect of any Loans into which Lender may enter on its own account as principal.

1.6 **Warranty of authority by Lender acting as Agent**

Agent warrants to Borrower that it will, on every occasion on which it enters or purports to enter into a Loan as an Agency Loan, have been duly authorised to enter into that Loan and perform the obligations arising under such Loan on behalf of the Principal in respect of that Loan and to perform on behalf of the Principal all the obligations of that person under the agreement referred to in paragraph 1.5(b) above.

ADDENDUM FOR POOLED PRINCIPAL AGENCY LOANS

1. SCOPE

This addendum applies where the Agent wishes to enter into an Agency Loan on behalf of more than one Principal. The Agency Annex shall apply to such a Loan subject to the modifications and additional terms and conditions contained in paragraph 2 to 7 below.

2. INTERPRETATION

2.1 In this addendum:

(a) *Collateral Transfer* has the meaning given in paragraph 5.1 below;

(b) if at any time on any Business Day the aggregate Market Value of Posted Collateral in respect of all Agency Loans outstanding with a Principal under the Agreement exceeds the aggregate of the Required Collateral Value in respect of such Agency Loans, Borrower has a *Net Loan Exposure* to that Principal equal to that excess; if at any time on any Business Day the aggregate Market Value of Posted Collateral in respect of all Agency Loans outstanding under the Agreement with a Principal falls below the aggregate of the Required Collateral Value in respect of such Agency Loans, that Principal has a *Net Loan Exposure* to Borrower for such Agency Loans equal to that deficiency;

(c) *Pooled Principal* has the meaning given in paragraph 6(a) below; and

(d) *Pooled Loan* has the meaning given in paragraph 6(a) below.

3. MODIFICATIONS TO THE AGENCY ANNEX

3.1 Paragraph 1.3(b) of the Agency Annex is deleted and replaced by the following:

"it enters into that Loan on behalf of one or more Principals and at or before the time when it enters into the Loan it discloses to Borrower the identity and the jurisdiction of incorporation, organisation or establishment of each such Principal (and such disclosure may be made either directly or by reference to a code or identifier which the Parties have agreed will be used to refer to a specified Principal);".

3.2 Paragraph 1.3(c) of the Agency Annex is deleted and replaced by the following:

"it has at the time when the Loan is entered into actual authority to enter into the Loan on behalf of each Principal and to perform on behalf of each Principal all of that Principal's obligations under the Agreement".

4. ALLOCATION OF AGENCY LOANS

4.1 The Agent undertakes that if, at the time of entering into an Agency Loan, the Agent has not allocated the Loan to a Principal, it will allocate the Loan before the Settlement Date for that Agency Loan either to a single Principal or to several Principals, each of whom shall be responsible for only that part of the Agency Loan which has been allocated to it. Promptly following such allocation, the Agent shall notify Borrower of the Principal or Principals (whether by name or reference to a code or identifier which the Parties have agreed will be used to refer to a specified Principal) to which that Loan or part of that Loan has been allocated.

4.2 Upon allocation of a Loan in accordance with paragraph 4.1 above or otherwise, with effect from the date on which the Loan was entered into:

(a) where the allocation is to a single Principal, the Loan shall be deemed to have been entered into between Borrower and that Principal; and

(b) where the allocation is to two or more Principals, a separate Loan shall be deemed to have been entered into between Borrower and each such Principal with respect to the appropriate proportion of the Loan.

4.3 If the Agent shall fail to perform its obligations under paragraph 4.2 above then for the purposes of assessing any damage suffered by Borrower (but for no other purpose) it shall be assumed that, if the Loan concerned (to the extent not allocated) had been allocated in accordance with that paragraph, all the terms of the Loan would have been duly performed.

5. ALLOCATION OF COLLATERAL

5.1 Unless the Agent expressly allocates (a) a deposit or delivery of Posted Collateral or (b) a repayment of Cash Collateral or a redelivery of Equivalent Collateral (each a ***Collateral Transfer***) before such time, the Agent shall, at the time of making or receiving that Collateral Transfer, be deemed to have allocated any Collateral Transfer in accordance with paragraph 6.3 below.

5.2 (a) If the Agent has made a Collateral Transfer on behalf of more than one Pooled Principal, that Collateral Transfer shall be allocated in proportion to Borrower's Net Loan Exposure in respect of each Pooled Principal at the Agent's close of business on the Business Day before the Collateral Transfer is made; and

(b) if the Agent has received a Collateral Transfer on behalf of more than one Pooled Principal, that Collateral Transfer shall be allocated in proportion to each Pooled Principal's Net Loan Exposure in respect of Borrower at the Agent's close of business on the Business Day before the Collateral Transfer is made.

(c) Sub-paragraphs (a) and (b) shall not apply in respect of any Collateral Transfer which is effected or deemed to have been effected under paragraph 6.3 below.

6. POOLED PRINCIPALS: REBALANCING OF MARGIN

6.1 Where the Agent acts on behalf of more than one Principal, the Parties may agree that, as regards all (but not some only) outstanding Agency Loans with those Principals, or with such of those Principals as they may agree (***Pooled Principals***, such Agency Loans being ***Pooled Loans***), any Collateral Transfers are to be made on an aggregate net basis.

6.2 Paragraphs 6.3 to 6.5 below shall have effect for the purpose of ensuring that Posted Collateral is, so far as is practicable, transferred and held uniformly, as between the respective Pooled Principals, in respect of all Pooled Loans for the time being outstanding under the Agreement.

6.3 At or as soon as practicable after the Agent's close of business on each Business Day on which Pooled Loans are outstanding (or at such other times as the Parties may from time to time agree) there shall be effected such Collateral Transfers as shall ensure that immediately thereafter:

(a) in respect of all Pooled Principals which have a Net Loan Exposure to Borrower, the amount of Collateral then deliverable or Cash Collateral then payable by Borrower to each such Pooled Principal is equal to such proportion of the aggregate amount of Collateral then deliverable or Cash Collateral then payable, to all such Pooled Principals as corresponds to the proportion which the Net Loan Exposure of the relevant Pooled Principal bears to the aggregate of the Net Loan Exposures of all Pooled Principals to Borrower; and

(b) in respect of all Pooled Principals to which Borrower has a Net Loan Exposure, the aggregate amount of Equivalent Collateral then deliverable or repayable by each such Pooled Principal to Borrower is equal to such proportion of the aggregate amount of Equivalent Collateral then deliverable or repayable by all such Pooled Principals as corresponds to the proportion which the Net Loan Exposure of Borrower to the relevant Pooled Principal bears to the aggregate of the Net Loan Exposures of Borrower to all Pooled Principals.

6.4 Collateral Transfers effected under paragraph 6.3 shall be effected (and if not so effected shall be deemed to have been so effected) by appropriations made by the Agent and shall be reflected by entries in accounting and other records maintained by the Agent. Accordingly, it shall not be necessary for payments of cash or deliveries of Securities to be made through any settlement system for the purpose of such Collateral Transfers. Without limiting the generality of the foregoing, the Agent is hereby authorised and instructed by Borrower to do all such things on behalf of Borrower as may be necessary or expedient to effect and record the receipt on behalf of Borrower of cash and Securities from, and the delivery on behalf of Borrower of cash and Securities to, Pooled Principals in the course or for the purposes of any Collateral Transfer effected under that paragraph.

6.5 Promptly following the Collateral Transfers effected under paragraph 6.3 above, and as at the Agent's close of business on any Business Day, the Agent shall prepare a statement showing in respect of each Pooled Principal the amount of cash Collateral which has been paid, and the amount of non-cash Collateral of each description which have been transferred, by or to that Pooled Principal immediately after those Collateral Transfers. If Borrower so requests, the Agent shall deliver to Borrower a copy of the statement so prepared in a format and to a timetable generally used in the market.

7. WARRANTIES

7.1 The Agent warrants to Borrower that:

(a) all notifications provided to Borrower under paragraph 4.1 above and all statements provided to the other party under paragraph 6.5 above shall be complete and accurate in all material respects;

(b) at the time of allocating an Agency Loan in accordance with paragraph 4.1 above, each Principal or Principals to whom the Agent has allocated that Agency Loan or any part of that Agency Loan is duly authorised to enter into the Agency Loans contemplated by this Agreement and to perform its obligations thereunder; and

(c) at the time of allocating an Agency Loan in accordance with paragraph 4.1 above, no Event of Default or event which would constitute an Event of Default with the service of a Default Notice or other written notice under paragraph 14 of the Agreement has occurred in relation to any Principal or Principals to whom the Agent has allocated that Agency Loan or any part of that Agency Loan.

GLOBAL MASTER SECURITIES LENDING AGREEMENT

2014 UK TAX ADDENDUM

(For use with the GMSLA 2010)

We hereby agree that the attached Global Master Securities Lending Agreement dated [date] (the *Agreement*) shall as from the date of this Addendum be subject to the following and supplemental terms:-

1. **DISAPPLICATION OF PREVIOUS ADDENDUM**

1.1 [The UK tax addendum dated [[date]]*/ [any previous UK tax addendum or equivalent or similar provision]* (the *Previous Addendum*) shall no longer apply insofar as it relates to the UK income tax treatment of any payment.

delete / complete as appropriate

1.2 For the avoidance of doubt, any undertaking made in the Agreement or the Previous Addendum pursuant to which a Party undertakes to notify the other Party about its status as an approved UK intermediary or an approved UK collecting agent shall no longer apply.

2. **APPLICATION OF THIS ADDENDUM**

The remaining provisions of this Addendum shall apply in relation to any payment made by Borrower under paragraph 6.2 or by Lender under paragraph 6.3 where:

(a) Borrower, in relation to any payment made under paragraph 6.2, or Lender, in relation to any payment made under paragraph 6.3, is either UK resident (except where the payment is an Exempt Branch Payment) or makes such payment in the course of a trade carried on in the UK through a branch or agency; and

(b) the Loaned Securities or Non-Cash Collateral (as the case may be) are REIT Shares, Net Paying UK Securities or PAIF Shares.

3. **DISAPPLICATION OF GROSS-UP**

3.1 Except as otherwise agreed, Borrower shall not be obliged to pay an additional amount under paragraph 12.2(d) in respect of any payment made under paragraph 6.2.

3.2 When determining whether any deduction or withholding is required under paragraph 12.1, Borrower, in relation to any payment made under paragraph 6.2, and Lender, in relation to any payment made under paragraph 6.3 shall (in each case acting reasonably) take account of:

Page 1

(a) any warranties made by the other Party under this Addendum; and

(b) any relevant documentation, warranty, certification or notice provided by the other Party.

4. APPLICATION OF WARRANTIES

Each Party shall specify in the Schedule to this Addendum which (if any) of paragraphs 5 to 7 below shall apply in relation to it and where or to the extent that no such specification is made it shall be assumed that such paragraphs do not apply in relation to Borrower and/or Lender, as the case may be.

5. MANUFACTURED PAYMENTS: NET PAYING UK SECURITIES

Lender, in relation to any Loan of Net Paying UK Securities, and Borrower, in relation to any Non-Cash Collateral in the form of any Net Paying UK Securities provided, warrants to the other Party on a continuing basis that, unless otherwise notified:

(a) the person beneficially entitled to any payment made under, as the case may be, paragraph 6.2 or 6.3 in respect of such Net Paying UK Securities is either:

   (i) a UK resident company; or

   (ii) a non-UK resident company carrying on a trade in the UK through a permanent establishment which is required to bring any such payment made to it into account in computing its chargeable profits for UK corporation tax purposes; or

(b) the person beneficially entitled to any payment made under, as the case may be, paragraph 6.2 or 6.3 in respect of such Net Paying UK Securities is a partnership each member of which is a company mentioned in (a)(i) or (ii) above; or

(c) the recipient of any payment made under, as the case may be, paragraph 6.2 or 6.3 in respect of such Net Paying UK Securities is either:

   (i) an ISA Manager or a PEP Manager, or the nominee of such a person, who receives such payment in respect of investments under the plan; or

   (ii) a scheme administrator of a Registered Pension Scheme.

6. MANUFACTURED PAYMENTS: REIT SHARES

Lender, in relation to any Loan of any REIT Shares, and Borrower, in relation to any Non-Cash Collateral in the form of any REIT Shares, warrants to the other Party on a continuing basis that, unless otherwise notified:

(a) the person beneficially entitled to any payment made under, as the case may be, paragraph 6.2 or 6.3 in respect of such shares is either:

> > (i) a UK resident company; or
> >
> > (ii) a non-UK resident company carrying on a trade in the UK through a permanent establishment which is required to bring any such payment made to it into account in computing its chargeable profits for UK corporation tax purposes; or
>
> (b) the recipient of any payment made under, as the case may be, paragraph 6.2 or 6.3 in respect of such shares is a partnership each member of which is a company mentioned in (a)(i) or (ii) above; or
>
> (c) the recipient of any payment made under, as the case may be, paragraph 6.2 or 6.3 in respect of such shares is either a scheme administrator of a Registered Pension Scheme or an ISA Manager or a PEP Manager and (in each case) any such payment is applied for the purposes of the scheme, account or plan in respect of which the recipient has duties.

7. MANUFACTURED PAYMENTS: PAIF SHARES

Lender, in relation to any Loan of any PAIF Shares, and Borrower, in relation to any Non-Cash Collateral in the form of any PAIF Shares, warrants to the other Party on a continuing basis that, unless otherwise notified, the warranties in paragraphs 5 and 6 of this Addendum shall apply in relation to any payment made under, as the case may be, paragraph 6.2 or 6.3 in respect of such shares as if such paragraphs referred to PAIF Shares.

8. INTERPRETATION

8.1 In this Addendum the following definitions shall apply:

Exempt Branch Payment means a payment where both (i) section 18A of the Corporation Tax Act 2009 has effect in relation to the payer for the accounting period in which the payment is made and (ii) the payment is made in the course of a trade carried on through a permanent establishment in a territory outside the UK;

ISA Manager means the account manager of an account within the meaning of regulation 4(1) of the Individual Savings Account Regulations 1998;

Net Paying UK Securities means securities (including any loan stock or any similar security, but excluding any shares) of the UK government or a local authority (or other public authority) in the UK or a UK resident company or other UK resident body, where such securities are neither gilt-edged securities nor other securities on which interest is payable without deduction of UK income tax;

PAIF Shares means shares in an open-ended investment company to which Part 4A of the Authorised Investment Funds (Tax) Regulations 2006 applies;

PEP Manager means the plan manager of a plan within the meaning of regulation 4(1) of the Personal Equity Plan Regulations 1989;

Previous Addendum has the meaning given to it in paragraph 1.1 of this Addendum;

REIT Shares means shares in a company UK REIT or the principal company of a group UK REIT (each as defined in Part 12 of the Corporation Tax Act 2010); and

Registered Pension Scheme means a registered pension scheme for the purposes of Part 4 of the Finance Act 2004.

8.2   Terms to which a defined meaning is given in the Agreement have the same meanings in this Addendum.

8.3   Unless otherwise specified, references to paragraphs in this Addendum are to paragraphs in the Agreement.

8.4   Any reference to a provision of law includes references to that provision as amended, consolidated or re-enacted.

Signed by)
)
Duly authorised for and on)
behalf of)

Signed by)
)
Duly authorised for and on)
behalf of)

SCHEDULE

1. PARTY A WARRANTIES

In relation to Party A:

(a)   paragraph 5 of this Addendum [shall/shall not]* apply;

(b)   paragraph 6 of this Addendum [shall/shall not]* apply; and

(c)   paragraph 7 of this Addendum [shall/shall not]* apply.

2. PARTY B WARRANTIES

In relation to Party B:

(a)   paragraph 5 of this Addendum [shall/shall not]* apply;

(b)   paragraph 6 of this Addendum [shall/shall not]* apply; and

(c)   paragraph 7 of this Addendum [shall/shall not]* apply.

delete as appropriate

GLOBAL MASTER SECURITIES LENDING AGREEMENT

2014 US TAX ADDENDUM

(For use with the GMSLA 2010)

We hereby agree that the attached Global Master Securities Lending Agreement dated [date] (the *Agreement*) shall as from the date of this Addendum be subject to the following and supplemental terms:-

1. APPLICATION OF THIS ADDENDUM

1.1   Paragraphs 2 to 6 of this Addendum shall apply in relation to any payment made by Borrower under paragraph 6.2 of the Agreement or by Lender under paragraph 6.3 of the Agreement where the Loaned Securities or Non-Cash Collateral (as the case may be) are US Equities.

1.2   Paragraphs 2 and 7 of this Addendum shall apply in relation to any payments made by Borrower or Lender under the Agreement.

2. DISAPPLICATION OF GROSS-UP

2.1   Where any of paragraphs 4, 5 or 6 of this Addendum apply, except as otherwise agreed, Borrower shall not be obliged to pay an additional amount under paragraph 12.2(d) of the Agreement in respect of any payment made under paragraph 6.2 of the Agreement.

2.2   Where any of paragraphs 4, 5 or 6 of this Addendum apply, when determining whether any deduction or withholding is required under paragraph 12.1 of the Agreement, Borrower, in relation to any payment made under paragraph 6.2 of the Agreement, and Lender, in relation to any payment made under paragraph 6.3 of the Agreement shall (in each case acting reasonably) take account of:

(a)   any warranties made by the other Party under this Addendum; and

(b)   any relevant form, documentation, warranty, representation, certification or notice provided by the other Party.

2.3   Where paragraph 7 of this Addendum applies, except as otherwise agreed, Borrower or, as the case may be, Lender shall not be obliged to pay an additional amount under paragraph 12.2(d) of the Agreement in respect of any payment made under the Agreement.

2.4 Where paragraph 7 of this Addendum applies, when determining whether any deduction or withholding is required under paragraph 12.1 of the Agreement, Borrower and Lender shall (in each case acting reasonably) take account of:

(a) any warranties made by the other Party under this Addendum; and

(b) any relevant form, documentation, warranty, representation, certification or notice provided by the other Party

3. APPLICATION OF WARRANTIES

The Parties shall specify in the Schedule to this Addendum which (if any) of paragraphs 4 to 6 below shall apply in relation to Borrower and Lender and where or to the extent that no such specification is made it shall be assumed that such paragraphs do not apply in relation to Borrower and/or Lender, as the case may be.

4. MANUFACTURED PAYMENTS TO US PERSONS

4.1 Lender, in relation to any Loan, and Borrower, in relation to any Non-Cash Collateral, warrants to the other Party on a continuing basis that, unless otherwise notified, the person Receiving any payment made under, as the case may be, paragraph 6.2 or 6.3 of the Agreement, is a US Person.

4.2 Where this paragraph 4 applies, Lender, in relation to any Loan, and Borrower, in relation to any Non-Cash Collateral, agrees that it will deliver to the other Party the Prescribed Form (so long as the completion, execution or submission of such form, document or representation would not materially prejudice the legal or commercial position of the Party in receipt of such demand). Any such form, document or representation shall be accurate and completed in a manner reasonably satisfactory to such other Party and shall be executed and delivered with any reasonably required certification by such date as is agreed between the Parties or, failing such agreement, as soon as reasonably practicable.

4.3 Where this paragraph 4 applies, Borrower, in relation to any payment made under paragraph 6.2 of the Agreement, or Lender, in relation to any payment made under paragraph 6.3 of the Agreement, agrees that it will deliver to the other Party Sufficient Evidence of any US Tax previously withheld by another party (so long as the completion, execution or submission of such documentation would not materially prejudice the legal or commercial position of the Party in receipt of such demand). Any such documentation shall be accurate and completed in a manner reasonably satisfactory to such other Party and shall be executed and delivered with any reasonably required certification by such date as is agreed between the Parties or, failing such agreement, as soon as reasonably practicable.

5. MANUFACTURED PAYMENTS TO NON-US PERSONS THAT ARE QUALIFIED SECURITIES LENDERS

5.1 Lender, in relation to any Loan, and Borrower, in relation to any Non-Cash Collateral, warrants to the other Party on a continuing basis that, unless otherwise notified, the person Receiving any payment made under, as the case may be, paragraph 6.2 or 6.3 of the Agreement, is a Non-US Person and a Qualified Securities Lender.

5.2 Where this paragraph 5 applies, Lender, in relation to any Loan, and Borrower, in relation to any Non-Cash Collateral, agrees that it will deliver to the other Party Written Certification (so long as the completion, execution or submission of such documentation would not materially prejudice the legal or commercial position of the Party in receipt of such demand). Any such documentation shall be accurate and completed in a manner reasonably satisfactory to such other Party and shall be executed and delivered with any reasonably required certification by such date as is agreed between the Parties or, failing such agreement, as soon as reasonably practicable.

5.3 Where this paragraph 5 applies, Borrower, in relation to any payment made under paragraph 6.2 of the Agreement, or Lender, in relation to any payment made under paragraph 6.3 of the Agreement, agrees that it will deliver to the other Party Sufficient Evidence of any US Tax previously withheld by another party (so long as the completion, execution or submission of such documentation would not materially prejudice the legal or commercial position of the Party in receipt of such demand). Any such documentation shall be accurate and completed in a manner reasonably satisfactory to such other Party and shall be executed and delivered with any reasonably required certification by such date as is agreed between the Parties or, failing such agreement, as soon as reasonably practicable.

6. **MANUFACTURED PAYMENTS TO NON-US PERSONS OTHER THAN QUALIFIED SECURITIES LENDERS**

6.1 Lender, in relation to any Loan, and Borrower, in relation to any Non-Cash Collateral, warrants to the other Party on a continuing basis that, unless otherwise notified, the person Receiving any payment made under, as the case may be, paragraph 6.2 or 6.3 of the Agreement is a Non-US Person but not a Qualified Securities Lender.

6.2 Where this paragraph 6 applies, Borrower, in relation to any payment made under paragraph 6.2 of the Agreement, or Lender, in relation to any payment made under paragraph 6.3 of the Agreement, agrees that in determining the amount of US Tax required to be withheld it will properly take into account any US Tax that has previously been withheld and in respect of which it has received Sufficient Evidence.

6.3 Where this paragraph 6 applies, Borrower, in relation to any payment made under paragraph 6.2 of the Agreement, or Lender, in relation to any payment made under paragraph 6.3 of the Agreement, agrees that it will deliver to the other Party Evidence of US Tax withheld by it or Sufficient Evidence of US Tax previously withheld by another party (as the case may be) (so long as the completion, execution or submission of such documentation would not materially prejudice the legal or commercial position of the Party in receipt of such demand). Any such documentation shall be accurate and completed in a manner reasonably satisfactory to such other Party and shall be executed and delivered with any reasonably required certification by such date as is agreed between the Parties or, failing such agreement, as soon as reasonably practicable.

Appendices

7. FATCA WITHHOLDING TAX

7.1 Where this paragraph 7 applies, Borrower or, as the case may be, Lender in determining the amount, if any, of FATCA Withholding Tax required to be deducted or withheld from any payment it makes agrees that it will properly take into account any FATCA Certification provided by the other Party.

7.2 Where this paragraph 7 applies, the recipient of any payment agrees that it will deliver to the other Party the FATCA Certification referred to in paragraph 7.1 of this Addendum (so long as the completion, execution or submission of such form, document or representation would not materially prejudice the legal or commercial position of the Party in receipt of such demand). Any such form, document or representation shall be accurate and completed in a manner reasonably satisfactory to such other Party and shall be executed and delivered with any reasonably required certification by such date as is agreed between the Parties or, failing such agreement, as soon as reasonably practicable.

7.3 Where this paragraph 7 applies and FATCA Withholding Tax is required to be deducted or withheld from any payment, the payer agrees that it will deliver to the other Party FATCA Evidence (so long as the completion, execution or submission of such form, document or representation would not materially prejudice the legal or commercial position of the Party in receipt of such demand). Any such form, document or representation shall be accurate and completed in a manner reasonably satisfactory to such other Party and shall be executed and delivered with any reasonably required certification by such date as is agreed between the Parties or, failing such agreement, as soon as reasonably practicable.

8. INTERPRETATION

8.1 In this Addendum the following definitions shall apply:

IRS means the Internal Revenue Service of the United States of America.

Code means the Internal Revenue Code of 1986, as amended, of the United States of America.

Evidence means the form, document or representation prescribed by the IRS from time to time so that the recipient of a payment has evidence of US Tax withheld or deducted. To the extent that Evidence consists, in whole or in part, of any payee statement within the meaning of Section 6724(d)(2) of the Code, the party required to provide such payee statement need not provide it currently but such party undertakes to provide such payee statement promptly when it becomes available to such party (in no event before the due date for providing such payee statement set forth in the Code and IRS guidance thereunder).

FATCA Certification means the form, document or representation prescribed by the IRS from time to time to confirm status for the purposes of FATCA Withholding Tax, and also includes any renewals that the IRS may require from time to time.

FATCA Evidence means the form, document or representation prescribed by the IRS from time to time so that the recipient of a payment has evidence of FATCA Withholding Tax withheld or deducted. To the extent that FATCA Evidence consists, in whole or in part, of any payee statement within the meaning of Section 6724(d)(2) of the Code, the party required to provide such payee statement need not provide it currently but such party undertakes to provide such payee statement promptly when it becomes available to such party (in no event before the due date for providing such payee statement set forth in the Code and IRS guidance thereunder).

FATCA Withholding Tax means tax required to be withheld under sections 1471 to 1474 of the Code, any current or future regulations or official interpretations thereof, any agreement entered into pursuant to section 1471(b) of the Code, or any fiscal or regulatory legislation, rules or practices adopted pursuant to any intergovernmental agreement entered into in connection with the implementation of such sections of the Code.

Non-US Person means any person other than a US Person.

Prescribed Form means the form, document or representation prescribed by the IRS from time to time to confirm status as a US Person, and also includes any renewals that the IRS may require from time to time.

Qualified Securities Lender means a Qualified Securities Lender for the purposes of Part II A i. of IRS Notice 2010-46, as published in volume 2010-2, pages 757 *et. seq.*, of the "Cumulative Bulletin" of the IRS, or any successor guidance.

Receiving means receiving a payment as the proper party to receive such payment, regardless of whether the person is receiving such payment as a principal or agent (disclosed or undisclosed), and regardless of whether the person receiving such payment is fiscally transparent for US tax purposes.

Substitute Dividends means a Substitute Dividend for the purposes of section 871(m) of the Code which is treated by that section as a dividend from sources within the United States of America and so is subject to withholding of US Tax.

Sufficient Evidence means written documentation that identifies amounts of US Tax previously withheld by another party with respect to actual dividends or substitute dividends in the same series of securities lending transactions and so provides sufficient evidence of prior withholding for the purposes of Part II B ii. of IRS Notice 2010-46, as published in volume 2010-2, pages 757 *et. seq.*, of the "Cumulative Bulletin" of the IRS, or any successor guidance. To the extent that Sufficient Evidence consists, in whole or in part, of any payee statement within the meaning of Section 6724(d)(2) of the Code), the Party required to provide such payee statement need not provide it currently but such Party undertakes to provide such payee statement promptly when it becomes available to such Party (in no event before the due date for providing such payee statement set forth in the Code and IRS guidance thereunder). Sufficient Evidence also includes such written documentation that may be reasonably requested by a Party as is reasonably necessary to further document amounts of US Tax previously withheld by any party with respect to Income in the same series of securities lending transactions, including information to assist with reconciliations, provided that in all cases the information requested is reasonably available to the Party receiving the request (or that the Party receiving the request determines, in its sole discretion, can be compiled without significant effort). For the avoidance of doubt, a request made after 15 May of a year for a copy of IRS Form 1042-S received by the Party receiving the demand with respect to a prior year is presumed to be reasonable.

US Equities means equity securities issued by a United States of America corporation that pay dividends that are from sources within the United States of America under Section 861(a)(2)(A), unless exempted from US Tax under the Code.

US Person means any individual, trust, estate, partnership, association, company or corporation that is a "United States Person" within the meaning of Section 7701(a)(30) of the Code.

US Tax means tax required to be withheld from dividends from sources within the United States of America under any of sections 1441, 1442 or 1443 and Chapter 4 of the Code.

Written Certification means written documentation provided by a Qualified Securities Lender for the purposes of Part II A ii. of IRS Notice 2010-46, as published in volume 2010-2, pages 757 *et. seq.*, of the "Cumulative Bulletin" of the IRS, or any successor guidance, in such form as may be prescribed by the IRS from time to time, attesting to the status of the recipient of the payment as a Qualified Securities Lender and that it will properly withhold US Tax from Substitute Dividends that it receives and/or makes. This term includes any renewals that may be required by the IRS from time to time.

8.2   Terms to which a defined meaning is given in the Agreement have the same meanings in this Addendum.

8.3   Unless otherwise specified, references to paragraphs in this Addendum are to paragraphs in the Agreement.

8.4   Any reference to a provision of law includes references to that provision as amended, consolidated or re-enacted.

Signed by   )
)
Duly authorised for and on   )
behalf of   )

Signed by   )
)
Duly authorised for and on   )
behalf of   )

SCHEDULE

1.   PARTY A WARRANTIES

In relation to Party A:

(a)   paragraph 4 of this Addendum [shall/shall not]* apply;

(b)   paragraph 5 of this Addendum [shall/shall not]* apply;

(c)   paragraph 6 of this Addendum [shall/shall not]* apply; and

(d)   paragraph 7 of this Addendum [shall/shall not]* apply.

2.   PARTY B WARRANTIES

In relation to Party B:

(a)   paragraph 4 of this Addendum [shall/shall not]* apply;

(b)   paragraph 5 of this Addendum [shall/shall not]* apply;

(c)   paragraph 6 of this Addendum [shall/shall not]* apply; and

(d)   paragraph 7 of this Addendum [shall/shall not]* apply.

delete as appropriate

Glossary

adjustment
A method that can be used to eliminate a transaction exposure by terminating a repo and creating a replacement repo for the remaining term to maturity by adjusting the amount of the purchased securities. Cf *repricing*.

agency repo/stock loan
A repo or stock loan executed with a counterparty on behalf of a client or clients by an agent.

agent lender
A person who provides the service of lending out the securities owned by its clients in order to generate additional income for those clients on its holding of securities.

beneficial owner
The expression used in an agency lending context to refer to the person owning the securities being lent by the agent lender and who is therefore the lender of them. This person would also generally be the legal owner of the securities but for technicalities arising from modern custodial arrangements.

borrower
The party to a stock loan who borrows securities against delivery to the lender of an agreed amount of collateral. Cf *lender*.

buyer
The party to a repo who buys the purchased securities at the purchase price on the purchase date. The buyer is effectively a lender of cash and is said to be doing a reverse repo. Cf *seller*.

buy-in
A right to purchase securities in the market and pass on the cost and which is exercisable by a purchaser of securities against a person who has agreed to sell those securities to it but who has failed to deliver them within a certain period following the settlement date.

buy/sell-back
Another term for a sell/buy-back. Strictly speaking, this is a sell/buy-back from the point of view of the buyer. Sometimes abbreviated to 'buy/sell'.

CCP
A central counterparty or central clearing counterparty. A CCP is a specialist intermediary that interposes itself into every transaction registered with it by its members, to become the seller to every buyer and the buyer to every seller.

classic repo
Another name for a repurchase agreement where the repo securities are not 'special'. Cf *special repo*.

clean price
The price of a fixed-income security as generally quoted in the secondary cash market for that security. It reflects the market value of the security but excludes accrued interest. Cf *dirty price*.

collateral
The assets for which cash (in the case of a repo) or loaned securities (in the case of a stock loan) are exchanged at inception of the relevant transaction. In a repo this collateral is initially the purchased securities. Variation margin is also a form of collateral. Although referred to as 'collateral', in securities financing it is not provided by way of security as such but by way of outright transfer of ownership.

committed repo
An arrangement under which the seller or the buyer is committed to enter into repo (typically term repo) transactions. Stock loans may also be committed in nature.

corporate actions or events
A term used to describe events (such as conversions, mergers, take-overs and successions, often, but not always, involving an election by the holder) which occur in respect of securities.

credit-linked repo
A repo into which is embedded a credit derivative. Stock loans may also be credit-linked.

dirty price
The price of a fixed-income security including accrued interest on it. Cf *clean price*.

DvP
Delivery-versus-payment, which means settlement of the sale or other transfer of a security by means of the simultaneous exchange of that security for cash. If not DvP then the transfer of securities is made 'free of payment'.

equivalent

In respect of securities, securities of the same issue but not necessarily the identical securities. This term is used to reflect the fact that the recipient of securities (or collateral) in a securities financing transaction is free to re-use the actual securities it receives and so may source other securities of the same type in order to return them to the other party. The definitions in the GMRA and GMSLA also have an extended meaning to deal with conversions, redemptions, corporate actions, etc on the securities in question.

ERC

The European Repo Council, which is a regional subcouncil of the International Repo Council, established by ICMA to represent member firms active in the repo market in Europe.

evergreen repo/stock loan

A fixed-term repo or stock loan in which the parties have the right to terminate the transaction before maturity, or an open repo/stock loan with a right to terminate, but subject to giving several days' or weeks' notice of termination.

floating rate repo

A repo in which the repo rate is periodically re-fixed by reference to an interest rate benchmark. The repo rate may incorporate a spread under or over the benchmark.

forward repo

A repo which settles on a forward date (ie, after the next-nearest money market value date).

general collateral (GC) repo

Where the seller in a repo has some choice about precisely what collateral to deliver to the buyer. GC repos are driven by the need to borrow and/or lend cash, rather than the precise identity of the collateral, which means there will be a common GC repo rate for each currency and term to maturity.

GMRA

The Global Master Repurchase Agreement, which is the master agreement for repurchase agreements published by ICMA. It can be extended to include sell/buy-backs by applying the Buy/Sell-Back Annex. The latest edition of the GMRA was published in 2011, and is expected to supersede the 2000 edition, which itself superseded the 1995 edition. See http://www.icmagroup.org.

GMSLA

The Global Master Securities Lending Agreement, which is the master agreement for securities lending transactions published by ISLA. The latest edition of the GMSLA was published in 2010, and superseded the 2000 edition, which itself superseded earlier master agreements such as the Overseas Securities Lending Agreement (or OSLA). See www.isla.co.uk.

haircut
An agreed percentage discount applied to the market value of collateral to determine the purchase price on the purchase date of a repo or the margin value of collateral under a stock loan.

hold-in-custody (HIC) repo
A repo in which the seller retains possession of the collateral, even though legal title passes to the buyer. The seller will, however, be required to segregate the collateral from its own assets.

ICMA
The International Capital Market Association, an industry association which represents financial institutions active in the international capital markets worldwide. ICMA's market standards and conventions provide a framework of rules governing market practice which facilitate the orderly functioning of the primary and secondary markets in securities. See http://www.icmagroup.org.

initial margin
The excess of the required market value of the purchased securities to be delivered on the purchase date of a repo over the purchase price. Also applied daily during the term of a repo to determine the amount of margin required to maintain the collateral for the cash loan at the requisite level. In the GMRA the initial margin percentage is called the margin ratio. A margin ratio of 100% means that no initial margin is required.

ISLA
The International Securities Lending Association, a trade association representing the interests of participants in the European securities lending market. ISLA publishes the Global Master Securities Lending Agreement (GMSLA). See http://www.isla.co.uk.

lender
The party to a stock loan which lends the loaned securities against delivery by the borrower of an agreed amount of collateral.

lending fee
The fee payable by the borrower to the lender for the loaned securities. Often comprised as part of a rebate.

loaned securities
The securities that are loaned by the lender to the borrower under a stock loan.

manufactured dividend or payment
The term used to describe the contractual payment under a repo or stock loan made by the buyer to the seller or by the relevant stock loan party to the other, which arises due to the payment of a coupon, dividend or other income on securities by the

underlying issuer. In a repo or stock loan, the manufactured payment is made on the same day as and is equal in value to the real income payment. In a sell/buy-back, the manufactured payment (plus interest) is deferred until the repurchase date and deducted from the repurchase price.

margin
A word used to describe collateral, particularly in a repo context, that encompasses initial margin and variation margin.

mini close-out
The remedy available to the seller under a GMRA of terminating an individual repo on which there has been a failure to deliver equivalent purchased securities by the buyer on the repurchase date. A similar remedy exists for both the lender and the borrower under a GMSLA where there is a failure to deliver equivalent loaned securities or equivalent collateral on the return leg of a stock loan.

on demand
A transaction which continues until one of the parties terminates it by providing notice to the other at any time.

purchase date
The initial settlement date under a repo on which the buyer purchases the purchased securities in exchange for the purchase price.

purchase price
The price payable by the buyer for the purchased securities at inception of a repo.

purchased securities
The securities which are purchased by the buyer under a repo and which constitute the initial collateral for the cash lent to the seller.

rebate
A reduction in the amount of interest which would otherwise be payable by the lender on cash collateral provided under a stock loan to reflect the lending fee which is due in respect of the stock loan.

repricing
A method that can be used to eliminate a transaction exposure under a repo by accelerating the repurchase date of an existing repo and entering into a repriced transaction on the same date. The repriced transaction will have a new purchase price that is calculated to maintain the margin ratio under the transactions instead of the margin being posted. Cf *adjustment*.

repo
The generic term for repurchase agreements and sell/buy-backs.

repo rate
The term for the rate of return to the buyer on the cash lent through a reverse repo. The repo interest is the difference between the purchase price and the repurchase price and the repo rate is the rate at which that return accrues (ie, the return divided by the term of the transaction).

repurchase agreement
Also known as a classic repo.

repurchase date
The term for the maturity date of a repo.

repurchase price
The term for the sum of money paid by the seller to the buyer on the repurchase date to buy back equivalent securities to the purchased securities. It is equal to the purchase price plus interest at the repo rate for the term of the transaction.

reverse repo
The buyer's side of a repo. The buyer is said to 'reverse in' collateral (whereas the seller is said to 'repo out' collateral).

securities financing
The entering into of transactions under which securities are provided against a payment of cash or collateral and which includes both repo and stock lending transactions. Securities financing transactions are often referred to as 'SFTs'.

securities lending
The activity of entering into transactions, under which one party (the lender) transfers title to securities to another party (the borrower) in exchange for either title to other securities or cash as collateral and the payment of a fee with an obligation to return equivalent securities at maturity.

SLRC
The Securities Lending and Repo Committee, a UK committee of international repo and securities lending practitioners and representatives of trade organisations, together with bodies such as the UK Debt Management Office, London Stock Exchange and Financial Conduct Authority and administered by the Bank of England. See http://www.bankofengland.co.uk/markets/Pages/gilts/slrc.aspx.

sell/buy-back
A type of repo which differs from a repurchase agreement in its treatment of accrued income. Now often traded under the GMRA but originally traded as separate purchase and repurchase transactions.

seller
The party to a repo who sells purchased securities for cash in the form of the purchase price on the purchase date and commits to buy back equivalent purchased securities on the repurchase date. The seller is effectively borrowing cash. Cf *buyer*.

special repo
A repo the purchased securities under which are 'special'.

special securities
Securities which are in demand and so command a premium borrowing fee in the market. In a repo the repo rate would be below the GC repo rate for the same term to reflect the fact that the purchased securities can be re-used by the buyer at a premium. Cf *general collateral*.

stock loan
Another term for a securities lending transaction. The term is used more narrowly to refer to loans of equities but was broadened to reflect the fact that the market has developed to extend to the lending of fixed-income securities.

substitution
The recall by the buyer or by the lender of collateral during the term of the transaction and substitution of collateral of equal quality and value that is acceptable to the buyer or the lender.

term repo
A repo with a fixed term, often of one or more years. Term repos are structured, floating-rate and often have larger haircuts and enhanced rights of substitution.

tri-party repo
A repurchase agreement in which a third-party agent (who is normally the custodian bank for both the parties) undertakes the settlement, custody and post-trade management of the transaction. Stock loans may also be transacted on a tri-party basis.

variation margin
The term applied to a cash payment or transfer of securities as collateral made by one party – in response to a margin call by the other – to eliminate the net credit exposure across transactions between them. Under both the GMRA and the GMSLA, either party is entitled to call for a margin to eliminate such exposure.

About the authors

Eric Bystrom
Director
Eric.g.bystrom@gmail.com

Eric Bystrom has worked in the investment banking industry for the past nine years. He specialises in collateral management, liquidity and funding and securities services. He is currently a director at a major European investment bank, where he is developing a securities services business.

Eric holds a BSc in international management.

Iain Colquhoun
Head of repo marketing, ICBC Standard Bank
Iain.Colquhoun@icbcstandard.com

Iain Colquhoun is head of repo marketing at ICBC Standard Bank, the global markets entity within the ICBC group. He has worked in a variety of roles within the repo industry for the last 15 years. This includes experience working with a large securities lending operation, a globally focused European bank and a Japanese securities house. Currently he is responsible for developing the international client financing franchise at ICBC Standard Bank.

Marissa Dearden
Senior associate, Fieldfisher
Marissa.Dearden@fieldfisher.com

Marissa Dearden is a senior associate in the derivatives and structured finance group at Fieldfisher, specialising in over-the-counter derivatives, structured repo/securities lending and prime brokerage. She qualified into the team in 2009 and undertakes transactional and advisory work for a range of clients, including asset managers, prime brokers, securities dealers and custodians. Ms Dearden has spent time on secondment with a broker dealer and two US investment banks, supporting their securities financing and prime brokerage desks.

Samit Desai
Principal consultant, Capco UK
Samit.Desai@capco.com

Samit Desai is a principal consultant in the capital markets practice at Capco, based in London. He holds a degree in economics and business and has more than 10 years experience in financial services across a range of banking and consulting roles. Mr Desai participates in key industry forums and is a collateral management specialist. He has led global collateral teams in fixed-income financing, central clearing, over-the-counter derivatives and prime brokerage. Most recently, he managed a large regulatory project through to completion at a large Tier 1 investment bank.

Ivelina Dimtscheva
Principal consultant, Capco UK
Ivelina.Dimtscheva@capco.com

Ivelina Dimtscheva is a principal consultant in the capital markets practice at Capco UK. She has expertise in strategy definition, operational transformation and IT realisation. Ms Dimtscheva

About the authors

has delivered multiple complex regulatory, profitability and efficiency driven projects across both sell-side and market infrastructure providers.

Ms Dimtscheva has broad capital markets experience, spanning post-trade derivatives and securities processing, regulatory compliance, central clearing and collateral management. She holds a master's degree in business administration from the University of Mannheim, Germany.

Daniel Franks
Partner, Norton Rose Fulbright
daniel.franks@nortonrosefulbright.com

Daniel Franks is a partner in Norton Rose Fulbright's capital markets department in London. He has extensive experience of a broad range of capital markets transactions, with a particular focus on OTC derivatives, repos, securities lending, structured products and structured finance transactions and advising on collateral, set-off, netting and derivatives enforceability.

Mr Franks has extensive experience advising in relation to a wide variety of complex secured financing transactions, including liquidity swaps, repos, securities lending and secured lending arrangements. He has a particular interest in advising on the enforceability and characterisation of derivatives, repos, stock lending and collateral arrangements against a range of counterparty types, including private individuals, partnerships, trustees, charities and statutory and charter corporations.

He has also been involved in the drafting of industry standard documentation relating to collateral and is an active member of the International Swaps and Derivatives Association's legal, collateral and documentation committees.

Mr Franks was, at the time of authoring the chapters on structured transactions, partner at Fieldfisher.

Edward Miller
Partner, Fieldfisher
Edward.Miller@fieldfisher.com

Edward Miller has been a partner in the Fieldfisher derivatives and structured finance team since 2003. His practice encompasses over-the-counter and exchange-traded derivatives (over all types of underlying), repos and stock lending, with a particular focus on collateral issues – including tri-party structures – and structured repo and stock lending. His clients include global banks, regional banks, institutional asset managers and broker-dealers. Mr Miller regularly speaks on derivatives, repos and stock lending across Europe.

Nicholas Noble
Partner, Fieldfisher
Nicholas.Noble@fieldfisher.com

Nicholas Noble is a partner at Fieldfisher based in London, specialising in the taxation of financial transactions and funds.

He has advised investment banks regarding repos and stock lending transactions over many years. He was a member of the International Swaps and Derivatives Association Tax Sub-committee, which agreed the Credit Support Annex.

He also advises various institutional stock lenders regarding the tax effects of stock lending.

He has dealt with Her Majesty's Revenue and Customs frequently regarding the tax effects of repos and stock lending transactions.

Jamie Pullen
Associate, Fieldfisher
Jamie.Pullen@fieldfisher.com

Jamie Pullen is an associate in the derivatives and structured finance group at Fieldfisher. He focuses on advising on documentation and regulatory issues relating to OTC derivatives, repos and stock lending, together with prime brokerage, custody and tri-party arrangements. His client base comprises predominantly sell-side institutions. Mr

Pullen has spent more than 12 months on secondment at the London offices of two major US banking groups.

Sarah Reid
Senior associate, Fieldfisher
Sarah.Reid@fieldfisher.com

Sarah Reid qualified into the derivatives and structured finance group at Fieldfisher in 2008. She undertakes a variety of work, for both banks and buy-side clients, including advising on and negotiating derivatives master agreements, credit support arrangements, master confirmation agreements and long-form trade confirmations, prime brokerage agreements, repo and stock lending documentation and tri-party collateral arrangements. Ms Reid has spent time on secondment at the London offices of three US broker dealers.

Emma Spiers
Senior associate, Fieldfisher
Emma.Spiers@fieldfisher.com

Emma Spiers is a senior associate at Fieldfisher and qualified into the firm's derivatives and structured finance group in 2006.

Her practice covers derivatives and structured products, including credit, equity and funds, as well as securities financing. Ms Spiers advises a wide range of clients on derivatives and collateral documentation, repo and stock lending documentation, over-the-counter and futures clearing, synthetic prime brokerage and currency overlay arrangements. She has a particular focus on investment managers and has a comprehensive knowledge of the derivatives issues facing Undertakings for Collective Investment in Transferable Securities. She also has experience in a range of structured finance transactions, including synthetic securitisations and putting derivatives into structured finance transactions.

Andrew Spooner
Partner, Deloitte LLP
aspooner@deloitte.co.uk

Andrew Spooner is the lead International Financial Reporting Standards (IFRS) financial instruments partner globally at Deloitte. He is also a partner in Deloitte UK's national accounting and auditing group.

Mr Spooner is the Deloitte's lead specialist in financial instruments accounting and advises financial institutions and corporations on accounting for financial instruments and structured transactions. He is the lead liaison with the International Accounting Standards Board and other key regulators, such as the UK Prudential Regulatory Authority on interpretative issues of IFRS for financial instruments.

Mr Spooner is a member of the Technical Expert Group of the European Financial Reporting Advisory Group; a member of the consultative group of the Corporate Reporting Standing Committee of the European Securities and Markets Authority; and a member of the Financial Reporting Faculty Board of the Institute of Chartered Accountants in England and Wales.

Mr Spooner is author of the two volumes of Deloitte's iGAAP Financial Instruments series, now in its tenth edition.

Guy Usher
Partner and head of derivatives and structured finance, Fieldfisher
guy.usher@fieldfisher.com

Guy Usher is a partner and head of the derivatives and structured finance group at Fieldfisher based in London. He joined the firm over 25 years ago and has practised in derivatives, repo and stock lending since then.

He advises banks, brokers, asset managers and agent lenders on flow and structured repo and securities lending transactions in both developed and emerging markets. He has advised on asset-backed securities and loan repo, liquidity swaps, cashless repos and stock loans, committed and term facilities, repo to maturity, extinguishable and credit contingent transactions. These transactions may alternatively be documented as total return swaps or forwards.

As well as advising on transactions, Mr Usher provides project advice on setting up new trading and collateral transformation operations and infrastructure, outsourcing, netting issues and bespoke collateral structures.

He has also advised on some major and high profile close-outs and has deep understanding of the intricacies of the standard documentation on close-outs and corporate actions.

Swen Werner
Securities services and collateral management expert
swen.werner@gmail.com

Swen Werner began his career with Deutsche Bank in 1999, working for the capital markets policy unit at the bank's head office in Frankfurt. Between 2005 and 2006 he worked for Deutsche Börse as a member of its market policy division (now part of group strategy). He re-joined Deutsche Bank's global transaction banking division in 2006, heading up market advocacy and business strategy for its direct securities services unit.

Between 2011 and 2015 Mr Werner headed up the regulatory change and strategy function, as well as the product management function for Asia-Pacific for JP Morgan's collateral management division. Mr Werner currently provides consulting services to financial organisations in securities services and collateral management.

Mr Werner has an (executive) MBA from Cass Business School, London.

Index

ABSs *see* **asset-backed securities (ABSs)**
accounting, 183–198
    see also **Financial Reporting Standards (FRSs); International Financial Reporting Standards (IFRS)**
    continued recognition, examples, 189–190
    control, 191–194
    credit-linked repo, 76
    credit-linked securities transaction, 95
    derecognition
        decision tree, 185–188
        definitions, 183
        examples, 189
        principles, 184–185, 195, 196
    Financial Reporting Standard for Smaller Entities, 194
    reporting entities applying sections 11 and 12 of FRS 102, 195, 197
    risks and rewards
        applying test to repos, 190–191
        applying test to stock lending, 191–194
        transfer or retention of, 187–188
    UK Generally Accepted Accounting Practice (UK GAAP) *see* **UK Generally Accepted Accounting Practice (UK GAAP)**
Act of Insolvency
    Global Master Repurchase Agreement, 129–130
    Global Master Securities Lending Agreement, 157–158
adjustment of transactions
    definitions, 379
    Global Master Repurchase Agreement, 123–124
agency agreement
    see also **agency relationship; agent lending/agency repo**
    approved counterparties, 45
    available assets, 45
    borrower default, 45–46
    collateral, 45
    commitment, 44
    fees, 45
    indemnities, 46
    liability, 45
    reporting, 45
    scope of authority, 44
Agency Annex
    Global Master Repurchase Agreement, 137–139
    Global Master Securities Lending Agreement, 164–166
agency relationship
    agency agreement, 44–46
    agency lending documentation framework, 43
    agent and borrower, 43–44
    tri-party repo, 49
agent lending/agency repo
    Agency Annex
        Global Master Repurchase Agreement, 137–139
        Global Master Securities Lending Agreement, 164–168
        modifications to, 167
    agency relationship *see* **agency relationship**
    Agent Disclosure Code of Guidance (SLRC), 108
    agent lender
        and beneficial owners, 65–66
        definition of role, 379
        disclosure, 46–47
        power to enter into loan as agent, 164
        third party, 42, 43
        warranty of authority by lender acting as agent, 166
    allocation
        collateral, 167
        effect, 167, 168
        express, 168
        obligation to allocate, 167
    allocation of agency loans, 167
    allocation of margin, 139
    beneficial owner, 42
    borrowers, 42–43
    central clearing perspectives, 65–66
    conditions for agency loan, 165
    conditions for agency transactions, 137
    confirmation, 137
    defined, 379
    documentation framework, 43
    global custodians, 42
    initiation, 137
    market background, 41
    multiple principals, 137, 138–139
    net loan exposure, 167
    non-custodian agents, 42
    notification, 137, 166
    participants, 42–43
    pooled principals, 47, 139, 165, 167–168
    rebalancing of margin, 168
    representations, 138
    separate agreement, 138
    single agents, 137
    status of agency loans, 166
    third-party agent lender/repo agents, 42, 43
    warranties, 138, 168

Index

warranty of authority by lender acting as agent, 166
amortisation
  asset-backed securities, 80, 96
anonymous trading
  central clearing counterparties connected to, 55
asset-backed securities (ABSs)
  amortisation, 80, 96
  background, 95
  background to repos of, 79
  haircut, 80
  illiquidity, 80, 95–96
  loans, 95–96
  purchased by central banks, 24
  repos, 24, 79–80
  valuation, 80, 96
assets
  agency agreement, 45
  determination of whether rights to have expired, 187
  loan repo, 78
  material transfer, 159
  subject to transfer, identification, 186–187
  types, 11, 19
assignment
  without consent, not permitted, 134–135
  Global Master Repurchase Agreement, 134–135
  Global Master Securities Lending Agreement, 163
  non-assignability, 134
authorised investment funds (AIFs), tax treatment, 229–236
  financial transaction tax, 233–235
  of interest on cash collateral, 232
  of manufactured payments, 230–231
  of movement of securities in each direction, 232–233
  Value Added Tax, 235
authority
  and capacity, 100–101

balance sheets
  central clearing counterparties, 55–56, 65
Bank for International Settlements (BIS)
  regulatory framework, 103
Bank of England
  see also **central banks**
  on central clearing counterparties, 65
  Gilt Repo Code of Best Practice, 108
  Securities Lending and Repo Committee *see* **Securities Lending and Repo Committee (SLRC)**
  securities lending markets, 17
banks
  see also **Basel Committee on Banking Supervision; Basel II framework; central banks**
  central clearing perspectives, 65
  custodian, 41
  shadow banking, 67, 110, 111
base currency
  defined, 116
base erosion and profit shifting (BEPS), 222, 250–251
Basel Committee on Banking Supervision (BCBS)

netting and set-off, 100
reforms following Global Financial Crisis, 109
regulatory framework, 103
Basel II framework
  agent lender disclosure, 46
Basel III framework
  central clearing counterparties, 55
  impetus for, 109–110
basic life assurance and general annuity business *see* **BLAGAB (basic life assurance and general annuity business), tax treatment**
beneficial owner
  central clearing perspectives, 65–66
  defined, 30, 379
  participants in agent lending/repos, 42
bilateral trading
  agency relationship, 43
  repos, 63–64
BLAGAB (basic life assurance and general annuity business), tax treatment
  interest on cash collateral, 244
  manufactured payments, 242–244
  taxation of stock loans, 223
Bond Market Association (TBMA), 114
borrower
  see also **default; lender**
  agency lending, 42–44
  borrower-side obligations, default-and close-out 39
  default, 45–46
  defined, 379
  failure to deliver equivalent securities, 155–156
  of stock, 17
  tax position of, 248, 250
  termination rights, 155
  warranties, 161–162
breakage costs
  floating rate repo, 70
  floating rate securities lending transaction, 82
brokers
  central clearing perspectives, 65
business day
  defined, 116–117
  Global Master Securities Lending Agreement, 145–146
buyer
  see also **seller**
  buyer- and seller-side obligations, 27, 38
  defined, 379
  failure to deliver equivalent securities, 131
buy-in
  defined, 379
  delivery failures, 36
Buy/Sell-Back Annex, GMRA
  accrued interest, 140, 141
  application, 381
  confirmation, 141
  income payments, 141
  initiation, 141
  interpretation, 140
  margin/margin maintenance, 141
  purpose of creation, 13
  repricing, 141
  scope, 140
  sell back price, 140, 141
buy/sell-back transactions
  buyer- and seller-side obligations, 27

392

Index

corporate actions/events, 32
default and close-out, 39
definitions, 13, 380
delivery failures, 35–36
income/manufactured dividends, 30–31
interest/fee accrual, 26
margin/collateral maintenance, 27–29
pricing rates, 25
repurchase date, 30
repurchase price, 30–31
settlement at maturity, 34
substitutions and recalls, 33

calculation agent
floating rate repo, 70
floating rate securities lending transaction, 82
capacity
and authority, 100–101
capital gains tax, 217–218
Capital Requirements Directive IV (CRD IV), 114
Capital Requirements Regulation (CRR), 114
capital usage
central clearing counterparties, 55–56
cash
default of cash lender, 55–56
failure to pay, 128, 128–129
financing *see* cash financing
full transfer of title in, 125
Global Master Repurchase Agreement, 125, 128–129
margin *see* **cash margin**
settlement amount, failure to pay, 128–129
cash financing
uses of repo, 14
uses of stock lending, 22
cash margin
currency, 122
nature of payment, 122
CCPs *see* **central clearing counterparties (CCPs)**
CCR *see* **counterparty credit risk (CCR)**
central banks
see also **Bank of England**; **banks**
asset-backed securities purchased by, 24
liquidity schemes, 79
pricing rates, 24
reverse repo transactions, 15
central clearing counterparties (CCPs)
anonymous trading, connection to, 55
in Asia, 53
balance sheet and capital usage, 55–56
and central counterparty clearing, 53–68
agent lenders and beneficial owners, 65–66
banks and brokers, 65
central counterparties, 64–65
drivers for central counterparty clearing in repo market, 54–56
drivers for repo and securities lending central clearing counterparties, 53–54
perspectives on central clearing, 64–66
securities lending, 59–62
transaction lifecycle, 56–59
tri-party agents, 65
compared to tri-party and bilateral trading of repo and securities lending, 63–64
cost challenges, 61, 63
definitions, 380
electronic platforms, connection to, 55, 59

eligibility to be counterparties, 60
in Europe, 53
industry outlook
shadow banking, 67
unintended consequences for securities financing as result of OTC derivatives regulations, 66–67
margining, 61
market participants, 60
market transparency, 56
mitigating counterparty credit risk, 54–55
in North America, 53
operational efficiency, 56
operational requirements, 61
over-collateralisation and haircuts posted to, 55
over-collateralisation and haircuts removed from a default of cash lender, 55–56
participation in, 61
securities lending
active repos, 59–60
CCPs in securities lending markets, 60–61, 62
challenges facing a securities lending CCP, 61, 63
electronic platforms, 59
specials, importance, 61
and term nature of trades, 60–61
transaction lifecycle, 56–59
collateral management, 58
corporate events, 58
default management, 58
lines of defence for CCPs, 58–59
maturity, 59
post-trade matching, 58
pre-trade, 56
settlement, 58
trade execution, 58
central counterparty clearing *see under* **central clearing counterparties (CCPs)**
Central Moneymarkets Unit (CMU), 60
Central Securities Depositories Regulation (CSDR) (909/2014), 112
delivery failures, 36
chargeable gains
corporation tax on, 217–218
charitable trusts, tax treatment
interest on cash collateral, 237
manufactured payments, 236–237
movement of securities in each direction, 238–239
stock lending fees, 241
Value Added Tax, 240–241
City Code on Takeovers and Mergers (Takeover Code), 107–108
classic repo
see also **special repo**
buyer- and seller-side obligations, 27, 38
collateral, 25
corporate actions/events, 32
default and close-out, 36–39
defined, 380
delivery failures, 35–36
haircut (agreed percentage discount), 24, 25
income/manufactured dividends, 30
initial margin, 25
initial purchase price, 24
interest/fee accrual, 26

393

Index

margin/collateral maintenance, 27–29
pricing rates, 24–25
settlement at maturity, 34
substitutions and recalls, 33
clean price
  see also **dirty price**
  defined, 380
Clearstream Repurchase Conditions (CRC)
  tri-party repo, 51
close of business
  defined, 163
close-out
  Global Master Repurchase Agreement, 130
  netting, 170–179
collateral
  see also **Financial Collateral Arrangements Directive (Directive 2002/47/EC)**
  agency agreement, 45
  allocation, agency loans, 167
  cash, tax treatment, 226, 232, 237, 244
  classic repo, 25
  committed securities lending facilities compared with secured cash lending facilities, 85
  constant collateral amount securities lending transaction, 87–90
    additional events of default, 89
    background, 87–88
    consequences of failure to transfer loaned securities on settlement date, 89
    double counting, 89
    initial transfer, 88
    marking to market of collateral, 89
    marking to market of loaned securities, 88
    rates in respect of loaned securities, 90
    return of excess loaned securities, 89–90
    settlement risk, 90
    timing of delivery of additional loaned securities, 89–90
  credit-linked securities transaction, 94
  defined, 380
  delivery on commencement of loan, 149
  economic factors, 19
  excess, requirements to deliver, 151
  Global Master Securities Lending Agreement
    delivery of equivalent collateral on termination, 155
    delivery on commencement of loan, 149
    eligible forms, 146
    equivalent collateral, lender's failure to deliver, 156
    excess collateral, 151
    indemnity for failure to redeliver equivalent non-cash collateral, 153
    marking to market during currency of loan on loan by loan basis, 151
    marking to market of during currency of loan on aggregated basis, 150–151
    non-cash collateral, manufactured payments in respect of, 152
    substitution of collateral, 149–150
    timing of repayments of excess collateral, 151
  haircut, 19
  interest/fee accrual, 26
  maintenance, 27–30
  management, 58
  marking to market of

on aggregated basis, 150–151
    constant collateral amount securities lending transaction, 89
    on loan by loan basis, 151
  security financial collateral arrangements, 101
  stock loan, 25, 26, 29
  substitution of, 149–150
  title transfer collateral arrangements, 101–102
  uncollateralised securities lending *see* **uncollateralised securities lending**
commencement of trade
  repos, 8–9
  stock loans, 18
commitment fees
  agency agreement, 45
  failure to pay, 72–73, 85
committed repo facilities
  background, 71
  commercial terms, 72
  commitment fee, failure to pay, 72–73
  committed party, commercial terms, 72
  comparison with secured lending facilities, 73–74
  defined, 380
  evergreen repo, 71
  extent of commitment, 72
  facility annex, 71
  facility transaction, 71
  failure under, consequences 72–73
  non-committed party, commercial terms, 72
  revolving transaction, 71
  standalone facility document, 71
committed securities lending facilities
  background, 83
  breach of eligibility criteria, concentration limits or portfolio guidelines, 85
  commercial terms, 84
  commitment fee, failure to pay, 85
  committed party 84, 85
  compared to secured lending facilities, 83, 85–86
  'drawdown,' 83
  evergreen transaction, 83
  extent of commitment, 84
  facility annex, 83
  facility transaction, 83
  failure under, consequences, 85
  non-committed party, commercial terms, 84
  revolving transaction, 83
  standalone facility document, 84
commodity repo
  allocation of risks and insurance, 79
  background, 78
  environmental liability, 79
  regulatory impact, 79
  transfer mechanics, 78–79
Companies Act 2006
  regulatory issues, 108
  title transfer and recharacterisation risk, 98
confidentiality
  loan repo, 77
confirmations
  Global Master Repurchase Agreement, 120
constant collateral amount securities lending transaction *see under* **collateral**
Contracts (Rights of Third Parties) Act 1999
  Global Master Repurchase Agreement, 135
corporate actions/events

buy/sell-back transaction, 32
central clearing counterparties, 58
classic repo, 32
defined, 380
Global Master Repurchase Agreement, 142–143
Global Master Securities Lending Agreement, 151, 153–154
notice of proposed action, 142–143
ownership transfer, 11, 12, 20
stock loan, 32–33
corporation tax provisions
chargeable gains, 217–218
manufactured payments, 215–216
repos, 208–216
tax position of borrower, 248
costs
central clearing counterparties, 61, 63
counterparties
agency agreement, 45
counterparty credit risk (CCR)
Basel III framework, 109
mitigating, 54–55
covenants
committed repo, comparison with secured lending facilities, 73
committed securities lending facilities compared with secured cash lending facilities, 85
Credit Derivative Definitions, ISDA
credit-linked provisions, 75, 93, 94
Credit Events and Deliverable Obligation Characteristics
ISDA Credit Derivatives Definitions, 75, 94
credit risk
see also **counterparty credit risk (CCR)**
counterparty, mitigated, 54–55
ownership transfer, 11, 12, 20–21
credit-linked repo
accelerated repurchase date following occurrence of credit event, 75
accounting, 76
additional termination provisions, 76
background, 74
Credit Events and Deliverable Obligation Characteristics, ISDA Derivatives Definitions, 75
credit-linked provisions, 75
default consequences, 76
defined, 380
early termination consequences, 76
hedging, 75
margining, 76
no intervening credit event, repurchase date where, 75
primary cash flows, 74
termination, 76
credit-linked securities transaction
accelerated termination date following occurrence of credit event, 93
accounting, 95
background, 92–93
collateral, 94
common types of trade, 92–93
Credit Events and Deliverable Obligation Characteristics, ISDA Derivatives Definitions, 94
default, consequences, 94

early termination consequences, 94
hedging, 94
no intervening credit event, termination date where, 93
provisions, 93–94
settlement date, 93
vanilla, 92
CSDR *see* **Central Securities Depositories Regulation (CSDR)**
currency
base, 116, 145
cash margin, 122
contractual, 126
conversion, 148
custodian banks
agent lending, 41

deductions
lack of, in GMRA, 125
default
agency agreement, 45–46
being declared in default by an exchange or regulatory authority, 159
central clearing counterparties, 58
and close-out, 170–179
buy/sell-back transaction, 39
classic repo, 36–39
consequences of events of default, 171–172
default valuation notice, 174
default valuation time, 173–174
determination of default market values of securities, 172–173
determination of net amount, 177–178
events of default, 170–172
heads of loss, other, 178
legal expenses, 178
net value, 175–176
receivable securities, 172
set-off, 179
standard of care, 176–177
stock loan, 39–40
valuation notice (GMRA only), 174–175
committed repo, comparison with secured lending facilities, 74
consequences, credit-linked repo, 76
constant collateral amount securities lending transaction, 89
credit-linked securities transaction, 94
default market value, 37, 38
events of *see* **events of default**
floating rate repo, 70
floating rate securities lending transaction, 82
Global Master Repurchase Agreement, 127, 128
lender
committed repo transaction, 74
committed securities lending facilities compared with secured cash lending facilities, 86
management, 58
notice of, 128
delivery
of additional loaned securities, 89–90
amendment to obligations, 86–87
credit-linked repo, 75
of excess collateral, 151
failures *see* **delivery failures**

395

Index

Global Master Securities Lending Agreement
  borrower's failure to deliver equivalent securities, 155–156
  delivery failures, 36, 155
  delivery of collateral on commencement of loan, 149
  delivery of equivalent securities, 154
  delivery of further collateral, 151
  delivery through securities settlement systems generating automatic payments, 149
  failure by either party, 156
  lender's failure to deliver equivalent collateral, 156
  reciprocal obligations, 155
  requirements to effect delivery, 148
  versus payment *see* **delivery-versus-payment (DvP)**
  requirements to effect, 148
  simultaneous, 149
  through securities settlement systems generating automatic payments, 149
delivery failures
  buyer's failure to deliver equivalent securities, 131
  buy/sell-back transactions, 35–36
  classic repo, 35–36
  by either party, 156
  Global Master Repurchase Agreement, 128
  Global Master Securities Lending Agreement, 155, 156, 157
  mini close-out, 35–36
  securities, 128
  seller's failure to deliver purchased securities, 131
  stock loan, 36
delivery-versus-payment (DvP)
  defined, 380
  settlement at the outset, 26
derecognition
  see also **accounting**
  consolidation, 185
  decision tree, 185–188
  definitions, 183
  determination of whether rights to assets have expired, 187
  examples, 189
  identification of asset subject to transfer, 186–187
  principles, 184–185, 195, 196
  transfer of contractual rights to receive cash flows, 187
  transfer or retention of risk and rewards, 187–188
Developments in the Global Lending Market (*Quarterly Bulletin*), 2011, 17
dirty price, 380
  see also **clean price**
disclosure
  acquisition or disposal of equities, 106–107
  agent lender, 46–47
  FCA Disclosure Rules and Transparency Rules Sourcebook (DTRs), 107
  industry codes of practice, 108
  interests in shares, 108
  takeover requirements, 107–108
  Transparency Directive (Directive 2004/109/EC), 107

distributions
  Global Master Securities Lending Agreement, 151
  non-cash, 31
dividends *see* **manufactured dividends/payments**
documentation
  agency lending, 43
  Foreign Account Tax Compliance Act (FATCA), US, 143–144
  Global Master Repurchase Agreement *see* **Global Master Repurchase Agreement (GMRA), ICMA**
  Global Master Securities Lending Agreement *see* **Global Master Securities Lending Agreement (GMSLA), ISLA**
  industry standard, 113–181
  notices/other communications, 133
  repos under securities lending agreement, 86–87
  standalone facility document, 71
  standard, reasons for, 113–114
  tri-party repo, 50–51
double counting
  avoiding, 82
  constant collateral amount securities lending transaction, 89
DvP *see* **delivery-versus-payment (DvP)**

economic factors
  commencement of repo, 8–9
  commencement of stock loan, 18
  interest, 9–10
  lending fees, 19
  margining, 10
  term of repo, 10–11
  termination, 9, 18
electronic platforms
  central clearing counterparties connected to, 55, 59
enforcement procedures
  title transfer and recharacterisation risk, 98
equities
  disclosure on acquisition or disposal, 106–107
  voting rights, 31
Equities Annex, GMRA, 33
  corporate actions and voting, 142
  equivalent margin securities/equivalent securities, 141–142
  income payments, 142
  interpretation, 141
  scope, 141
  transfer, 143
  voting, 142, 143
equity of redemption
  title transfer and recharacterisation risk, 99
equity repo
  corporate events, 32–33
equivalence
  assets, 78
  borrower's failure to deliver equivalent securities, 155–156
  buyer's failure to deliver equivalent securities, 131
  definition of 'equivalent,' 117, 146–147, 381
  equivalent margin securities/equivalent securities, 141–142
  lender's failure to deliver equivalent collateral, 156

396

ERC *see* **European Repo Council (ERC), ICMA**
European Repo Council (ERC), ICMA
  see also **International Capital Market Association (ICMA)**
  definition of role, 381
  delivery failures, 36
  Guide to Best Practice in the European Repo Market, 23, 35, 108
  industry codes of practice, 108
European Securities and Markets Authority (ESMA), 111, 112
events of default
  see also **default**
  close-out netting, 170–171
  consequences, 159–160, 171–172
  floating rate repo, 70
  floating rate securities lending transaction, 82
  Global Master Repurchase Agreement, 127, 132
  Global Master Securities Lending Agreement, 156–157
  notification, 132, 159
  potential, notification, 132
evergreen repo/stock loan
  and committed repo, 71
  defined, 381

facility transaction
  committed repo, 71
FCA Amendment Regulations (FCARs) 2010 (SI 2010/2993)
  and Financial Collateral Arrangements Directive, 102
  title transfer and recharacterisation risk, 98
fee accrual
  see also **interest**
  buy/sell-back transactions, 26
  classic repo, 26
  stock loan, 26–27
fees
  agency agreement, 45
  commitment *see* **commitment fees**
  economic factors, 19
  lending, 19, 24, 382
    tax treatment, 229, 235–236, 241, 247–248
  pricing rates, 24
  rebates, 24
Financial Collateral Arrangements Directive (Directive 2002/47/EC)
  and Financial Collateral Arrangements Regulations 2003, 102
  implementation in UK, 102
  purpose, 101
  regulatory framework, 103
  security financial collateral arrangements, 101
  title transfer and recharacterisation risk, 97
  title transfer collateral arrangements, 101–102
Financial Collateral Arrangements Regulations 2003
  title transfer and recharacterisation risk, 98
Financial Conduct Authority (FCA), 114
  Disclosure Rules, 107
  FCA Amendment Regulations (FCARs) 2010 (SI 2010/2993), 98, 102
  regulated activities and authorisation, 104
  regulatory framework, 103
Financial Reporting Standard for Smaller Entities (FRSSE), 194

Financial Reporting Standards (FRSs)
  FRS 5 (*Reporting the Substance of Transactions*), 195–196, 198
    Application Note B, 196–197
  FRS 26 (*Financial Instruments: Recognition and Measurement*), 194, 198
    exclusion, 195–196, 197
  FRS 101 (*Reduced Disclosure Framework*), 194
  FRS 102 (*Financial Reporting Standard Applicable in the UK and Republic of Ireland*), 194
    ss 11 and 12, 195
Financial Stability Board (FSB)
  regulatory framework, 103
  shadow banking, 110, 111
financial transaction tax (FTT)
  see also **taxation**
  authorised investment funds, 233–235
  basic life assurance and general annuity business, 246–247
  charitable trusts, 239–240
  registered pension schemes, 227–228
  repo transactions, 220–221
  tax position of borrower, 249–250
floating rate repo
  additional events of default, 70
  ancillary amendments, 70
  background, 69
  calculation agent, 70
  defined, 381
  interest breakage, 70
  periodic payments, 69–70
floating rate securities lending transaction
  additional events of default, 82
  ancillary amendments, 82
  background, 81
  breakage costs, 82
  calculation agent, 82
  periodic payments, 81–82
Foreign Account Tax Compliance Act (FATCA), US, 169
  approaches of, 143–144
forward repo
  defined, 381
forward transactions
  Global Master Repurchase Agreement, 136
freedom to deal
  ownership transfer, 11, 19
FTT *see* **financial transaction tax (FTT)**

general collateral (GC)
  cash financing, 14
general collateral (GC) repo
  defined, 381
general collateral rate (GC rate)
  cash financing, 14
  securities financing, 15
Gilt Repo Code of Best Practice
  Bank of England, 108
Global Financial Crisis (GFC) 2008
  Basel III framework following, 109
  short selling regulations, 106
Global Master Repurchase Agreement (GMRA), ICMA, 114–144
  see also **repurchase transactions (repos)**
  1992 version, 114
  1995 version, 114, 381
  2000 version, 23, 114, 115–135, 254–288, 381

397

Index

2011 version, 25, 28, 31, 35, 36, 37, 114, 179–181, 289–324, 381
Act of Insolvency, 129–130
adjustment of transactions, 123–124
admission of inability/intention not to perform obligations, 130
agent lending/agency repo
  pooled principals, 47
Annexes, 114–115
  Agency, 137–138
  Buy/Sell-Back, 140–141, 381
  standard form, 115
assignment without consent, not permitted, 134–135
breach of representation, 130
buyer's failure to deliver equivalent securities, 131
buy/sell-back transactions, 13, 28, 29
cash, failure to pay, 128
cash margin, 122
cash settlement, failure to pay, 128–129
central clearing counterparties, 56
classic repo, 29
close-out, 130
close-out netting, 170–179
confirmations, 120
contractual currency, 126
default
  consequences, 171
  determination of default market values of securities, 172–173
  determination of net amount, 177–178
  events of, 127, 170–171
  heads of loss, other, 178
  legal expenses, 178
  net value, 175–176
  notice of, 128
  notification of event, 132
  potential event, notification, 132
  set-off, 179
  special notice, 134
  standard of care, 176–177
  timing of sales, purchases and quotations, 174–175
  valuation notice, 174
  valuation time, 173–174
definitions, 116–120
on demand transactions, 121
entire agreement, 134
Equities Annex, 33, 141–143
failure to perform any other obligations, 130
formalities of payment and transfer, 124–125
forward transactions, 136
governing law, 135
immunity, waiver of, 135
income payments, 124
initiation, 120
interest, 132–133
lifecycle of transactions, 23, 56
  classic repo, 25
  corporate actions/events, 32, 33
  delivery failures, 35
  income/manufactured dividends, 30, 31
  margin/collateral maintenance, 27, 28, 29
  substitutions and recalls, 33
margin maintenance, 121
margin provisions, failure to comply with, 129

margin transfer
  composition, 122
  right to if net exposure, 121
  time for, 122–123
margining, 10
'master agreement' structure, 114–115
net exposure, 121–122
  forward transactions, 136
no withholdings or deductions, 125
non-assignability, 134
notices/other communications, 133
optional condition precedent to payment/transfer obligation, 126
payment
  cash settlement, failure to pay, 128–129
  formalities, 124–125
  income, 124
  manufactured payments, failure to make, 129
  netting, 125–126
  optional condition precedent to payment/transfer obligation, 126
  simultaneous transfer and payment, 125
  and transfer, 124–125
pre-printed form ('front-end'), 114
recording of telephone conversations, 135
representations, 127
  breach of representation, 130
repricing, 123
securities, failure to deliver, 128
seller's failure to deliver purchased securities, 131
separate margining for transactions, 123
settlement netting, 126
severability, 134
simultaneous transfer and payment, 125
single agreement, 133
substitution, 126, 127
suspension/expulsion from exchange, etc, 130
tax event, 132
termination of transactions, 120, 134
  on notice, 135
third party rights, 135
transfer
  full transfer of title in cash and securities, 125
  margin *see* **margin transfer above**
  optional condition precedent to payment/transfer obligation, 126
  and payment, 124–125
  on purchase date, 120
  on repurchase date, 121
  simultaneous, on variation, 127
tri-party repo, 51
variation of purchased securities, 126, 127
waivers, lack of, 135
Global Master Securities Lending Agreement (GMSLA), ISLA, 144–169
  see also **securities lending**
  2000 version, 381
  2010 version, 23, 29, 39, 114, 144, 145–166, 325–364, 381
  admission of inability/intention not to perform obligations under, 159
  Agency Annex, 164–166
    Addendum for pooled principal agency loans, 167–168
  agency loans

398

Index

agency relationship, 43
   pooled principals, 167–168
applicability, 115, 145
assignment, 163
base currency, 145
being declared in default by an exchange or regulatory authority, 159
borrower's warranties, 161–162
breach of warranties, 158
business day, 145–146
close-out netting, 170–179
collateral
   delivery of equivalent on termination, 155
   delivery on commencement of loan, 149
   eligible forms, 146
   equivalent, failure to deliver, 156
   excess, 151
   indemnity for failure to redeliver equivalent non-cash collateral, 153
   marking to market during currency of loan on loan by loan basis, 151
   marking to market of during currency of loan on aggregated basis, 150–151
   non-cash, manufactured payments in respect of, 152
   substitution, 149–150
   timing of repayments of excess, 151
conforming, responsibility for, 164
corporate actions, 151, 153–154
currency conversion, 148
default
   consequences, 171–172
   determination of default market values of securities, 172–173
   determination of net amount, 177–178
   events of, 156–157, 170–171
   legal expenses, 178
   net value, 175–176
   set-off, 179
   standard of care, 176–177
   valuation time, 173–174
delivery
   borrower's failure to deliver equivalent securities, 155–156
   of collateral on commencement of loan, 149
   of equivalent securities, 154
   failures, 36, 155, 156, 157
   of further collateral, 151
   lender's failure to deliver equivalent collateral, 156
   reciprocal obligations, 155
   requirements to effect, 148
   through securities settlement systems generating automatic payments, 149
economic factors, 18
equivalence, 146–147
existing securities lending agreements, 164
failure to perform any other obligations, 159
governing law, 163–164
immunity, waiver of, 164
income, in form of securities, 153
interest on outstanding payments, 162
interpretation, 145
jurisdiction, 163–164
lender's warranties, 160–161
Letters of Credit, substitutions and extensions, 151

lifecycle of transactions, 23
   corporate actions/events, 33
   default and close-out, 39
   delivery failures, 36
   income/manufactured dividends, 31
   margin/collateral maintenance, 29
   pricing rates, 25
   substitutions and recalls, 33
   voting rights, 32
loans of securities, 148
manufactured payments, loaned securities, 152
margin, 147–148
market terminology, 148
market value, 147
'master agreement' structure, 144
material transfer of assets, 159
non-waiver, 163
notices, 162–163
notification of event of default, 159
payment
   failure, 157
   interest, 162
   of rates, 154
pooled principals, 47
rate applicable to loaned securities and cash collateral, 154
recording of telephone conversations, 164
retrospective changes in law, 160
severability, 162
single agreement, 162
specific performance, 162
structured securities lending transactions, 87
taxation, 160
   UK Tax Addendum 2014, 169, 365–370
   US Tax Addendum 2014, 169, 371–377
termination rights, 154–155, 162
time considerations, 164
trade-specific terms of individual transactions, 144
voting rights, 153
written notice of events of default, 156–157
GMRA *see* Global Master Repurchase Agreement (GMRA), ICMA
GMSLA *see* Global Master Securities Lending Agreement (GMSLA), ISLA
'gold-plating'
   regulatory framework, 103
governing law
   Global Master Repurchase Agreement, 135
   Global Master Securities Lending Agreement, 163–164
Group of Twenty (G20) forum
   financial regulatory reform agenda agreed by, 103
Guide to Best Practice in the European Repo Market (ERC), 23, 35, 108

haircut (agreed percentage discount)
   asset-backed securities, repo of, 80
   central clearing counterparty, posted to, 55
   classic repo, 24, 25
   collateral, 19
   commencement of loan, 18
   commencement of repo trade, 9
   description, 9, 382
   leverage, 15
   margin/collateral maintenance, 27

399

Index

market conventions, 16
removed from a default of cash lender, 55–56
tri-party repos, 50
hedging
credit-linked repos, 75
credit-linked securities transaction, 94
Herstatt settlement risk
constant collateral amount securities lending transaction, 90
High-level Expert Group
final report, 110
hold-in-custody (HIC) repo
defined, 382
tri-party repo, 51

ICMA *see* **International Capital Market Association (ICMA)**
illiquidity
asset-backed securities, 80, 95–96
immunity
waiver of, 135, 164
income
see also **manufactured dividend/payment**
buy/sell-back transactions, 30–31
classic repo, 30
Global Master Repurchase Agreement, 124
Global Master Securities Lending Agreement, 153
non-cash distributions, 31
ownership transfer, 12, 20
payments, 141, 142
stock loan, 31
title transfer and recharacterisation risk, 99
indemnities
agency agreement, 46
failure to redeliver equivalent non-cash collateral, 153
industry codes of practice
disclosure, 108
industry documentation *see* **documentation**
initial margin
classic repo, 25
defined, 382
initial purchase price
classic repo, 24
insolvency *see* **Act of Insolvency**
institutional asset managers
agent lending, 41
insurance
commodity repo, 79
interest
buy/sell-back transactions, 26
cash collateral, tax treatment, 226, 232, 237, 244
classic repo, 26
economic factors, 9–10
Global Master Repurchase Agreement, 132–133
Global Master Securities Lending Agreement, 162
'repo rate,' 9
short-term rates, US, 46
stock loan, 26
interest breakage
floating rate repo, 70
International Accounting Standards Board (IASB), 184
International Accounting Standards (IAS)

IAS 18 (*Revenue*), 184
IAS 39 (*Financial Instruments: Recognition and Measurement*), 184, 192, 193, 195, 197, 198
International Capital Market Association (ICMA)
see also **European Repo Council (ERC), ICMA; Global Master Repurchase Agreement (GMRA), ICMA**
bi-annual survey, 8, 11
delivery failures, 36
'frequently asked questions,' 8
general role, 11, 382
Global Master Repurchase Agreement 2011, 179
GMRA published by, 114
netting and set-off, 100
recent developments, 112
repo market, 8
tri-party repo, 51
International Financial Reporting Standards (IFRS), 183
accounting requirements, 184
IFRS 9 (*Financial Instruments*), 184, 189, 192, 193, 195, 197, 198
IFRS 15 (*Revenue from Contracts with Customers*), 184
in United Kingdom, 183–194
International Organisation of Securities Commissions (IOSCO)
Technical Committee, 17, 106
International Primary Market Association (IPMA), 114
International Repo Council, 381
see also **European Repo Council (ERC)**
International Securities Identification Number (ISIN), 97
International Securities Lending Association (ISLA)
see also **Global Master Securities Lending Agreement (GMSLA), ISLA**
agent lender disclosure, 46
general role, 382
netting and set-off, 100
recent developments, 112
International Securities Market Association (ISMA), 114
International Swaps and Derivatives Association (ISDA)
Credit Derivative Definitions, 75, 93, 94
Master Agreement, 95
Physical Settlement Matrix, 75, 93–94
ISDA *see* **International Swaps and Derivatives Association (ISDA)**
ISLA *see* **International Securities Lending Association (ISLA)**

Korean Exchange (KRX), 59

legal issues
capacity and authority, 100–101
due diligence requirements, 101
Financial Collateral Arrangements Directive 2002 *see* **Financial Collateral Arrangements Directive (Directive 2002/47/EC)**
nature of transactions, 97
netting and set-off, 100
title transfer and recharacterisation risk, 97–99

Lehman Brothers
  collapse, 59
Lehman's Repo 105 and 108 transactions
  Basel III framework, 109
lender
  see also **borrower**
  agent
    and beneficial owners, 65–66
    definition of role, 379
    disclosure, 46–47
    power to enter into loan as agent, 164
    third-party, 42, 43
    warranty of authority by lender acting as agent, 166
  cash, over-collateralisation and haircuts removed from a default of, 55–56
  default
    cash lender, 55–56
    committed repo transaction, 74
    committed securities lending facilities compared with secured cash lending facilities, 86
    lender-side obligations, 39
  equivalent collateral, failure to deliver, 156
  termination rights, 154–155
  warranties, 160–161
lender-side obligations
  default and close-out, 39
lending fees *see* **fees**
Letters of Credit
  substitutions and extensions, 151
leverage
  uses of repo, 15
leverage ratio
  Basel III framework, 109
liability
  agency agreement, 45
  environmental, commodity repo, 79
life assurance *see* **BLAGAB (basic life assurance and general annuity business), tax treatment**
lifecycle of transactions
  central clearing counterparties, 56–59
    collateral management, 58
    corporate actions/events, 58
    default management, 58
    execution of trade, 58
    post-trade matching, 58
    pre-trade, 56
    settlement, 58
  corporate actions/events, 32–33
  default and close-out
    buy/sell-back transactions, 39
    classic repo, 36–39
    stock loan, 39–40
  delivery failures, 35–36
  Global Master Repurchase Agreement, 23, 25, 28, 29, 33
  Global Master Securities Lending Agreement, 23, 29, 33
  income/manufactured dividends
    buy/sell-back transactions, 30–31
    classic repo, 30
    non-cash distributions, 31
    stock loan, 31
  interest/fee accrual
    buy/sell-back transactions, 26
    classic repo, 26
    stock loan, 26–27
  margin/collateral maintenance
    buy/sell-back transactions, 27–29
    classic repo, 27–29
    stock loan, 29–30
  maturity, 34–35, 59
  pricing rates
    buy/sell-back transactions, 25
    classic repo, 24–25
    stock loan, 25–26
  settlement
    at maturity, 34–35
    at the outset, 26
  substitutions and recalls, 33–34
  trade, performing, 23–24
  voting rights, 31–32
Liikanen Report 2012
  shadow banking, 110
liquidity ratios
  Basel III framework, 109
loan repo
  additional payment obligations, 77–78
  background, 76–77
  confidentiality, 77
  equivalent assets, 78
  syndicated loans, 78
  taxation, 78
  transfer restrictions, 77
  valuation, 78
loaned securities
  defined, 382
lock-in
  defined, 156
London Clearing House (LCH)
  RepoClear service, 53

manufactured dividends/payments
  see also **income**
  authorised investment funds (AIFs), tax treatment, 230–231
  basic life assurance and general annuity business, 242–244
  buy/sell-back transactions, 30–31
  charitable trusts, tax treatment, 236–237
  classic repo, 30
  defined, 382–383
  failure to make, 129
  income tax provisions, 205–208
  loaned securities, 152
  non-cash collateral, 152
  non-cash distributions, 31
  registered pension schemes, 224–225
  stock loan, 31
  taxation, 205–208, 215–216, 236–237
margin
  see also **margin ratio; margin securities; margin transfer; margining; variation margin**
  Agency Annex, Addendum to, 139
  allocation, for agency transactions, 139
  buyer- and seller-side obligations, 27
  buy/sell-back transactions, 27–29
    Buy/Sell-Back Annex, GMRA, 141
  calculation methodology, 28
  cash, 122
  classic repo, 27–29
  and collateral maintenance, 27–30
  defined, 383
  general rule for transfer or receipt of, 139

401

Index

Global Master Securities Lending Agreement, 147–148
initial, 25, 382
maintenance, 121, 141
provisions, failure to comply with, 129
rebalancing of, 139, 168
stock loan, 29–30
margin ratio
defined, 117
margin securities
defined, 117
substitution, 127
margin transfer
composition, 122
defined, 117
right to if net exposure, 121
time for, 122–123
margining
see also **margin; margin ratio; margin securities; margin transfer**
central clearing counterparties, 61
credit-linked repo, 76
economic factors, 10
forward transactions, 28
repricing as alternative to, 10
separate, for transactions, 123
market conventions
and uses of repo, 15–16
market value
defined, 117–118
Global Master Securities Lending Agreement, 147
markets
see also **market conventions; repurchase transactions (repos); securities lending; stock lending transactions**
repo, 7–8
securities lending, 17
terminology, 148
Markets in Financial Instruments Directive (MiFID) (Directive 2004/39/EC), 111
Markets in Financial Instruments II Directive (MiFID II), (Directive 2014/65/EU), 111, 112
Markets in Financial Instruments Regulation (MiFIR), 2014, 111, 112
MF Global 'rep to maturity' product
Basel III framework, 109–110
mini close-out
defined, 383
delivery failures, 35, 35–36
failure to pay cash settlement amount following, 157
Model Double Taxation Convention, 222, 250

negative pledge
title transfer and recharacterisation risk, 99
net exposure
forward transactions, 136
Global Master Repurchase Agreement, 121–122, 136
net margin
defined, 118
net stocklending
see also **stock lending transactions**
characterisation, 92
shortfall and excess, 92
tax treatment, 92
netting

close-out, 170–179
payment, 125–126
and set-off, 100
settlement, 126
non-cash distributions
income/manufactured dividends, 31

OATs (French government bonds)
default and close-out, 39, 40
margin/collateral maintenance, 29
pricing rates, 25
settlement at maturity, 35
settlement at outset, 26
on-demand transactions
definitions, 383
on-demand ('open') stock loans, 27
Global Master Repurchase Agreement, 121
Options Clearing Corporation (OCC), 59
OTC (over-the-counter) derivatives see **over-the-counter (OTC) derivatives**
outsourcing
and non-custodian agents, 42
over-collateralisation
central clearing counterparty, posted to, 55
removed from a default of cash lender, 55–56
terms of stock loan not providing for, 21
terms of repo transaction not providing for, 12–13
tri-party repos, 50
overnight indexed swap (OIS)
market conventions, 16
Overseas Securities Lending Agreement (OSLA), 381
see also **Global Master Securities Lending Agreement (GMSLA), ISLA**
over-the-counter (OTC) derivatives
drivers for repo and securities lending counterparties, 53
liquidity squeeze on 'safe assets,' 68
recent developments, 112
regulations, unintended consequences for securities financing as result of, 66–67
standard documents, reasons for, 113
ownership transfer
corporate actions/events, 11, 12, 20
credit risk, 11, 12, 20–21
freedom to deal, 11, 19
income, 12, 20
outright, in repo market, 11
over-collateralisation risk
terms of stock loan not providing for, 21
terms of repo transaction not providing for, 12–13
payment on securities, 11, 20
repos, 11–12
restrictions on dealing, 12, 21
securities lending, 19–21
terms of stock loan, excluded provisions, 21
terms of repo transaction, excluded provisions, 12–13
terms of transactions, 12
voting rights, 11, 12, 20

payment considerations
delivery-versus-payment, 26, 380
floating rate repos, 69–70
Global Master Repurchase Agreement Buy/Sell-Back Annex, 141

cash settlement, failure to pay, 128–129
formalities, 124–125
income payments, 124, 141, 142
optional condition precedent to payment/transfer obligation, 126
payment netting, 125–126
simultaneous transfer and payment, 125
transfer and payment, 124–125
Global Master Securities Lending Agreement
failure to make manufactured payments, 157
failure to pay cash settlement amount following mini close-out, 157
failure to pay or deliver, 157
interest on outstanding payments, 162
payment of rates, 154
income payments, 124, 141, 142
loan repo, obligations under, 77–78
manufactured payments *see* **manufactured dividends/payments**
netting, 125–126
optional condition precedent to payment/transfer obligation, 126
ownership transfer, 11, 20
periodic payments *see* **periodic payments**
securities lending agreement, documenting repos under, 86–87
securities settlement systems generating automatic payments, 149
simultaneous transfer and payment, 125
transfer and payment, 124–125
pensions *see* **registered pension schemes, tax treatment**
periodic payments
floating rate repo, 69–70
floating rate securities lending transaction, 81–82
Physical Settlement Matrix, ISDA
credit-linked provisions, 75, 93–94
pledge
negative, 99
preferential creditors
title transfer and recharacterisation risk, 98
price differential
defined, 118–119
pricing rates
buy/sell-back transactions, 25
classic repo, 24–25
definitions, 119
floating rate repos, 69
OATs (French government bonds), 25
stock loan, 25–26
Prudential Regulation Authority (PRA), 114
regulated activities and authorisation, 104
regulatory framework, 103
purchase date
defined, 383
purchased securities
defined, 119, 383

Quadriserv (US electronic platform), 59

Real Estate Investment Trust (REIT), 207, 243
rebates, 24, 383
recalls
buy/sell-back transactions, 33
classic repo, 33
stock loan, 33–34

recharacterisation risk
and title transfer, 97–99
registered pension schemes, tax treatment, 224–229
cash collateral, 226
financial transaction tax, 227–228
manufactured payments, 224–225
movement of securities in each direction, 226–227
stock lending fees, 229
Value Added Tax, 229
registration
title transfer and recharacterisation risk, 98
Regulated Activities Order (SI 2001/544)
regulated activities and authorisation, 104
regulatory issues
Companies Act 2006, 108
disclosure and transparency
acquisition or disposal of equities, 106–107
interests in shares, 108
takeover requirements, 107–108
framework, 103
national regulators, 103
regulated activities and authorisation, 104
short selling regulations, 104–106
rehypothecation
potential risks, 111
repo rate
defined, 384
RepoClear service
London Clearing House, 53
reports
agency agreement, 45
repos *see* **repurchase transactions (repos)**
representations
breach, 130
Global Master Repurchase Agreement, 127, 130
Agency Annex, 138
repricing
defined, 383
Global Master Repurchase Agreement, 123
repurchase agreement *see* **classic repo**
repurchase date
buy/sell-back transactions, 30
credit-linked repo, 75
defined, 384
economic factors, 9
repurchase price
buy/sell-back transactions, 30–31
defined, 119
repurchase transactions (repos)
see also **European Repo Council (ERC); Global Master Repurchase Agreement (GMRA), ICMA; International Repo Council; securities lending; stock lending transactions**
agency repo/stock loan, 379
asset-backed securities, 79–80
bilateral trading, 63–64
classic repo *see* **classic repo**
commencement of trade, 8–9
committed repo *see* **committed repo**
commodity *see* **commodity repo**
credit-linked *see* **credit-linked repo**
creditor quasi-repo, 211
creditor repo, 209, 211

403

Index

debtor quasi repo, 212, 213, 214
debtor repo, 212
defined, 7, 383
drivers for central clearing counterparties, 53–54
drivers for central counterparty clearing in repo market, 54–56
economic factors, 8–11
equity repo, 32–33
evergreen repo, 381
floating rate repo *see* **floating rate repo**
forward repo, 381
general collateral (GC) repo, 381
Gilt Repo Code of Best Practice (Bank of England), 108
hold-in-custody (HIC) repo, 51, 382
loan repo *see* **loan repo**
market, 7–8
market conventions, 15–16
medium- and long-term, 69
origins, 7–8
pricing rates, 24–26
reverse repo, 7, 384
risks and rewards test, applying, 190–191
as sale and repurchase transactions, 97
as secured loans, 97, 98
as securities financing transactions, 110
securities lending CCPs and active repos, 59–60
simple (vanilla), 7, 9, 74, 76
special repo, 380
spot rate, 8–9
standard documents, reasons for, 113–114
taxation
  accrued income scheme, 208
  corporation tax provisions, 208–216
  general principles, 200–201
  income tax provisions, 202–208
  manufactured payments, 205–208, 215–216
  mixed party repos, 216–217
  summary of issues, 199
  in United Kingdom, 202–222
term repo, 385
tri-party repo *see* **tri-party repo**
uses
  cash financing, 14
  and central banks, 15
  leverage, 15
  securities lending, 14–15
uses of, 14–15
vanilla, 74
restrictions on dealing
  terms of stock loan not providing for, 21
  terms of repo transaction not providing for, 12
retention
  of risk and rewards, 187–188
return leg
  redelivery of securities, 9
reverse repo
  defined, 7, 384
revolving transaction
  committed repo, 71
risks
  allocation, commodity repos, 79
  commodity repo, 79
  counterparty credit, mitigating, 54–55
  credit *see* **credit risk**

over-collateralisation, 12–13, 21
recharacterisation, 97–99
rehypothecation, potential risks, 111
short selling, 105–106
risks and rewards
  applying test to repos, 190–191
  applying test to stock lending, 191–194
  transfer or retention of, 187–188

sales tax
  Global Master Securities Lending Agreement, 160
SecFinex, Europe (electronic platform), 59
Securities and Exchange Commission (SEC)
  agent lender disclosure, 46
securities financing *see* **securities lending**
Securities Industry and Financial Markets Association (SIFMA), 18, 114, 179
securities lending
  see also **Global Master Securities Lending Agreement (GMSLA), ISLA; stock lending transactions; repurchase transactions (repos)**
  central clearing counterparties, 59–62
    markets, 60–61, 62
  committed repo facilities compared, 73–74
  credit-linked transaction *see* **credit-linked securities transaction**
  definitions, 384
  drivers for central clearing counterparties, 53–54
  economic factors, 18–19
  floating rate securities lending transaction, 81–82
  markets, 17, 60–61, 62
  medium- and long-term transactions, 81
  net stocklending, 91–92
  Securities Borrowing and Lending Code of Guidance, 108
  stock loan, 16–17
  transactions, 110
  uncollateralised
    background, 90
    disapplication of provisions, 91
    set-off, 90–91
  uses of stock lending, 21–22
securities lending agreement, documenting repos under
  amendment to payment and delivery obligations, 86–87
  background, 86
  characterisation, 87
  reliance on opinions, 87
Securities Lending and Repo Committee (SLRC)
  Code of Guidance, 23, 32, 108
  general role, 384
Securities Lending Transactions, Market Development and Implications (Technical Committee of IOSCO), 17
sell/buy-back
  defined, 384
seller
  see also **buyer**
  buyer- and seller-side obligations, 27, 38
  failure to deliver purchased securities, 131
set-off
  and netting, 100, 179

404

uncollateralised securities lending, 90–91
settlement
  cash, failure to pay under GMRA, 128–129
  central clearing counterparties, 58
  constant collateral amount securities lending transaction, 89, 90
  at maturity, 34–35
  netting, 126
  OATs (French government bonds), 26
  at the outset, 26
  securities settlement systems generating automatic payments, 149
settlement date
  consequences of failure to transfer loaned securities on, 89
  credit-linked securities transaction, 93
  repos, 24
severability
  Global Master Repurchase Agreement, 134
  Global Master Securities Lending Agreement, 162
shadow banking
  central clearing counterparties, 67
  credit activities, 110
  securities financing transactions, 110
shares
  disclosure of interests in, 108
short selling regulations, 104–106
  'covered' short sales, 105
  'naked' short sales, 105
  risks in short selling, 105–106
  Short Selling Regulation (236/2012), 106
SIFMA Master Securities Loan Agreements (1993 and 2000), 18, 114, 179
SLRC see **Securities Lending and Repo Committee (SLRC)**
special repo
  see also **classic repo**
  classic repo distinguished, 380
  defined, 385
  securities financing, 15
special securities
  defined, 385
specific performance
  Global Master Securities Lending Agreement, 162
spot rate, 8–9, 119
stamp duty and stamp duty reserve tax, 219–220
  Global Master Securities Lending Agreement, 160
  tax position of borrower, 248
stock lending transactions
  agency repo/stock loan, 379
  borrowers of stock, 17
  borrower-side obligations, 39
  corporate actions/events, 32–33
  default and close-out, 39–40
  definition of stock loan, 16–17, 385
  on-demand ('open') stock loans, 27
  evergreen repo/stock loan, 381
  fees see **fees**
  income/manufactured dividends, 31
  interest/fee accrual, 26–27
  lender-side obligations, 39
  margin/collateral maintenance, 29–30
  pricing rates, 25–26
  risks and rewards test, applying, 191–194

as sale and repurchase transactions, 97
as secured loans, 97, 98
as securities financing transactions, 110
settlement at maturity, 34–35
standard documents, reasons for, 113–114
substitutions and recalls, 33–34
taxation, 222–251
  general principles, 201–202
  summary of issues, 200
uses of stock lending, 21–22
structured transactions
  repos
    asset-backed securities, 79–80
    committed, 71–74, 380
    commodity, 78–79
    credit-linked, 74–76, 380
    floating rate, 69–70, 381
    loan, 76–78
  securities lending
    asset-backed securities, loans, 95–96
    committed facilities, 83–86
    constant collateral amount securities lending transaction, 87–90
    credit-linked transactions, 92–95
    documenting repos under securities lending agreement, 86–87
    floating rate, 81–82
    net stocklending, 91–92
    uncollateralised, 90–91
substitutions
  buy/sell-back transactions, 33
  classic repo, 33
  of collateral, 149–150
  definitions, 385
  Global Master Repurchase Agreement, 126
  Global Master Securities Lending Agreement, 149–150
  Letters of Credit, 151
  margin securities, 127
  stock loan, 33–34
supranational bodies
  regulatory framework, 103
syndication
  committed repo, comparison with secured lending facilities, 74
  committed securities lending facilities compared with secured cash lending facilities, 86
  loan repo, 78

takeovers
  disclosure requirements, 107–108
taxation, 199–251
  accrued income scheme, 208, 216
  authorised investment funds see **authorised investment funds (AIFs), tax treatment**
  avoidance schemes, 202
  base erosion and profit shifting, 222, 250–251
  BLAGAB see **BLAGAB (basic life assurance and general annuity business), tax treatment**
  borrower, tax position, 248–250
  capital gains tax, 217–218
  charitable trusts see **charitable trusts, tax treatment**
  corporation tax provisions, 208–216
    chargeable gains, 217–218
    manufactured payments, 215–216

405

Index

tax position of borrower, 248
financial transaction tax *see* **financial transaction tax (FTT)**
Global Master Repurchase Agreement, 132
Global Master Securities Lending Agreement, 160
    UK Tax Addendum 2014, 169, 365–370
    US Tax Addendum 2014, 169, 371–377
loan repo, 78
Model Double Taxation Convention, 222, 250
net stocklending, 92
registered pension schemes *see* **registered pension schemes, tax treatment**
repo transactions
    corporation tax provisions, 208–216
    creditor quasi-repo, 211
    creditor repo, 209, 211
    debtor quasi repo, 212, 213, 214
    debtor repo, 212
    general taxation principles, 200–201
    income tax provisions, 202–208
    manufactured payments, 205–208, 215–216
    mixed party repos, 216–217
    summary of tax issues, 199
    in United Kingdom, 202–222
sales tax, 160
stamp duty and stamp duty reserve tax, 160, 219–220, 248
stock lending transactions, 222–251
    general principles, 201–202
    summary of tax issues, 200
summary of tax issues, 199 200
UK legislation
    Corporation Tax Act (CTA) 2009, 208, 209, 211, 214, 215, 216, 217, 218, 230, 231, 232, 235, 242, 243, 244, 248
    Corporation Tax Act (CTA) 2010, 215, 222, 230, 231, 242, 243
    Finance Act (FA) 1986, 202, 219, 232, 238, 245, 248
    Finance Act (FA) 2004, 224, 229
    Finance Act (FA) 2013, 202, 217
    Income and Corporation Taxes Act (ICTA) 1988, 202, 229, 235, 247
    Income Tax Act (ITA) 2007, 202, 204, 205–206, 207, 208, 215, 216, 217, 222, 224, 225, 230, 232, 236, 237, 241, 242, 244, 248
    Income Tax (Trading and Other Income) Act (ITTOIA) 2005, 202, 203–204, 216, 241
    Taxation of Chargeable Gains Act (TCGA) 1985, 244
    Taxation of Chargeable Gains Act (TCGA) 1992, 202, 217, 218, 226, 229, 232, 238, 248
    Value Added Tax Act 1994, 202
US legislation
    Foreign Account Tax Compliance Act (FATCA), 143–144, 169
Value Added Tax *see* **Value Added Tax (VAT)**
withholding, gross-up and information provision, 160
term of repo
economic factors, 10–11, 19
term repo
defined, 385

termination
borrower's right to terminate, 155
credit-linked repo, 76
credit-linked securities transaction, 93, 94–95
delivery of equivalent securities or collateral on loan termination, 155
early, consequences, 38, 76, 94
economic factors, 9
Global Master Repurchase Agreement, 120
Global Master Securities Lending Agreement, 154–155, 162
lender's right to terminate, 154–155
of repo, 9
of stock loan, 18
terms of transactions
ownership transfer, 12
third party rights
Global Master Repurchase Agreement, 135
title transfers
committed repo, comparison with secured lending facilties, 73
committed securities lending facilities compared with secured cash lending facilities, 85
enforcement procedures, 98
full transfer in cash and securities, 125
preferential creditors, 98
and recharacterisation risk, 97–99
registration, 98
trade
agreement, 23–24
anonymous trading, 55
arising of, 23
central clearing counterparties, 58
commencement of repo trade, 8–9
confirmations (doing the trade), 23–24
execution of, 58
performing, lifecycle of transactions, 23–24
post-trade matching, 58
pre-trade, 58
vanilla on-demand, 81, 83
transaction exposure
defined, 119–120
transfer
of contractual rights to receive cash flows, 187
formalities, 124–125
Global Master Repurchase Agreement, 121, 124
    Equities Annex, 143
loan repo, transfer restrictions, 77
margin *see* **margin transfer**
material transfer of assets, 159
optional condition precedent to payment/transfer obligation, 126
ownership *see* **ownership transfer**
and payment, 124–125
on purchase date, 120
on repurchase date, 121
of risk and rewards, 187–188
transfers
commodity repo, 78–79
failure, constant collateral amount securities lending transaction, 89
identification of asset subject to transfer, 186–187
title *see* **title transfers**
Transparency Directive (Directive 2004/109/EC), 107

Index

tri-party repo
  agency lending, 49, 65, 67, 68
  CCPs compared, 63–64
  defined, 49, 385
  documentation, 50–51
  hold-in-custody (HIC) repo, 51
  market participants, 51
  recent developments, 51–52
  role, 49–50

UCITS management companies
  shadow banking, 111
UK Generally Accepted Accounting Practice (UK GAAP), 183, 194–196
  see also **accounting**; **Financial Reporting Standards (FRSs)**
  changes to, 184
  compared to IFRS, 197–198
  reporting entities applying 'old' UK GAAP excluding FRS 26, 195–196, 197
  taxation, 209, 210, 211, 212, 213, 214
uncollateralised securities lending
  background, 90
  disapplication of provisions, 91
  set-off, 90–91
United States
  custodian banks, 41
  Federal Reserve and repo market, 7
  Foreign Account Tax Compliance Act (FATCA), 143–144, 169
  SEC and agent lender disclosure, 46
  short-term interest rates, 46
  treasury market, 7–8

valuation
  asset-backed securities, 80, 96
  close-out netting, 173–174
  loan repo, 78
Value Added Tax (VAT)
  authorised investment funds, 235
  basic life assurance and general annuity business, 247
  case law, 219, 229
  charitable trusts, 240–241
  registered pension schemes, 229
  repo transactions, tax of, 218–219
  tax position of borrower, 250
vanilla repos, 7, 9, 74, 76
variation margin
  see also **margin**
  and collateral, 380
  defined, 385
  posting of, 27, 28
  settlement at maturity, 34
variation of purchased securities
  effect, 127
  Global Master Repurchase Agreement, 126, 127
  simultaneous transfer on, 127
voting rights
  direction, 21
  direction, terms of repo transaction not providing for, 12
  Global Master Repurchase Agreement, 142, 143
  Global Master Securities Lending Agreement, 153
  lifecycle of transactions, 31–32

  ownership transfer, 11, 12, 20
  title transfer and recharacterisation risk, 99

waivers
  Global Master Repurchase Agreement, 135
  Global Master Securities Lending Agreement, 163–164
warranties
  agent lending, 138, 168
  borrower's, 161–162
  breach, 158
  Global Master Repurchase Agreement Agency Annex, 138
  Global Master Securities Lending Agreement, 158, 160–162
  lender's, 160–161
withholdings
  lack of, in GMRA, 125